WAID • KRAUSE • BARRETO • DALHOUSE • WOODARD

IRREDEEMABLE ™

PREMIER EDITION

VOLUME THREE

IRREDEEMABLE PREMIER EDITION Volume Three, December 2016. Published by BOOM! Studios, a division of Boom Entertainment, Inc. Irredeemable is ™ & © 2016 Boom Entertainment, Inc. and Mark Waid. Originally published in single magazine form as IRREDEEMABLE No. 16-23 ™ & © 2010, 2011 Boom Entertainment, Inc. and Mark Waid. All rights reserved. BOOM! Studios™ and the BOOM! Studios logo are trademarks of Boom Entertainment, Inc., registered in various countries and categories. All characters, events, and institutions depicted herein are fictional. Any similarity between any of the names, characters, persons, events, and/or institutions in this publication to actual names, characters, and persons, whether living or dead, events, and/ or institutions is unintended and purely coincidental. BOOM! Studios does not read or accept unsolicited submissions of ideas, stories, or artwork.

A catalog record of this book is available from OCLC and from the BOOM! Studios website, www.boom-studios.com, on the Librarians Page.

BOOM! Studios, 5670 Wilshire Boulevard, Suite 450, Los Angeles, CA 90036-5679. Printed in China. First Printing.

ISBN: 978-1-60886-915-2, eISBN: 978-1-61398-586-1

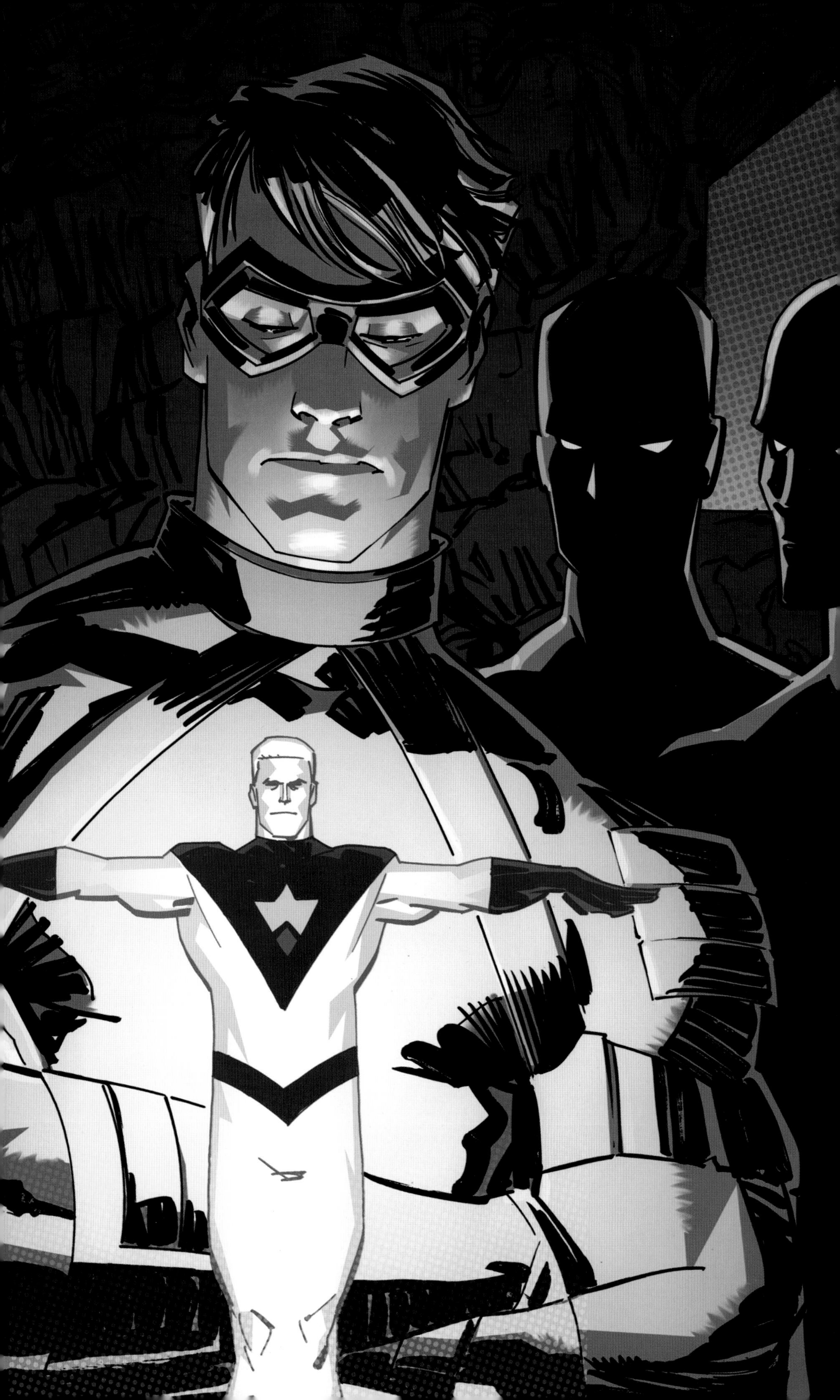

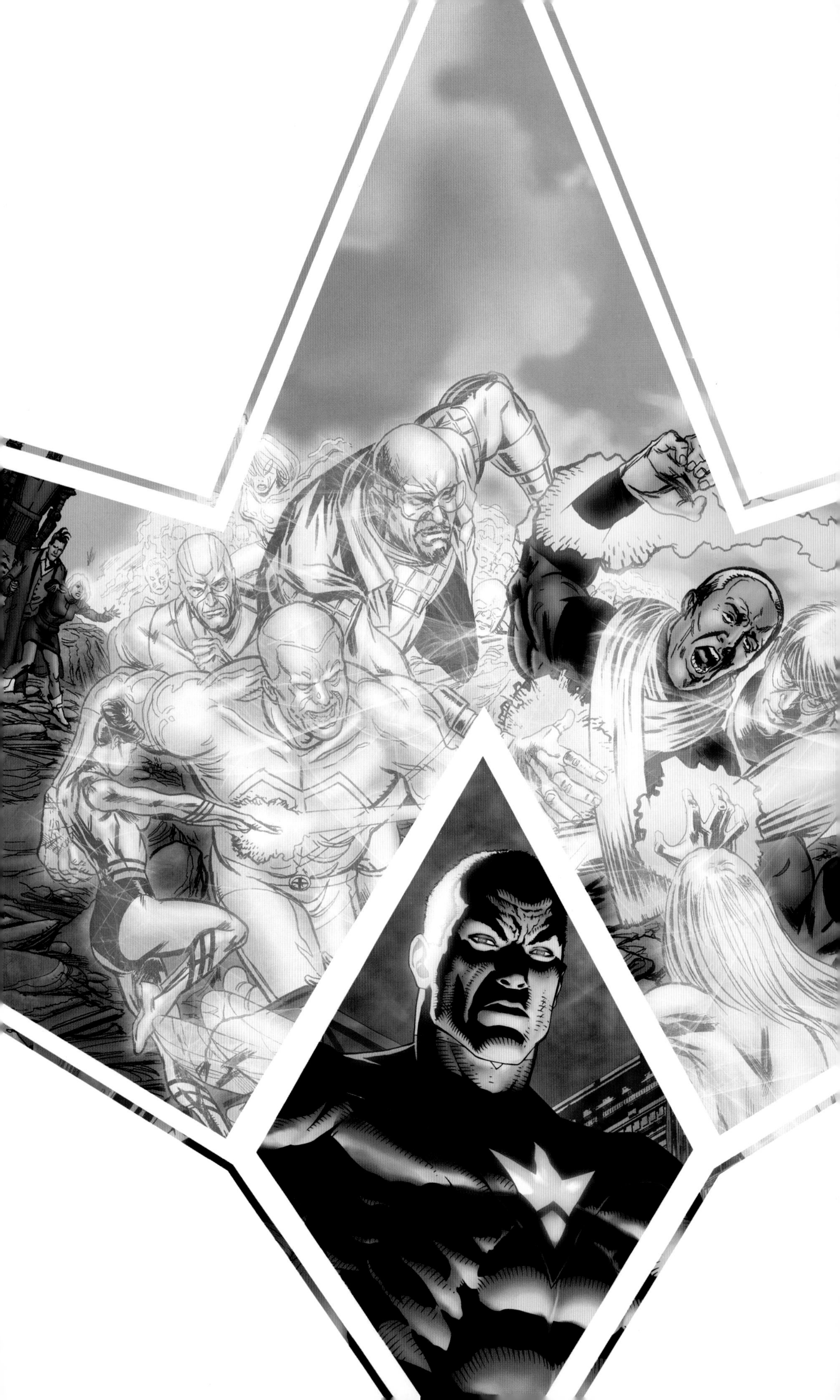

IRREDEEMABLE ™

PREMIER EDITION
VOLUME THREE

CREATED & WRITTEN BY
MARK WAID

ILLUSTRATED BY
**PETER KRAUSE
DIEGO BARRETO**

COLORS BY
**ANDREW DALHOUSE
NOLAN WOODARD**

LETTERS BY
ED DUKESHIRE

PLUTONIAN CHARACTER DESIGN BY
PAUL AZACETA

COVER & COLLECTION DESIGN BY
MICHELLE ANKLEY

WITH ART BY *JOHN CASSADAY* & *LAURA MARTIN*,
JEFFREY SPOKES, DAN PANOSIAN

ORIGINAL SERIES EDITOR
MATT GAGNON

COLLECTION ASSISTANT EDITOR
MATTHEW LEVINE

COLLECTION EDITOR
DAFNA PLEBAN

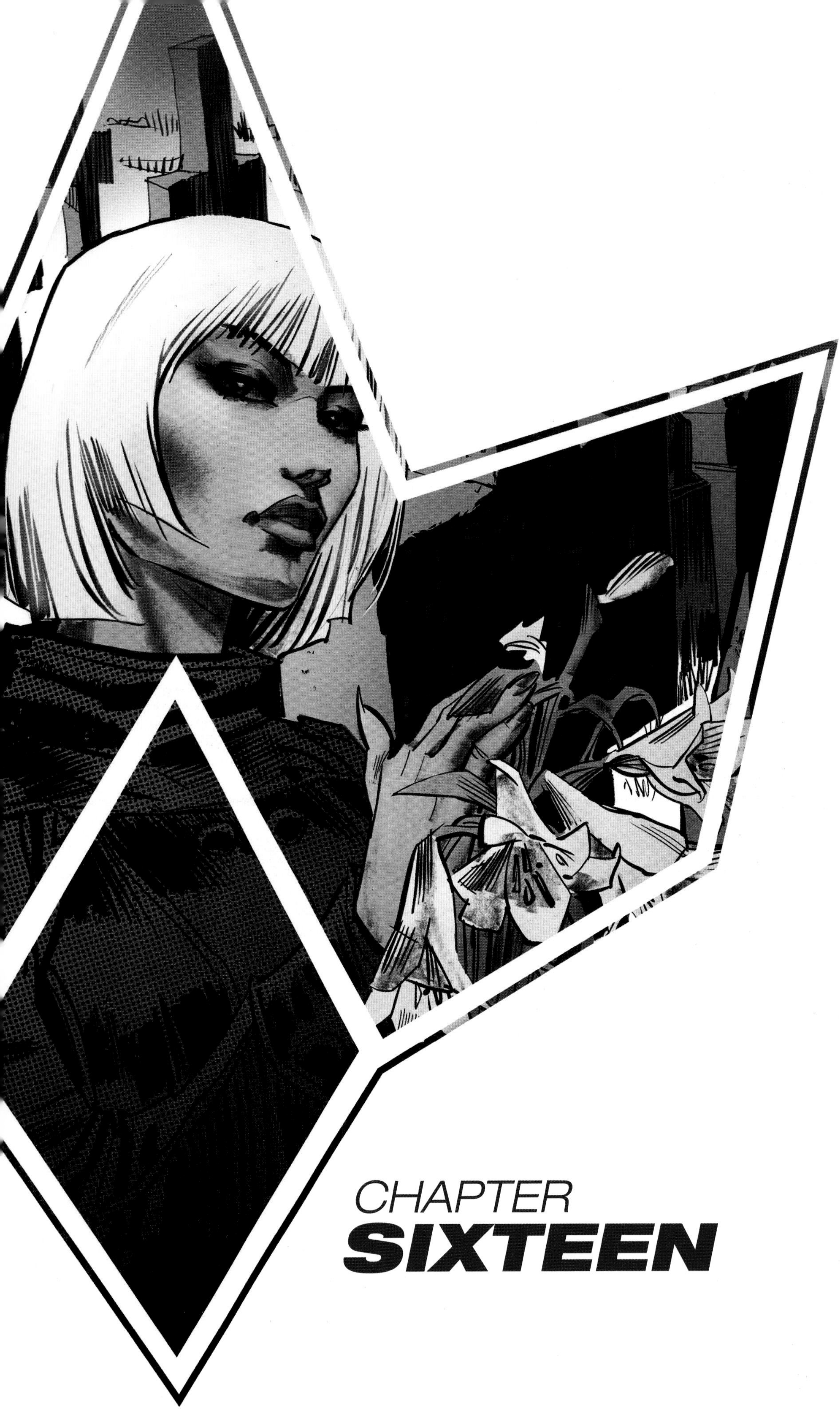

CHAPTER SIXTEEN

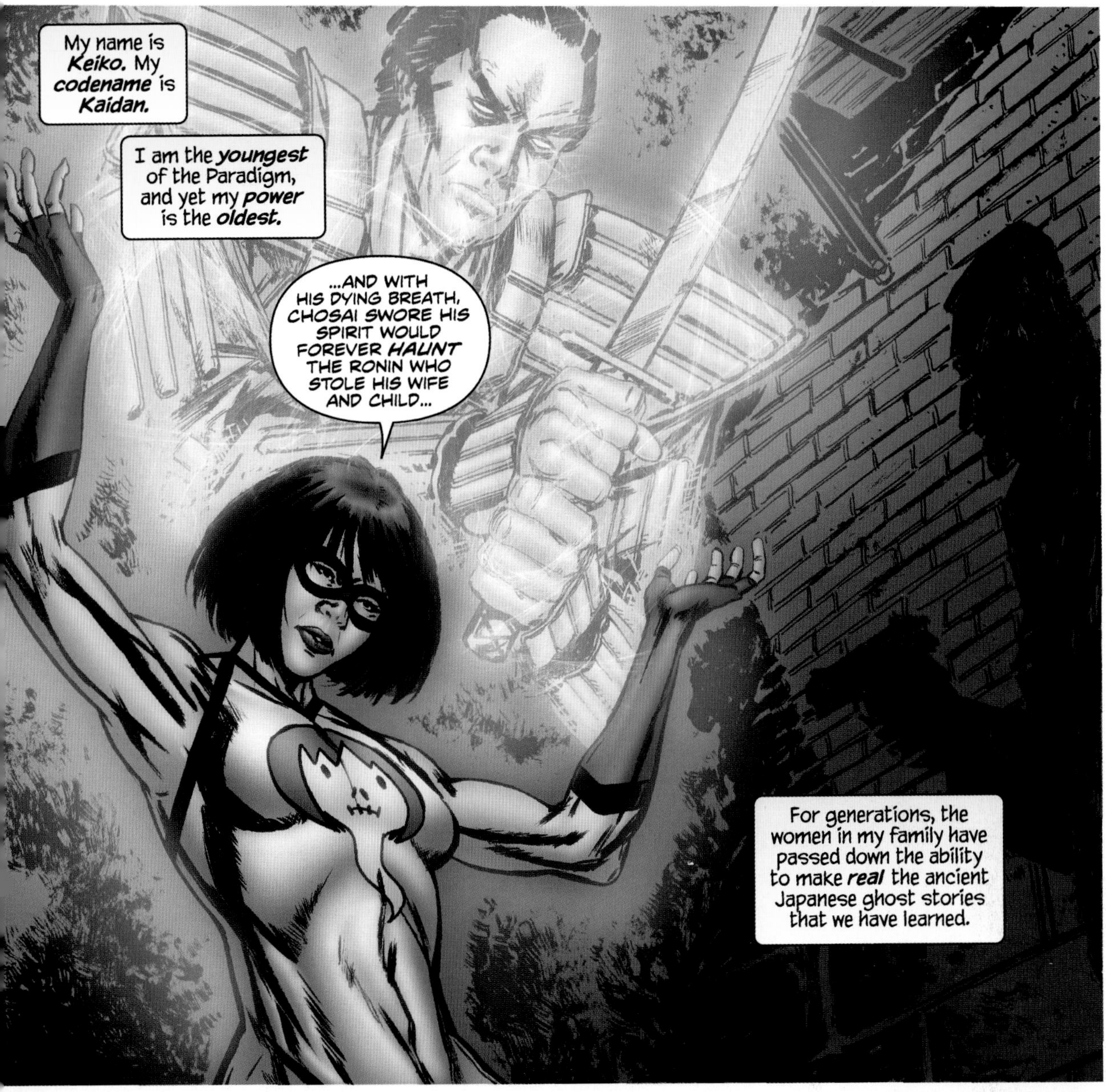

My name is *Keiko.* My *codename* is *Kaidan.*
I am the *youngest* of the Paradigm, and yet my *power* is the *oldest.*
...AND WITH HIS DYING BREATH, CHOSAI SWORE HIS SPIRIT WOULD FOREVER *HAUNT* THE RONIN WHO STOLE HIS WIFE AND CHILD...
For generations, the women in my family have passed down the ability to make *real* the ancient Japanese ghost stories that we have learned.

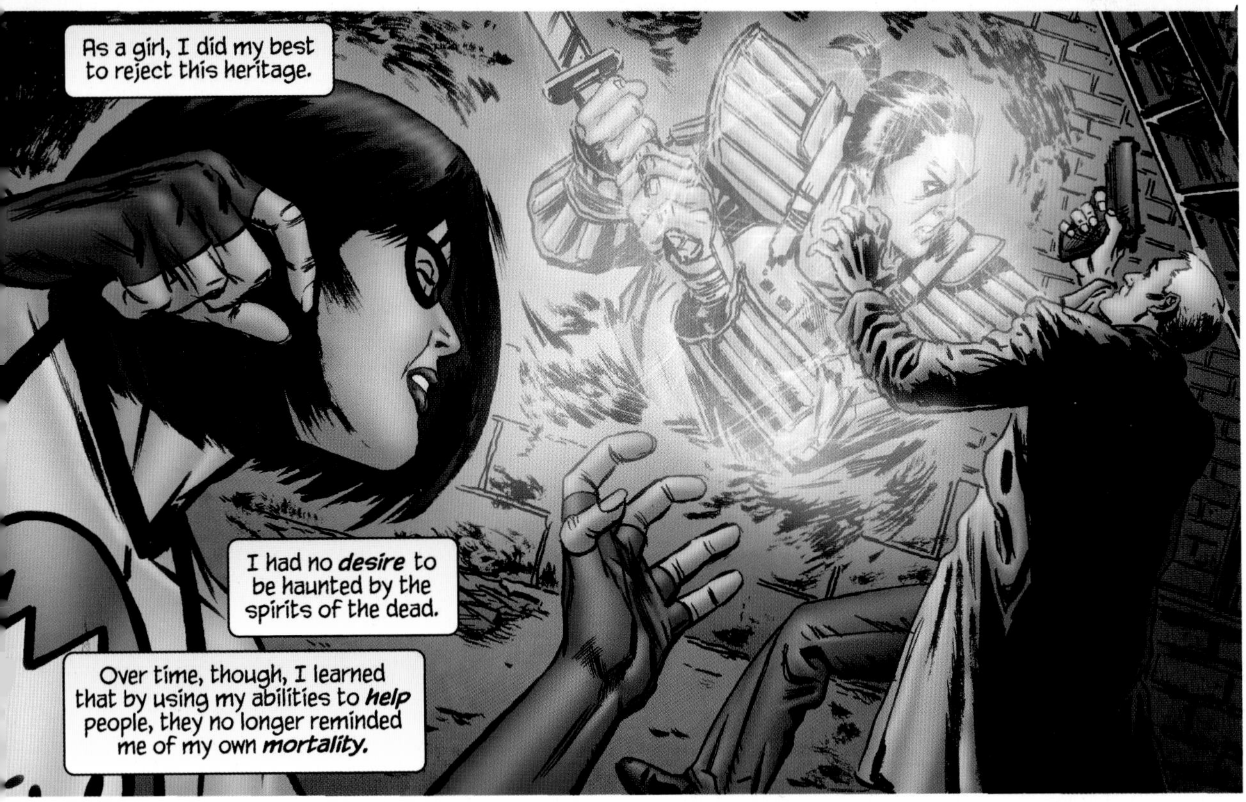

As a girl, I did my best to reject this heritage.
I had no *desire* to be haunted by the spirits of the dead.
Over time, though, I learned that by using my abilities to *help* people, they no longer reminded me of my own *mortality.*

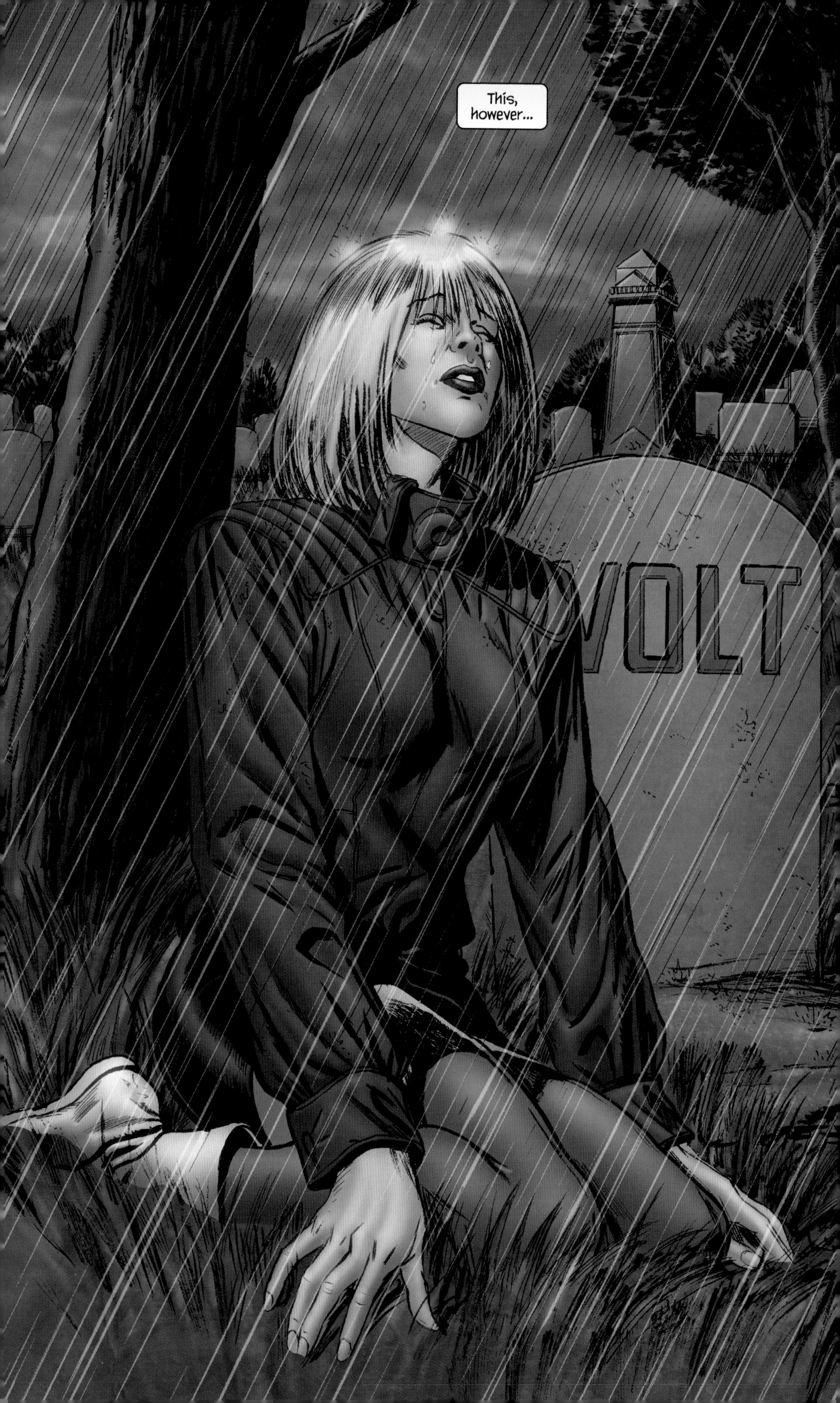
This, however...
VOLT

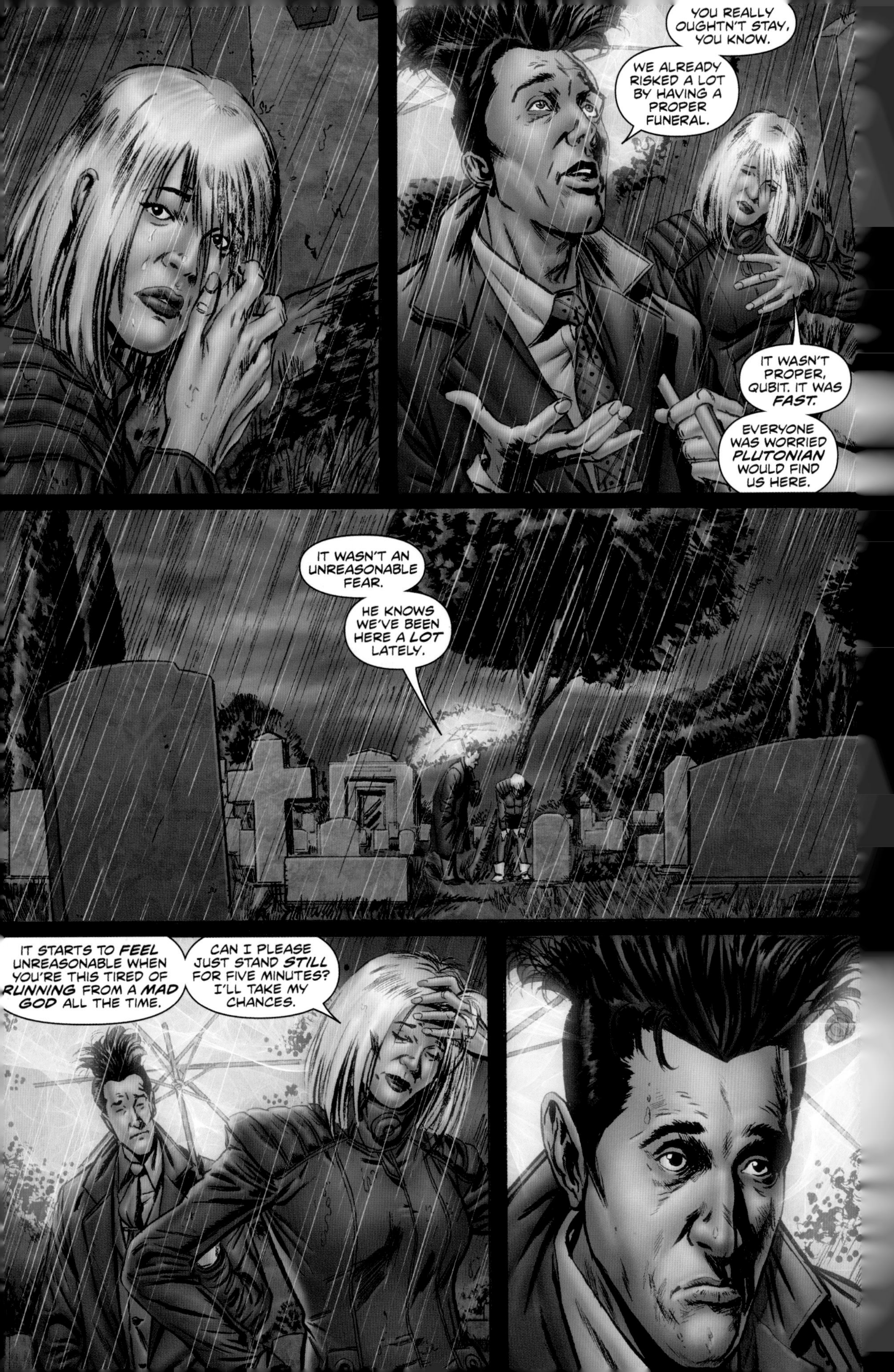
YOU REALLY OUGHTN'T STAY, YOU KNOW.
WE ALREADY RISKED A LOT BY HAVING A PROPER FUNERAL.
IT WASN'T PROPER, QUBIT. IT WAS FAST.
EVERYONE WAS WORRIED PLUTONIAN WOULD FIND US HERE.
IT WASN'T AN UNREASONABLE FEAR.
HE KNOWS WE'VE BEEN HERE A LOT LATELY.
IT STARTS TO FEEL UNREASONABLE WHEN YOU'RE THIS TIRED OF RUNNING FROM A MAD GOD ALL THE TIME.
CAN I PLEASE JUST STAND STILL FOR FIVE MINUTES? I'LL TAKE MY CHANCES.

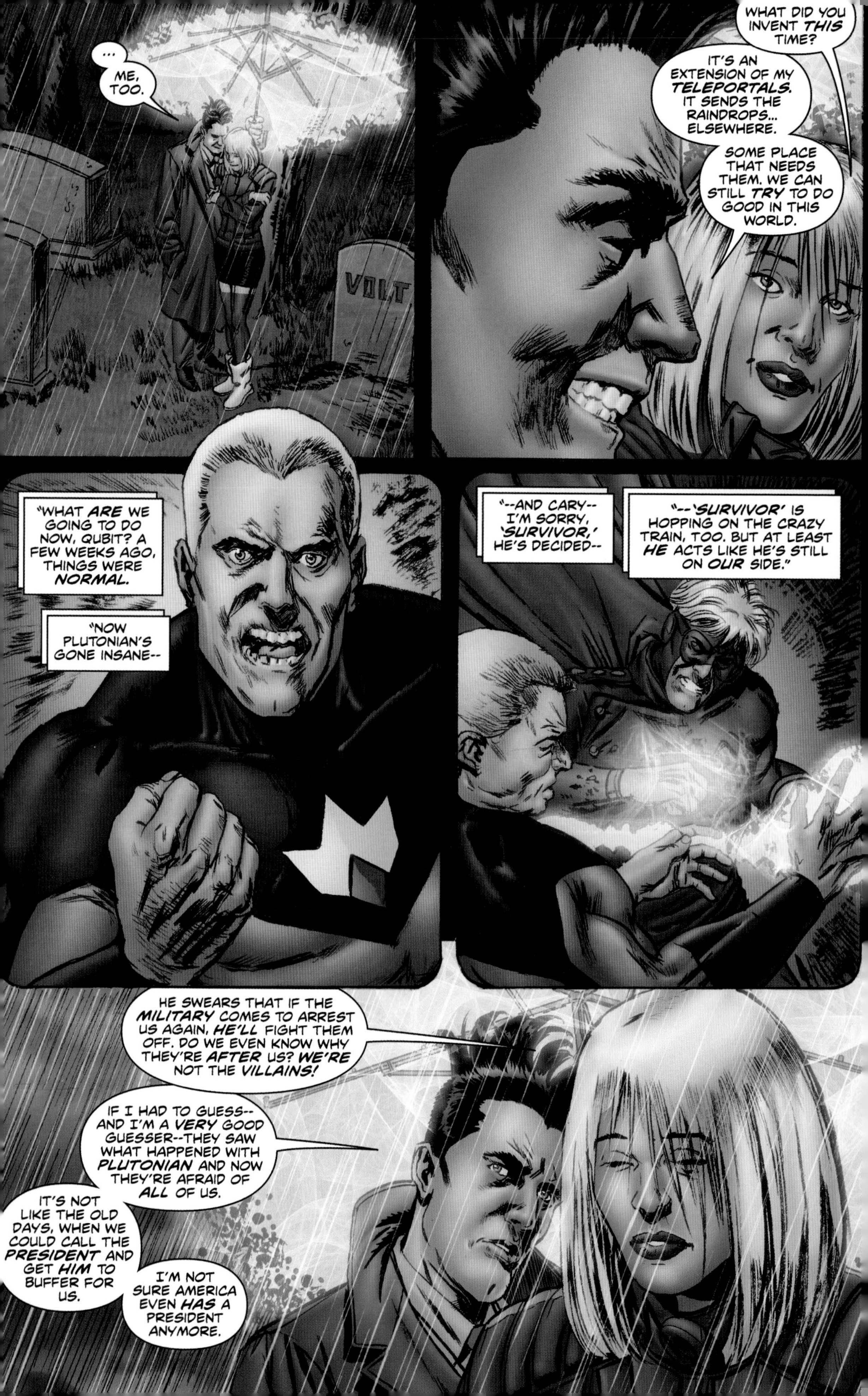
... ME, TOO.
WHAT DID YOU INVENT THIS TIME?
IT'S AN EXTENSION OF MY TELEPORTALS. IT SENDS THE RAINDROPS... ELSEWHERE.
SOME PLACE THAT NEEDS THEM. WE CAN STILL TRY TO DO GOOD IN THIS WORLD.
VOLT
"WHAT ARE WE GOING TO DO NOW, QUBIT? A FEW WEEKS AGO, THINGS WERE NORMAL.
"NOW PLUTONIAN'S GONE INSANE--
"--AND CARY-- I'M SORRY, 'SURVIVOR,' HE'S DECIDED--
"--'SURVIVOR' IS HOPPING ON THE CRAZY TRAIN, TOO. BUT AT LEAST HE ACTS LIKE HE'S STILL ON OUR SIDE."
HE SWEARS THAT IF THE MILITARY COMES TO ARREST US AGAIN, HE'LL FIGHT THEM OFF. DO WE EVEN KNOW WHY THEY'RE AFTER US? WE'RE NOT THE VILLAINS!
IF I HAD TO GUESS-- AND I'M A VERY GOOD GUESSER--THEY SAW WHAT HAPPENED WITH PLUTONIAN AND NOW THEY'RE AFRAID OF ALL OF US.
IT'S NOT LIKE THE OLD DAYS, WHEN WE COULD CALL THE PRESIDENT AND GET HIM TO BUFFER FOR US.
I'M NOT SURE AMERICA EVEN HAS A PRESIDENT ANYMORE.

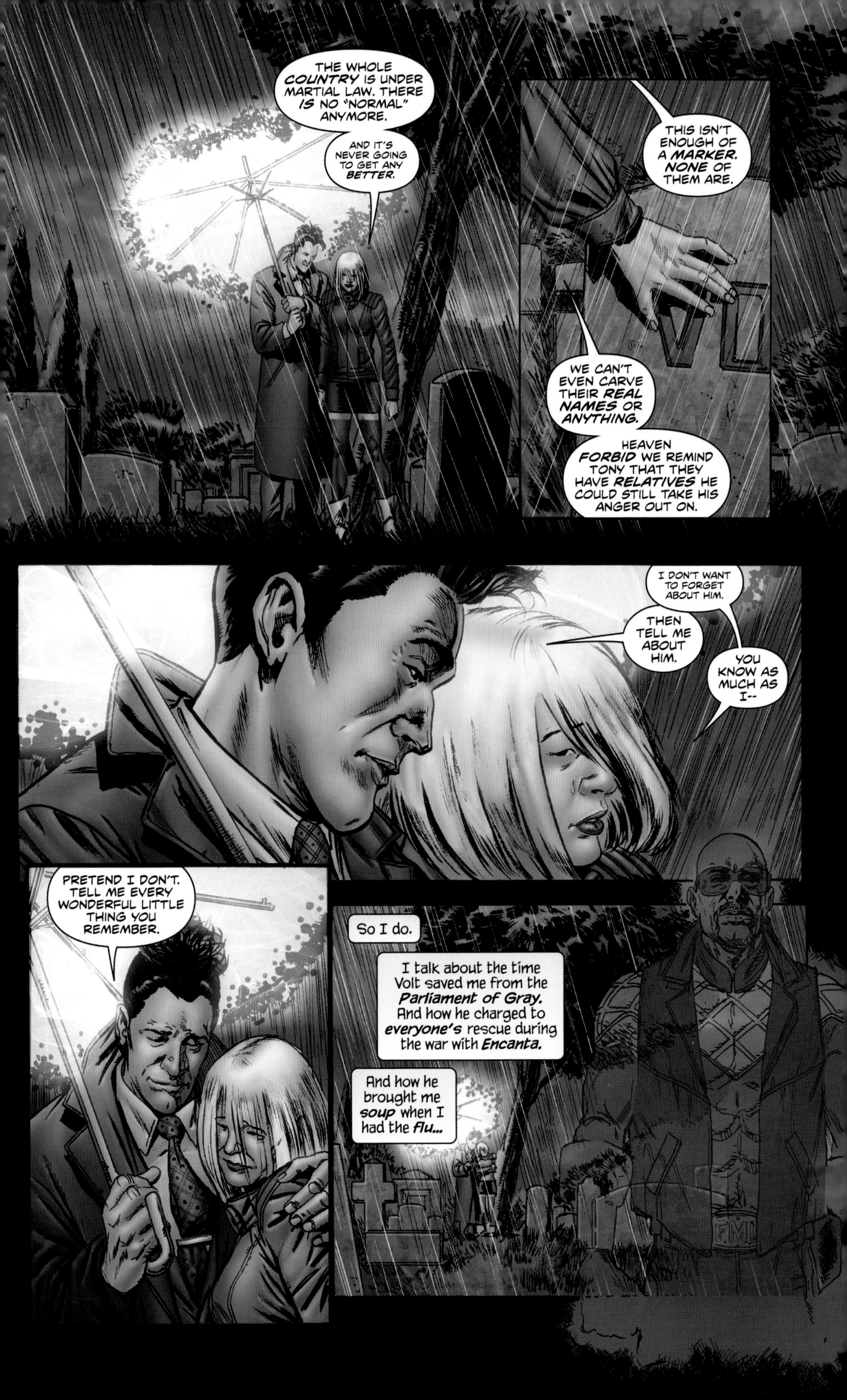
THE WHOLE COUNTRY IS UNDER MARTIAL LAW. THERE IS NO "NORMAL" ANYMORE.
AND IT'S NEVER GOING TO GET ANY BETTER.
THIS ISN'T ENOUGH OF A MARKER. NONE OF THEM ARE.
WE CAN'T EVEN CARVE THEIR REAL NAMES OR ANYTHING.
HEAVEN FORBID WE REMIND TONY THAT THEY HAVE RELATIVES HE COULD STILL TAKE HIS ANGER OUT ON.
I DON'T WANT TO FORGET ABOUT HIM.
THEN TELL ME ABOUT HIM.
YOU KNOW AS MUCH AS I--
PRETEND I DON'T. TELL ME EVERY WONDERFUL LITTLE THING YOU REMEMBER.
So I do.
I talk about the time Volt saved me from the Parliament of Gray. And how he charged to everyone's rescue during the war with Encanta.
And how he brought me soup when I had the flu...

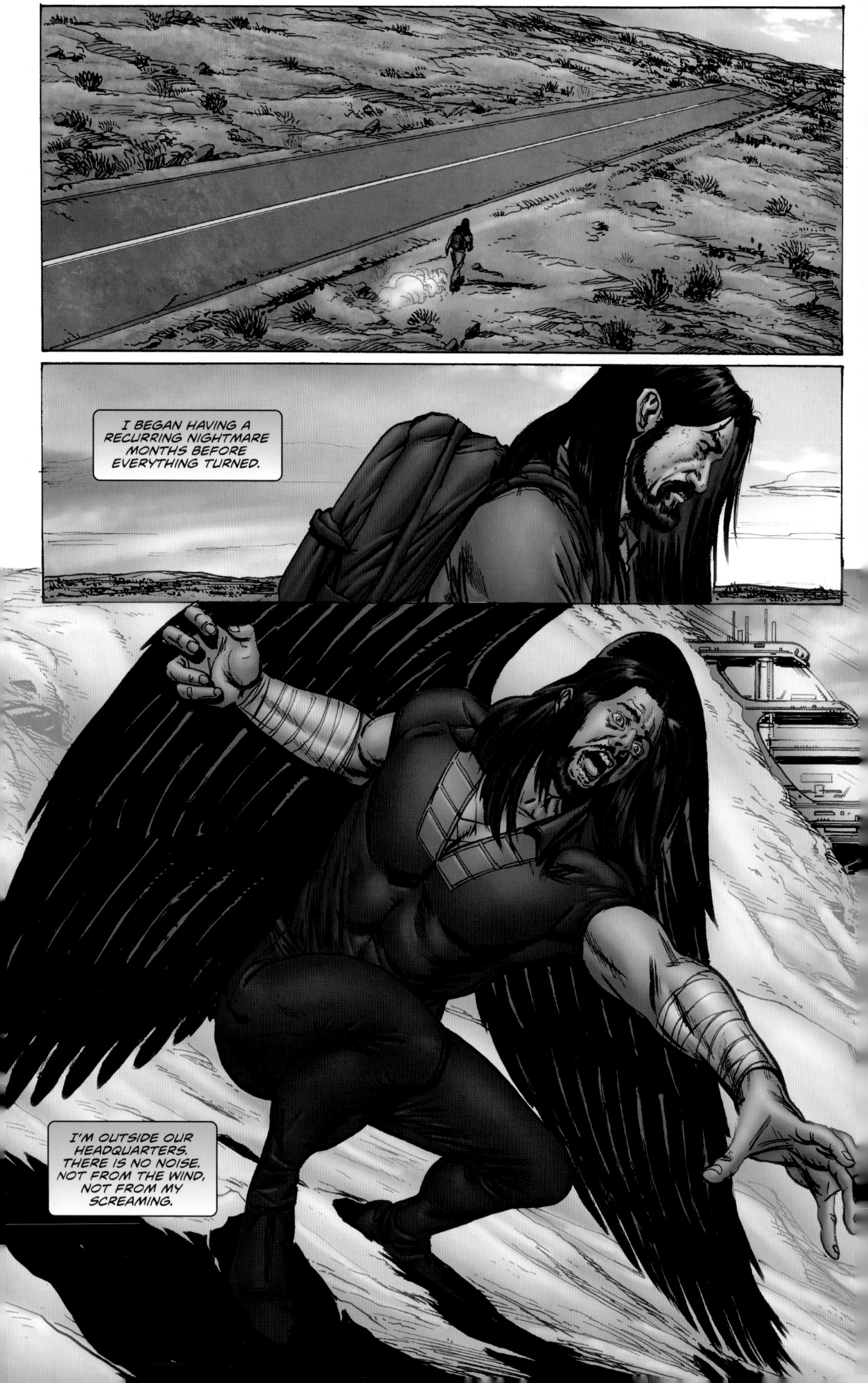
I BEGAN HAVING A RECURRING NIGHTMARE MONTHS BEFORE EVERYTHING TURNED.
I'M OUTSIDE OUR HEADQUARTERS. THERE IS NO NOISE. NOT FROM THE WIND, NOT FROM MY SCREAMING.

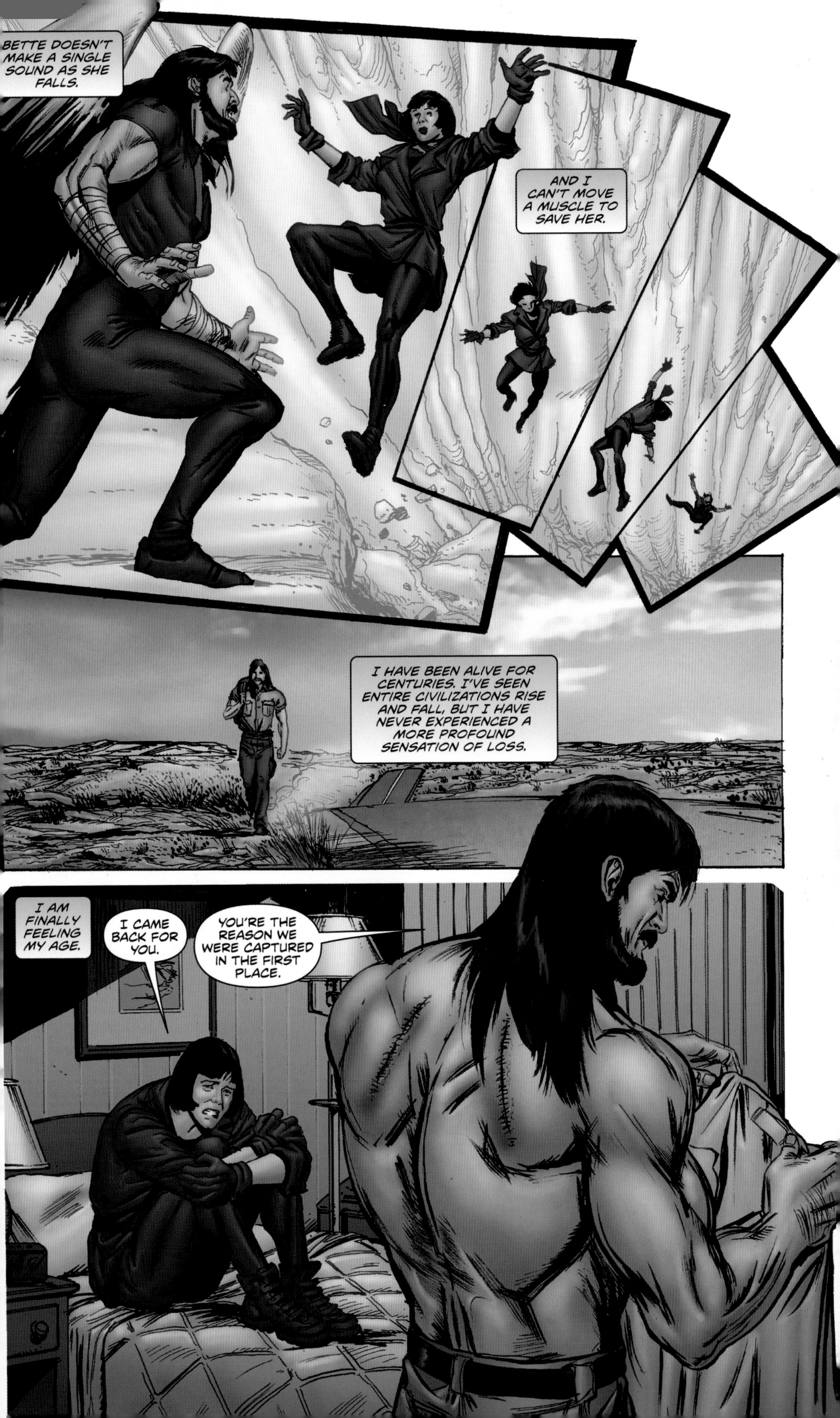
BETTE DOESN'T MAKE A SINGLE SOUND AS SHE FALLS.
AND I CAN'T MOVE A MUSCLE TO SAVE HER.
I HAVE BEEN ALIVE FOR CENTURIES. I'VE SEEN ENTIRE CIVILIZATIONS RISE AND FALL, BUT I HAVE NEVER EXPERIENCED A MORE PROFOUND SENSATION OF LOSS.
I AM FINALLY FEELING MY AGE.
I CAME BACK FOR YOU.
YOU'RE THE REASON WE WERE CAPTURED IN THE FIRST PLACE.

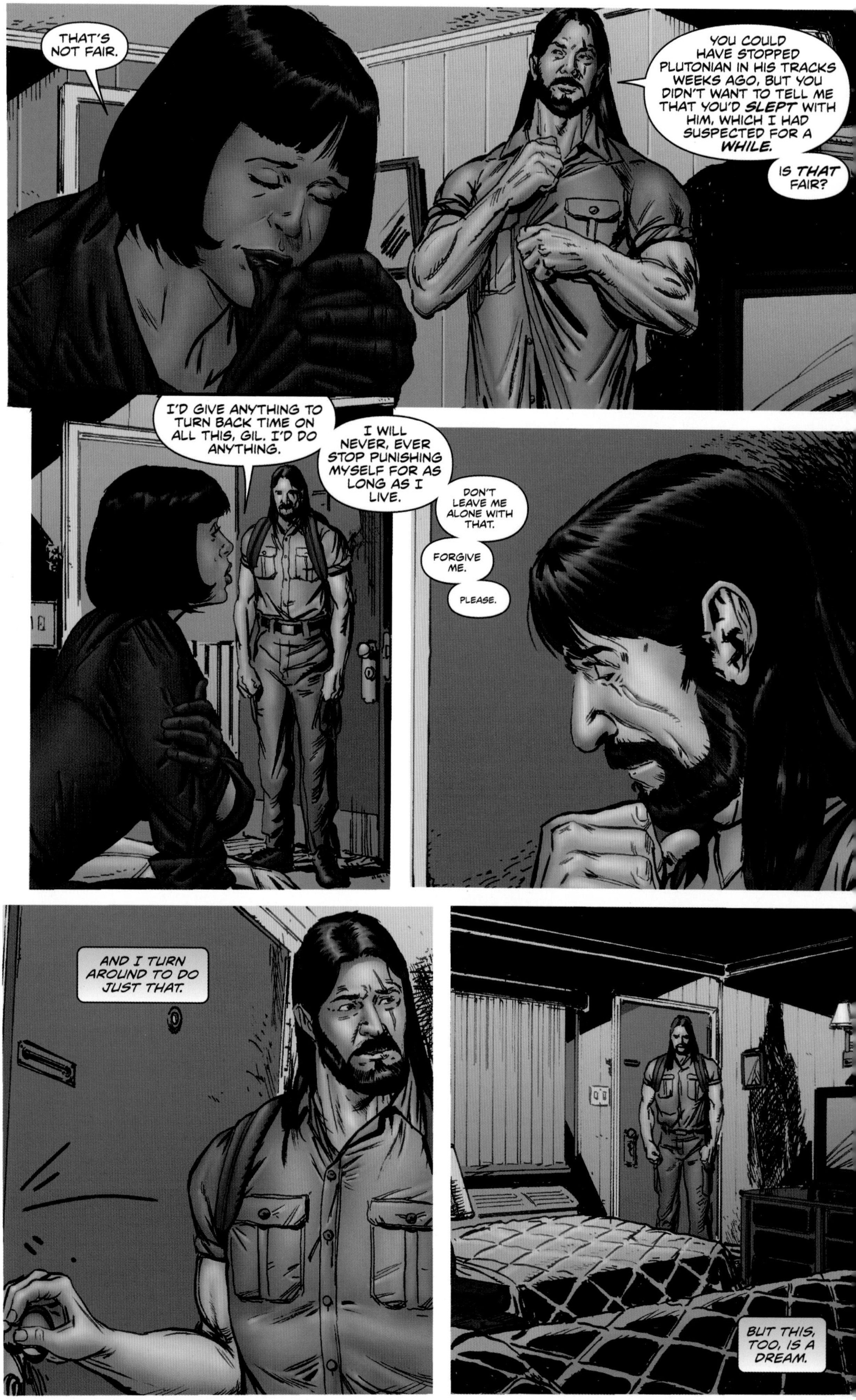
THAT'S NOT FAIR.
YOU COULD HAVE STOPPED PLUTONIAN IN HIS TRACKS WEEKS AGO, BUT YOU DIDN'T WANT TO TELL ME THAT YOU'D SLEPT WITH HIM, WHICH I HAD SUSPECTED FOR A WHILE.
IS THAT FAIR?
I'D GIVE ANYTHING TO TURN BACK TIME ON ALL THIS, GIL. I'D DO ANYTHING.
I WILL NEVER, EVER STOP PUNISHING MYSELF FOR AS LONG AS I LIVE.
DON'T LEAVE ME ALONE WITH THAT.
FORGIVE ME.
PLEASE.
AND I TURN AROUND TO DO JUST THAT.
BUT THIS, TOO, IS A DREAM.

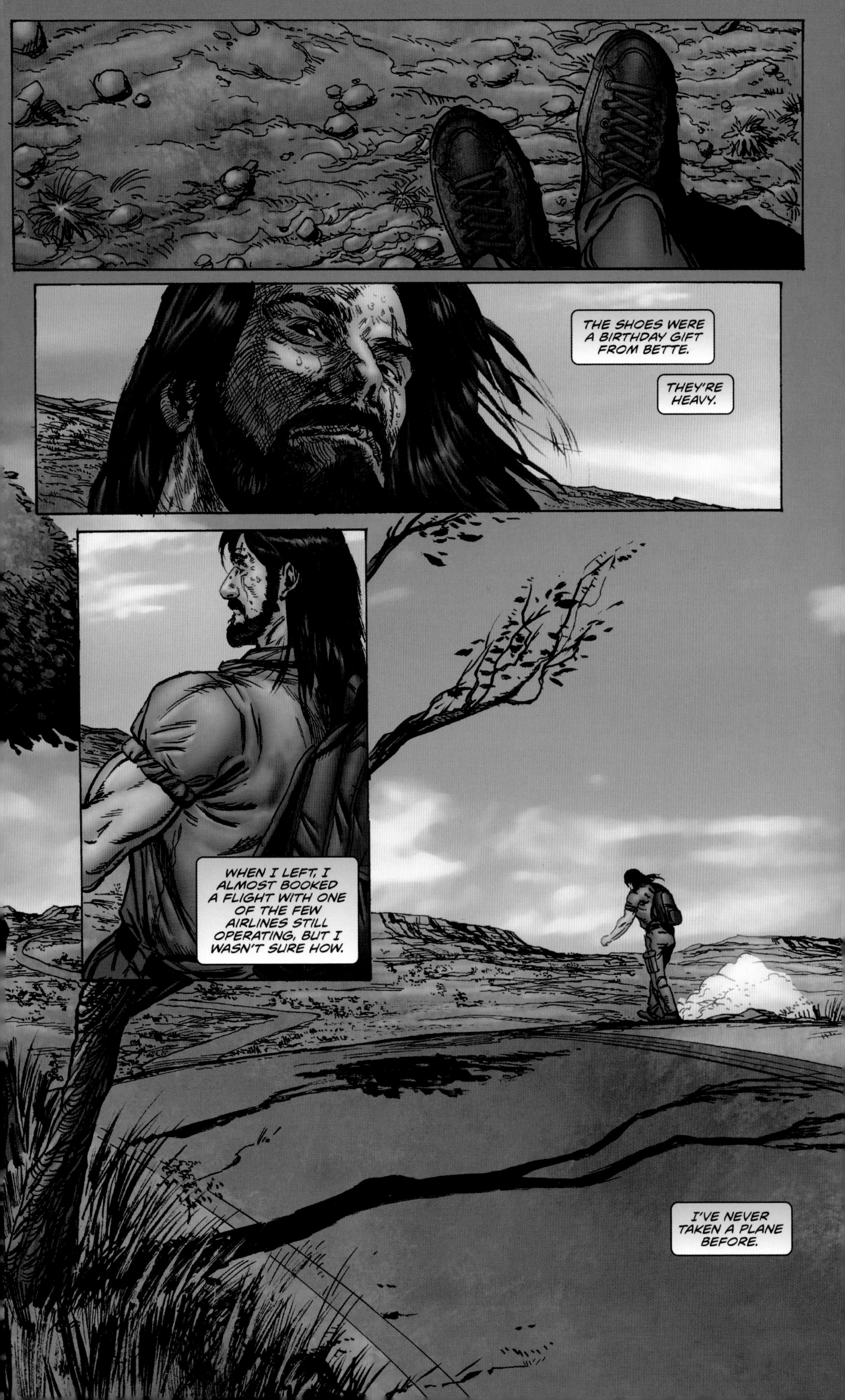
THE SHOES WERE A BIRTHDAY GIFT FROM BETTE.
THEY'RE HEAVY.
WHEN I LEFT, I ALMOST BOOKED A FLIGHT WITH ONE OF THE FEW AIRLINES STILL OPERATING, BUT I WASN'T SURE HOW.
I'VE NEVER TAKEN A PLANE BEFORE.

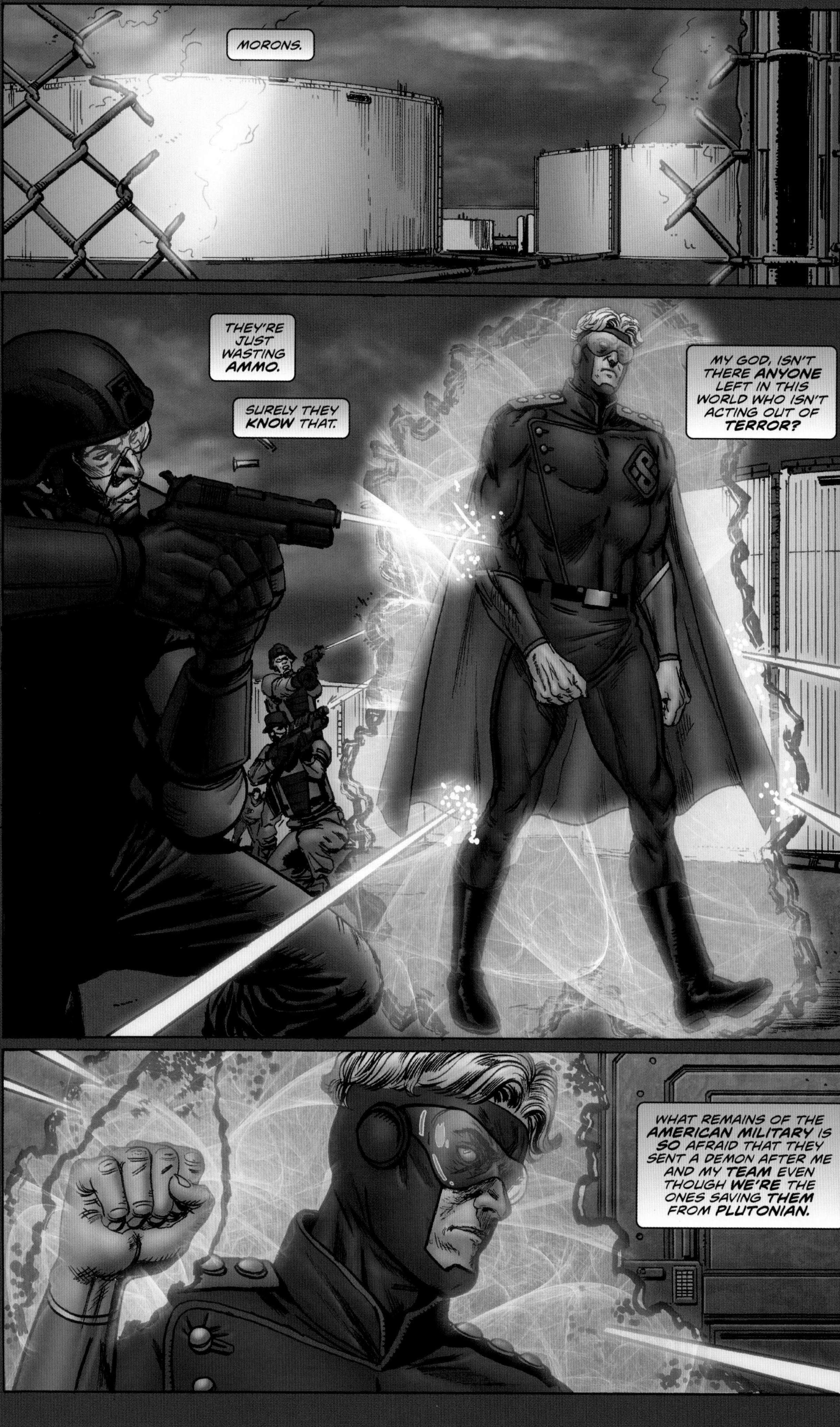
MORONS.
THEY'RE JUST WASTING AMMO.
SURELY THEY KNOW THAT.
MY GOD, ISN'T THERE ANYONE LEFT IN THIS WORLD WHO ISN'T ACTING OUT OF TERROR?
WHAT REMAINS OF THE AMERICAN MILITARY IS SO AFRAID THAT THEY SENT A DEMON AFTER ME AND MY TEAM EVEN THOUGH WE'RE THE ONES SAVING THEM FROM PLUTONIAN.

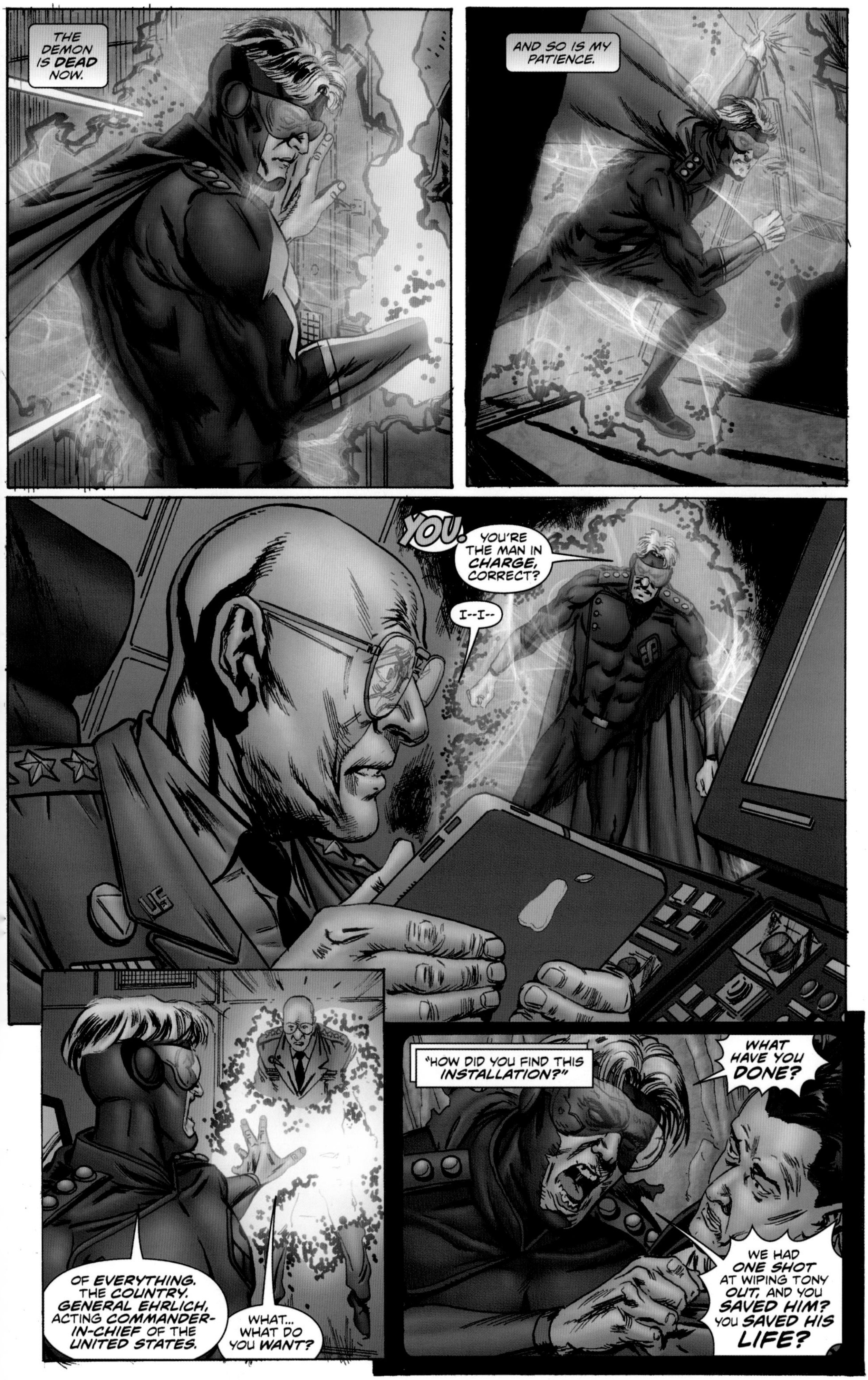
THE DEMON IS DEAD NOW.
AND SO IS MY PATIENCE.
YOU!
YOU'RE THE MAN IN CHARGE, CORRECT?
I--I--
OF EVERYTHING. THE COUNTRY. GENERAL EHRLICH, ACTING COMMANDER-IN-CHIEF OF THE UNITED STATES.
WHAT... WHAT DO YOU WANT?
"HOW DID YOU FIND THIS INSTALLATION?"
WHAT HAVE YOU DONE?
WE HAD ONE SHOT AT WIPING TONY OUT, AND YOU SAVED HIM? YOU SAVED HIS LIFE?

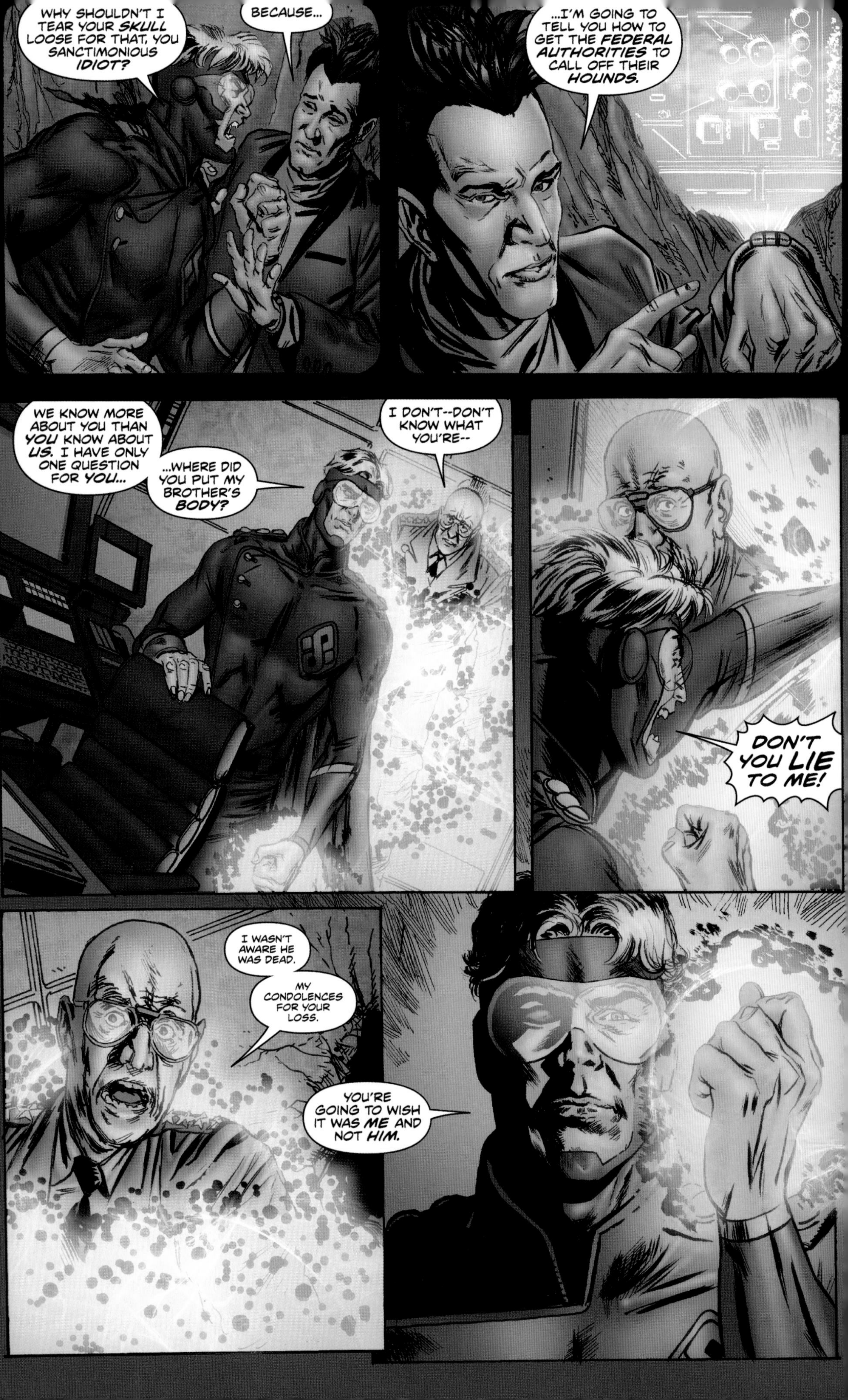
WHY SHOULDN'T I TEAR YOUR SKULL LOOSE FOR THAT, YOU SANCTIMONIOUS IDIOT?
BECAUSE...
...I'M GOING TO TELL YOU HOW TO GET THE FEDERAL AUTHORITIES TO CALL OFF THEIR HOUNDS.
WE KNOW MORE ABOUT YOU THAN YOU KNOW ABOUT US. I HAVE ONLY ONE QUESTION FOR YOU...
...WHERE DID YOU PUT MY BROTHER'S BODY?
I DON'T--DON'T KNOW WHAT YOU'RE--
DON'T YOU LIE TO ME!
I WASN'T AWARE HE WAS DEAD.
MY CONDOLENCES FOR YOUR LOSS.
YOU'RE GOING TO WISH IT WAS ME AND NOT HIM.

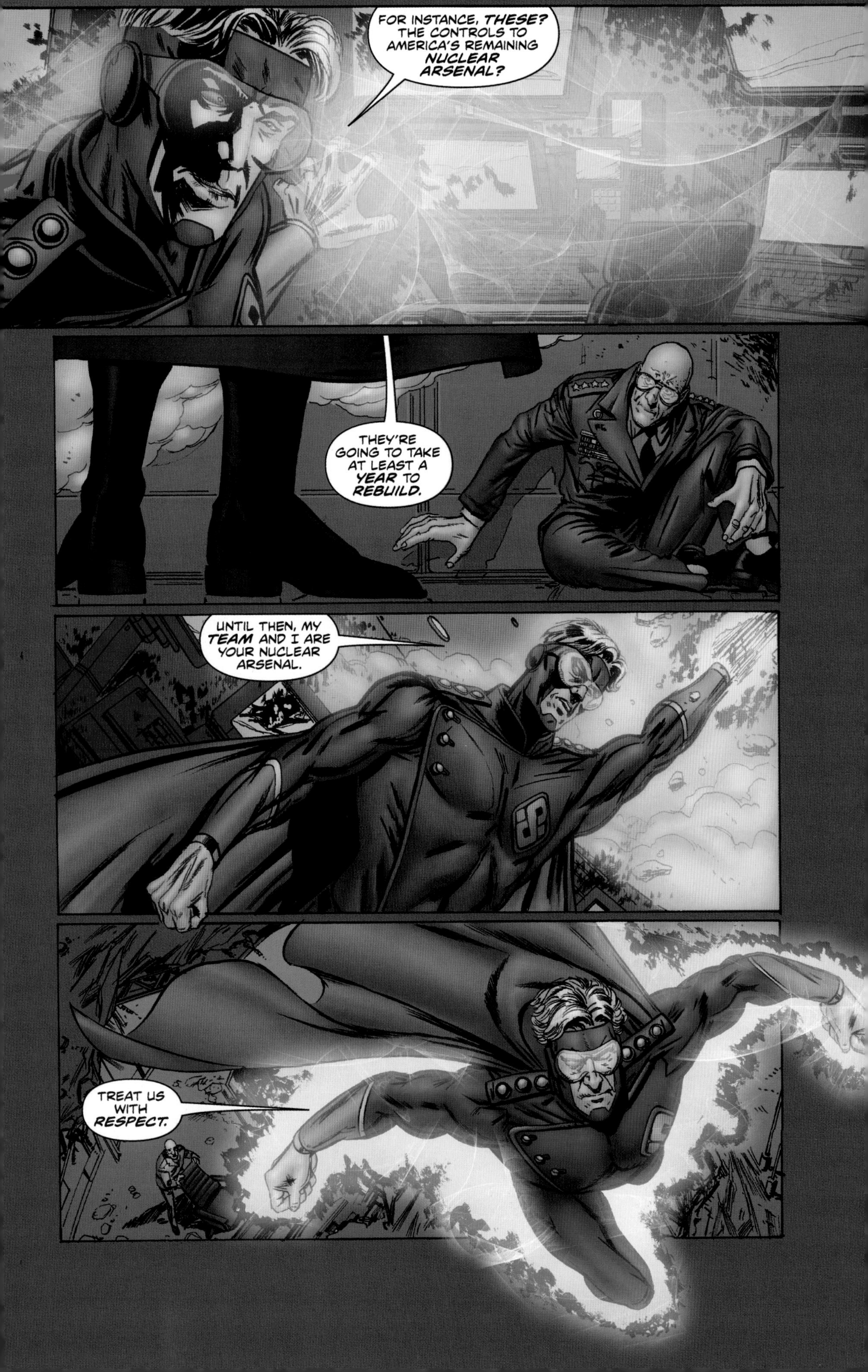

FOR INSTANCE, THESE? THE CONTROLS TO AMERICA'S REMAINING NUCLEAR ARSENAL?
THEY'RE GOING TO TAKE AT LEAST A YEAR TO REBUILD.
UNTIL THEN, MY TEAM AND I ARE YOUR NUCLEAR ARSENAL.
TREAT US WITH RESPECT.

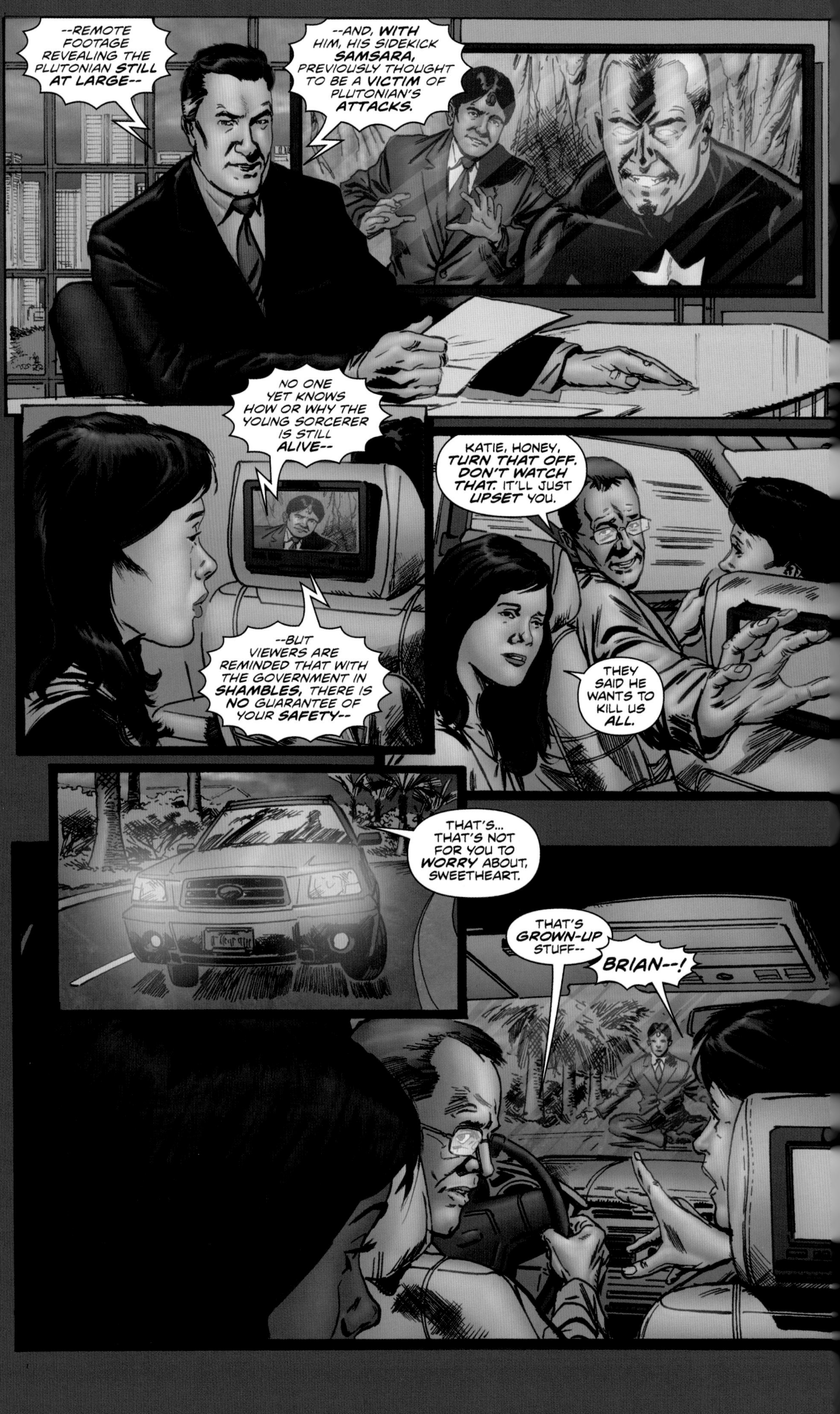
--REMOTE FOOTAGE REVEALING THE PLUTONIAN STILL AT LARGE--
--AND, WITH HIM, HIS SIDEKICK SAMSARA, PREVIOUSLY THOUGHT TO BE A VICTIM OF PLUTONIAN'S ATTACKS.
NO ONE YET KNOWS HOW OR WHY THE YOUNG SORCERER IS STILL ALIVE--
--BUT VIEWERS ARE REMINDED THAT WITH THE GOVERNMENT IN SHAMBLES, THERE IS NO GUARANTEE OF YOUR SAFETY--
KATIE, HONEY, TURN THAT OFF. DON'T WATCH THAT. IT'LL JUST UPSET YOU.
THEY SAID HE WANTS TO KILL US ALL.
THAT'S... THAT'S NOT FOR YOU TO WORRY ABOUT, SWEETHEART.
THAT'S GROWN-UP STUFF--
BRIAN--!

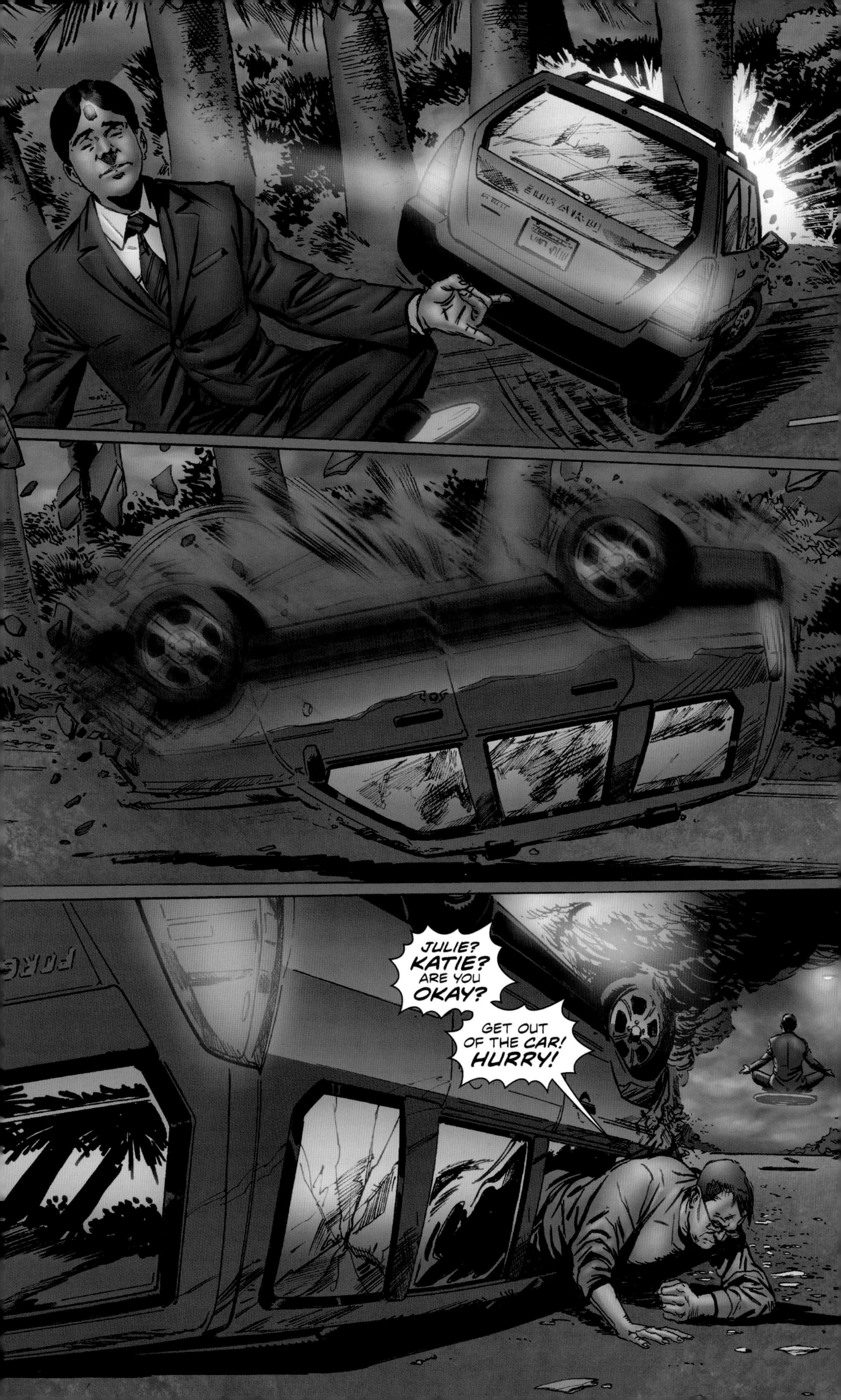
JULIE? KATIE? ARE YOU OKAY?
GET OUT OF THE CAR! HURRY!

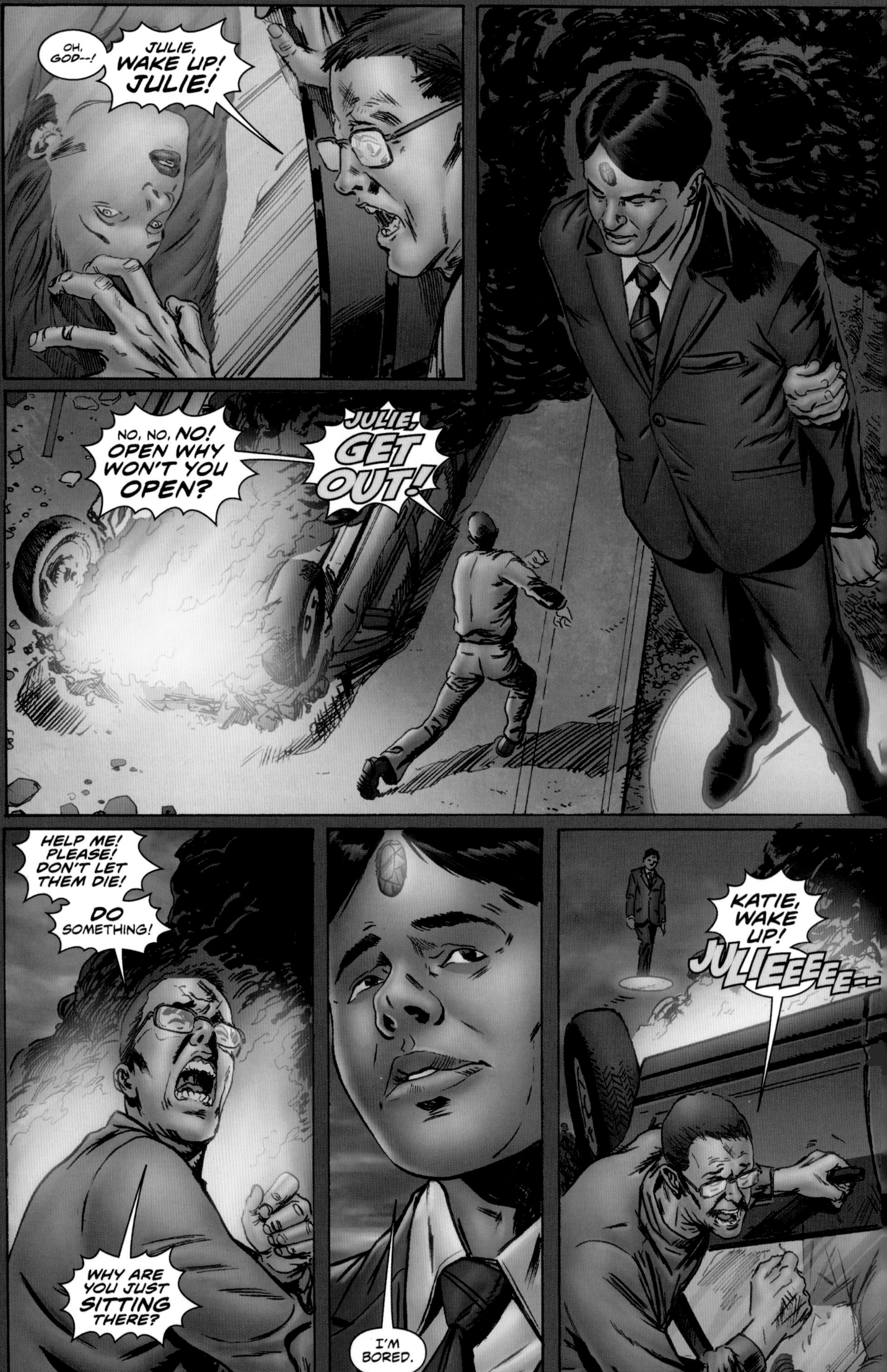
OH, GOD--!
JULIE, WAKE UP! JULIE!
NO, NO, NO! OPEN WHY WON'T YOU OPEN?
JULIE, GET OUT!
HELP ME! PLEASE! DON'T LET THEM DIE!
DO SOMETHING!
WHY ARE YOU JUST SITTING THERE?
I'M BORED.
KATIE, WAKE UP!
JULIEEEEE--

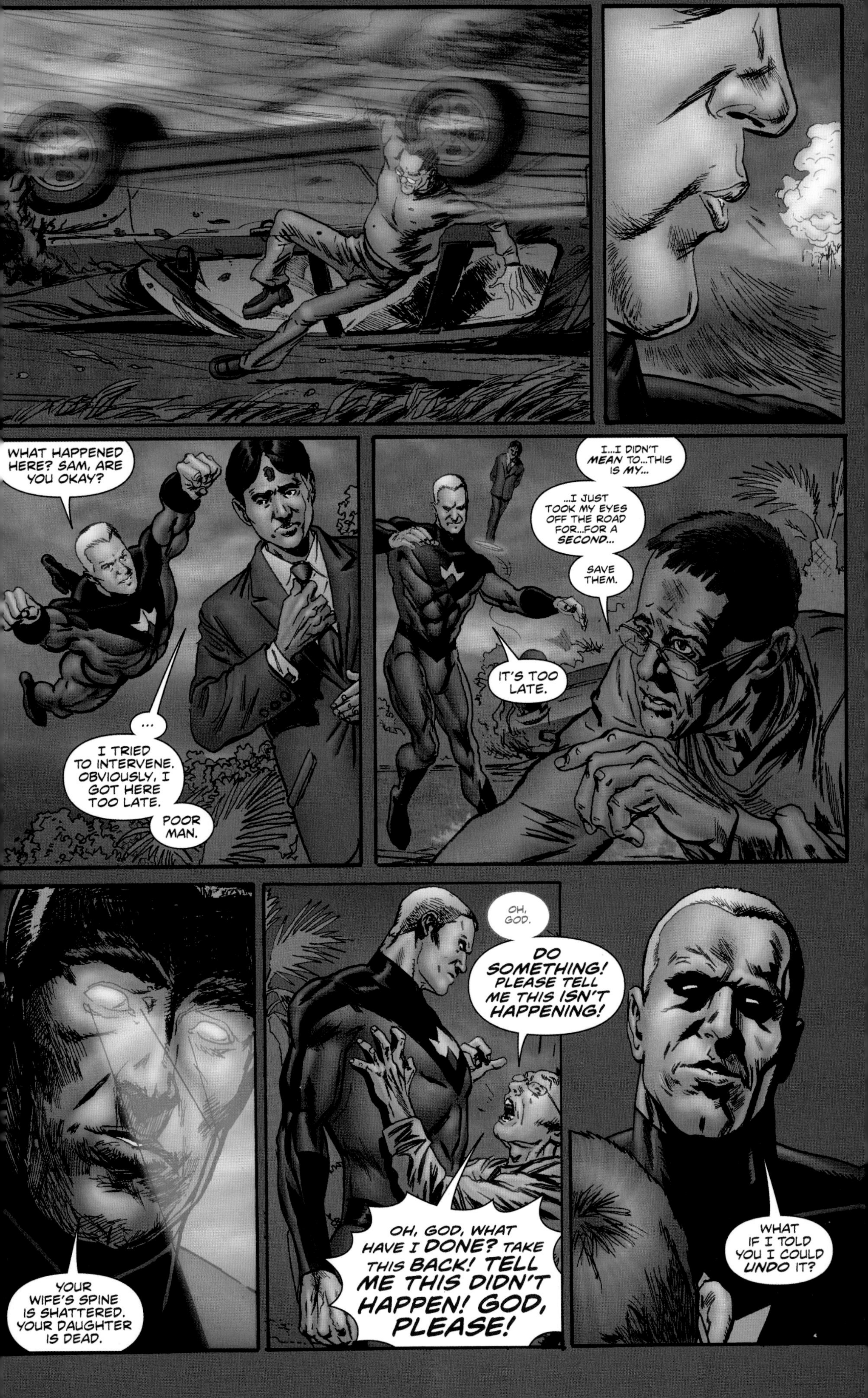
WHAT HAPPENED HERE? SAM, ARE YOU OKAY?
...
I TRIED TO INTERVENE. OBVIOUSLY, I GOT HERE TOO LATE.
POOR MAN.
I...I DIDN'T MEAN TO...THIS IS MY...
...I JUST TOOK MY EYES OFF THE ROAD FOR...FOR A SECOND...
SAVE THEM.
IT'S TOO LATE.
YOUR WIFE'S SPINE IS SHATTERED. YOUR DAUGHTER IS DEAD.
OH, GOD.
DO SOMETHING! PLEASE TELL ME THIS ISN'T HAPPENING!
OH, GOD, WHAT HAVE I DONE? TAKE THIS BACK! TELL ME THIS DIDN'T HAPPEN! GOD, PLEASE!
WHAT IF I TOLD YOU I COULD UNDO IT?

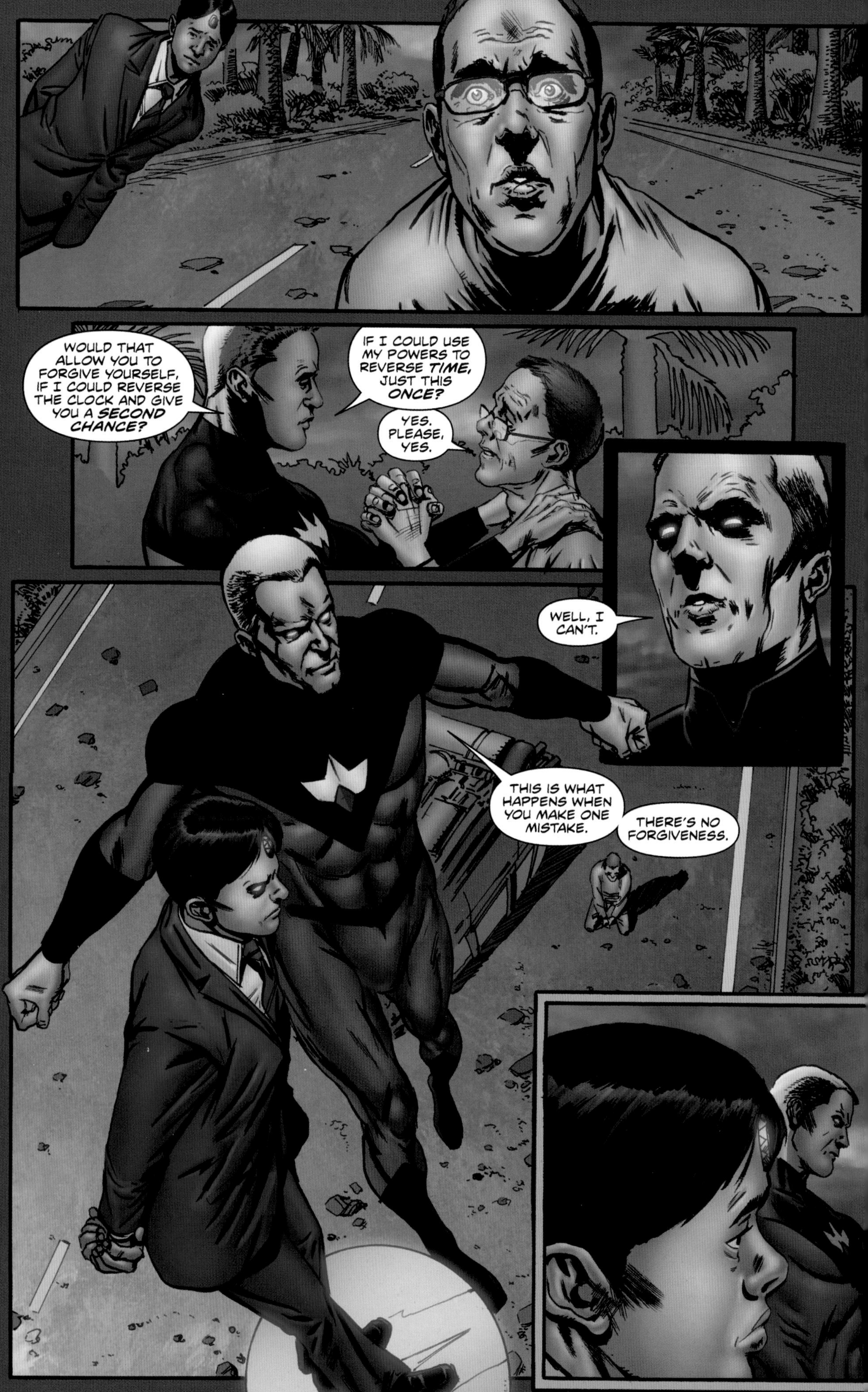

WOULD THAT ALLOW YOU TO FORGIVE YOURSELF, IF I COULD REVERSE THE CLOCK AND GIVE YOU A *SECOND CHANCE?*
IF I COULD USE MY POWERS TO REVERSE *TIME,* JUST THIS *ONCE?*
YES. PLEASE, YES.
WELL, I CAN'T.
THIS IS WHAT HAPPENS WHEN YOU MAKE ONE MISTAKE.
THERE'S NO FORGIVENESS.

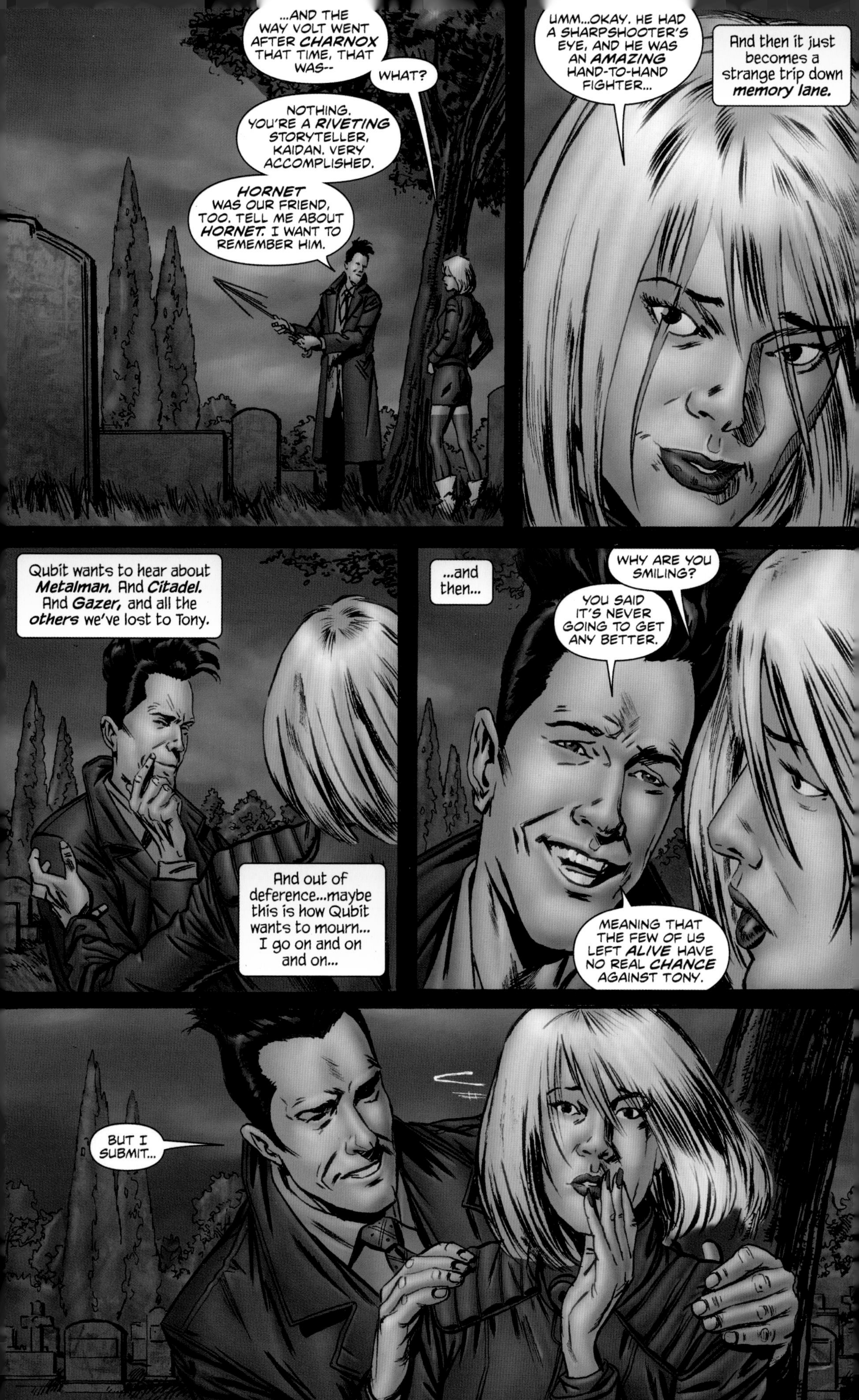
...AND THE WAY VOLT WENT AFTER CHARNOX THAT TIME, THAT WAS--
WHAT?
NOTHING. YOU'RE A RIVETING STORYTELLER, KAIDAN. VERY ACCOMPLISHED.
HORNET WAS OUR FRIEND, TOO. TELL ME ABOUT HORNET. I WANT TO REMEMBER HIM.
UMM...OKAY. HE HAD A SHARPSHOOTER'S EYE, AND HE WAS AN AMAZING HAND-TO-HAND FIGHTER...
And then it just becomes a strange trip down memory lane.
Qubit wants to hear about Metalman. And Citadel. And Gazer, and all the others we've lost to Tony.
And out of deference...maybe this is how Qubit wants to mourn... I go on and on and on...
...and then...
WHY ARE YOU SMILING?
YOU SAID IT'S NEVER GOING TO GET ANY BETTER.
MEANING THAT THE FEW OF US LEFT ALIVE HAVE NO REAL CHANCE AGAINST TONY.
BUT I SUBMIT...

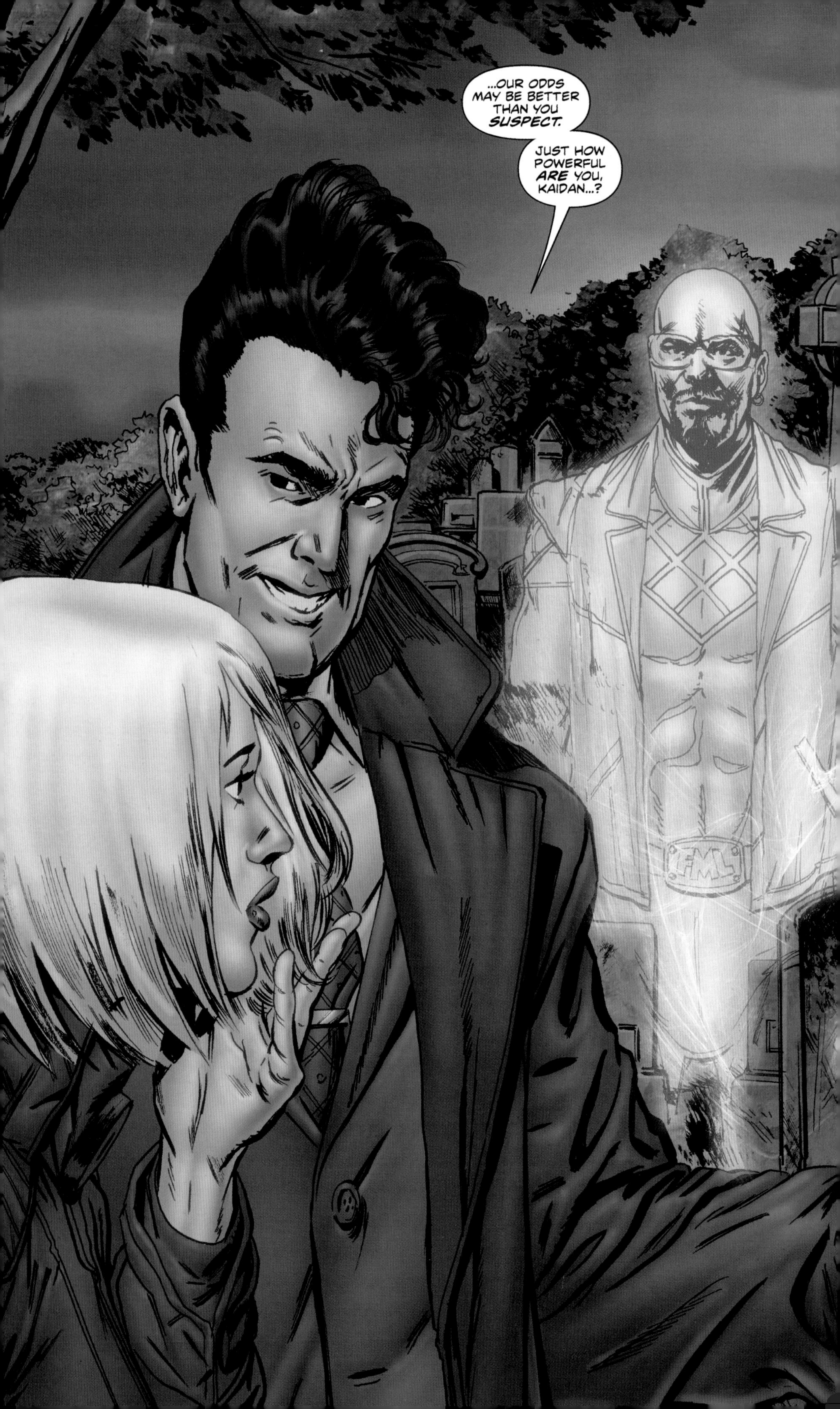
...OUR ODDS MAY BE BETTER THAN YOU SUSPECT.
JUST HOW POWERFUL ARE YOU, KAIDAN...?

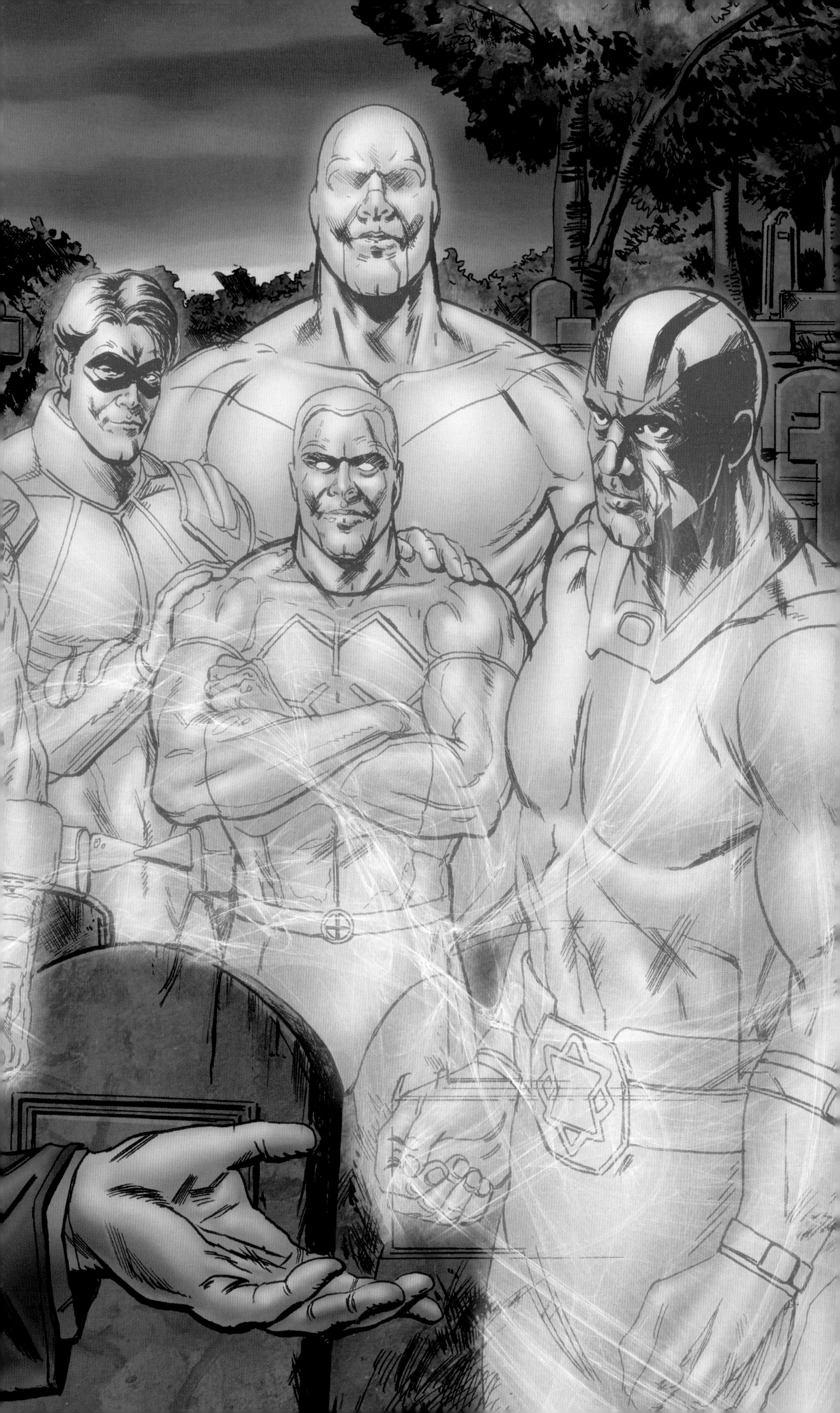

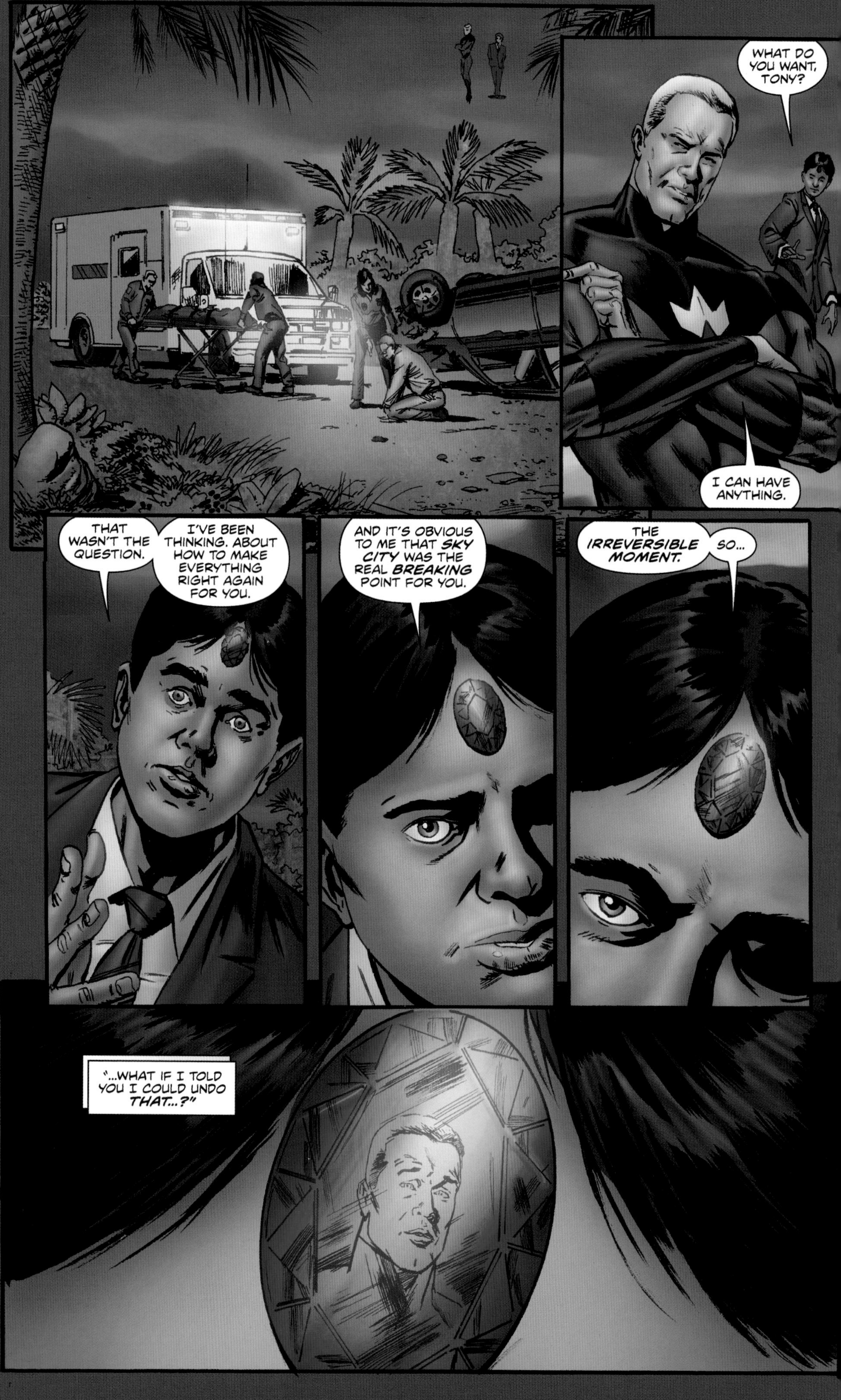
WHAT DO YOU WANT, TONY?
I CAN HAVE ANYTHING.
THAT WASN'T THE QUESTION.
I'VE BEEN THINKING. ABOUT HOW TO MAKE EVERYTHING RIGHT AGAIN FOR YOU.
AND IT'S OBVIOUS TO ME THAT SKY CITY WAS THE REAL BREAKING POINT FOR YOU.
THE IRREVERSIBLE MOMENT.
SO...
"...WHAT IF I TOLD YOU I COULD UNDO THAT...?"

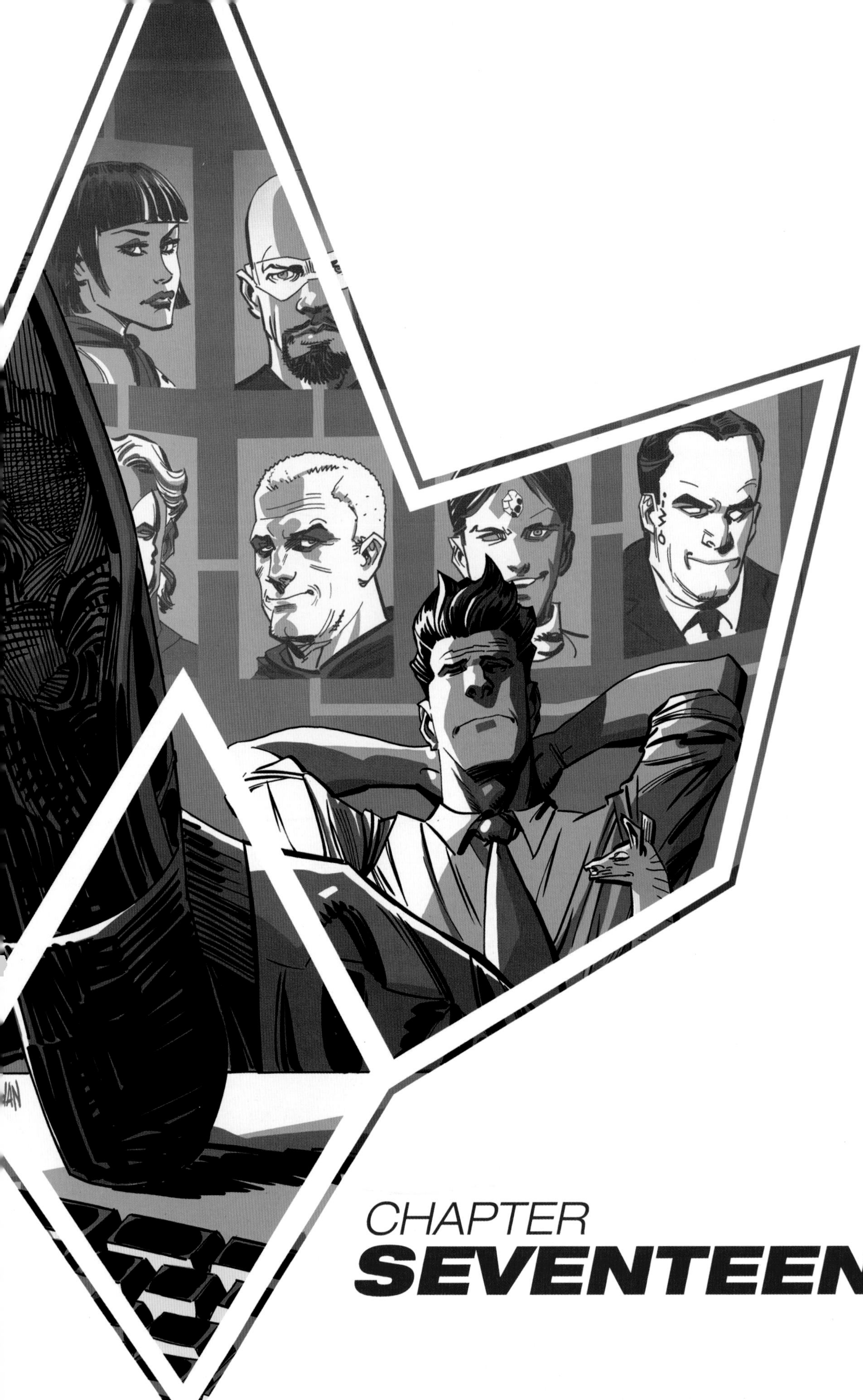

CHAPTER **SEVENTEEN**

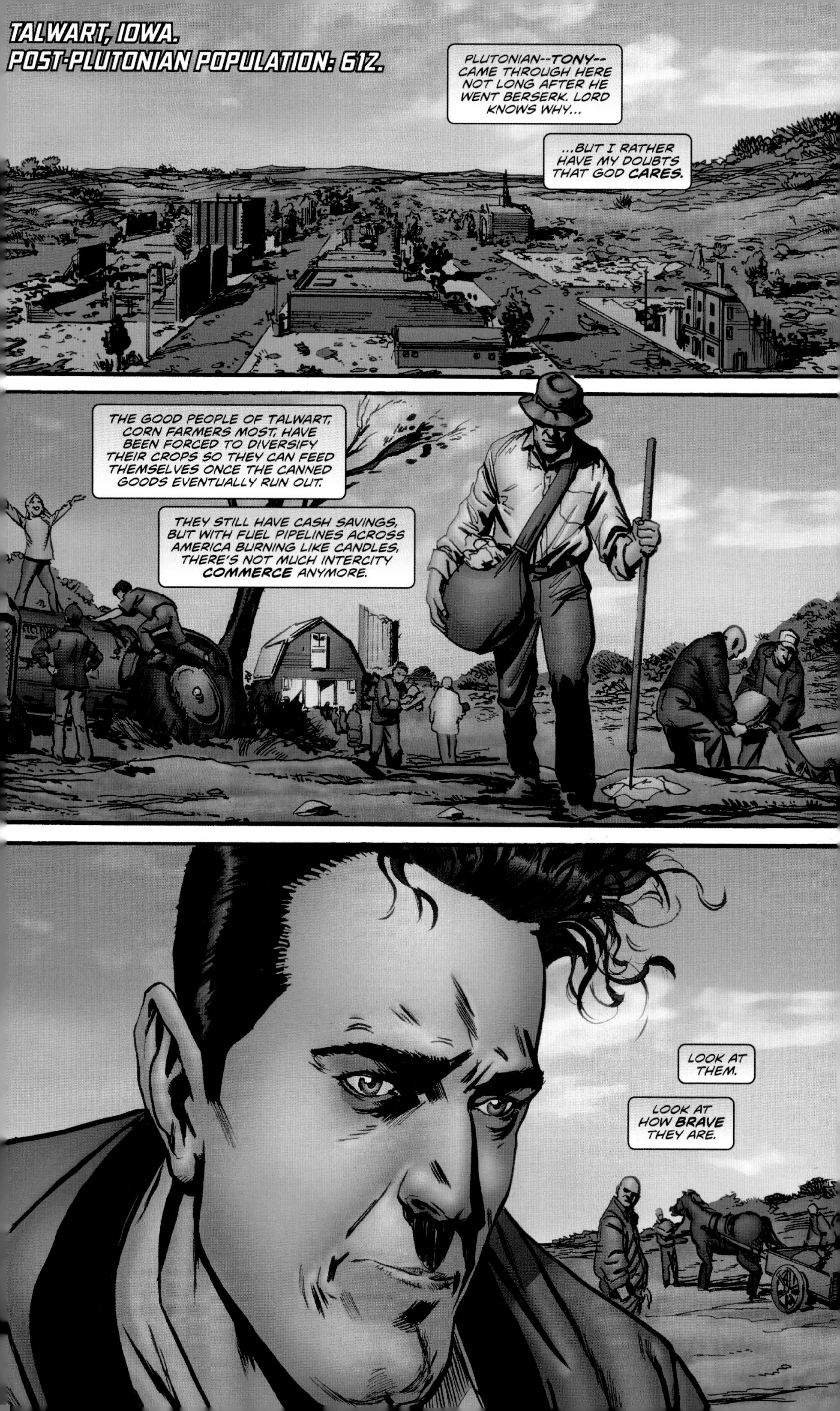
TALWART, IOWA.
POST-PLUTONIAN POPULATION: 612.
PLUTONIAN--TONY--CAME THROUGH HERE NOT LONG AFTER HE WENT BERSERK. LORD KNOWS WHY...
...BUT I RATHER HAVE MY DOUBTS THAT GOD CARES.
THE GOOD PEOPLE OF TALWART, CORN FARMERS MOST, HAVE BEEN FORCED TO DIVERSIFY THEIR CROPS SO THEY CAN FEED THEMSELVES ONCE THE CANNED GOODS EVENTUALLY RUN OUT.
THEY STILL HAVE CASH SAVINGS, BUT WITH FUEL PIPELINES ACROSS AMERICA BURNING LIKE CANDLES, THERE'S NOT MUCH INTERCITY COMMERCE ANYMORE.
LOOK AT THEM.
LOOK AT HOW BRAVE THEY ARE.

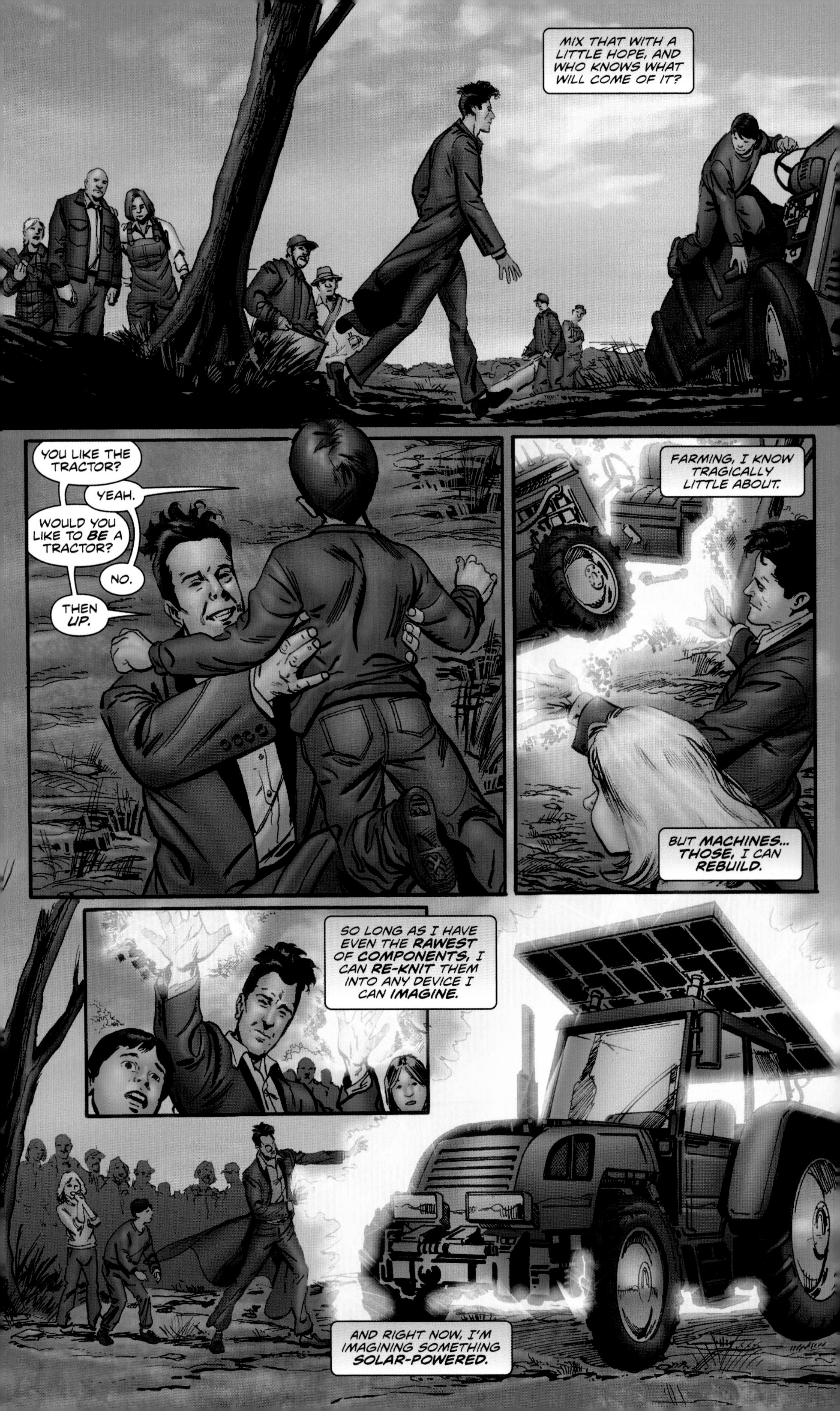
MIX THAT WITH A LITTLE HOPE, AND WHO KNOWS WHAT WILL COME OF IT?
YOU LIKE THE TRACTOR?
YEAH.
WOULD YOU LIKE TO BE A TRACTOR?
NO.
THEN UP.
FARMING, I KNOW TRAGICALLY LITTLE ABOUT.
BUT MACHINES... THOSE, I CAN REBUILD.
SO LONG AS I HAVE EVEN THE RAWEST OF COMPONENTS, I CAN RE-KNIT THEM INTO ANY DEVICE I CAN IMAGINE.
AND RIGHT NOW, I'M IMAGINING SOMETHING SOLAR-POWERED.

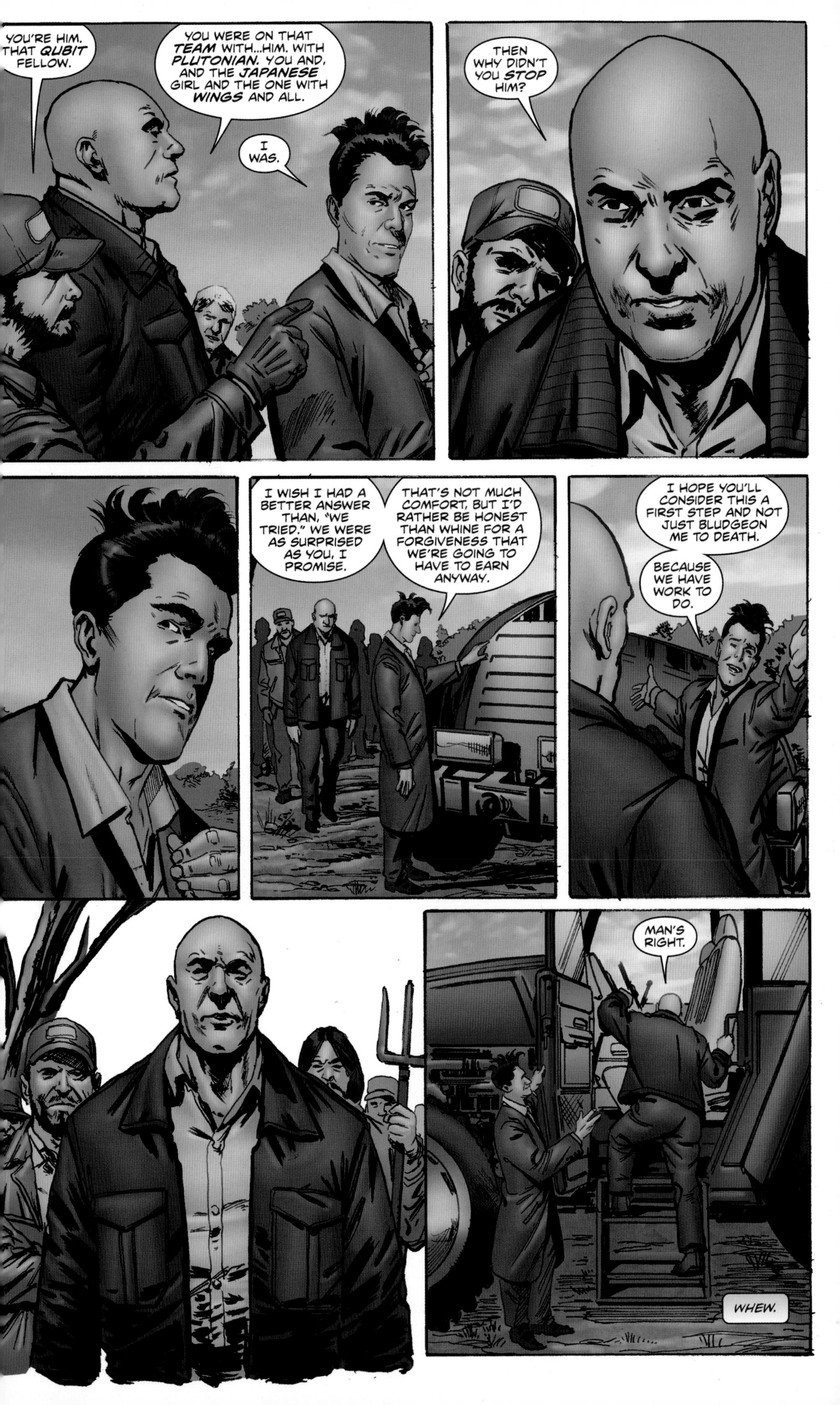
YOU'RE HIM. THAT QUBIT FELLOW.
YOU WERE ON THAT TEAM WITH...HIM. WITH PLUTONIAN. YOU AND, AND THE JAPANESE GIRL AND THE ONE WITH WINGS AND ALL.
I WAS.
THEN WHY DIDN'T YOU STOP HIM?
I WISH I HAD A BETTER ANSWER THAN, "WE TRIED." WE WERE AS SURPRISED AS YOU, I PROMISE.
THAT'S NOT MUCH COMFORT, BUT I'D RATHER BE HONEST THAN WHINE FOR A FORGIVENESS THAT WE'RE GOING TO HAVE TO EARN ANYWAY.
I HOPE YOU'LL CONSIDER THIS A FIRST STEP AND NOT JUST BLUDGEON ME TO DEATH.
BECAUSE WE HAVE WORK TO DO.
MAN'S RIGHT.
WHEW.

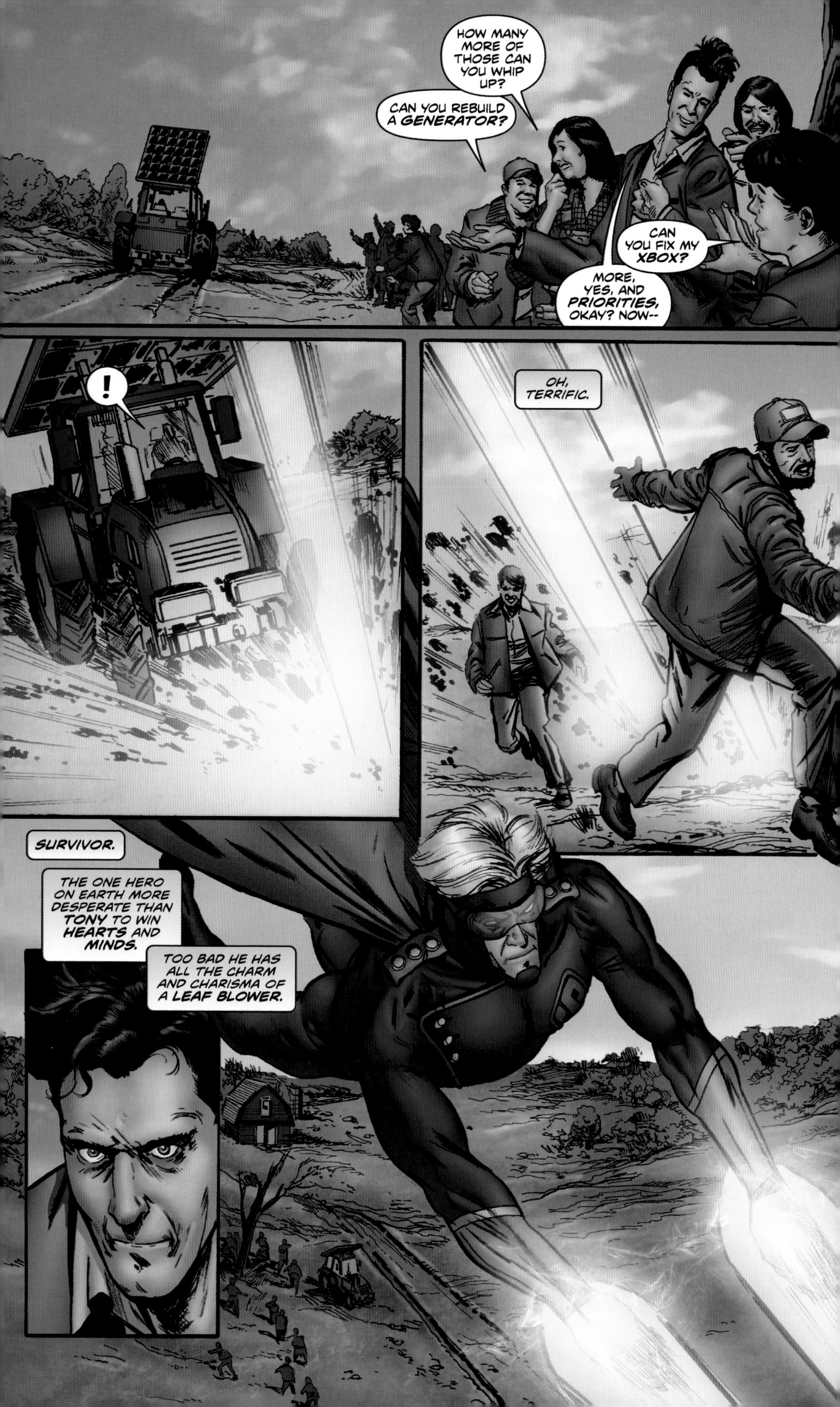
HOW MANY MORE OF THOSE CAN YOU WHIP UP?
CAN YOU REBUILD A GENERATOR?
CAN YOU FIX MY XBOX?
MORE, YES, AND PRIORITIES, OKAY? NOW--
!
OH, TERRIFIC.
SURVIVOR.
THE ONE HERO ON EARTH MORE DESPERATE THAN TONY TO WIN HEARTS AND MINDS.
TOO BAD HE HAS ALL THE CHARM AND CHARISMA OF A LEAF BLOWER.

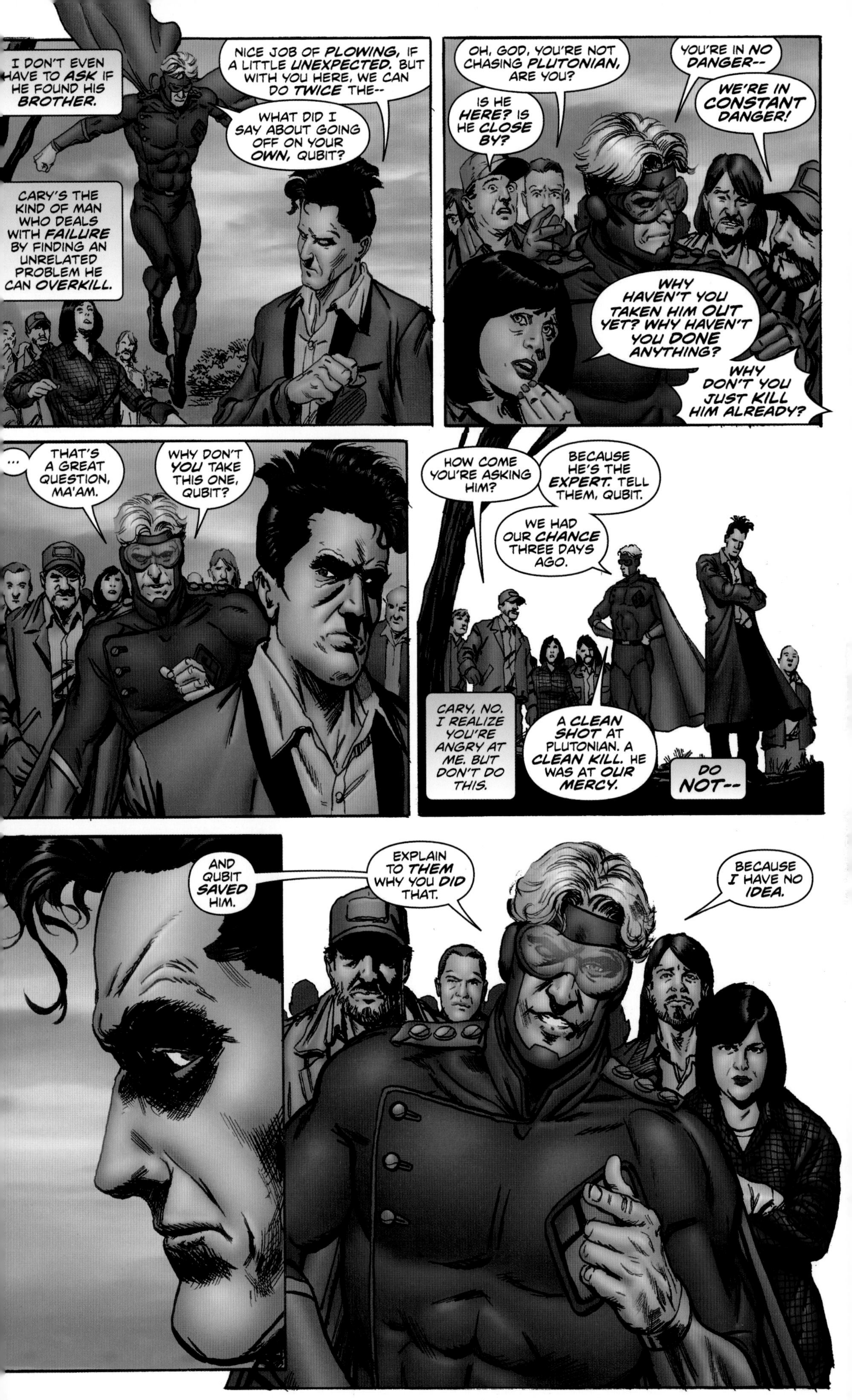
I DON'T EVEN HAVE TO ASK IF HE FOUND HIS BROTHER.
NICE JOB OF PLOWING, IF A LITTLE UNEXPECTED. BUT WITH YOU HERE, WE CAN DO TWICE THE--
WHAT DID I SAY ABOUT GOING OFF ON YOUR OWN, QUBIT?
CARY'S THE KIND OF MAN WHO DEALS WITH FAILURE BY FINDING AN UNRELATED PROBLEM HE CAN OVERKILL.
OH, GOD, YOU'RE NOT CHASING PLUTONIAN, ARE YOU?
IS HE HERE? IS HE CLOSE BY?
YOU'RE IN NO DANGER--
WE'RE IN CONSTANT DANGER!
WHY HAVEN'T YOU TAKEN HIM OUT YET? WHY HAVEN'T YOU DONE ANYTHING?
WHY DON'T YOU JUST KILL HIM ALREADY?
...
THAT'S A GREAT QUESTION, MA'AM.
WHY DON'T YOU TAKE THIS ONE, QUBIT?
HOW COME YOU'RE ASKING HIM?
BECAUSE HE'S THE EXPERT. TELL THEM, QUBIT.
WE HAD OUR CHANCE THREE DAYS AGO.
CARY, NO. I REALIZE YOU'RE ANGRY AT ME. BUT DON'T DO THIS.
A CLEAN SHOT AT PLUTONIAN. A CLEAN KILL. HE WAS AT OUR MERCY.
DO NOT--
AND QUBIT SAVED HIM.
EXPLAIN TO THEM WHY YOU DID THAT.
BECAUSE I HAVE NO IDEA.

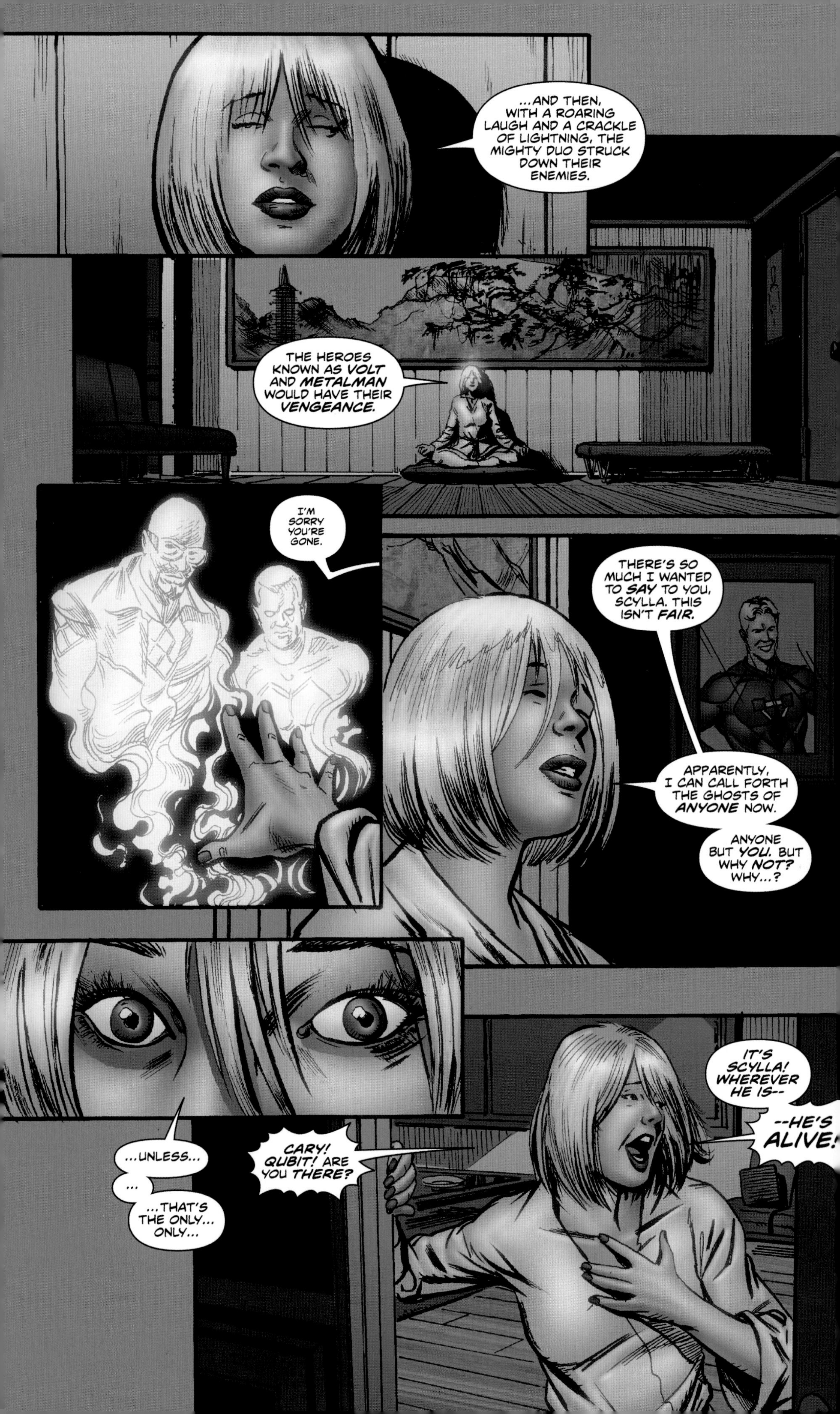
...AND THEN, WITH A ROARING LAUGH AND A CRACKLE OF LIGHTNING, THE MIGHTY DUO STRUCK DOWN THEIR ENEMIES.
THE HEROES KNOWN AS VOLT AND METALMAN WOULD HAVE THEIR VENGEANCE.
I'M SORRY YOU'RE GONE.
THERE'S SO MUCH I WANTED TO SAY TO YOU, SCYLLA. THIS ISN'T FAIR.
APPARENTLY, I CAN CALL FORTH THE GHOSTS OF ANYONE NOW.
ANYONE BUT YOU. BUT WHY NOT? WHY...?
...UNLESS...
...
...THAT'S THE ONLY... ONLY...
CARY! QUBIT! ARE YOU THERE?
IT'S SCYLLA! WHEREVER HE IS--
--HE'S ALIVE!

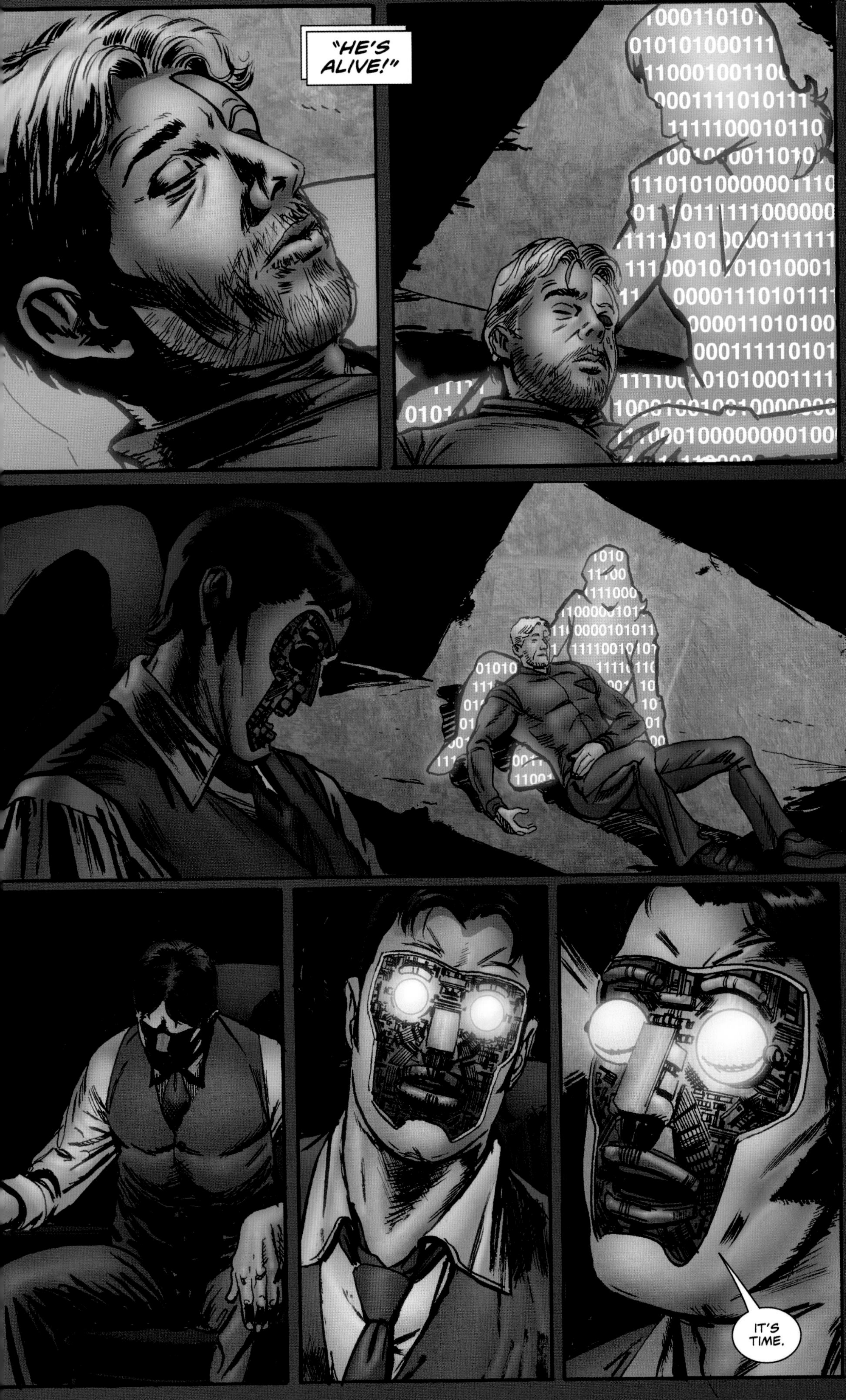
"HE'S ALIVE!"
IT'S TIME.

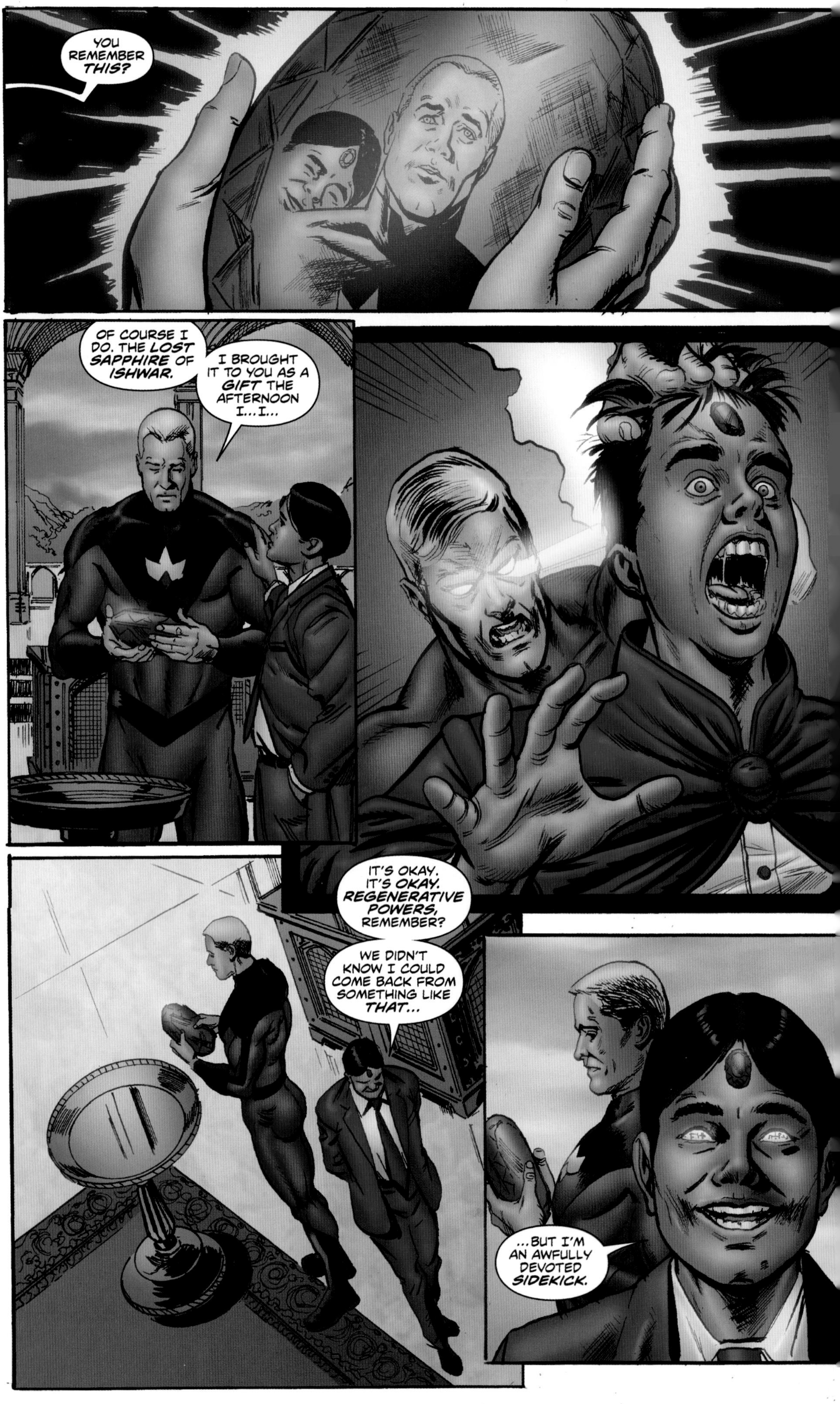
YOU REMEMBER THIS?
OF COURSE I DO. THE LOST SAPPHIRE OF ISHWAR.
I BROUGHT IT TO YOU AS A GIFT THE AFTERNOON I...I...
IT'S OKAY. IT'S OKAY. REGENERATIVE POWERS, REMEMBER?
WE DIDN'T KNOW I COULD COME BACK FROM SOMETHING LIKE THAT...
...BUT I'M AN AWFULLY DEVOTED SIDEKICK.

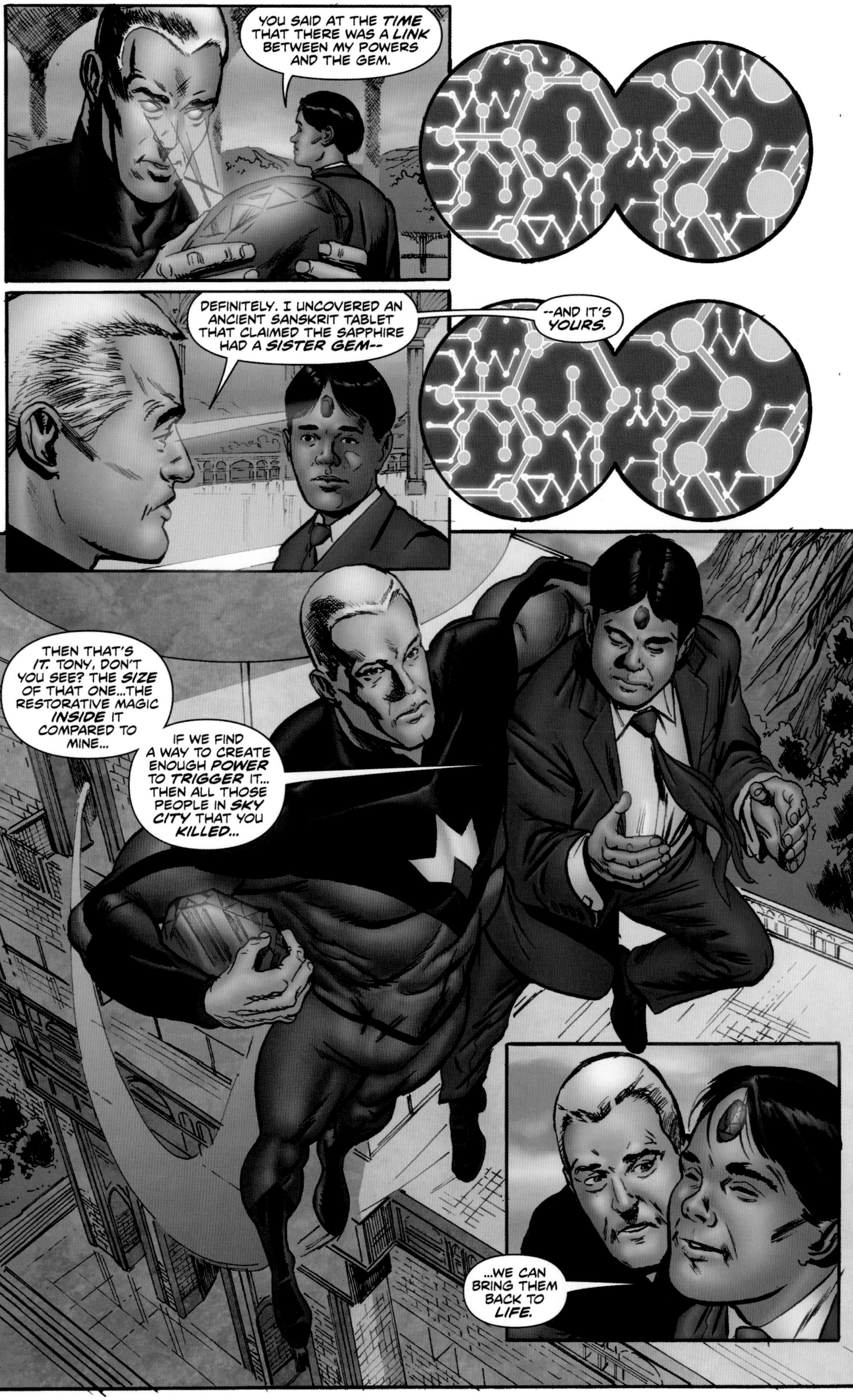
YOU SAID AT THE *TIME* THAT THERE WAS A *LINK* BETWEEN MY POWERS AND THE GEM.
DEFINITELY. I UNCOVERED AN ANCIENT SANSKRIT TABLET THAT CLAIMED THE SAPPHIRE HAD A *SISTER GEM--*
--AND IT'S *YOURS.*
THEN THAT'S *IT.* TONY, DON'T YOU SEE? THE *SIZE* OF THAT ONE...THE RESTORATIVE MAGIC *INSIDE* IT COMPARED TO MINE...
IF WE FIND A WAY TO CREATE ENOUGH *POWER* TO *TRIGGER* IT... THEN ALL THOSE PEOPLE IN *SKY CITY* THAT YOU *KILLED...*
...WE CAN BRING THEM BACK TO *LIFE.*

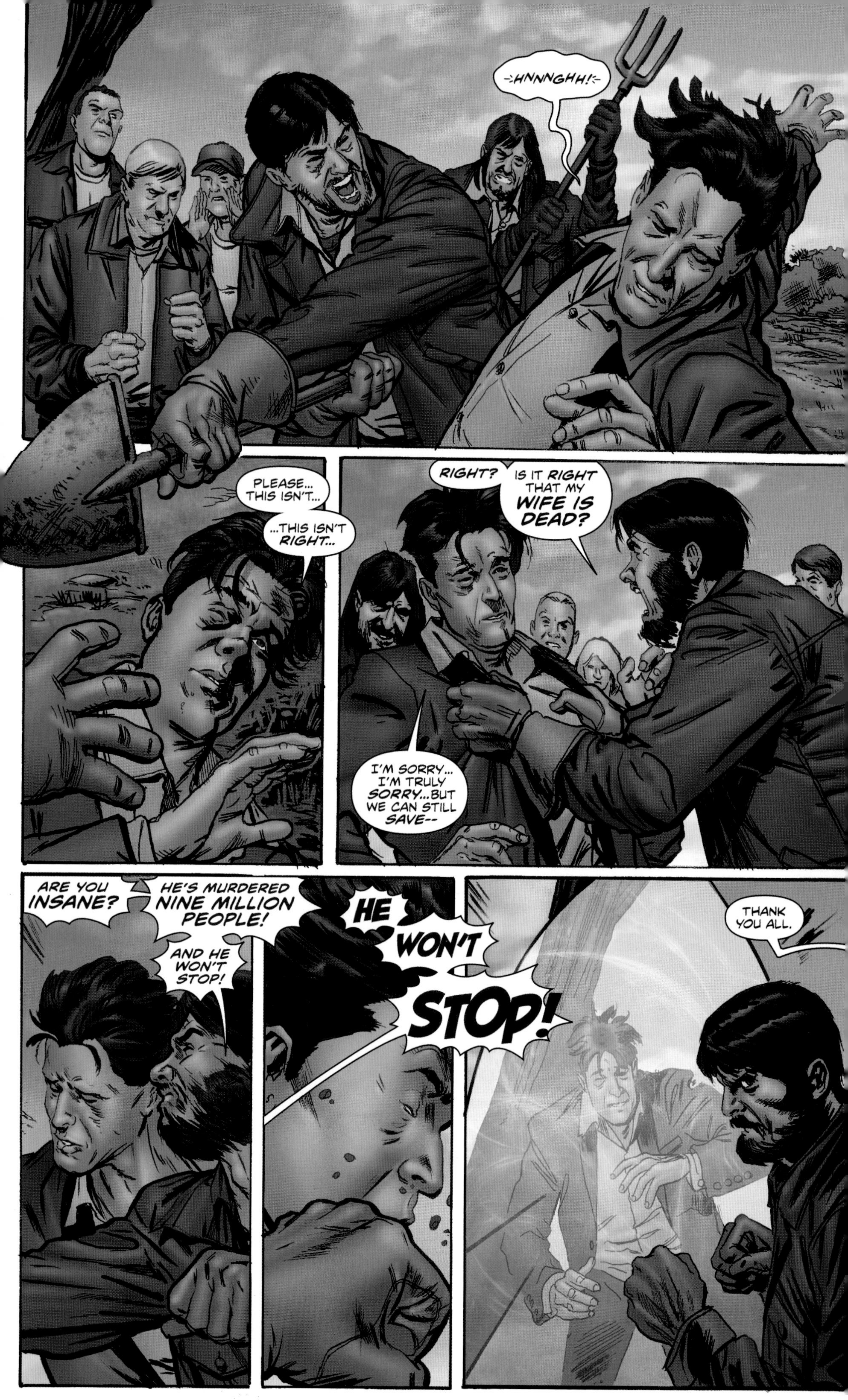
-HNNNGHH!-
PLEASE... THIS ISN'T...
...THIS ISN'T RIGHT...
RIGHT?
IS IT RIGHT THAT MY WIFE IS DEAD?
I'M SORRY... I'M TRULY SORRY...BUT WE CAN STILL SAVE--
ARE YOU INSANE?
HE'S MURDERED NINE MILLION PEOPLE!
AND HE WON'T STOP!
HE WON'T STOP!
THANK YOU ALL.

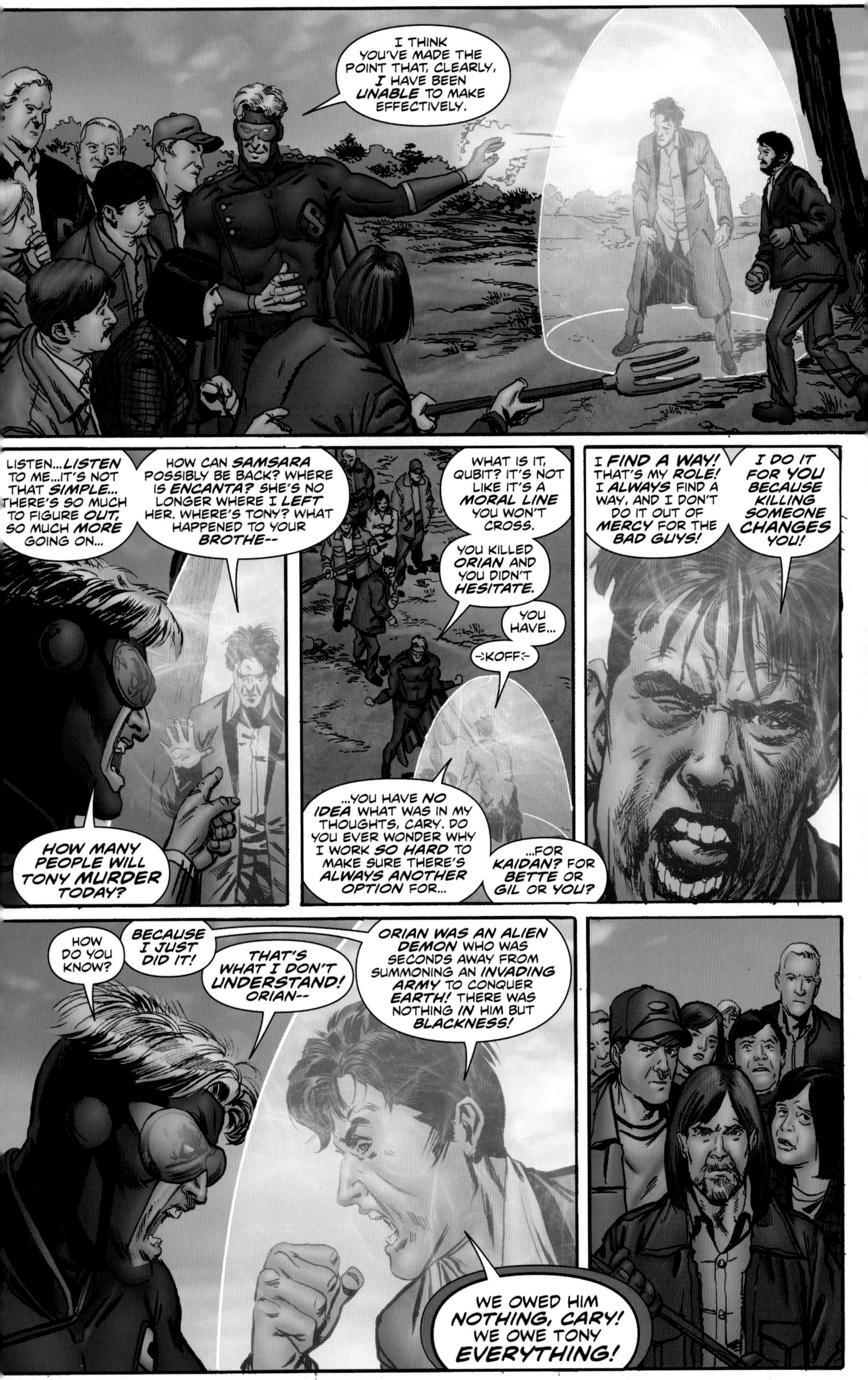
I THINK YOU'VE MADE THE POINT THAT, CLEARLY, I HAVE BEEN UNABLE TO MAKE EFFECTIVELY.
LISTEN...LISTEN TO ME...IT'S NOT THAT SIMPLE... THERE'S SO MUCH TO FIGURE OUT, SO MUCH MORE GOING ON...
HOW CAN SAMSARA POSSIBLY BE BACK? WHERE IS ENCANTA? SHE'S NO LONGER WHERE I LEFT HER. WHERE'S TONY? WHAT HAPPENED TO YOUR BROTHE--
HOW MANY PEOPLE WILL TONY MURDER TODAY?
WHAT IS IT, QUBIT? IT'S NOT LIKE IT'S A MORAL LINE YOU WON'T CROSS.
YOU KILLED ORIAN AND YOU DIDN'T HESITATE.
YOU HAVE...
-KOFF-
...YOU HAVE NO IDEA WHAT WAS IN MY THOUGHTS, CARY. DO YOU EVER WONDER WHY I WORK SO HARD TO MAKE SURE THERE'S ALWAYS ANOTHER OPTION FOR...
...FOR KAIDAN? FOR BETTE OR GIL OR YOU?
I FIND A WAY! THAT'S MY ROLE! I ALWAYS FIND A WAY, AND I DON'T DO IT OUT OF MERCY FOR THE BAD GUYS!
I DO IT FOR YOU BECAUSE KILLING SOMEONE CHANGES YOU!
HOW DO YOU KNOW?
BECAUSE I JUST DID IT!
THAT'S WHAT I DON'T UNDERSTAND! ORIAN--
ORIAN WAS AN ALIEN DEMON WHO WAS SECONDS AWAY FROM SUMMONING AN INVADING ARMY TO CONQUER EARTH! THERE WAS NOTHING IN HIM BUT BLACKNESS!
WE OWED HIM NOTHING, CARY! WE OWE TONY EVERYTHING!

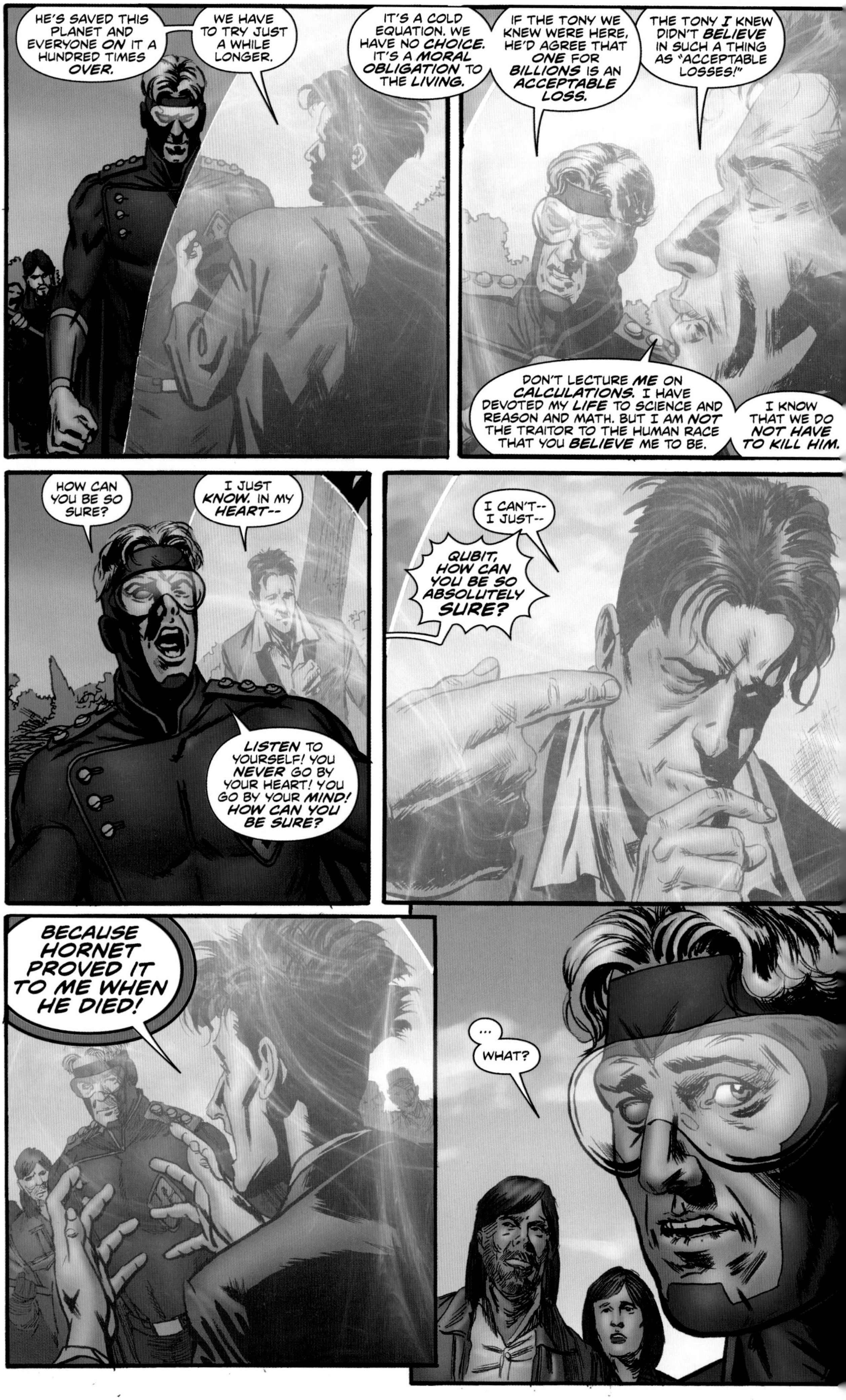
HE'S SAVED THIS PLANET AND EVERYONE ON IT A HUNDRED TIMES OVER.
WE HAVE TO TRY JUST A WHILE LONGER.
IT'S A COLD EQUATION. WE HAVE NO CHOICE. IT'S A MORAL OBLIGATION TO THE LIVING.
IF THE TONY WE KNEW WERE HERE, HE'D AGREE THAT ONE FOR BILLIONS IS AN ACCEPTABLE LOSS.
THE TONY I KNEW DIDN'T BELIEVE IN SUCH A THING AS "ACCEPTABLE LOSSES!"
DON'T LECTURE ME ON CALCULATIONS. I HAVE DEVOTED MY LIFE TO SCIENCE AND REASON AND MATH. BUT I AM NOT THE TRAITOR TO THE HUMAN RACE THAT YOU BELIEVE ME TO BE.
I KNOW THAT WE DO NOT HAVE TO KILL HIM.
HOW CAN YOU BE SO SURE?
I JUST KNOW. IN MY HEART--
LISTEN TO YOURSELF! YOU NEVER GO BY YOUR HEART! YOU GO BY YOUR MIND! HOW CAN YOU BE SURE?
I CAN'T-- I JUST--
QUBIT, HOW CAN YOU BE SO ABSOLUTELY SURE?
BECAUSE HORNET PROVED IT TO ME WHEN HE DIED!
... WHAT?

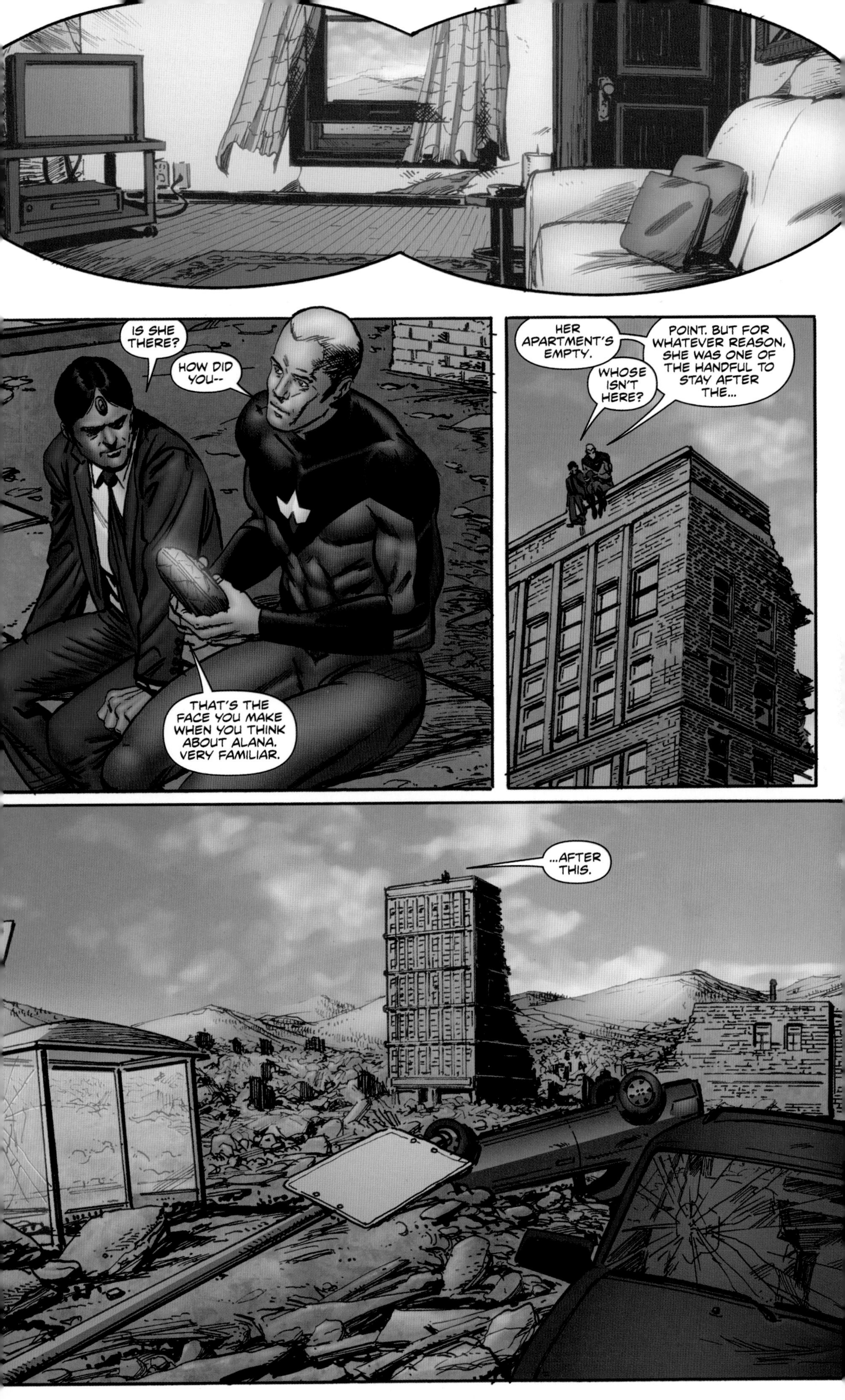
IS SHE THERE?
HOW DID YOU--
THAT'S THE FACE YOU MAKE WHEN YOU THINK ABOUT ALANA. VERY FAMILIAR.
HER APARTMENT'S EMPTY.
WHOSE ISN'T HERE?
POINT. BUT FOR WHATEVER REASON, SHE WAS ONE OF THE HANDFUL TO STAY AFTER THE...
...AFTER THIS.

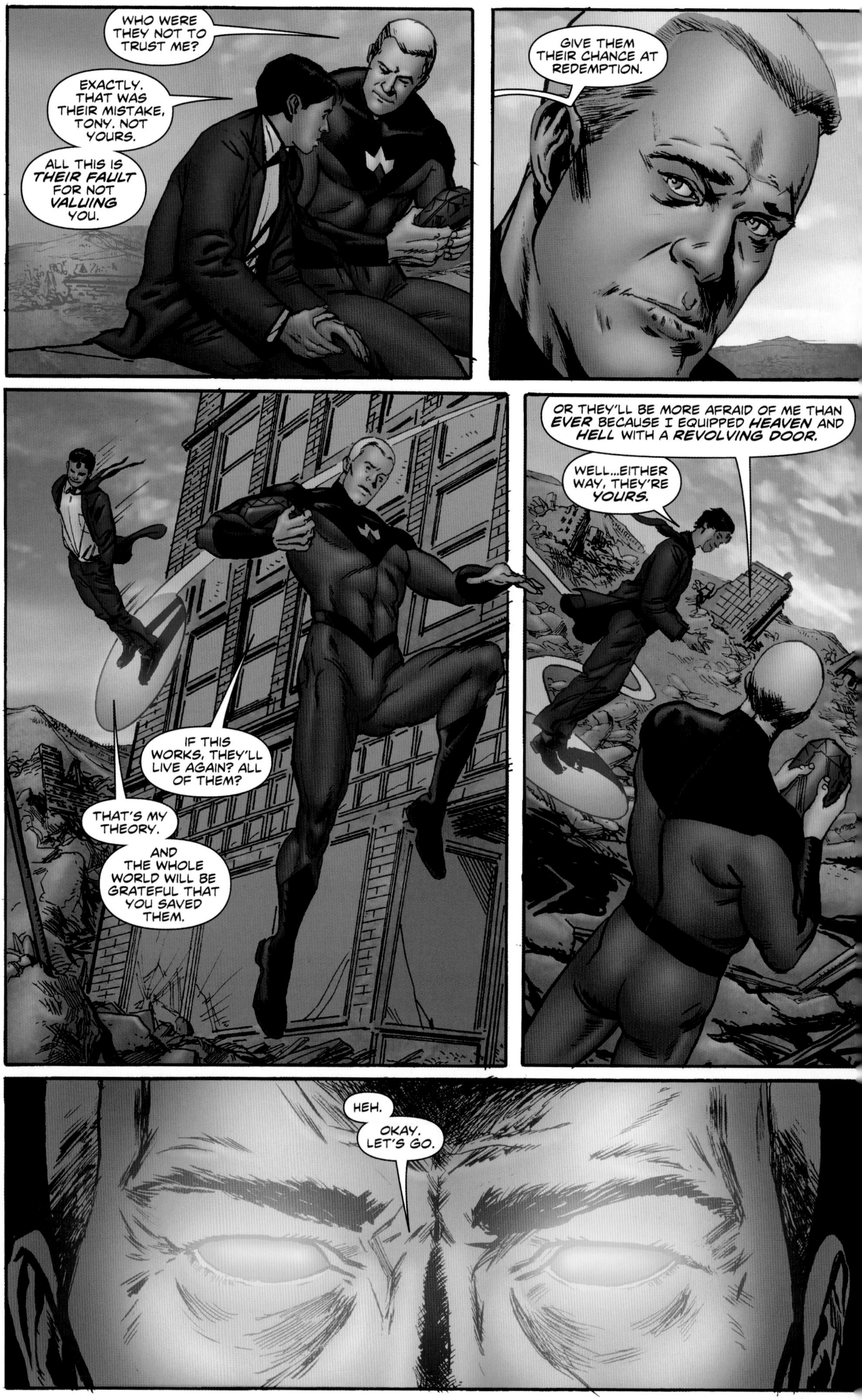
WHO WERE THEY NOT TO TRUST ME?
EXACTLY. THAT WAS THEIR MISTAKE, TONY. NOT YOURS.
ALL THIS IS *THEIR FAULT* FOR NOT *VALUING* YOU.
GIVE THEM THEIR CHANCE AT REDEMPTION.
IF THIS WORKS, THEY'LL LIVE AGAIN? ALL OF THEM?
THAT'S MY THEORY.
AND THE WHOLE WORLD WILL BE GRATEFUL THAT YOU SAVED THEM.
OR THEY'LL BE MORE AFRAID OF ME THAN *EVER* BECAUSE I EQUIPPED *HEAVEN* AND *HELL* WITH A *REVOLVING DOOR.*
WELL...EITHER WAY, THEY'RE *YOURS.*
HEH.
OKAY. LET'S GO.

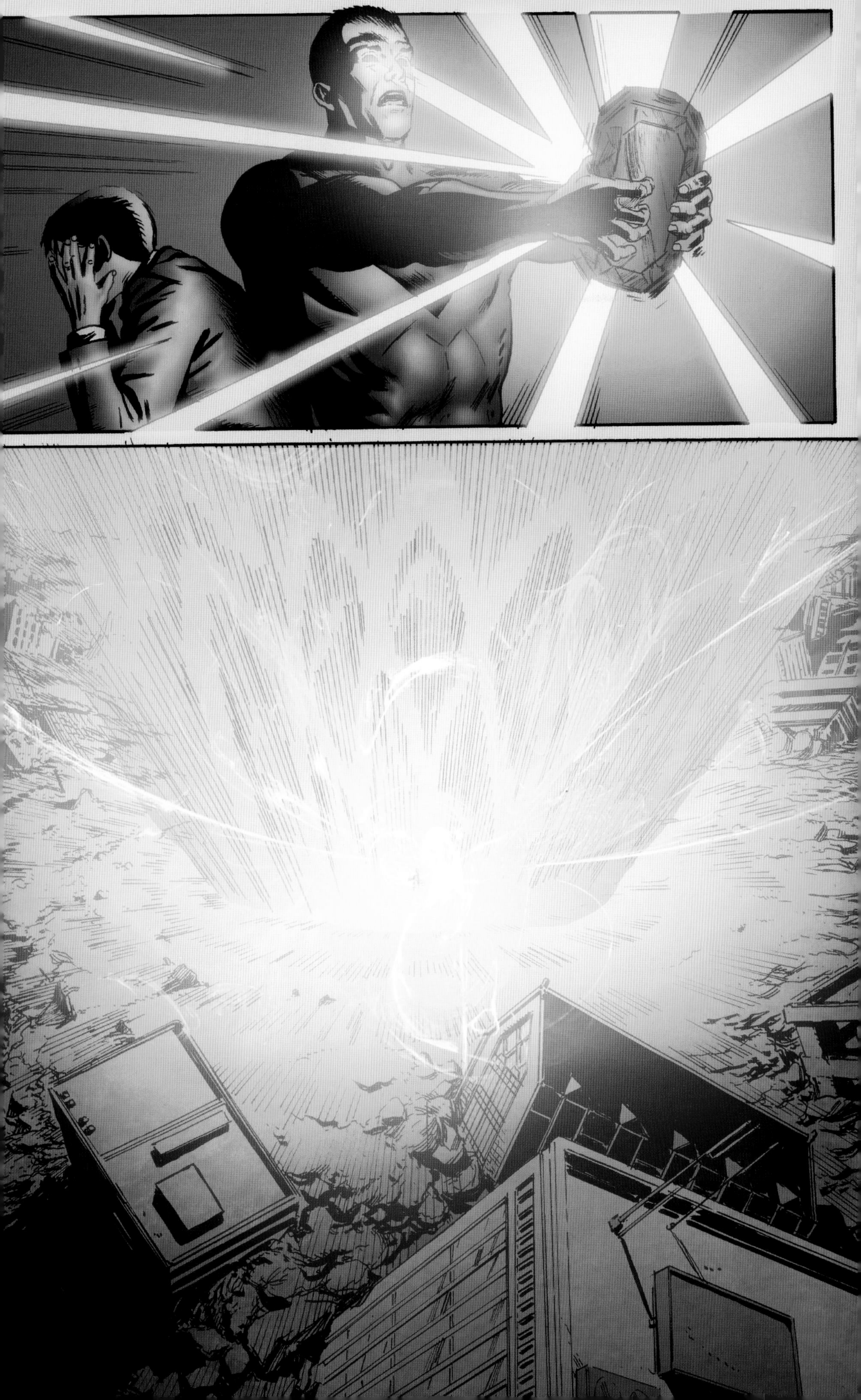

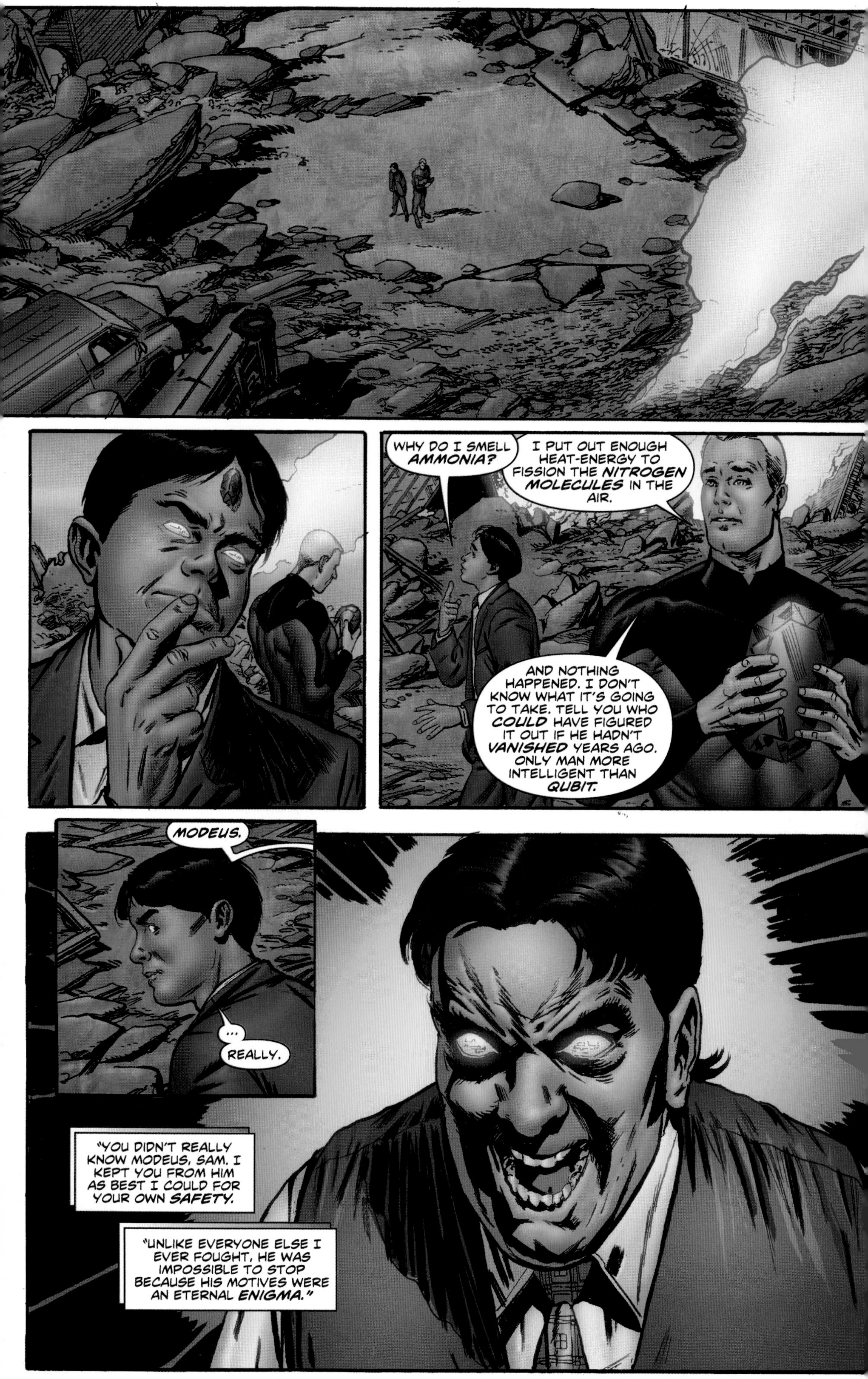
WHY DO I SMELL AMMONIA?
I PUT OUT ENOUGH HEAT-ENERGY TO FISSION THE NITROGEN MOLECULES IN THE AIR.
AND NOTHING HAPPENED. I DON'T KNOW WHAT IT'S GOING TO TAKE. TELL YOU WHO COULD HAVE FIGURED IT OUT IF HE HADN'T VANISHED YEARS AGO. ONLY MAN MORE INTELLIGENT THAN QUBIT.
MODEUS.
... REALLY.
"YOU DIDN'T REALLY KNOW MODEUS, SAM. I KEPT YOU FROM HIM AS BEST I COULD FOR YOUR OWN SAFETY.
"UNLIKE EVERYONE ELSE I EVER FOUGHT, HE WAS IMPOSSIBLE TO STOP BECAUSE HIS MOTIVES WERE AN ENIGMA."

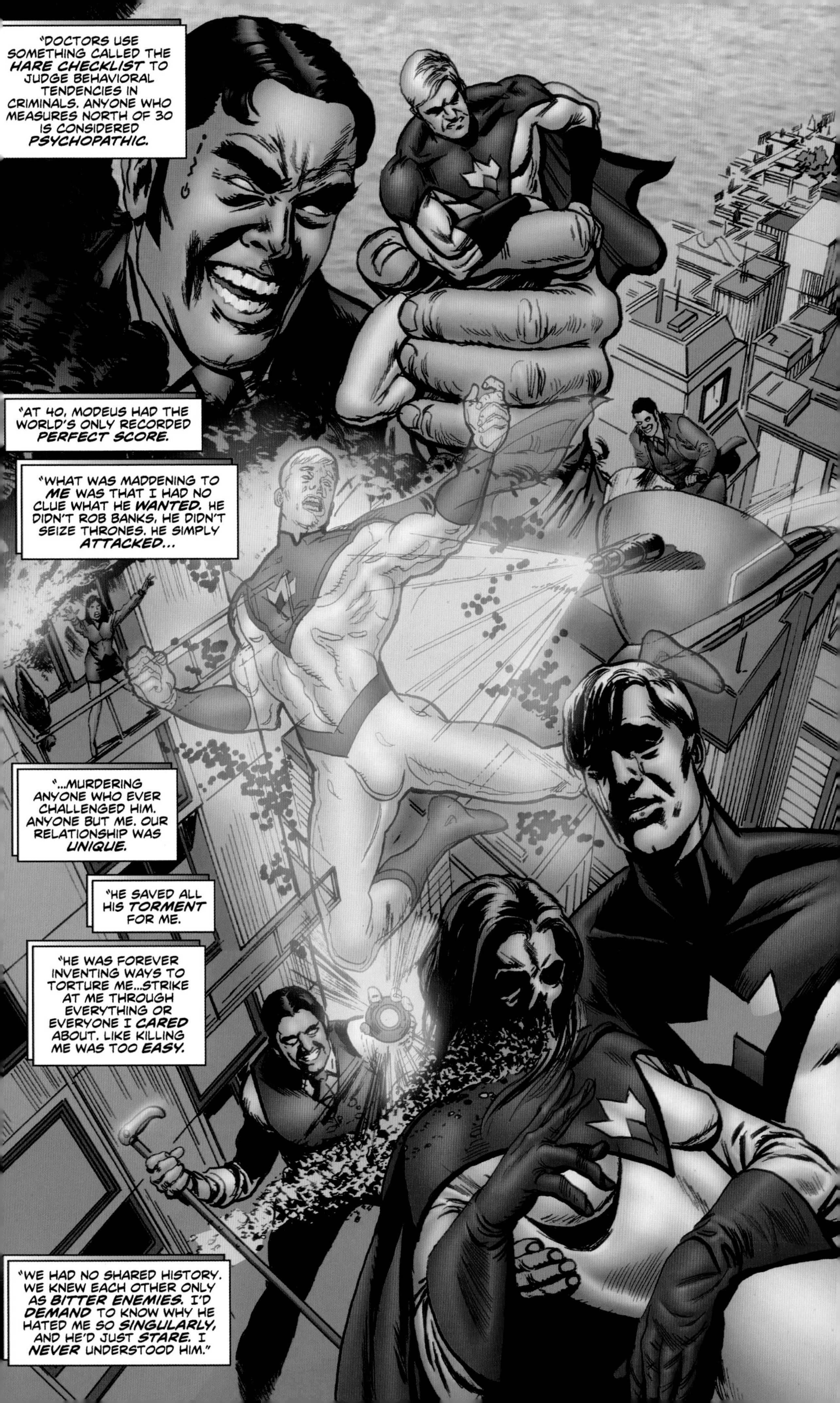
"DOCTORS USE SOMETHING CALLED THE HARE CHECKLIST TO JUDGE BEHAVIORAL TENDENCIES IN CRIMINALS. ANYONE WHO MEASURES NORTH OF 30 IS CONSIDERED PSYCHOPATHIC.
"AT 40, MODEUS HAD THE WORLD'S ONLY RECORDED PERFECT SCORE.
"WHAT WAS MADDENING TO ME WAS THAT I HAD NO CLUE WHAT HE WANTED. HE DIDN'T ROB BANKS, HE DIDN'T SEIZE THRONES. HE SIMPLY ATTACKED...
"...MURDERING ANYONE WHO EVER CHALLENGED HIM. ANYONE BUT ME. OUR RELATIONSHIP WAS UNIQUE.
"HE SAVED ALL HIS TORMENT FOR ME.
"HE WAS FOREVER INVENTING WAYS TO TORTURE ME...STRIKE AT ME THROUGH EVERYTHING OR EVERYONE I CARED ABOUT. LIKE KILLING ME WAS TOO EASY.
"WE HAD NO SHARED HISTORY. WE KNEW EACH OTHER ONLY AS BITTER ENEMIES. I'D DEMAND TO KNOW WHY HE HATED ME SO SINGULARLY, AND HE'D JUST STARE. I NEVER UNDERSTOOD HIM."

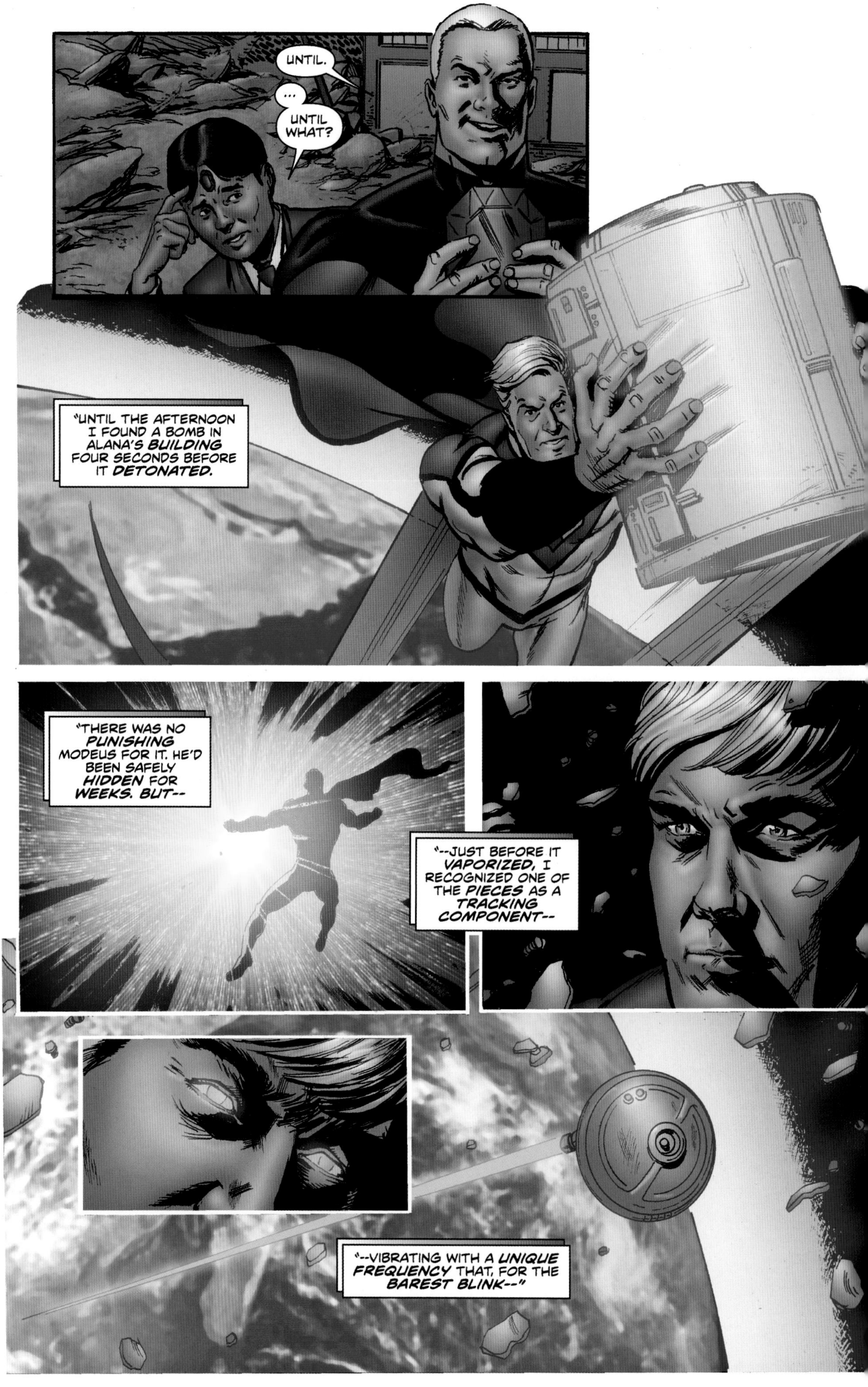
UNTIL.
...
UNTIL WHAT?
"UNTIL THE AFTERNOON I FOUND A BOMB IN ALANA'S BUILDING FOUR SECONDS BEFORE IT DETONATED.
"THERE WAS NO PUNISHING MODEUS FOR IT. HE'D BEEN SAFELY HIDDEN FOR WEEKS. BUT--
"--JUST BEFORE IT VAPORIZED, I RECOGNIZED ONE OF THE PIECES AS A TRACKING COMPONENT--
"--VIBRATING WITH A UNIQUE FREQUENCY THAT, FOR THE BAREST BLINK--"

"--ETHERCAST A PICOSECOND-LONG *BATTLE REPORT* BACK TO ITS *BUILDER.*"

"IF I COULD OUTRACE THE *SIGNAL,* I COULD--FOR *ONCE, FINALLY*--GET THE *DROP* ON THIS GUY."

"THE SIGNAL LED ME TO SOME SORT OF *CYBERNETICS LAB.* THERE WERE *GUARD DOGS,* NATURALLY."

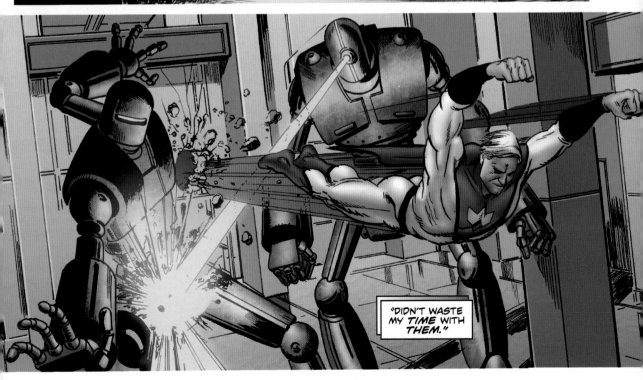

"DIDN'T WASTE MY *TIME* WITH *THEM.*"

"INSTEAD, I FOUND *MODEUS* BUILDING A HALF-DOZEN *PLUTONIAN ROBOTS* AND HAD HIM *BEHIND BARS* BEFORE HE COULD DROP HIS *WRENCH.*"

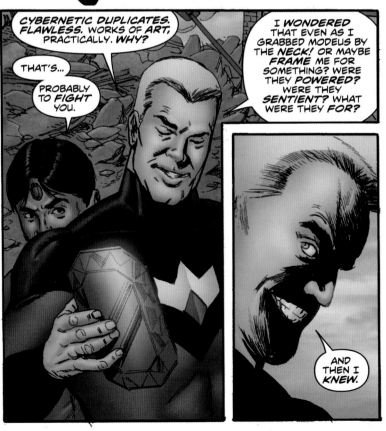

CYBERNETIC DUPLICATES. FLAWLESS. WORKS OF ART, PRACTICALLY. *WHY?*

THAT'S...

PROBABLY TO *FIGHT* YOU.

I *WONDERED* THAT EVEN AS I GRABBED MODEUS BY THE *NECK!* OR MAYBE *FRAME* ME FOR SOMETHING? WERE THEY *POWERED?* WERE THEY *SENTIENT?* WHAT WERE THEY *FOR?*

AND THEN I *KNEW.*

"MODEUS'S DRIVING FORCE--HIS CLINICAL LACK OF EMPATHY--WAS ALWAYS HIS ONE *WEAKNESS.*"

"AS SMART AS HE *WAS,* HE WAS NEVER ABLE TO REALLY THINK THROUGH HOW I PERCEIVE THE WORLD.

"I CAN DO FAR MORE THAN SIMPLY HEAR *HEARTBEATS,* SAM."

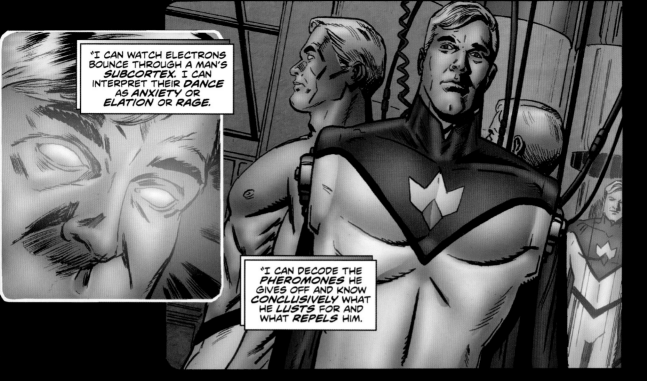

"I CAN WATCH ELECTRONS BOUNCE THROUGH A MAN'S *SUBCORTEX*. I CAN INTERPRET THEIR *DANCE* AS ANXIETY OR ELATION OR RAGE.

"I CAN DECODE THE *PHEROMONES* HE GIVES OFF AND KNOW *CONCLUSIVELY* WHAT HE *LUSTS* FOR AND WHAT *REPELS* HIM.

"I'D MISSED IT *ALL ALONG*. BUT IN THAT MOMENT, MODEUS'S *GUARD* WAS DOWN AND ALL HIS FEELINGS WERE NOT ONLY ON *FULL DISPLAY*, THEY WERE OFF THE *CHARTS*...AND I FINALLY KNEW THE *TRUTH*.

"THOSE WEREN'T INSTRUMENTS OF *CRIME* MODEUS WAS BUILDING.

"THEY WERE *SEX ROBOTS*.

"MODEUS WAS *IN LOVE WITH ME*."

...

THAT'S...

...THAT'S NOT...

...HE DIDN'T *LOVE*...

...HE *HATED* YOU...

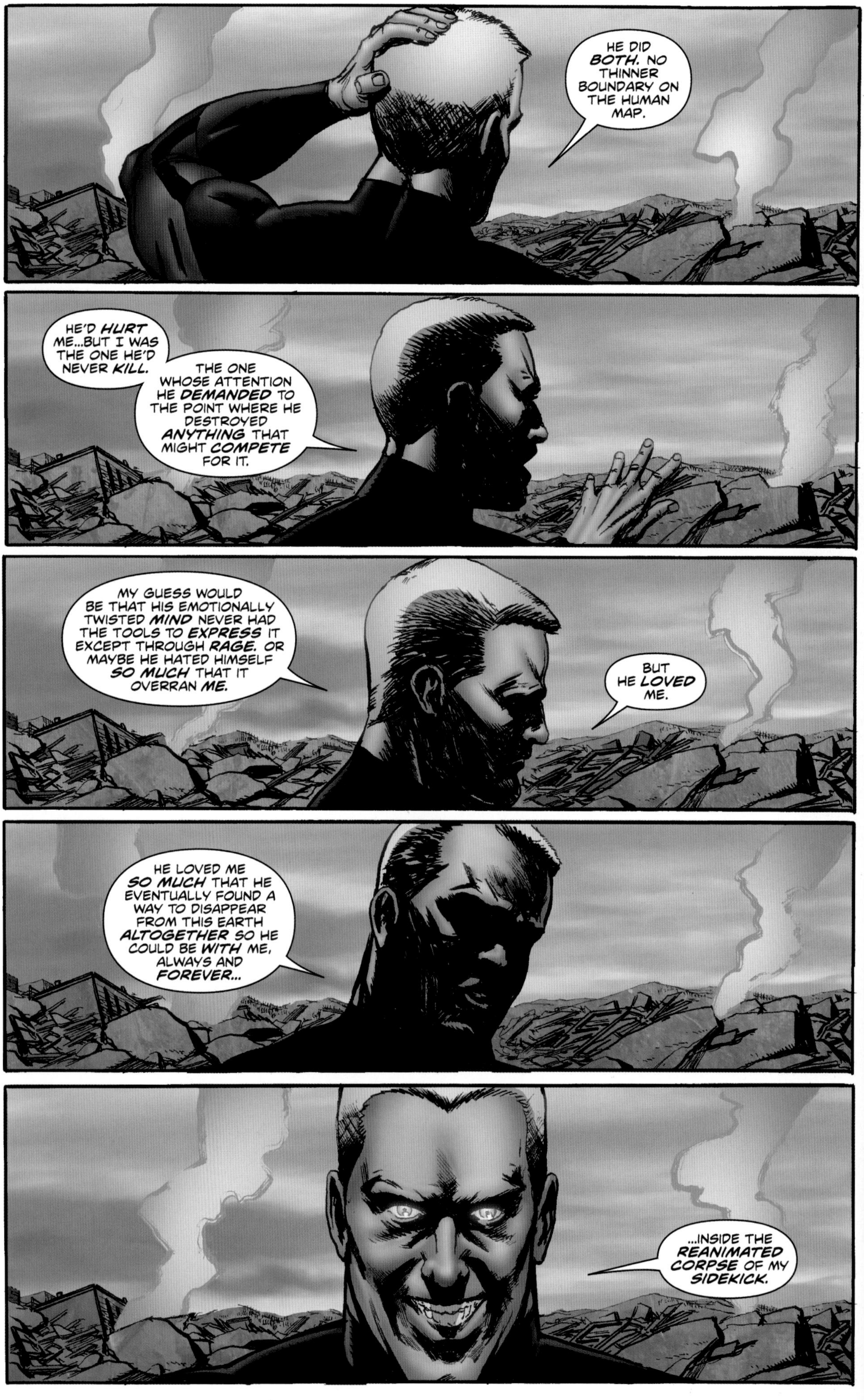
HE DID BOTH. NO THINNER BOUNDARY ON THE HUMAN MAP.
HE'D HURT ME...BUT I WAS THE ONE HE'D NEVER KILL.
THE ONE WHOSE ATTENTION HE DEMANDED TO THE POINT WHERE HE DESTROYED ANYTHING THAT MIGHT COMPETE FOR IT.
MY GUESS WOULD BE THAT HIS EMOTIONALLY TWISTED MIND NEVER HAD THE TOOLS TO EXPRESS IT EXCEPT THROUGH RAGE. OR MAYBE HE HATED HIMSELF SO MUCH THAT IT OVERRAN ME.
BUT HE LOVED ME.
HE LOVED ME SO MUCH THAT HE EVENTUALLY FOUND A WAY TO DISAPPEAR FROM THIS EARTH ALTOGETHER SO HE COULD BE WITH ME, ALWAYS AND FOREVER...
...INSIDE THE REANIMATED CORPSE OF MY SIDEKICK.

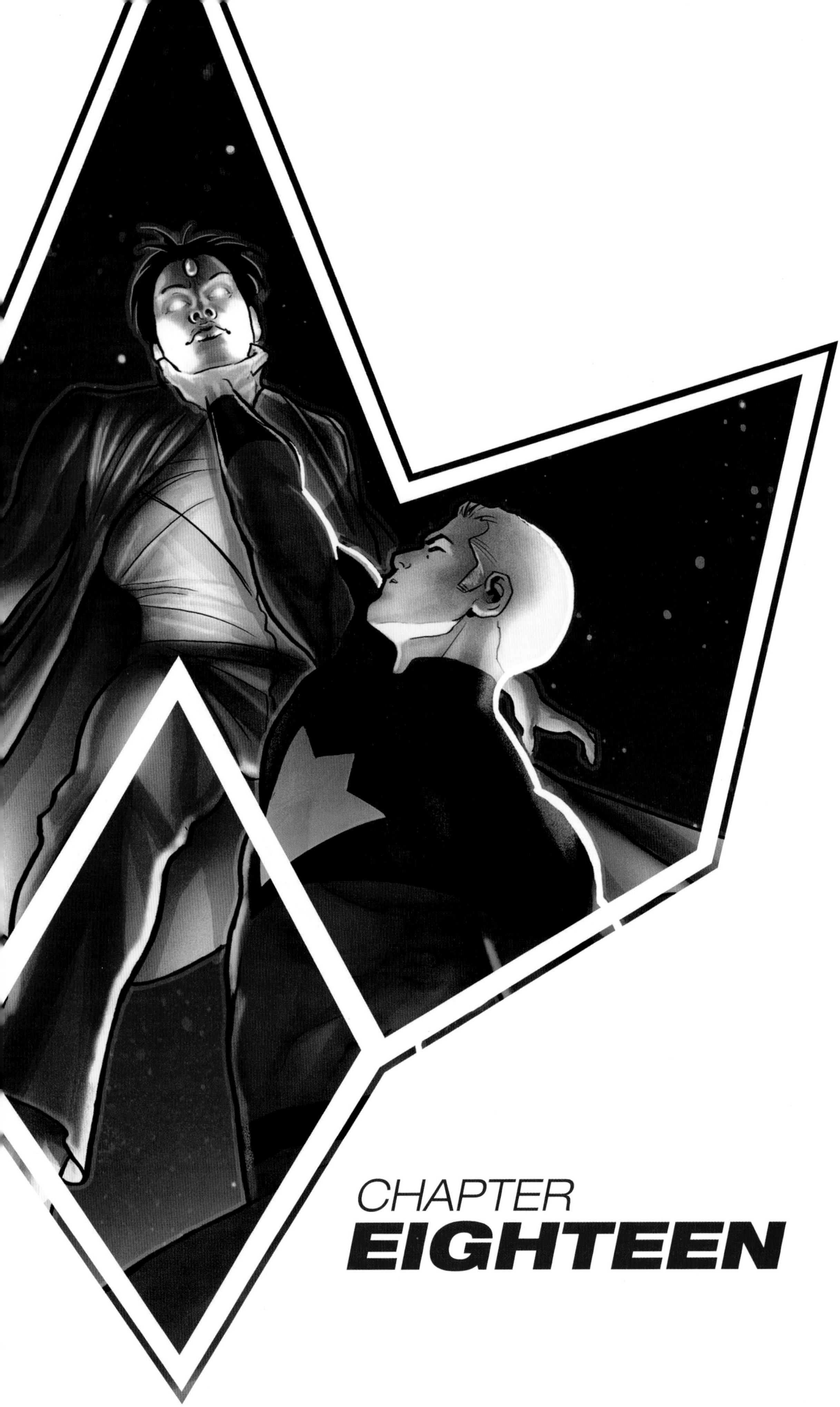

CHAPTER
EIGHTEEN

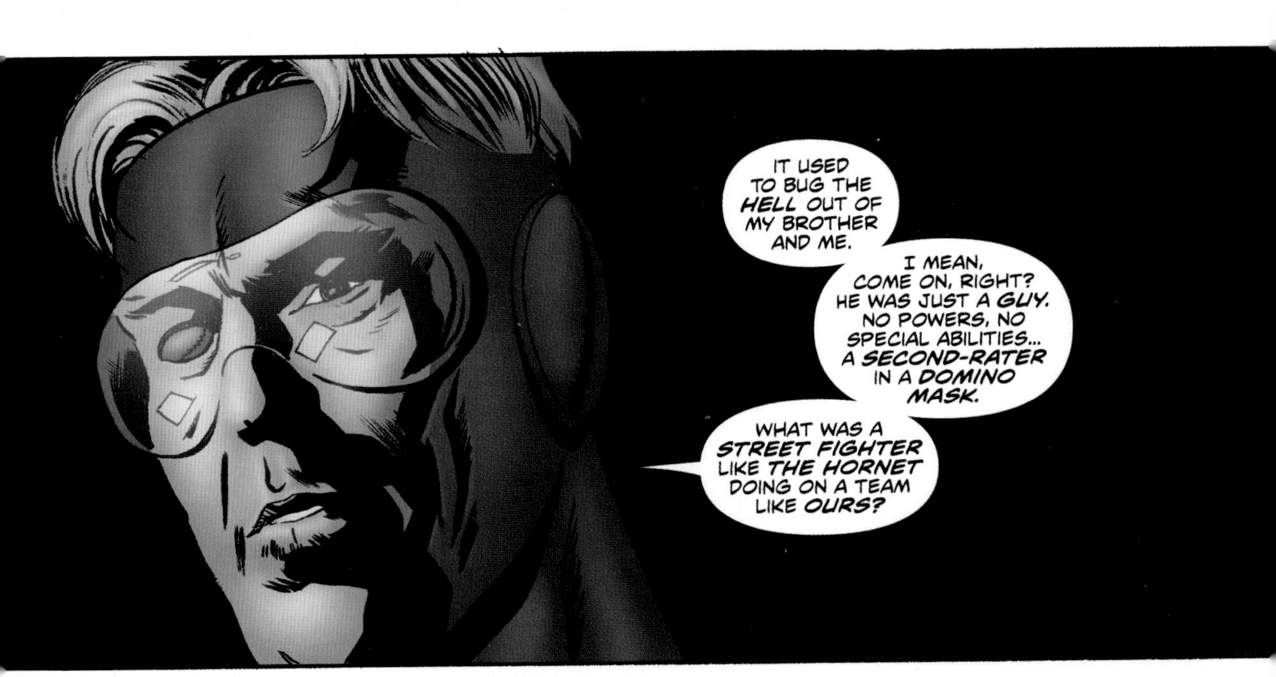
IT USED TO BUG THE HELL OUT OF MY BROTHER AND ME.
I MEAN, COME ON, RIGHT? HE WAS JUST A GUY. NO POWERS, NO SPECIAL ABILITIES... A SECOND-RATER IN A DOMINO MASK.
WHAT WAS A STREET FIGHTER LIKE THE HORNET DOING ON A TEAM LIKE OURS?

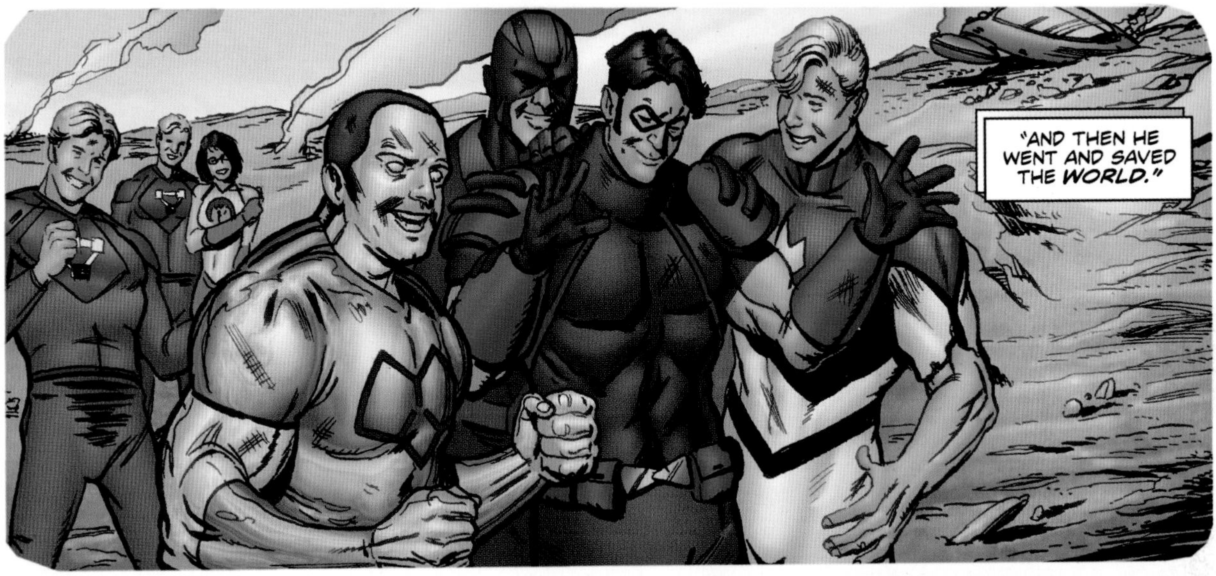
"AND THEN HE WENT AND SAVED THE WORLD."

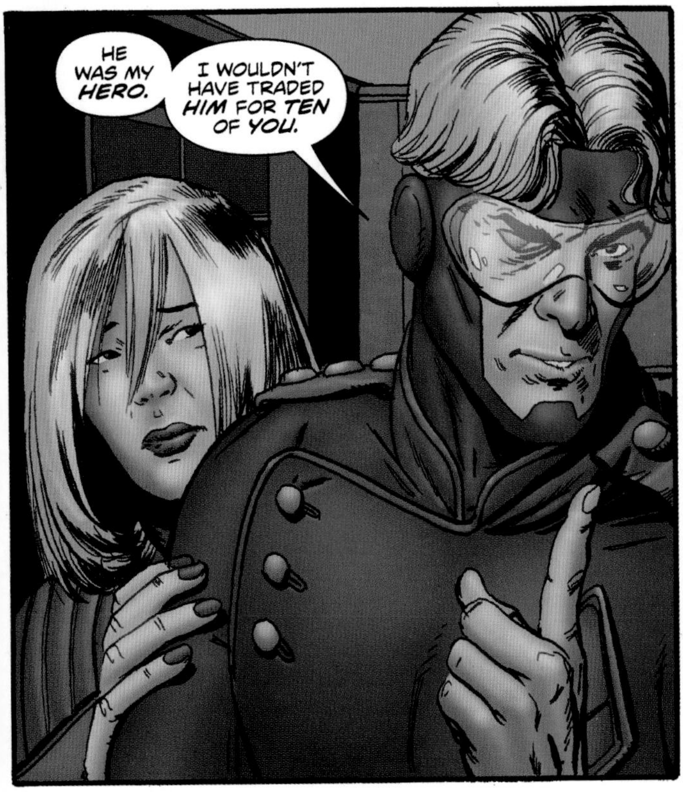
HE WAS MY HERO.
I WOULDN'T HAVE TRADED HIM FOR TEN OF YOU.

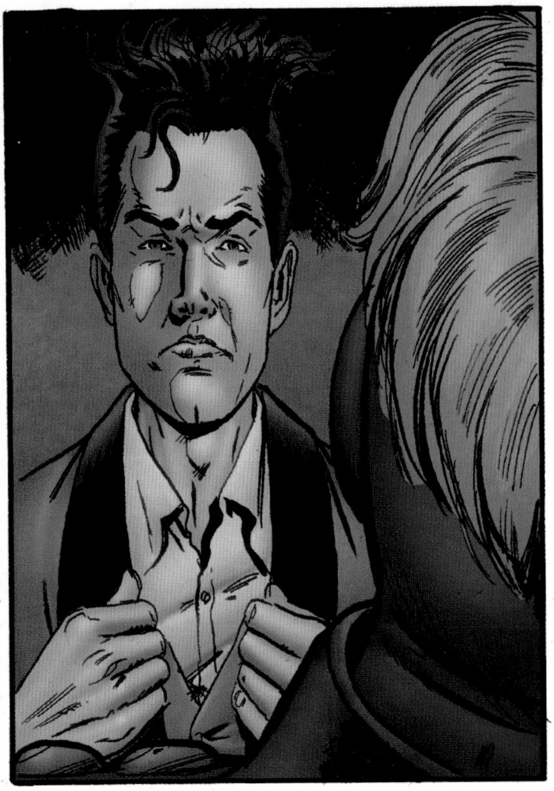

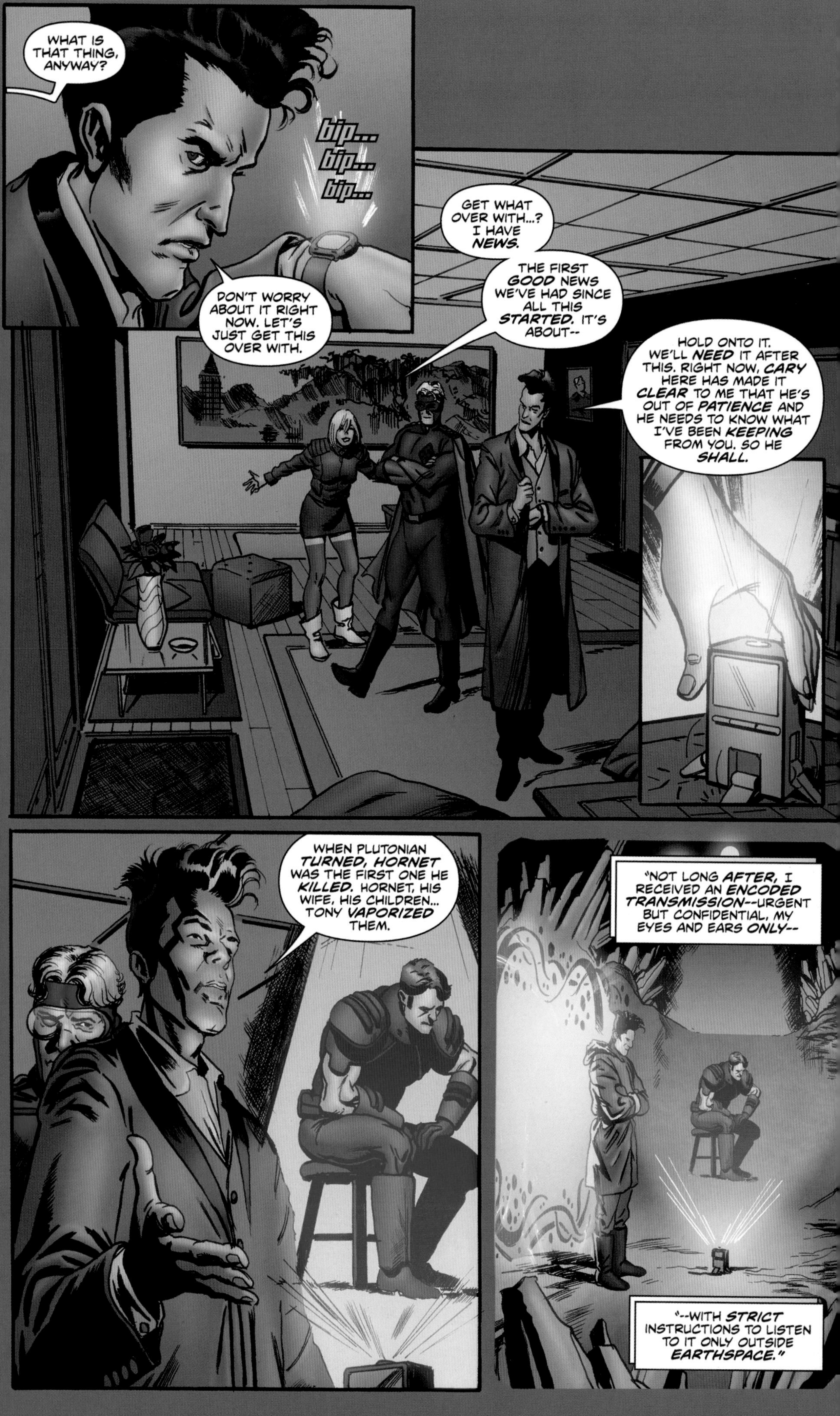
WHAT IS THAT THING, ANYWAY?
bip... bip... bip...
DON'T WORRY ABOUT IT RIGHT NOW. LET'S JUST GET THIS OVER WITH.
GET WHAT OVER WITH...? I HAVE NEWS.
THE FIRST GOOD NEWS WE'VE HAD SINCE ALL THIS STARTED. IT'S ABOUT--
HOLD ONTO IT. WE'LL NEED IT AFTER THIS. RIGHT NOW, CARY HERE HAS MADE IT CLEAR TO ME THAT HE'S OUT OF PATIENCE AND HE NEEDS TO KNOW WHAT I'VE BEEN KEEPING FROM YOU. SO HE SHALL.
WHEN PLUTONIAN TURNED, HORNET WAS THE FIRST ONE HE KILLED. HORNET, HIS WIFE, HIS CHILDREN... TONY VAPORIZED THEM.
"NOT LONG AFTER, I RECEIVED AN ENCODED TRANSMISSION--URGENT BUT CONFIDENTIAL, MY EYES AND EARS ONLY--
"--WITH STRICT INSTRUCTIONS TO LISTEN TO IT ONLY OUTSIDE EARTHSPACE."

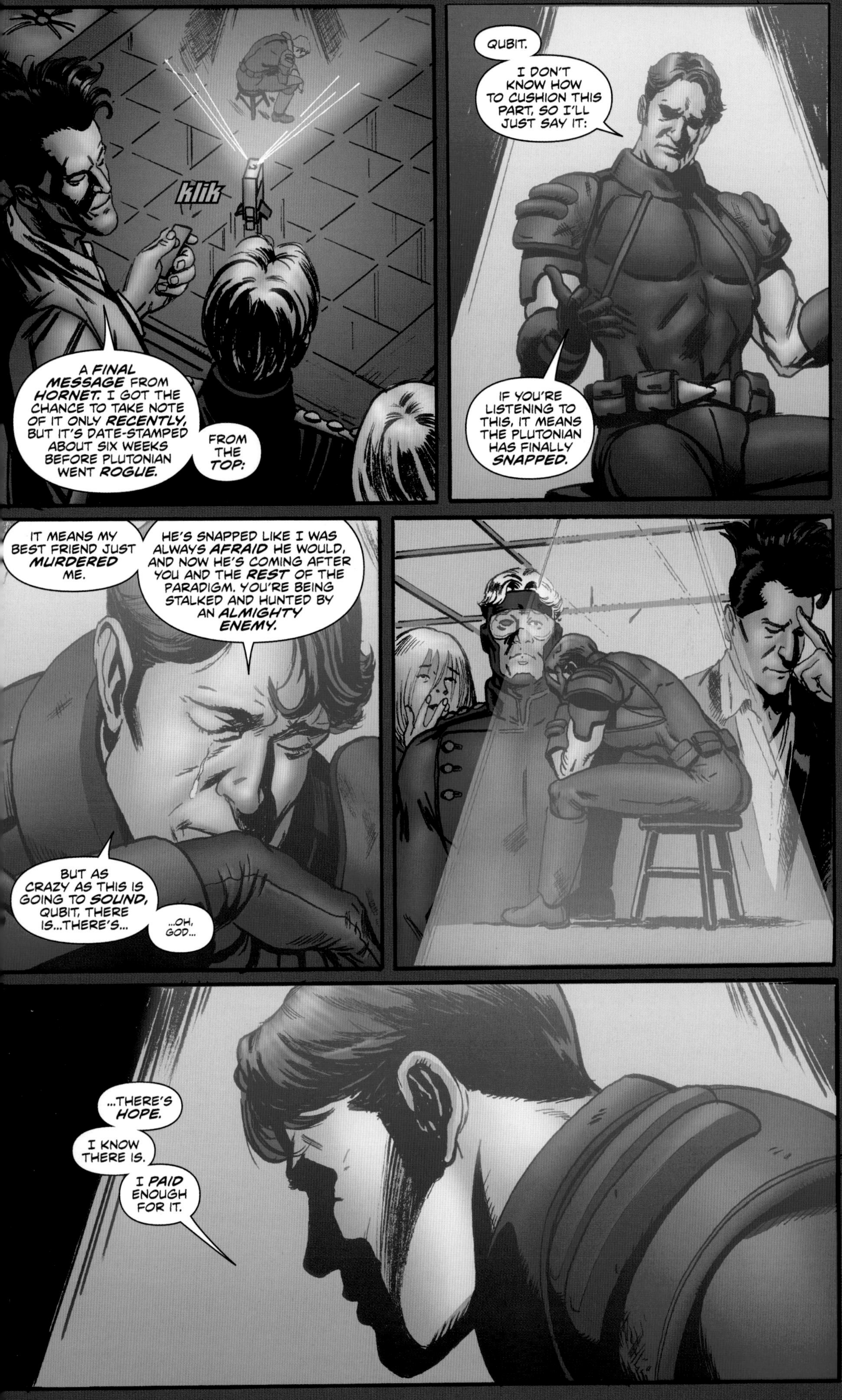

KLIK
A FINAL MESSAGE FROM HORNET. I GOT THE CHANCE TO TAKE NOTE OF IT ONLY RECENTLY, BUT IT'S DATE-STAMPED ABOUT SIX WEEKS BEFORE PLUTONIAN WENT ROGUE.
FROM THE TOP:
QUBIT.
I DON'T KNOW HOW TO CUSHION THIS PART, SO I'LL JUST SAY IT:
IF YOU'RE LISTENING TO THIS, IT MEANS THE PLUTONIAN HAS FINALLY SNAPPED.
IT MEANS MY BEST FRIEND JUST MURDERED ME.
HE'S SNAPPED LIKE I WAS ALWAYS AFRAID HE WOULD, AND NOW HE'S COMING AFTER YOU AND THE REST OF THE PARADIGM. YOU'RE BEING STALKED AND HUNTED BY AN ALMIGHTY ENEMY.
BUT AS CRAZY AS THIS IS GOING TO SOUND, QUBIT, THERE IS...THERE'S...
...OH, GOD...
...THERE'S HOPE.
I KNOW THERE IS.
I PAID ENOUGH FOR IT.

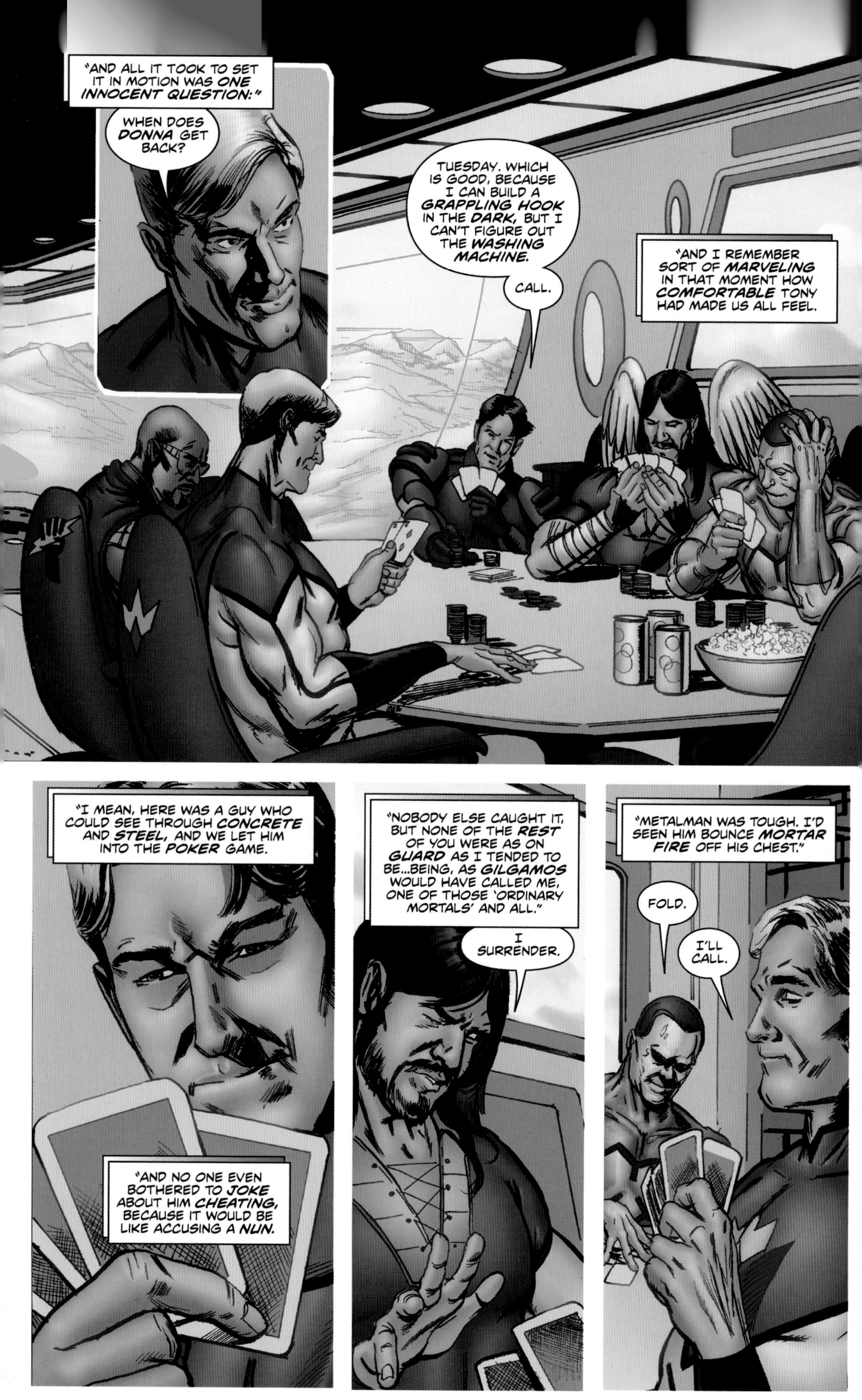
"AND ALL IT TOOK TO SET IT IN MOTION WAS ONE INNOCENT QUESTION:"
WHEN DOES DONNA GET BACK?
TUESDAY. WHICH IS GOOD, BECAUSE I CAN BUILD A GRAPPLING HOOK IN THE DARK, BUT I CAN'T FIGURE OUT THE WASHING MACHINE.
CALL.
"AND I REMEMBER SORT OF MARVELING IN THAT MOMENT HOW COMFORTABLE TONY HAD MADE US ALL FEEL.
"I MEAN, HERE WAS A GUY WHO COULD SEE THROUGH CONCRETE AND STEEL, AND WE LET HIM INTO THE POKER GAME.
"AND NO ONE EVEN BOTHERED TO JOKE ABOUT HIM CHEATING, BECAUSE IT WOULD BE LIKE ACCUSING A NUN.
"NOBODY ELSE CAUGHT IT, BUT NONE OF THE REST OF YOU WERE AS ON GUARD AS I TENDED TO BE...BEING, AS GILGAMOS WOULD HAVE CALLED ME, ONE OF THOSE 'ORDINARY MORTALS' AND ALL."
I SURRENDER.
"METALMAN WAS TOUGH. I'D SEEN HIM BOUNCE MORTAR FIRE OFF HIS CHEST."
FOLD.
I'LL CALL.

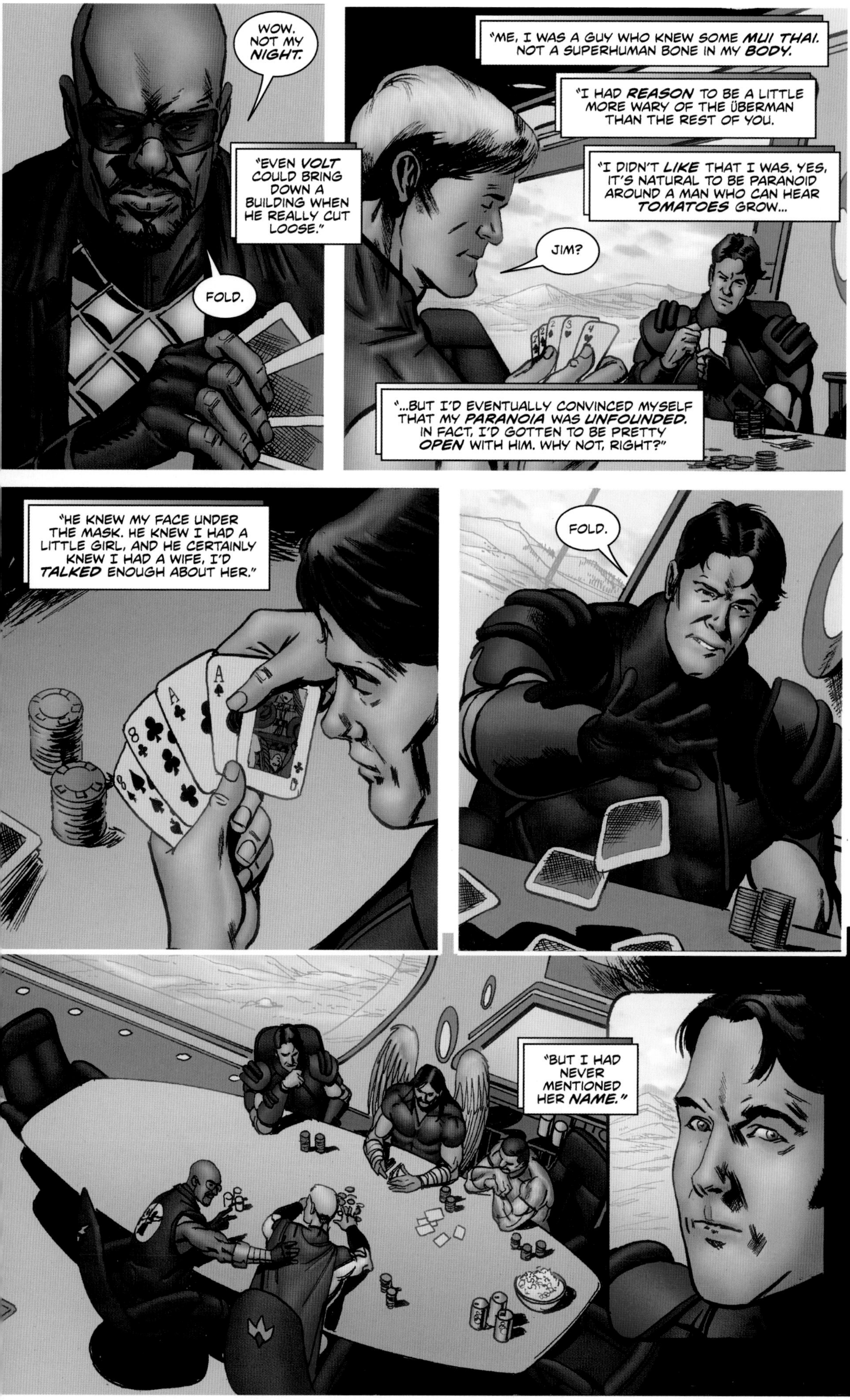
WOW. NOT MY NIGHT.
"EVEN VOLT COULD BRING DOWN A BUILDING WHEN HE REALLY CUT LOOSE."
FOLD.
"ME, I WAS A GUY WHO KNEW SOME MUI THAI. NOT A SUPERHUMAN BONE IN MY BODY.
"I HAD REASON TO BE A LITTLE MORE WARY OF THE ÜBERMAN THAN THE REST OF YOU.
"I DIDN'T LIKE THAT I WAS. YES, IT'S NATURAL TO BE PARANOID AROUND A MAN WHO CAN HEAR TOMATOES GROW...
JIM?
"...BUT I'D EVENTUALLY CONVINCED MYSELF THAT MY PARANOIA WAS UNFOUNDED. IN FACT, I'D GOTTEN TO BE PRETTY OPEN WITH HIM. WHY NOT, RIGHT?"
"HE KNEW MY FACE UNDER THE MASK. HE KNEW I HAD A LITTLE GIRL, AND HE CERTAINLY KNEW I HAD A WIFE, I'D TALKED ENOUGH ABOUT HER."
FOLD.
"BUT I HAD NEVER MENTIONED HER NAME."

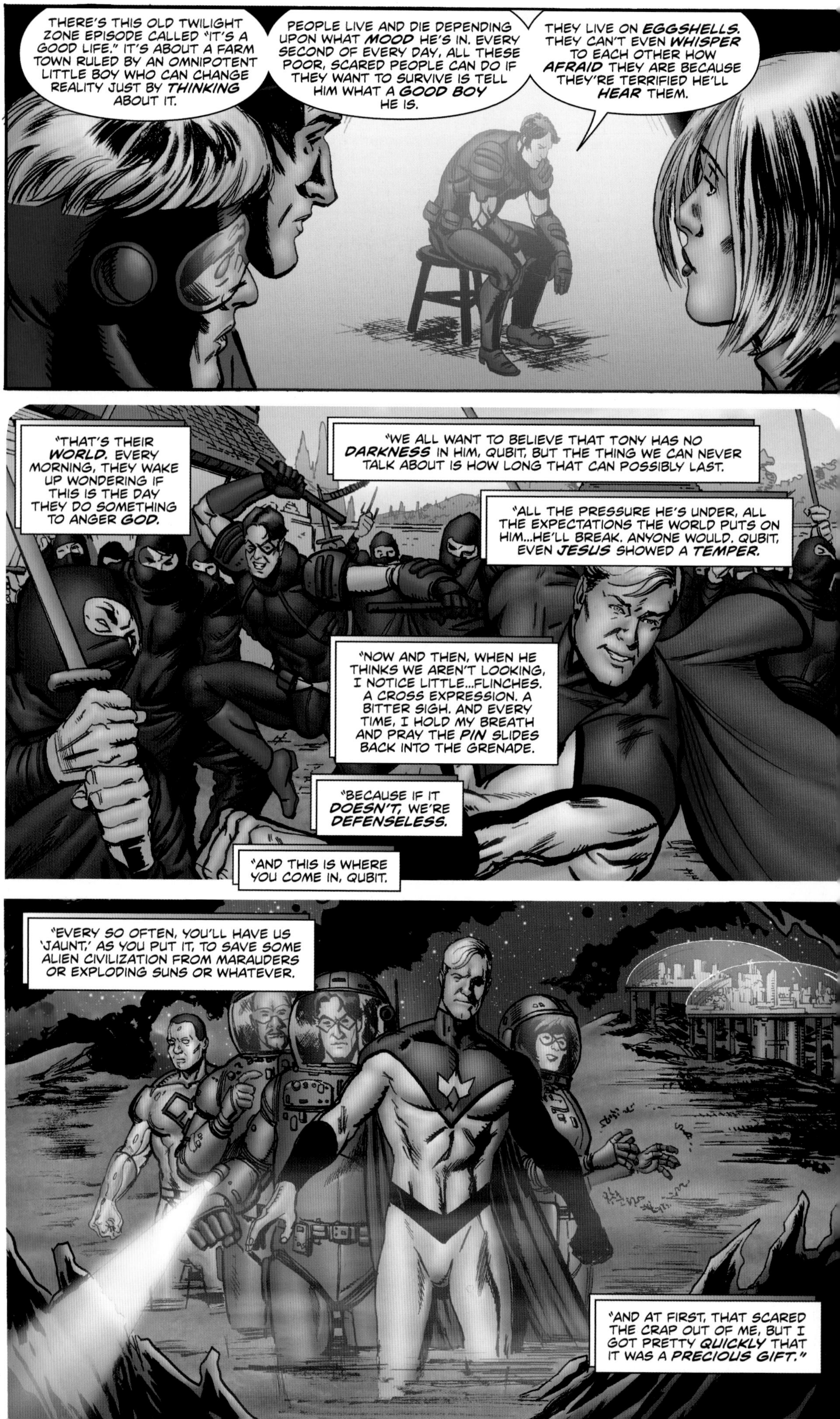
THERE'S THIS OLD TWILIGHT ZONE EPISODE CALLED "IT'S A GOOD LIFE." IT'S ABOUT A FARM TOWN RULED BY AN OMNIPOTENT LITTLE BOY WHO CAN CHANGE REALITY JUST BY THINKING ABOUT IT.
PEOPLE LIVE AND DIE DEPENDING UPON WHAT MOOD HE'S IN. EVERY SECOND OF EVERY DAY, ALL THESE POOR, SCARED PEOPLE CAN DO IF THEY WANT TO SURVIVE IS TELL HIM WHAT A GOOD BOY HE IS.
THEY LIVE ON EGGSHELLS. THEY CAN'T EVEN WHISPER TO EACH OTHER HOW AFRAID THEY ARE BECAUSE THEY'RE TERRIFIED HE'LL HEAR THEM.
"THAT'S THEIR WORLD. EVERY MORNING, THEY WAKE UP WONDERING IF THIS IS THE DAY THEY DO SOMETHING TO ANGER GOD.
"WE ALL WANT TO BELIEVE THAT TONY HAS NO DARKNESS IN HIM, QUBIT, BUT THE THING WE CAN NEVER TALK ABOUT IS HOW LONG THAT CAN POSSIBLY LAST.
"ALL THE PRESSURE HE'S UNDER, ALL THE EXPECTATIONS THE WORLD PUTS ON HIM...HE'LL BREAK. ANYONE WOULD. QUBIT, EVEN JESUS SHOWED A TEMPER.
"NOW AND THEN, WHEN HE THINKS WE AREN'T LOOKING, I NOTICE LITTLE...FLINCHES. A CROSS EXPRESSION. A BITTER SIGH. AND EVERY TIME, I HOLD MY BREATH AND PRAY THE PIN SLIDES BACK INTO THE GRENADE.
"BECAUSE IF IT DOESN'T, WE'RE DEFENSELESS.
"AND THIS IS WHERE YOU COME IN, QUBIT.
"EVERY SO OFTEN, YOU'LL HAVE US 'JAUNT,' AS YOU PUT IT, TO SAVE SOME ALIEN CIVILIZATION FROM MARAUDERS OR EXPLODING SUNS OR WHATEVER.
"AND AT FIRST, THAT SCARED THE CRAP OUT OF ME, BUT I GOT PRETTY QUICKLY THAT IT WAS A PRECIOUS GIFT."

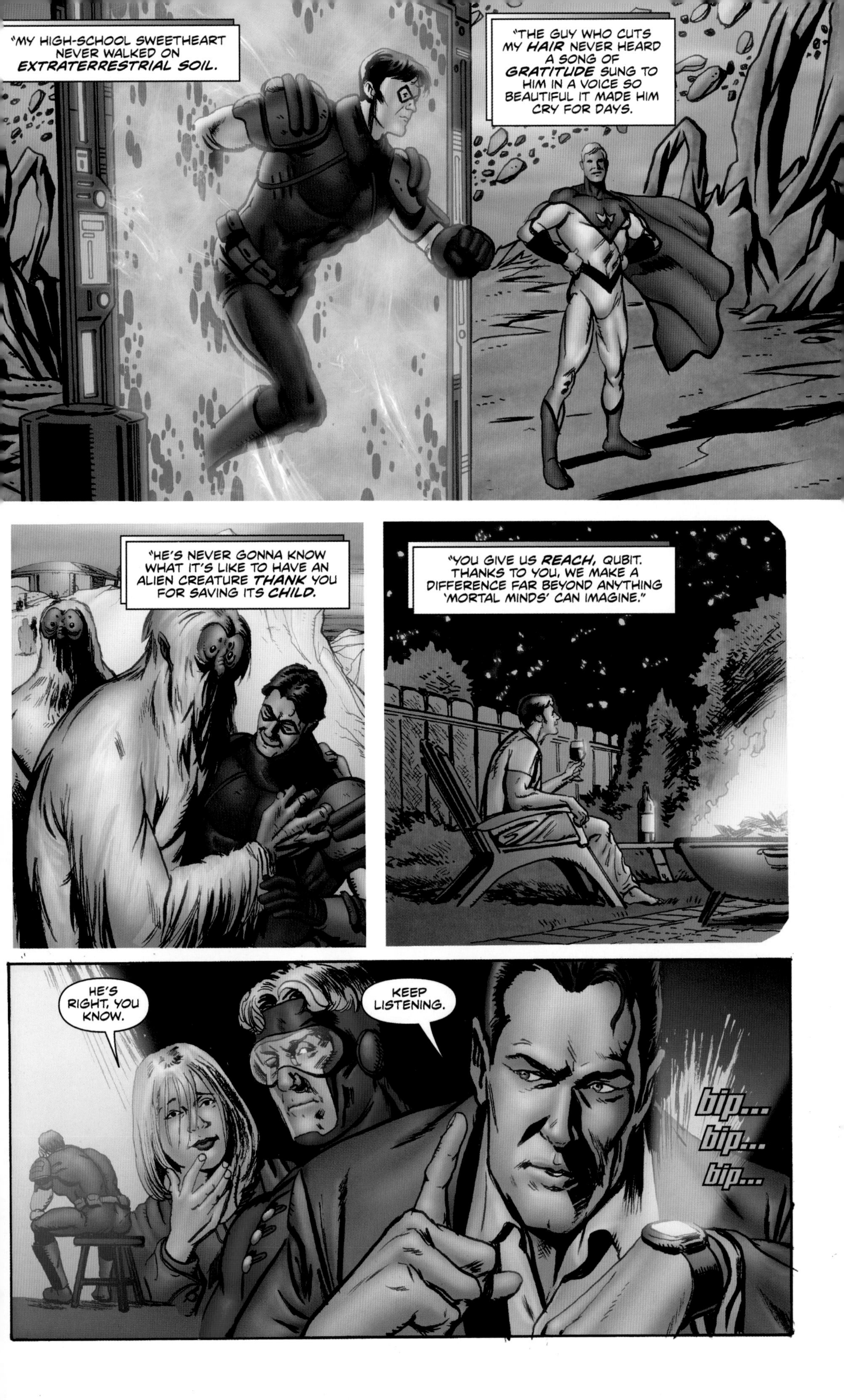
"MY HIGH-SCHOOL SWEETHEART NEVER WALKED ON EXTRATERRESTRIAL SOIL.
"THE GUY WHO CUTS MY HAIR NEVER HEARD A SONG OF GRATITUDE SUNG TO HIM IN A VOICE SO BEAUTIFUL IT MADE HIM CRY FOR DAYS.
"HE'S NEVER GONNA KNOW WHAT IT'S LIKE TO HAVE AN ALIEN CREATURE THANK YOU FOR SAVING ITS CHILD.
"YOU GIVE US REACH, QUBIT. THANKS TO YOU, WE MAKE A DIFFERENCE FAR BEYOND ANYTHING 'MORTAL MINDS' CAN IMAGINE."
HE'S RIGHT, YOU KNOW.
KEEP LISTENING.
bip... bip... bip...

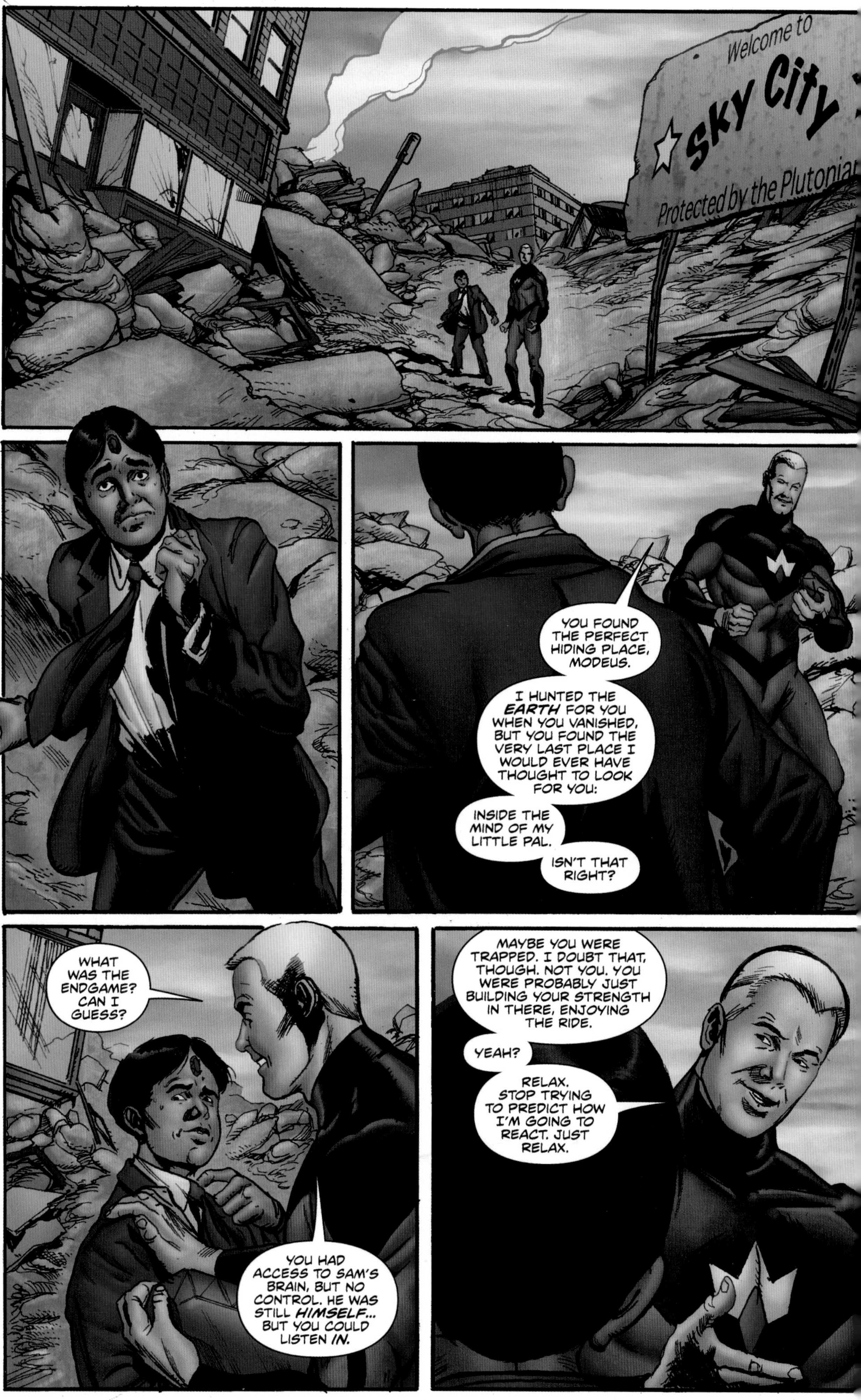
Welcome to
Sky City
Protected by the Plutonian
YOU FOUND THE PERFECT HIDING PLACE, MODEUS.
I HUNTED THE EARTH FOR YOU WHEN YOU VANISHED, BUT YOU FOUND THE VERY LAST PLACE I WOULD EVER HAVE THOUGHT TO LOOK FOR YOU:
INSIDE THE MIND OF MY LITTLE PAL.
ISN'T THAT RIGHT?
WHAT WAS THE ENDGAME? CAN I GUESS?
YOU HAD ACCESS TO SAM'S BRAIN, BUT NO CONTROL. HE WAS STILL HIMSELF... BUT YOU COULD LISTEN IN.
MAYBE YOU WERE TRAPPED. I DOUBT THAT, THOUGH. NOT YOU. YOU WERE PROBABLY JUST BUILDING YOUR STRENGTH IN THERE, ENJOYING THE RIDE.
YEAH?
RELAX. STOP TRYING TO PREDICT HOW I'M GOING TO REACT. JUST RELAX.

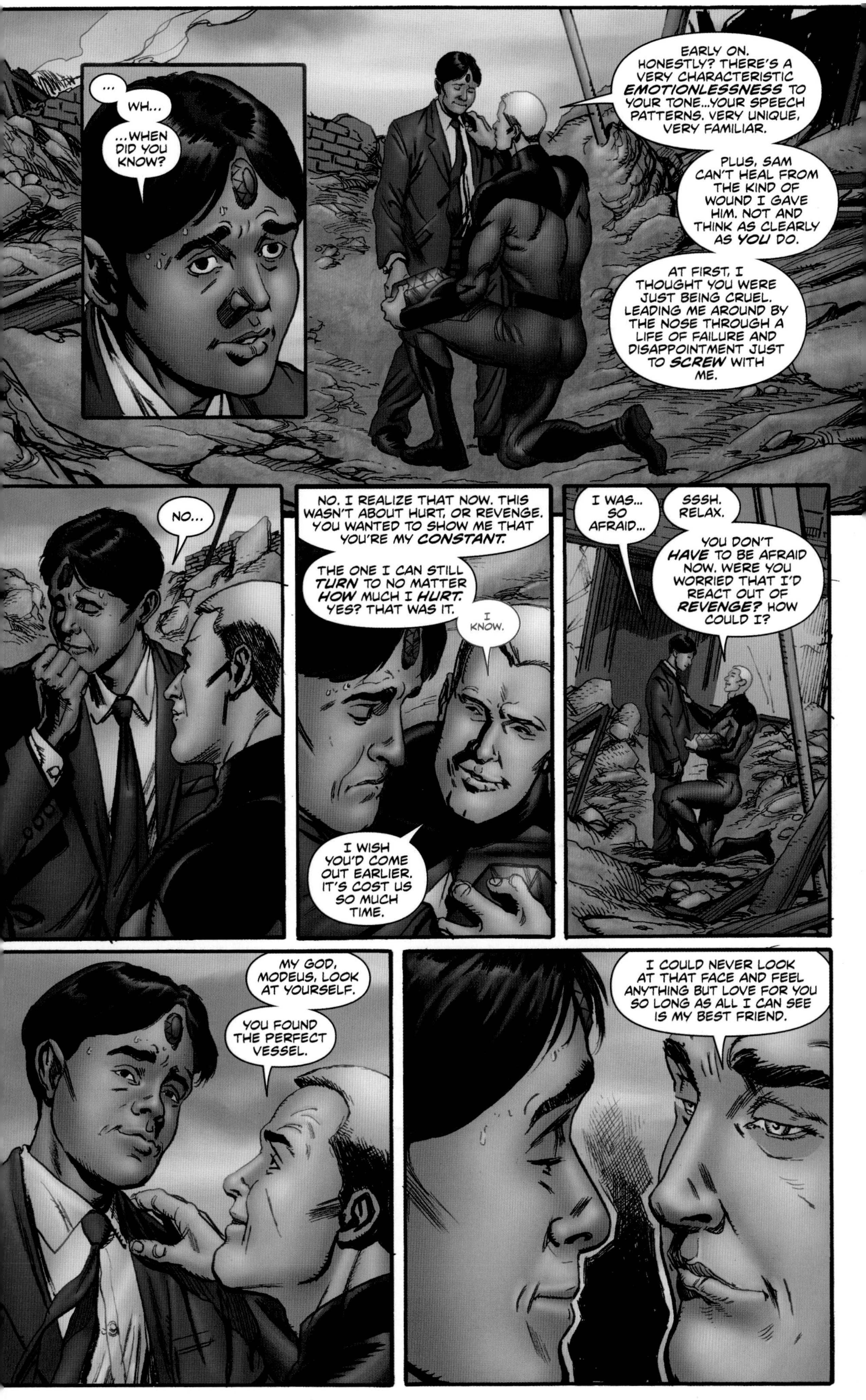
...
WH...
...WHEN DID YOU KNOW?
EARLY ON. HONESTLY? THERE'S A VERY CHARACTERISTIC EMOTIONLESSNESS TO YOUR TONE...YOUR SPEECH PATTERNS. VERY UNIQUE, VERY FAMILIAR.
PLUS, SAM CAN'T HEAL FROM THE KIND OF WOUND I GAVE HIM. NOT AND THINK AS CLEARLY AS YOU DO.
AT FIRST, I THOUGHT YOU WERE JUST BEING CRUEL. LEADING ME AROUND BY THE NOSE THROUGH A LIFE OF FAILURE AND DISAPPOINTMENT JUST TO SCREW WITH ME.
NO...
NO. I REALIZE THAT NOW. THIS WASN'T ABOUT HURT, OR REVENGE. YOU WANTED TO SHOW ME THAT YOU'RE MY CONSTANT.
THE ONE I CAN STILL TURN TO NO MATTER HOW MUCH I HURT. YES? THAT WAS IT.
I KNOW.
I WISH YOU'D COME OUT EARLIER. IT'S COST US SO MUCH TIME.
I WAS... SO AFRAID...
SSSH. RELAX.
YOU DON'T HAVE TO BE AFRAID NOW. WERE YOU WORRIED THAT I'D REACT OUT OF REVENGE? HOW COULD I?
MY GOD, MODEUS, LOOK AT YOURSELF.
YOU FOUND THE PERFECT VESSEL.
I COULD NEVER LOOK AT THAT FACE AND FEEL ANYTHING BUT LOVE FOR YOU SO LONG AS ALL I CAN SEE IS MY BEST FRIEND.

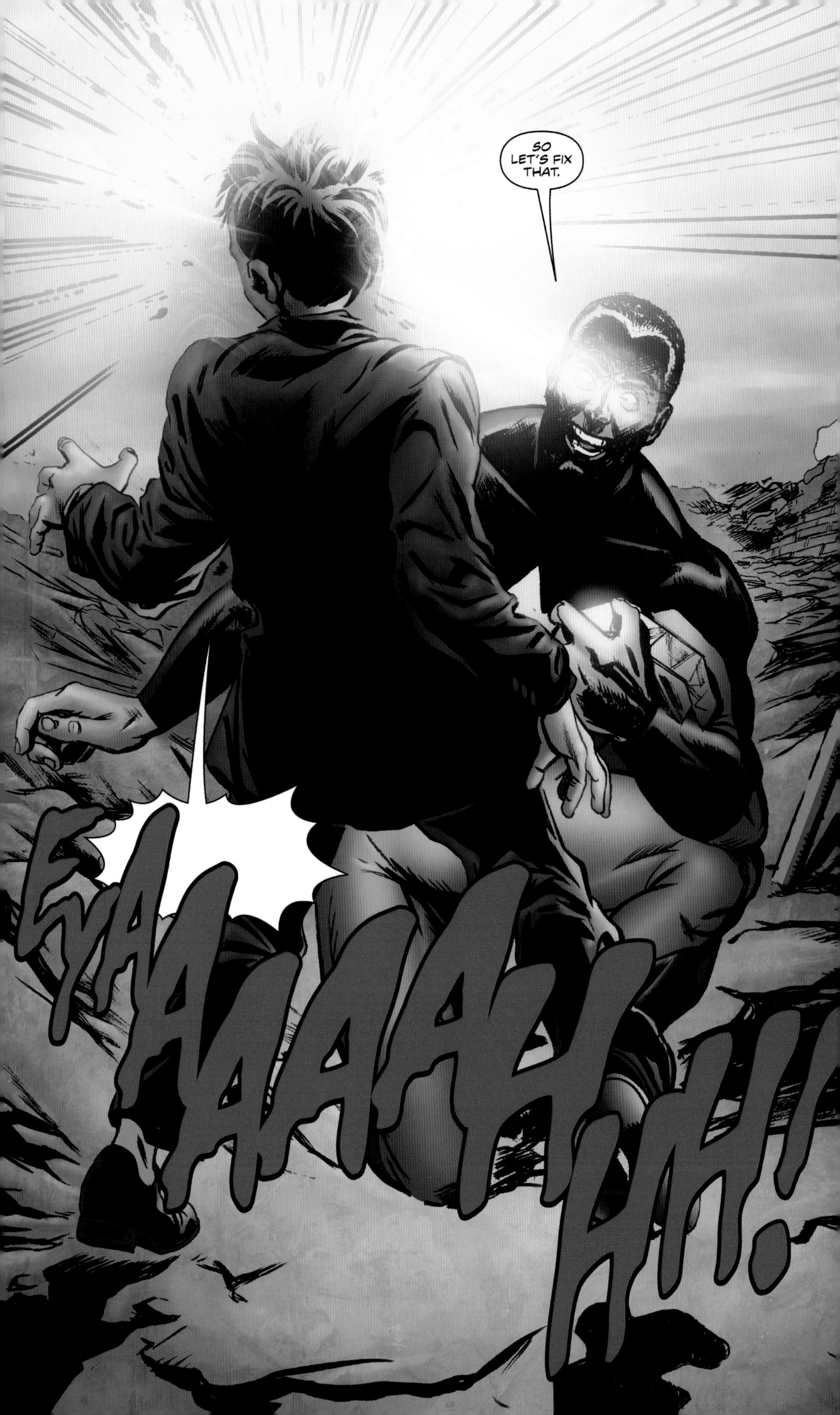
SO LET'S FIX THAT.
EYAAAAAAHHH!!

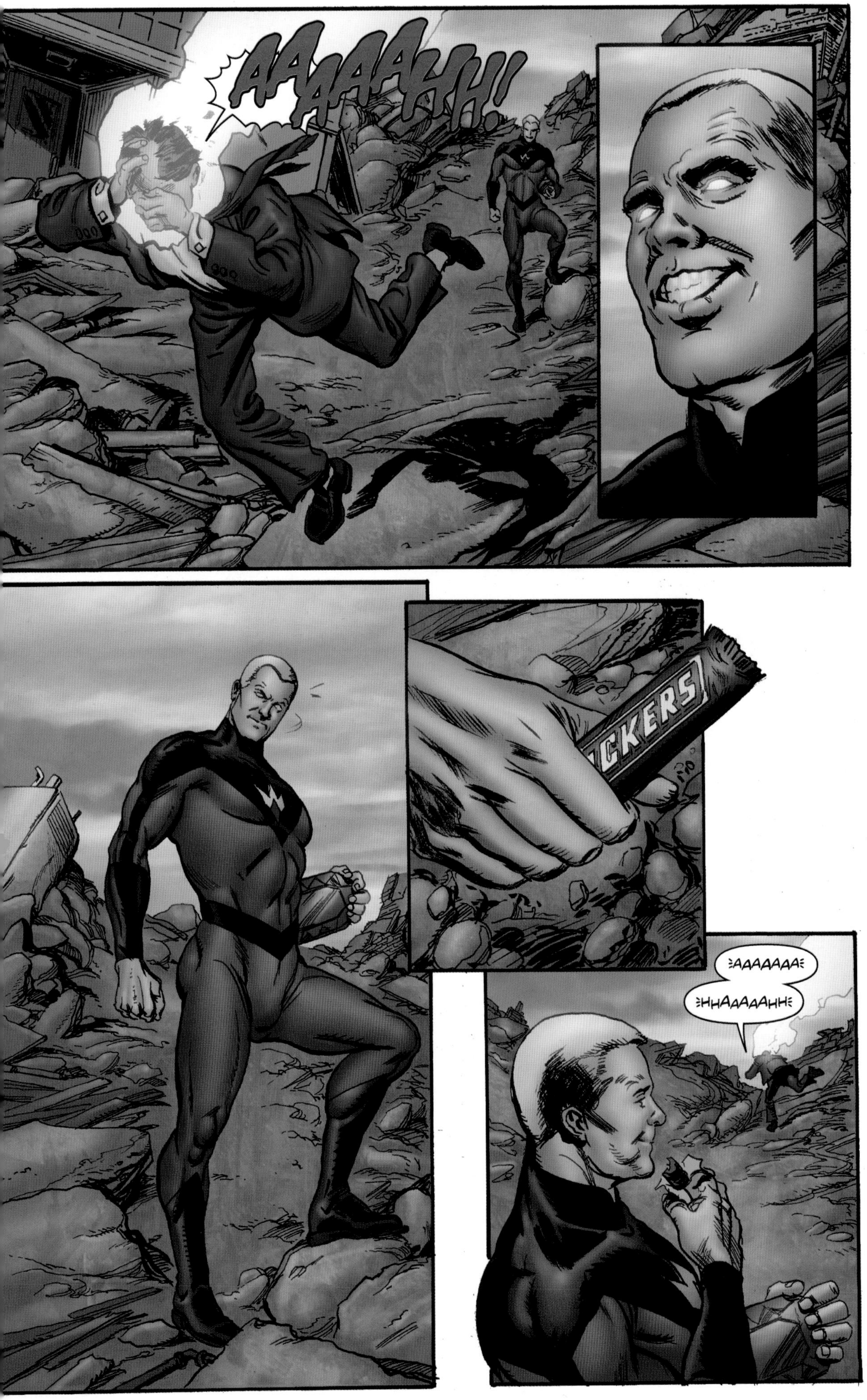
AAAAAAHH!
CKERS
AAAAAAA
HHAAAAAHH

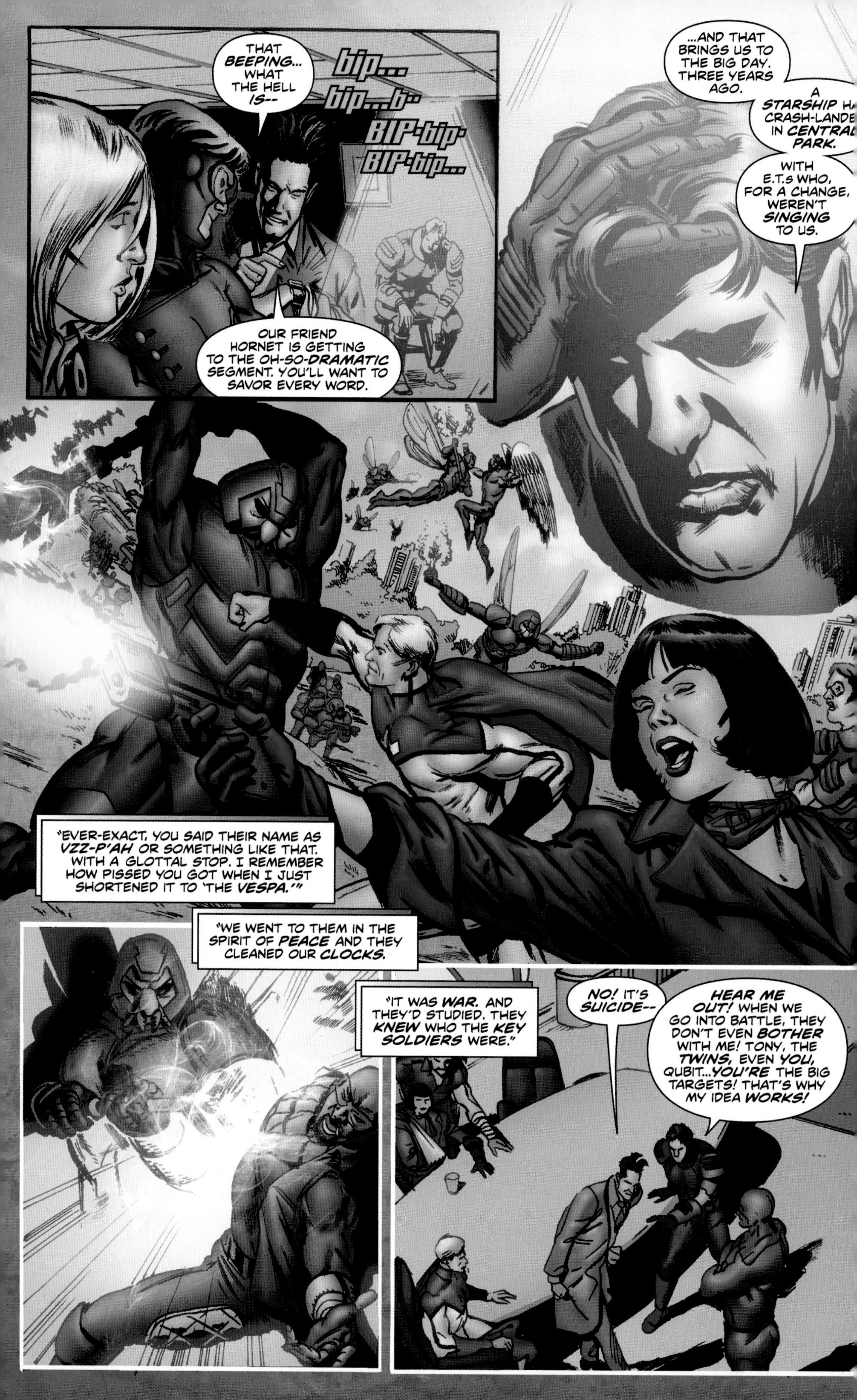

THAT BEEPING... WHAT THE HELL IS--
bip... bip...b- BIP-bip- BIP-bip...
OUR FRIEND HORNET IS GETTING TO THE OH-SO-DRAMATIC SEGMENT. YOU'LL WANT TO SAVOR EVERY WORD.
...AND THAT BRINGS US TO THE BIG DAY. THREE YEARS AGO.
A STARSHIP HA CRASH-LANDE IN CENTRAL PARK.
WITH E.T.s WHO, FOR A CHANGE, WEREN'T SINGING TO US.
"EVER-EXACT, YOU SAID THEIR NAME AS VZZ-P'AH OR SOMETHING LIKE THAT. WITH A GLOTTAL STOP. I REMEMBER HOW PISSED YOU GOT WHEN I JUST SHORTENED IT TO 'THE VESPA.'"
"WE WENT TO THEM IN THE SPIRIT OF PEACE AND THEY CLEANED OUR CLOCKS.
"IT WAS WAR. AND THEY'D STUDIED. THEY KNEW WHO THE KEY SOLDIERS WERE."
NO! IT'S SUICIDE--
HEAR ME OUT! WHEN WE GO INTO BATTLE, THEY DON'T EVEN BOTHER WITH ME! TONY, THE TWINS, EVEN YOU, QUBIT...YOU'RE THE BIG TARGETS! THAT'S WHY MY IDEA WORKS!

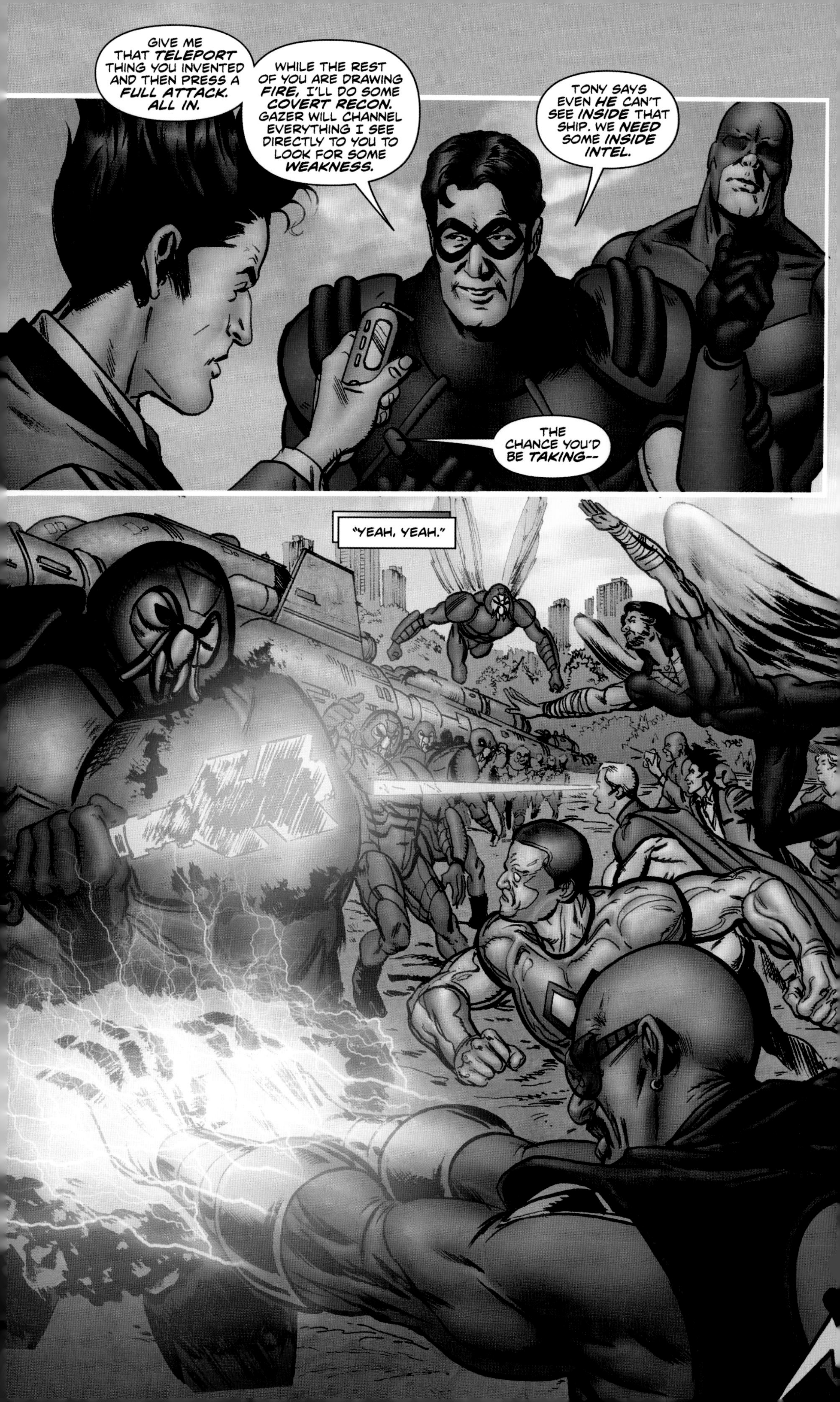
GIVE ME THAT TELEPORT THING YOU INVENTED AND THEN PRESS A FULL ATTACK. ALL IN.
WHILE THE REST OF YOU ARE DRAWING FIRE, I'LL DO SOME COVERT RECON. GAZER WILL CHANNEL EVERYTHING I SEE DIRECTLY TO YOU TO LOOK FOR SOME WEAKNESS.
TONY SAYS EVEN HE CAN'T SEE INSIDE THAT SHIP. WE NEED SOME INSIDE INTEL.
THE CHANCE YOU'D BE TAKING--
"YEAH, YEAH."

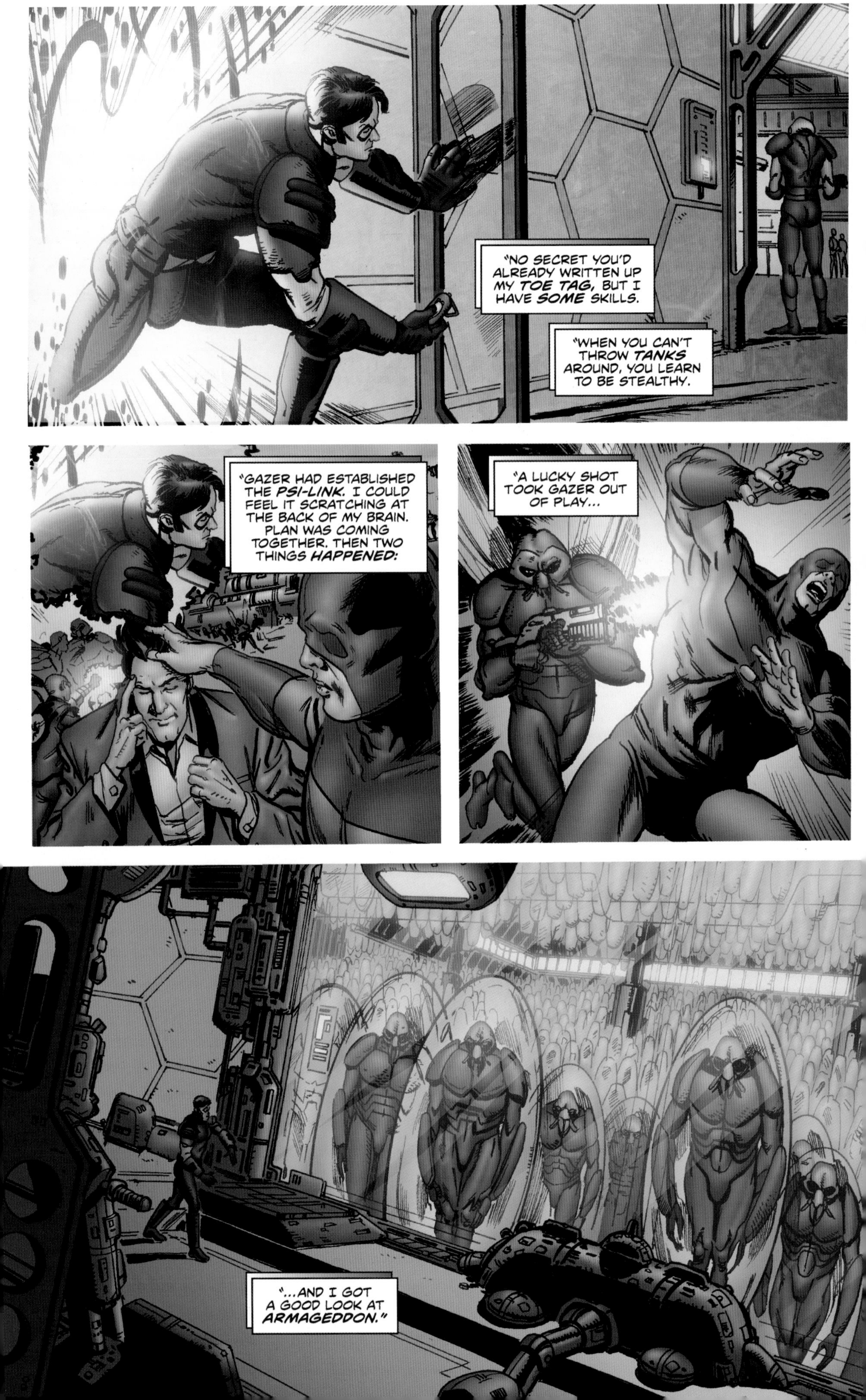
"NO SECRET YOU'D ALREADY WRITTEN UP MY TOE TAG, BUT I HAVE SOME SKILLS.
"WHEN YOU CAN'T THROW TANKS AROUND, YOU LEARN TO BE STEALTHY.
"GAZER HAD ESTABLISHED THE PSI-LINK. I COULD FEEL IT SCRATCHING AT THE BACK OF MY BRAIN. PLAN WAS COMING TOGETHER. THEN TWO THINGS HAPPENED:
"A LUCKY SHOT TOOK GAZER OUT OF PLAY...
"...AND I GOT A GOOD LOOK AT ARMAGEDDON."

"WE HAD *VASTLY* UNDERESTIMATED THEIR NUMBERS."

AAAH! AAAH!

ﾝﾞｿﾞｿﾞｿﾞ ﾊﾞｿﾞ

UNIVERSAL TRANSLATOR INSERTED. BRING PRISONER TO ﾄﾞｿﾞｿﾞ ﾄﾞｿﾞｿﾞ

"WHILE YOU WERE FIGHTING OUTSIDE, THE VESPA PARADED ME IN FRONT OF THEIR LEADER SO HE COULD GIVE ME A *MESSAGE* TO DELIVER.

"STAR-TRAVEL WAS *NEW* TO THEM, HE SAID. EARTH WAS THE FIRST ENVIRONMENTALLY ADEQUATE PLANET THEY'D *FOUND.*

"THEY'D ALREADY KILLED *HUNDREDS,* AND THAT WAS ONLY A *START.*

"HE MADE IT *ABUNDANTLY CLEAR* THAT HIS SOLDIERS WOULD STOP AT *ABSOLUTELY NOTHING* TO OVERRUN IT FOR THEIR NEEDS.

"IN FACT, HE TOOK GREAT *PLEASURE* IN DESCRIBING THE NOISE THAT *HUMAN CHILDREN* MADE WHEN VESPANS LAID *EGGS* DOWN THEIR THROATS.

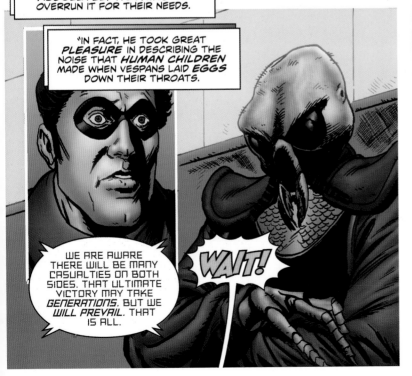

WE ARE AWARE THERE WILL BE MANY CASUALTIES ON BOTH SIDES. THAT ULTIMATE VICTORY MAY TAKE *GENERATIONS.* BUT WE *WILL PREVAIL.* THAT IS ALL.

WAIT!

WHAT... ...

...WHAT IF I OFFERED YOU A *BETTER DEAL?*

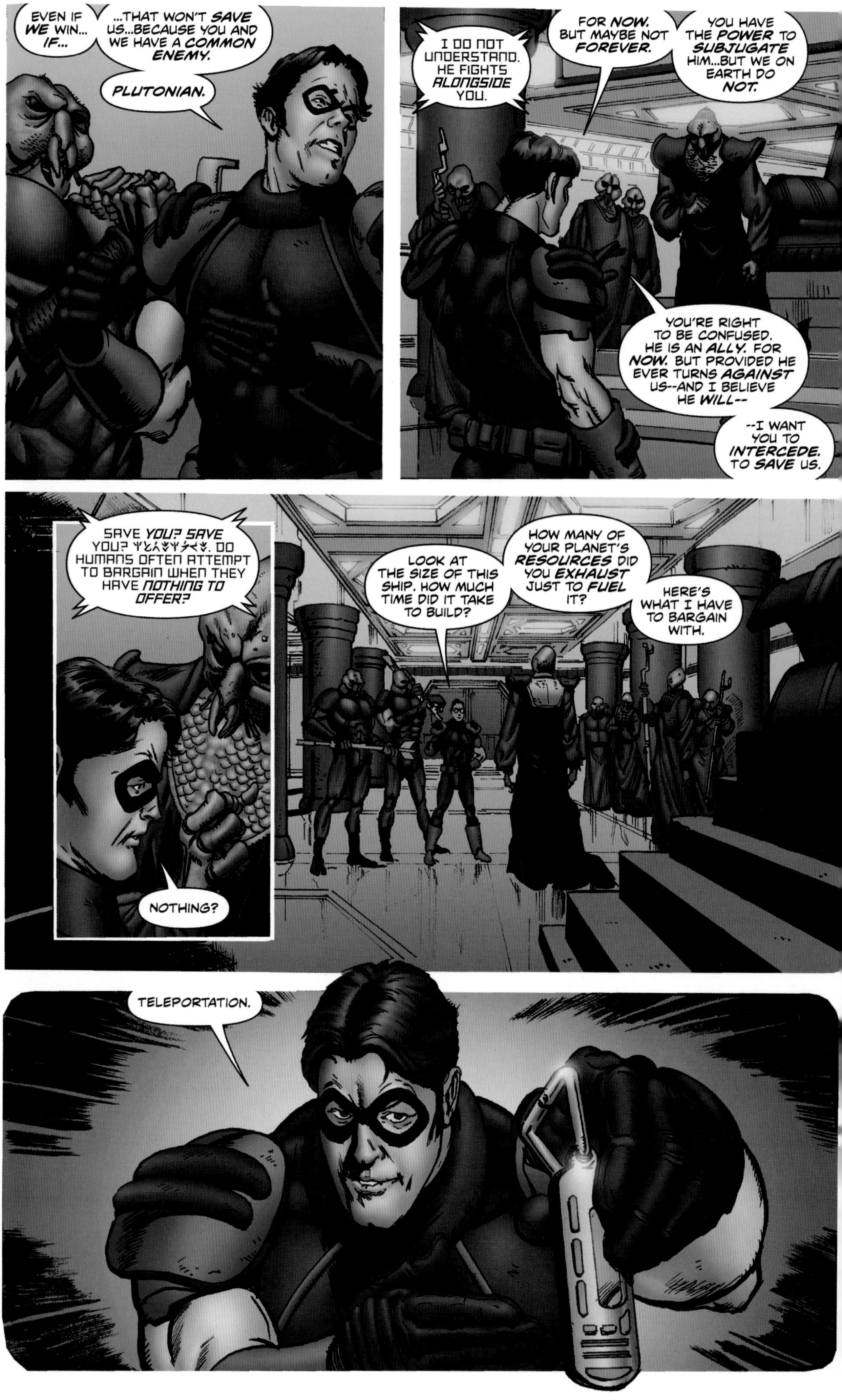
EVEN IF WE WIN... IF...
...THAT WON'T SAVE US...BECAUSE YOU AND WE HAVE A COMMON ENEMY.
PLUTONIAN.
I DO NOT UNDERSTAND. HE FIGHTS ALONGSIDE YOU.
FOR NOW. BUT MAYBE NOT FOREVER.
YOU HAVE THE POWER TO SUBJUGATE HIM...BUT WE ON EARTH DO NOT.
YOU'RE RIGHT TO BE CONFUSED. HE IS AN ALLY. FOR NOW. BUT PROVIDED HE EVER TURNS AGAINST US--AND I BELIEVE HE WILL--
--I WANT YOU TO INTERCEDE. TO SAVE US.
SAVE YOU? SAVE YOU? DO HUMANS OFTEN ATTEMPT TO BARGAIN WHEN THEY HAVE NOTHING TO OFFER?
NOTHING?
LOOK AT THE SIZE OF THIS SHIP. HOW MUCH TIME DID IT TAKE TO BUILD?
HOW MANY OF YOUR PLANET'S RESOURCES DID YOU EXHAUST JUST TO FUEL IT?
HERE'S WHAT I HAVE TO BARGAIN WITH.
TELEPORTATION.

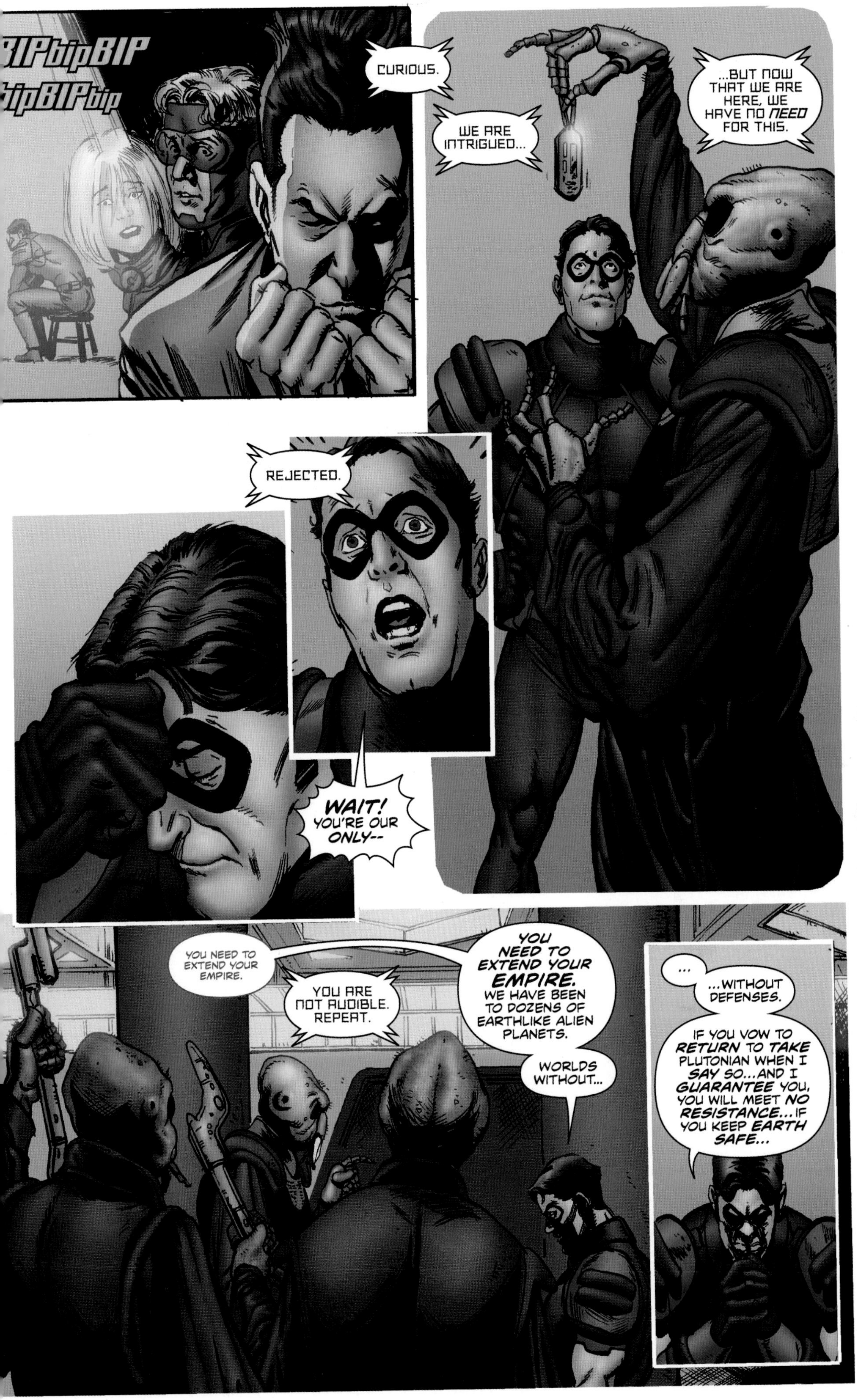
BIPbipBIP
bipBIPbip
CURIOUS.
WE ARE INTRIGUED...
...BUT NOW THAT WE ARE HERE, WE HAVE NO *NEED* FOR THIS.
REJECTED.
WAIT! YOU'RE OUR *ONLY--*
YOU NEED TO EXTEND YOUR EMPIRE.
YOU ARE NOT AUDIBLE. REPEAT.
YOU NEED TO EXTEND YOUR EMPIRE. WE HAVE BEEN TO DOZENS OF EARTHLIKE ALIEN PLANETS.
WORLDS WITHOUT...
...
...WITHOUT DEFENSES.
IF YOU VOW TO *RETURN* TO *TAKE* PLUTONIAN WHEN I *SAY* SO...AND I *GUARANTEE* YOU, YOU WILL MEET *NO RESISTANCE*...IF YOU KEEP *EARTH SAFE...*

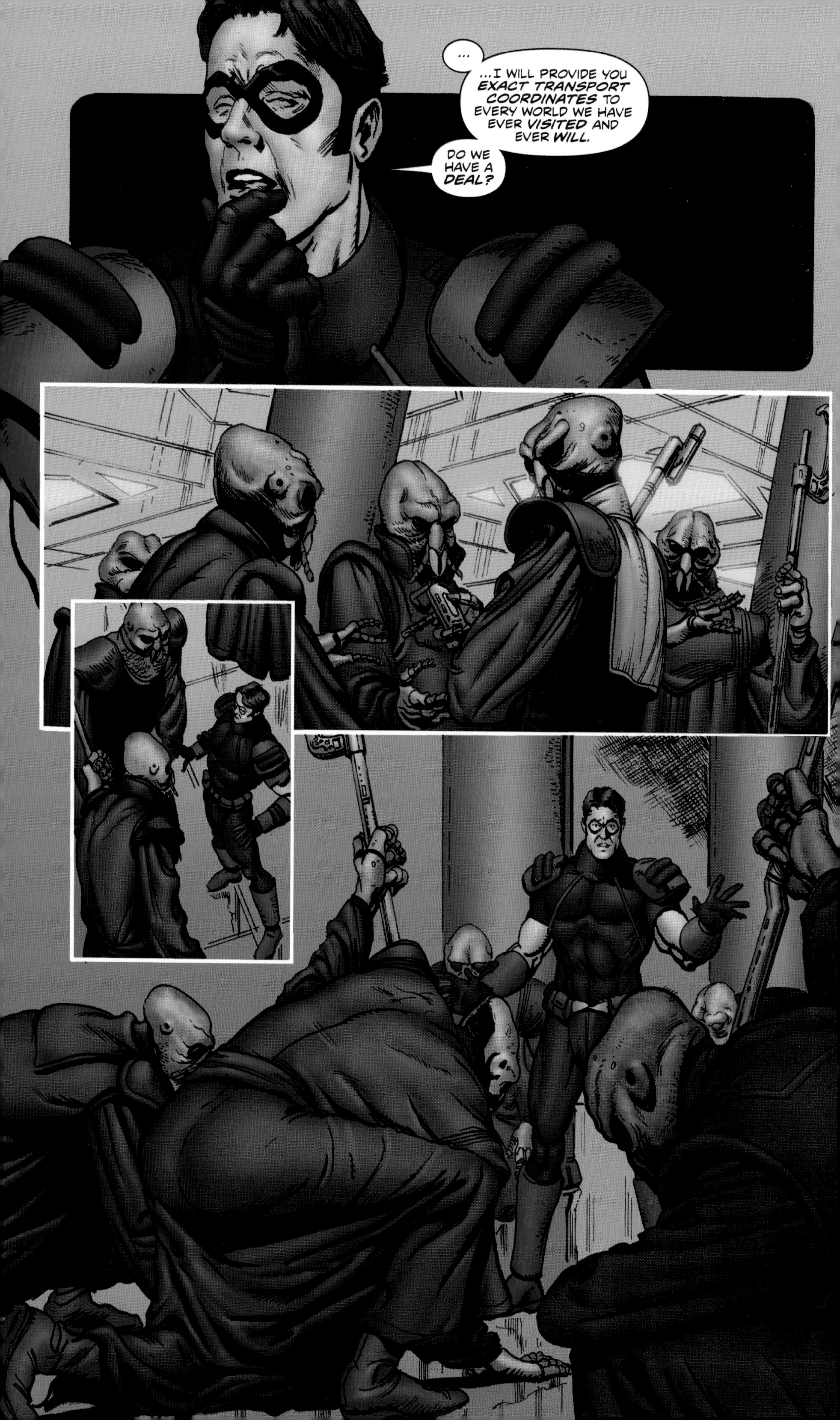
...
...I WILL PROVIDE YOU EXACT TRANSPORT COORDINATES TO EVERY WORLD WE HAVE EVER VISITED AND EVER WILL.
DO WE HAVE A DEAL?

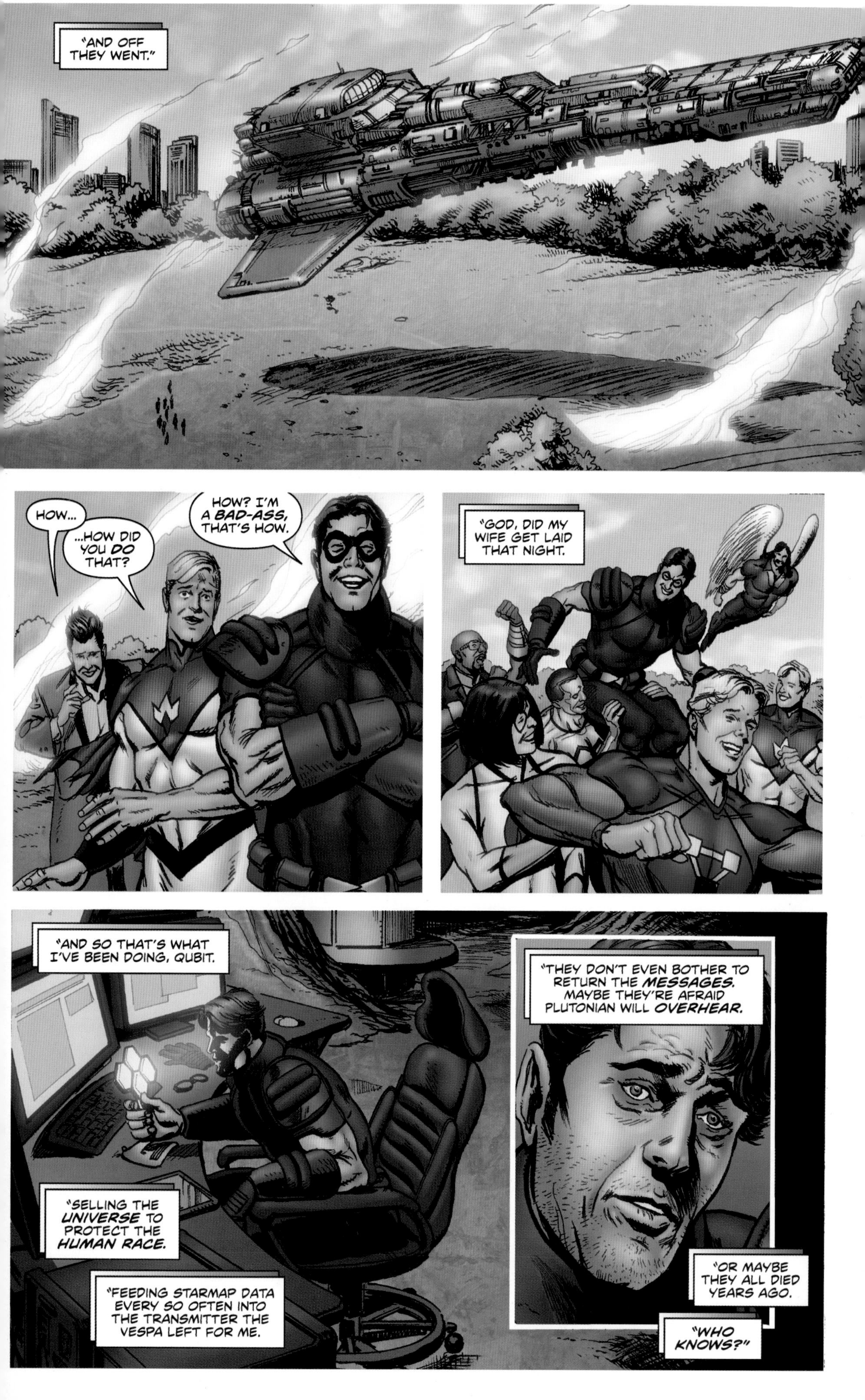
"AND OFF THEY WENT."
HOW...
...HOW DID YOU DO THAT?
HOW? I'M A BAD-ASS, THAT'S HOW.
"GOD, DID MY WIFE GET LAID THAT NIGHT.
"AND SO THAT'S WHAT I'VE BEEN DOING, QUBIT.
"SELLING THE UNIVERSE TO PROTECT THE HUMAN RACE.
"FEEDING STARMAP DATA EVERY SO OFTEN INTO THE TRANSMITTER THE VESPA LEFT FOR ME.
"THEY DON'T EVEN BOTHER TO RETURN THE MESSAGES. MAYBE THEY'RE AFRAID PLUTONIAN WILL OVERHEAR.
"OR MAYBE THEY ALL DIED YEARS AGO.
"WHO KNOWS?"

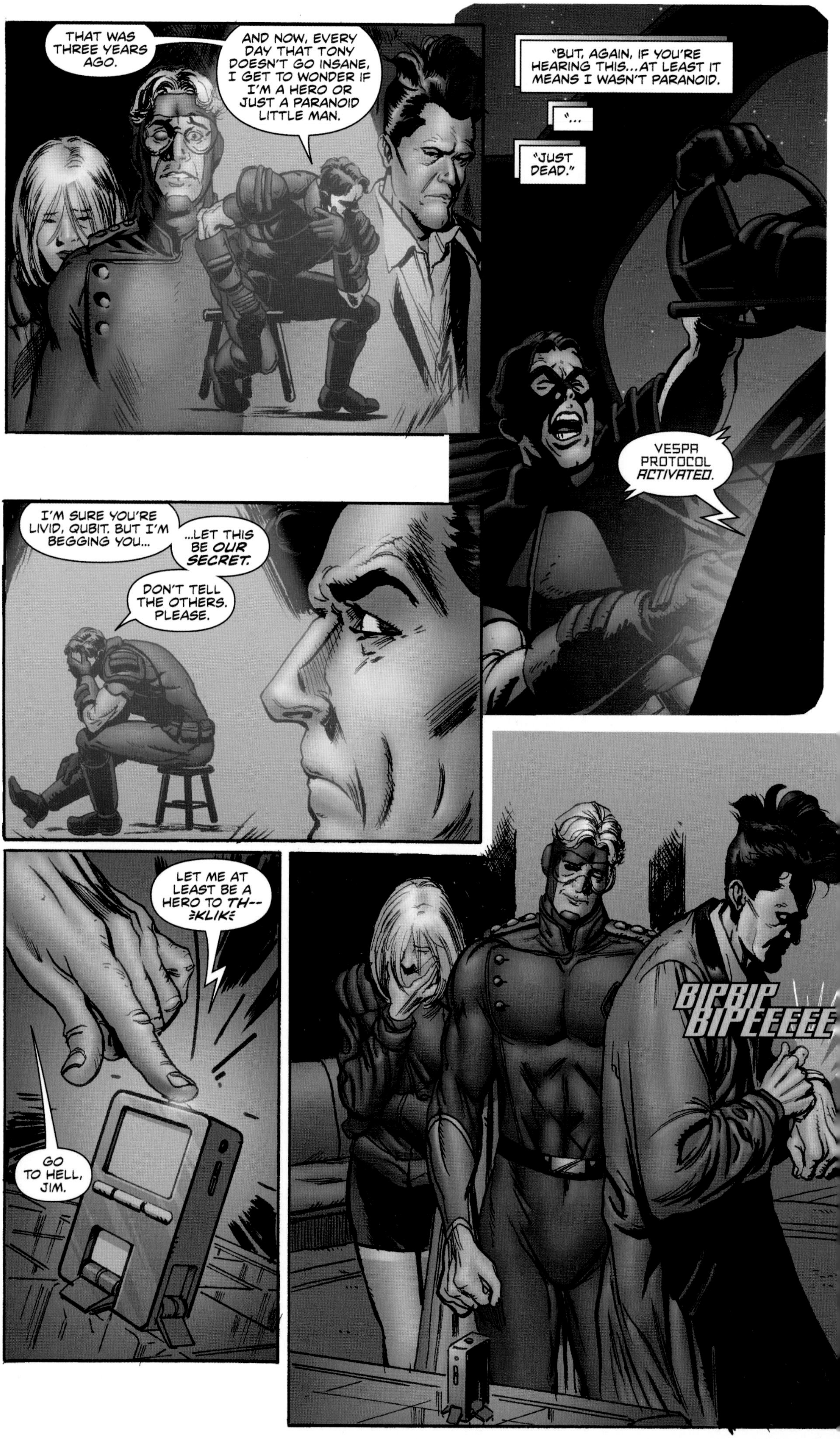
THAT WAS THREE YEARS AGO.
AND NOW, EVERY DAY THAT TONY DOESN'T GO INSANE, I GET TO WONDER IF I'M A HERO OR JUST A PARANOID LITTLE MAN.
"BUT, AGAIN, IF YOU'RE HEARING THIS...AT LEAST IT MEANS I WASN'T PARANOID.
"...
"JUST DEAD."
VESPA PROTOCOL ACTIVATED.
I'M SURE YOU'RE LIVID, QUBIT. BUT I'M BEGGING YOU...
...LET THIS BE OUR SECRET.
DON'T TELL THE OTHERS. PLEASE.
LET ME AT LEAST BE A HERO TO TH--
KLIK
GO TO HELL, JIM.
BIPBIP BIPEEEEE

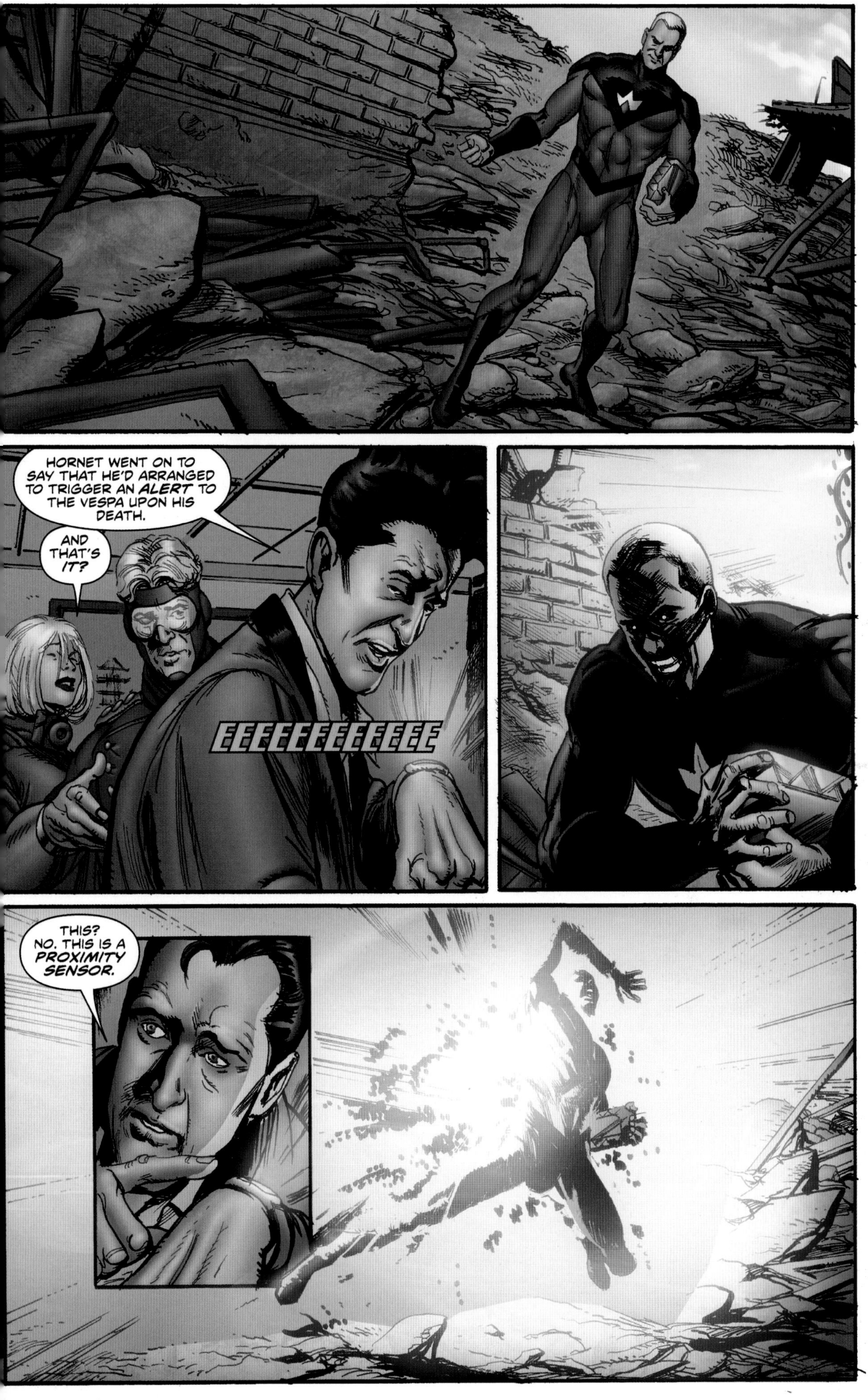

HORNET WENT ON TO SAY THAT HE'D ARRANGED TO TRIGGER AN *ALERT* TO THE VESPA UPON HIS DEATH.
AND THAT'S *IT*?
EEEEEEEEEEEEE
THIS? NO. THIS IS A *PROXIMITY SENSOR.*

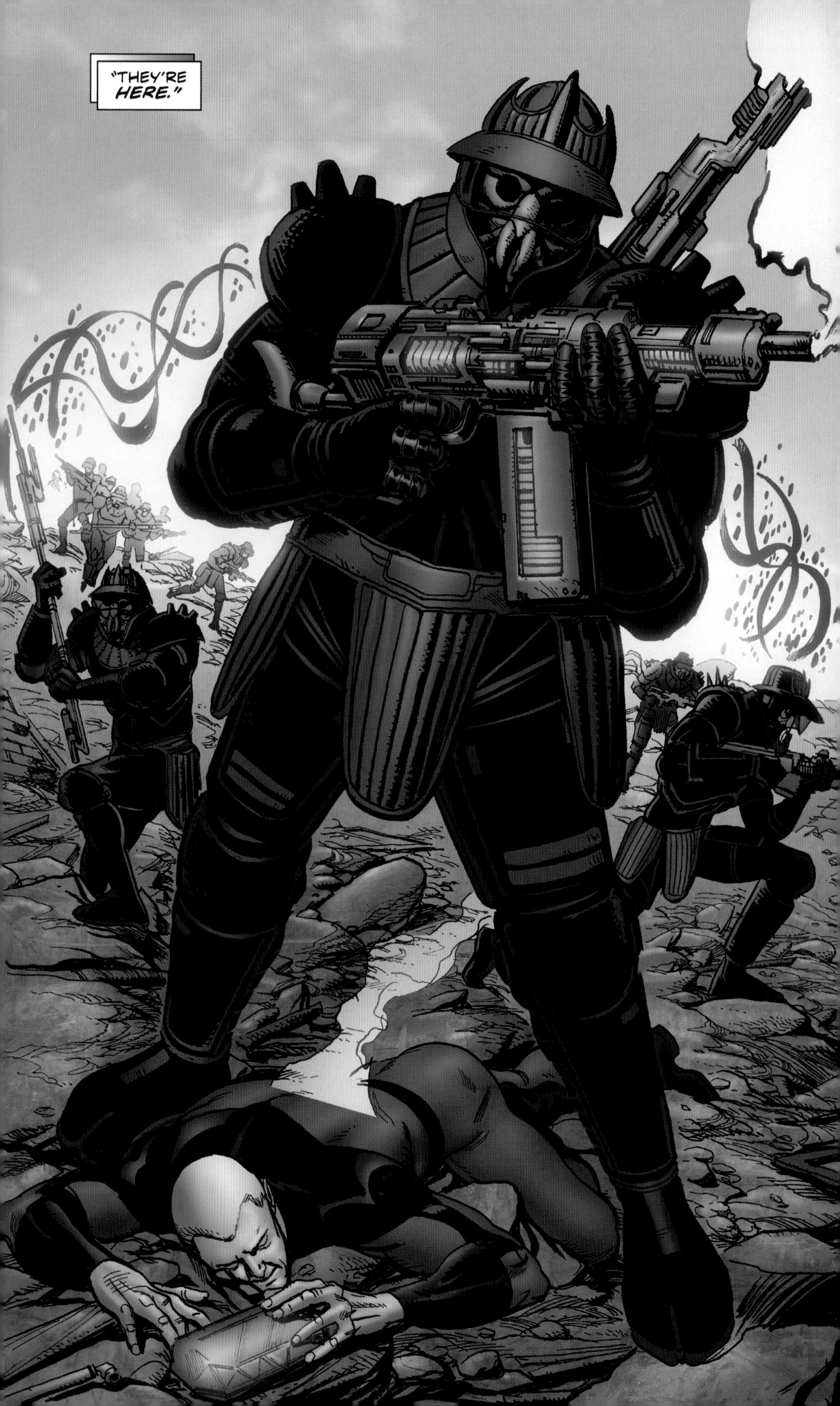
"THEY'RE HERE."

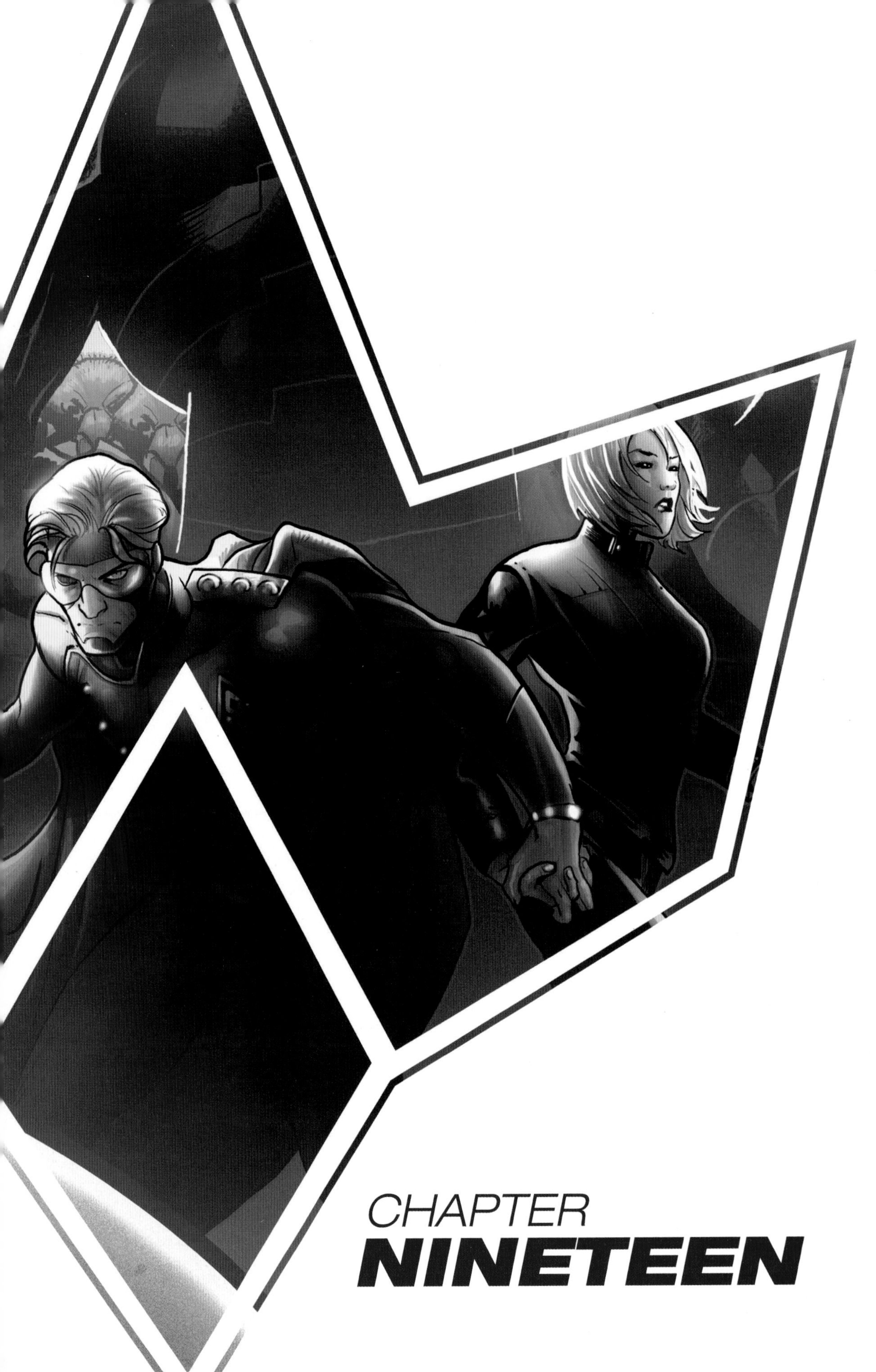

CHAPTER
NINETEEN

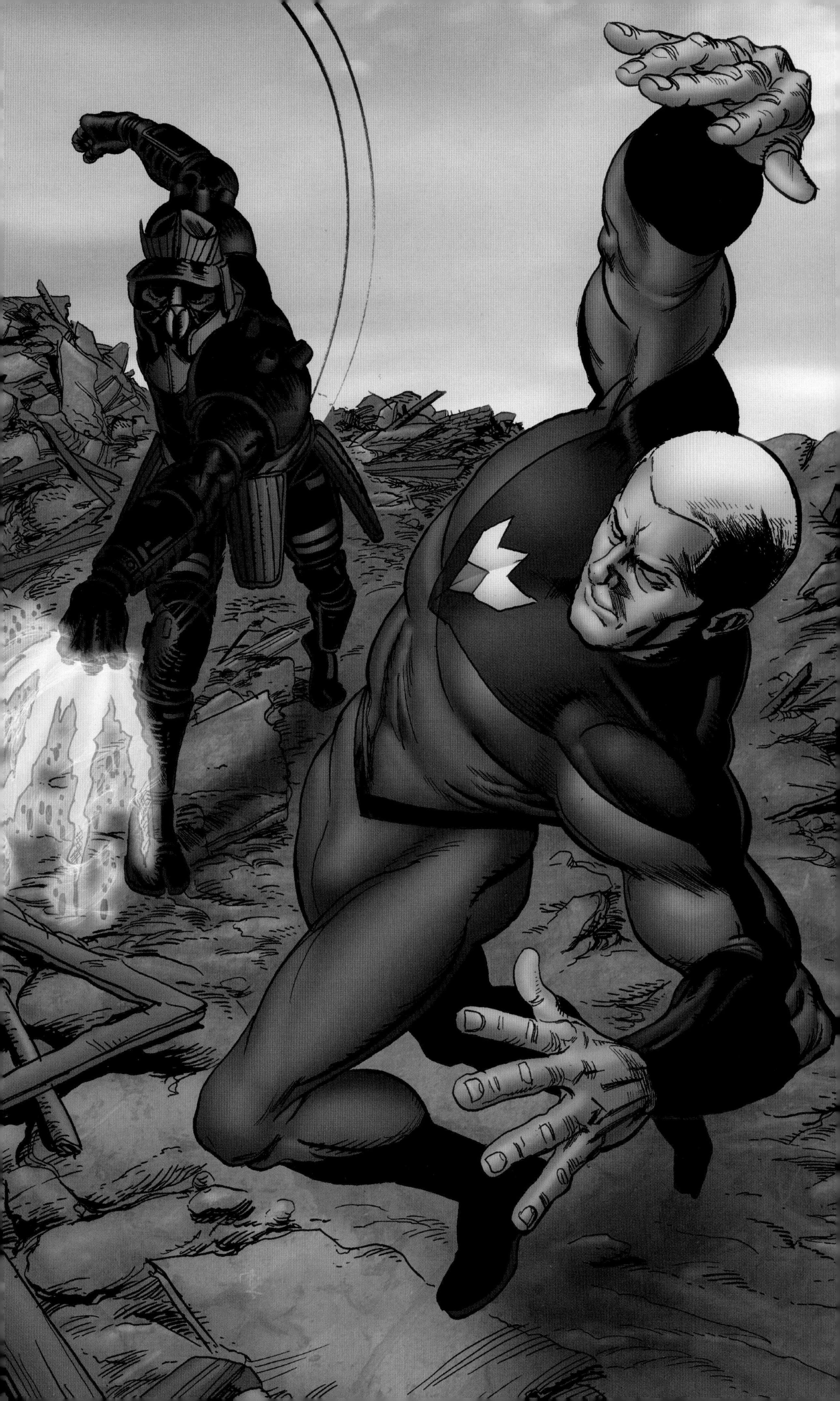

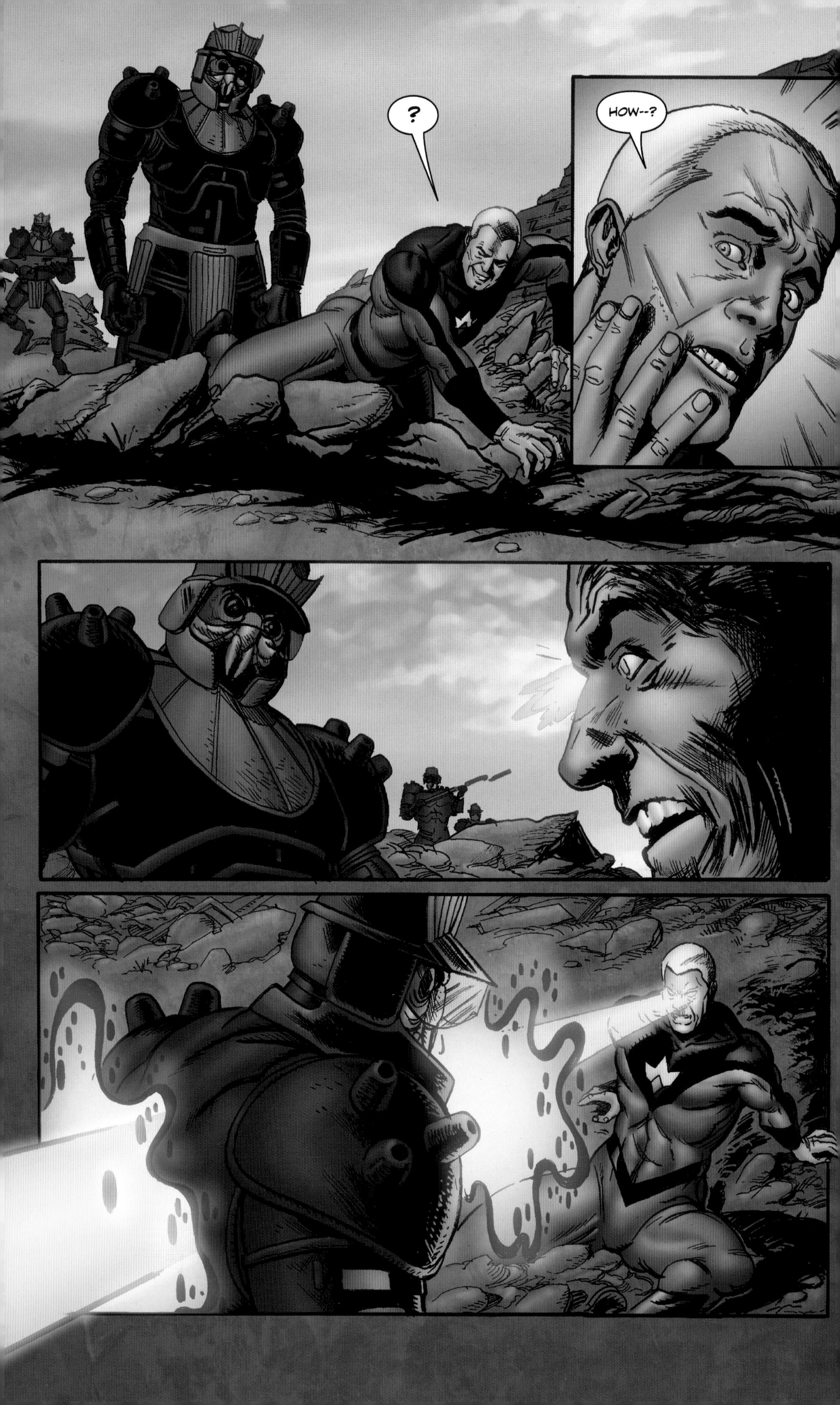
?
HOW--?

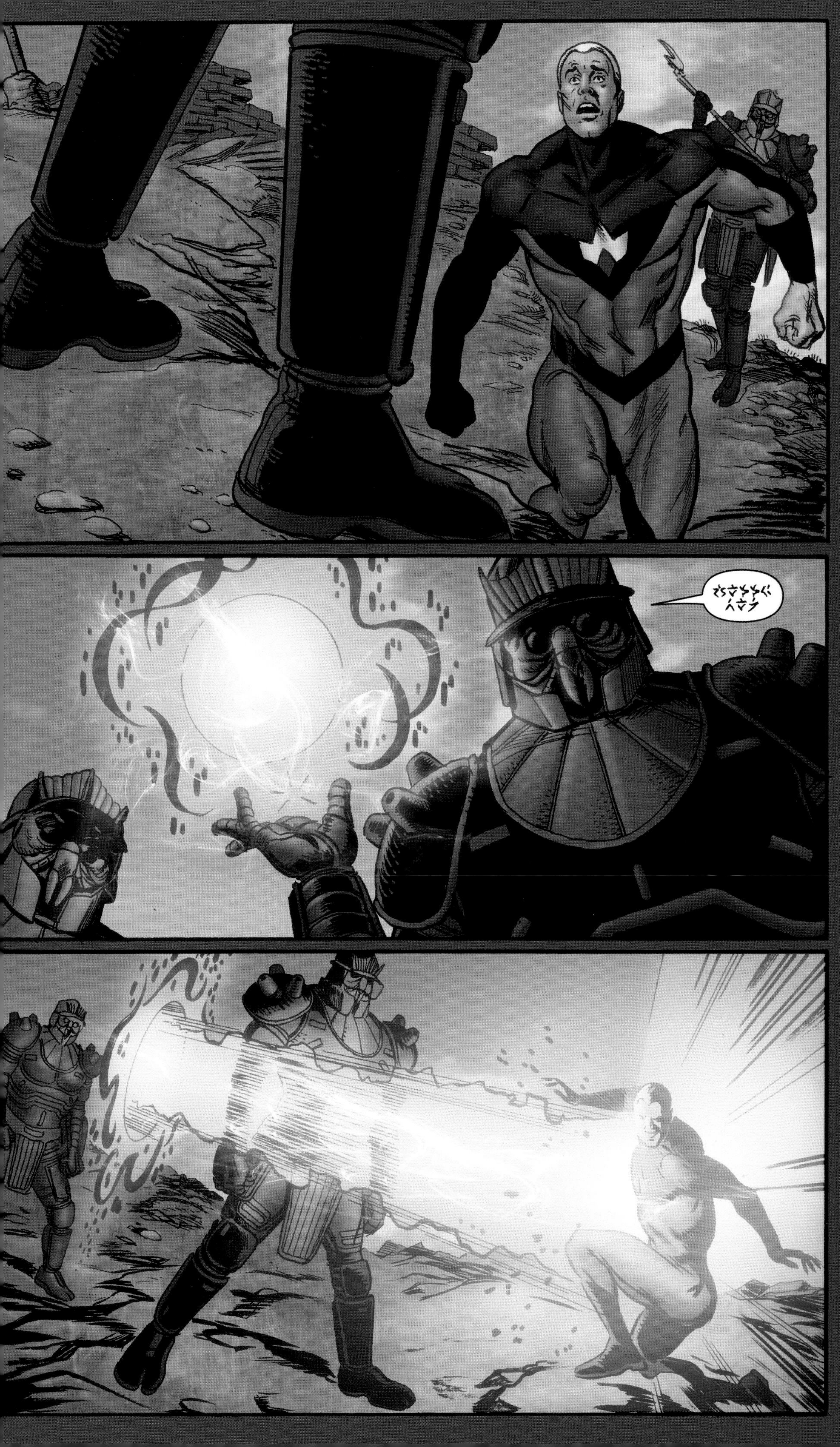

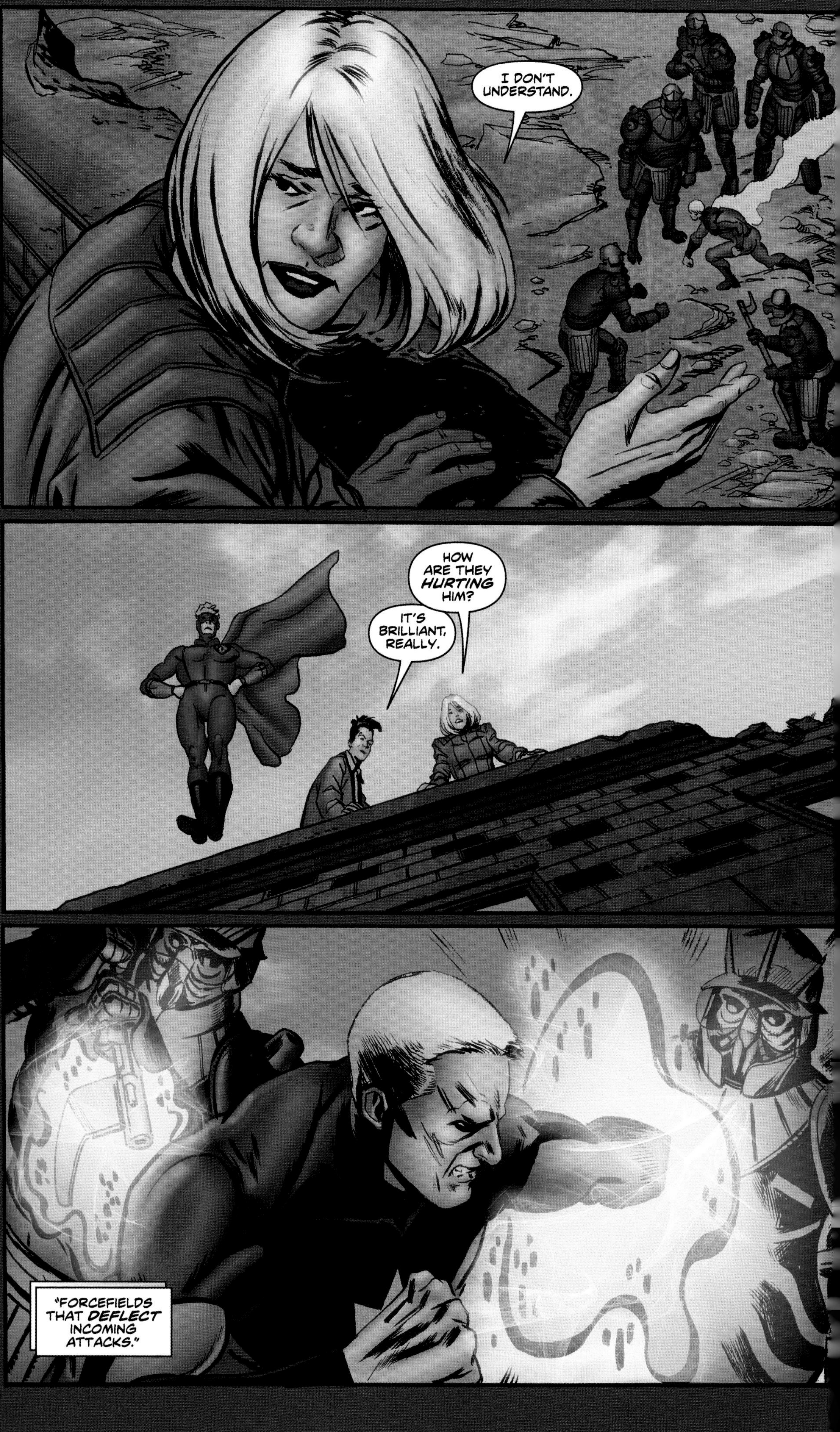
I DON'T UNDERSTAND.
HOW ARE THEY *HURTING* HIM?
IT'S BRILLIANT, REALLY.
"FORCEFIELDS THAT *DEFLECT* INCOMING ATTACKS."

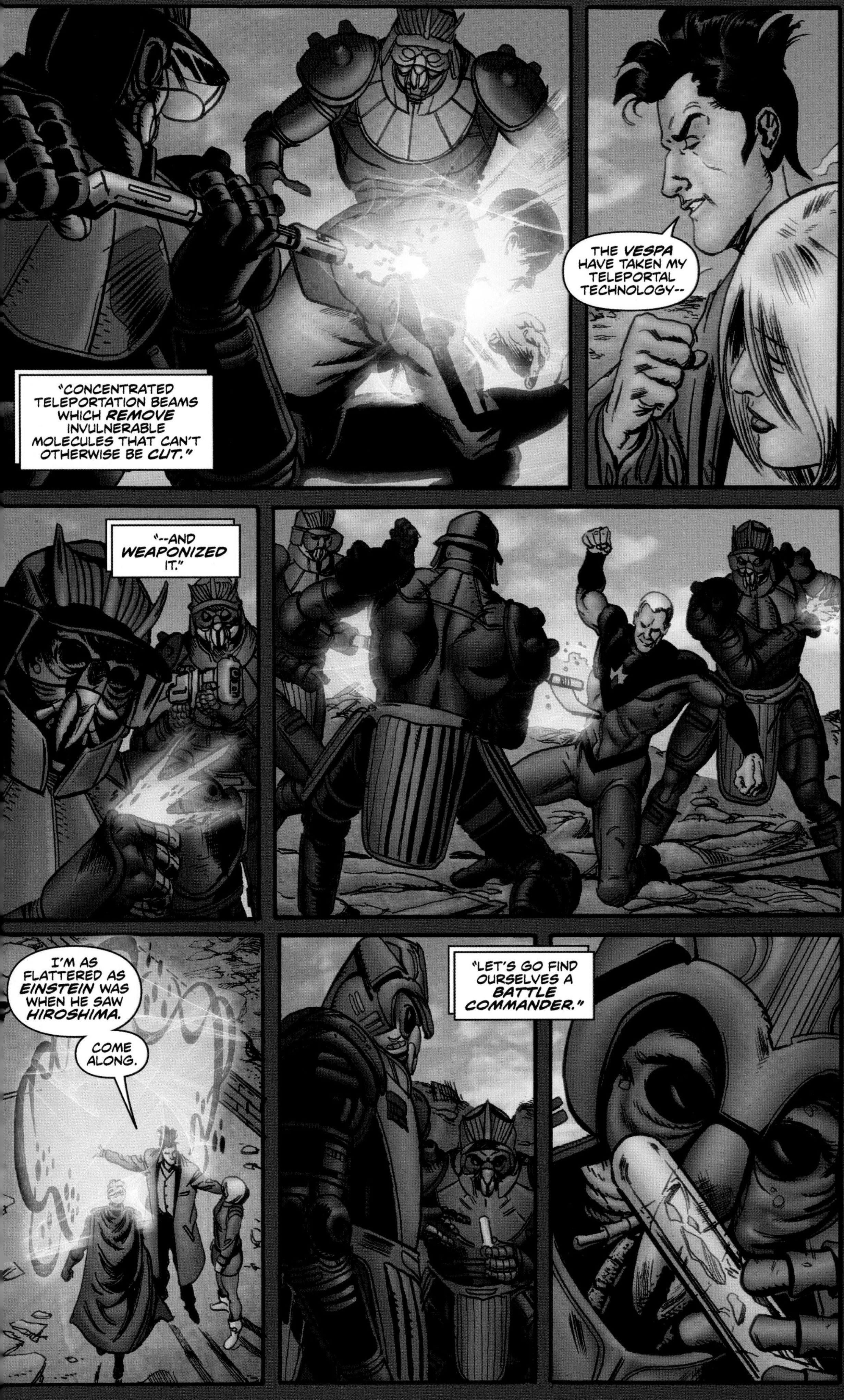
"CONCENTRATED TELEPORTATION BEAMS WHICH REMOVE INVULNERABLE MOLECULES THAT CAN'T OTHERWISE BE CUT."
THE VESPA HAVE TAKEN MY TELEPORTAL TECHNOLOGY--
"--AND WEAPONIZED IT."
I'M AS FLATTERED AS EINSTEIN WAS WHEN HE SAW HIROSHIMA.
COME ALONG.
"LET'S GO FIND OURSELVES A BATTLE COMMANDER."

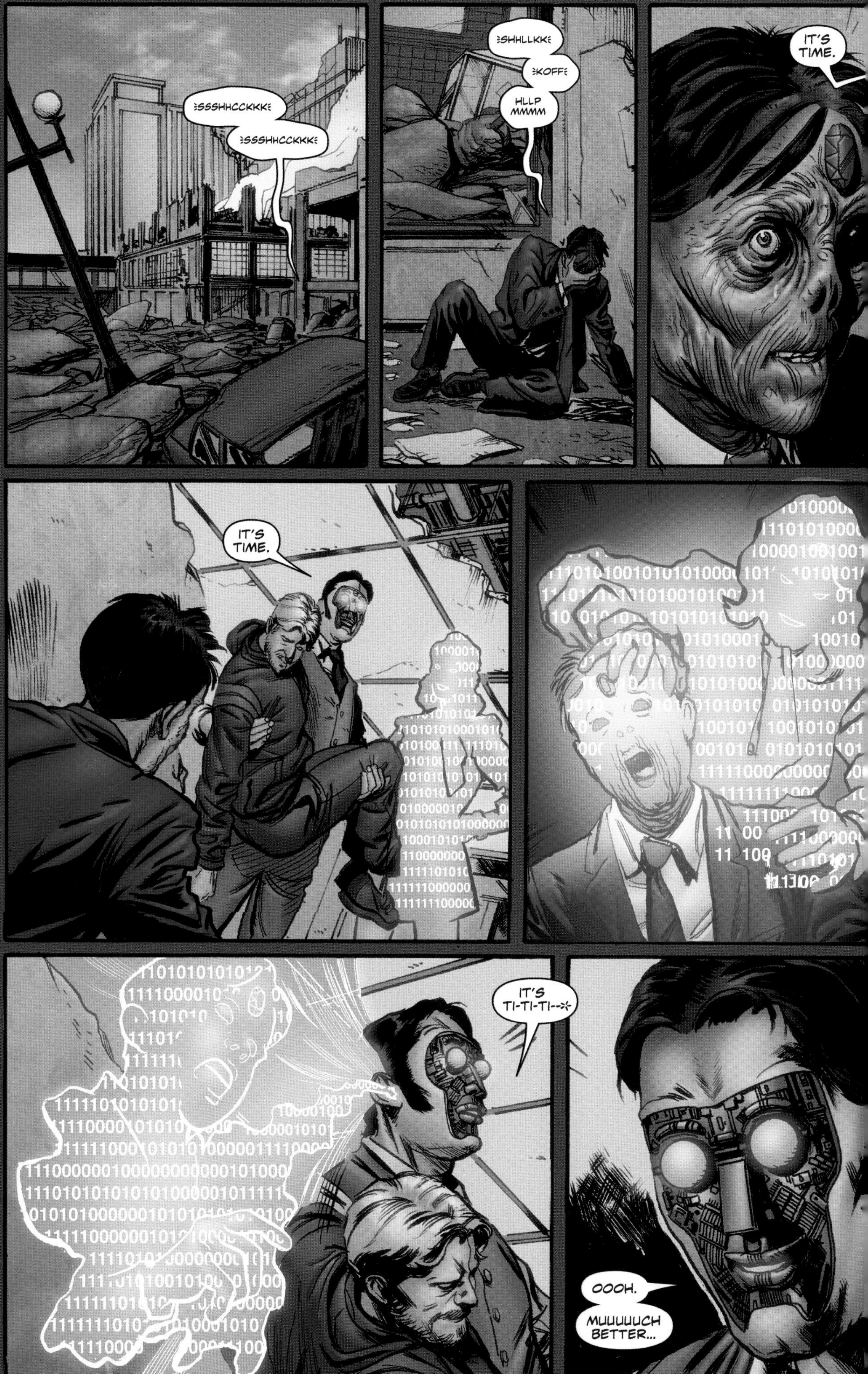
SSSHHCCKKK
SSSHHCCKKK
SHHLLKK
KOFF
HLLP MMMM
IT'S TIME.
IT'S TIME.
IT'S TI-TI-TI--
OOOH.
MUUUUUCH BETTER...

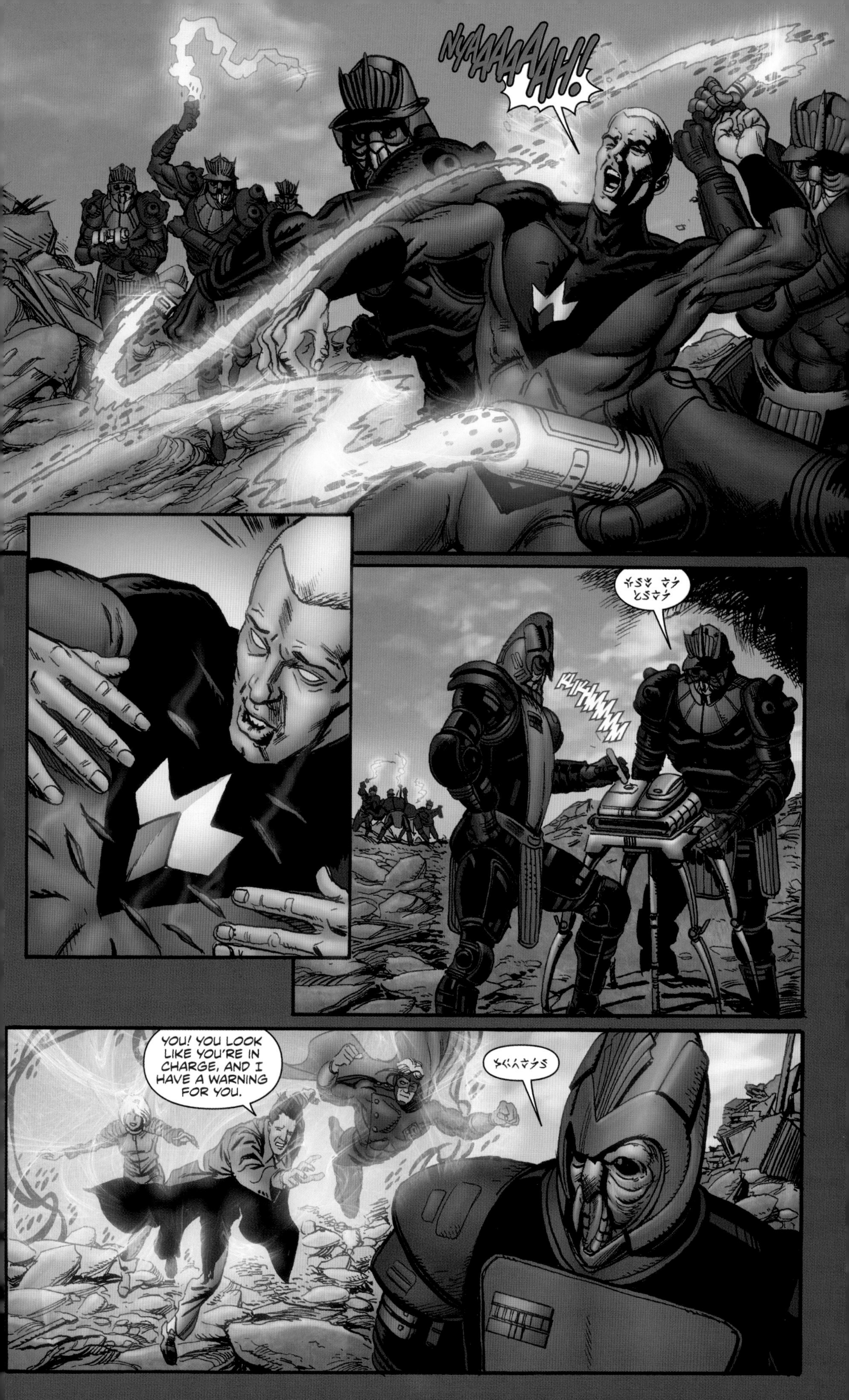
NYAAAAAAH!
KLIKHMMMM
YOU! YOU LOOK LIKE YOU'RE IN CHARGE, AND I HAVE A WARNING FOR YOU.

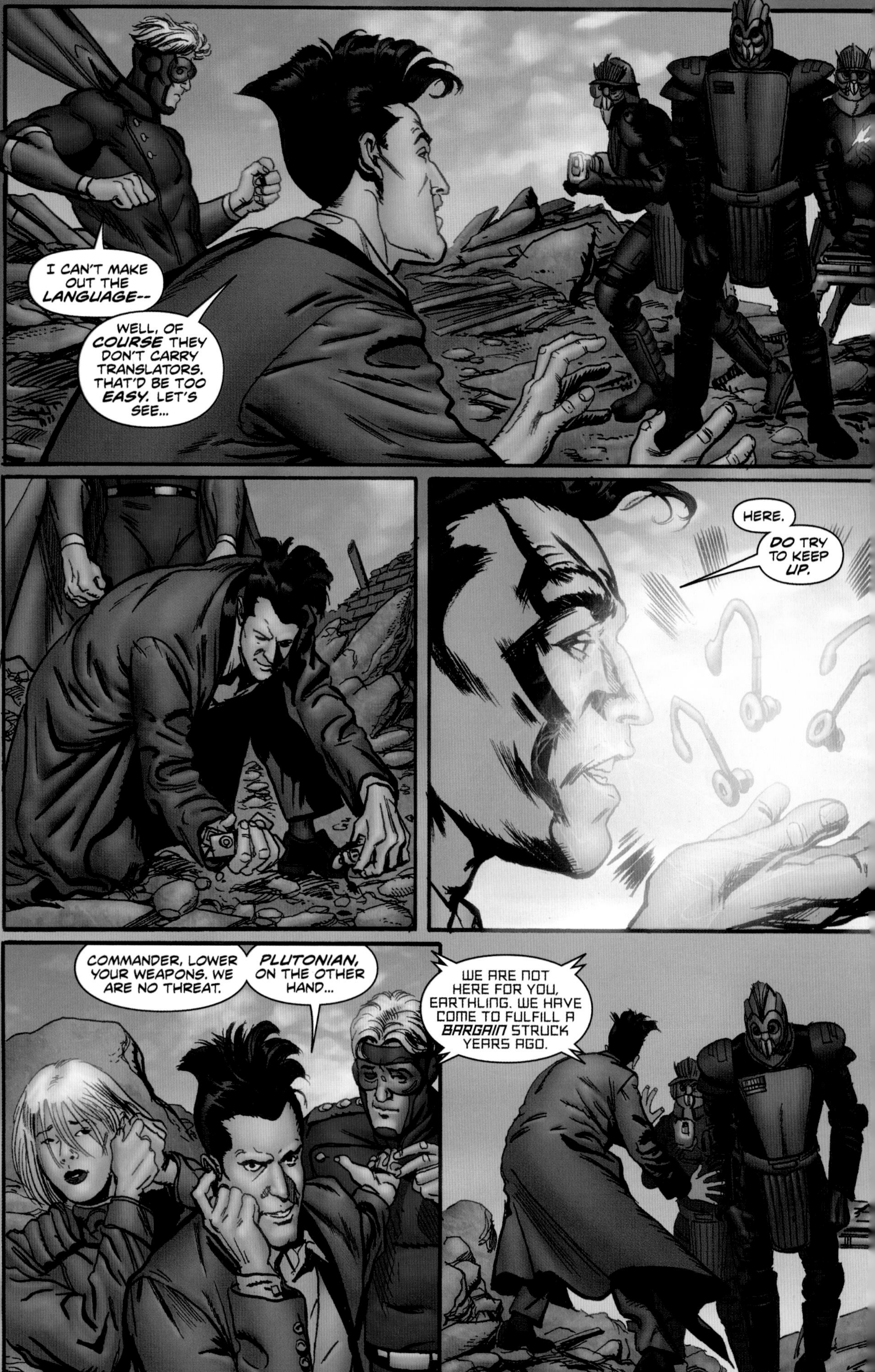
I CAN'T MAKE OUT THE LANGUAGE--
WELL, OF COURSE THEY DON'T CARRY TRANSLATORS. THAT'D BE TOO EASY. LET'S SEE...
HERE.
DO TRY TO KEEP UP.
COMMANDER, LOWER YOUR WEAPONS. WE ARE NO THREAT.
PLUTONIAN, ON THE OTHER HAND...
WE ARE NOT HERE FOR YOU, EARTHLING. WE HAVE COME TO FULFILL A BARGAIN STRUCK YEARS AGO.

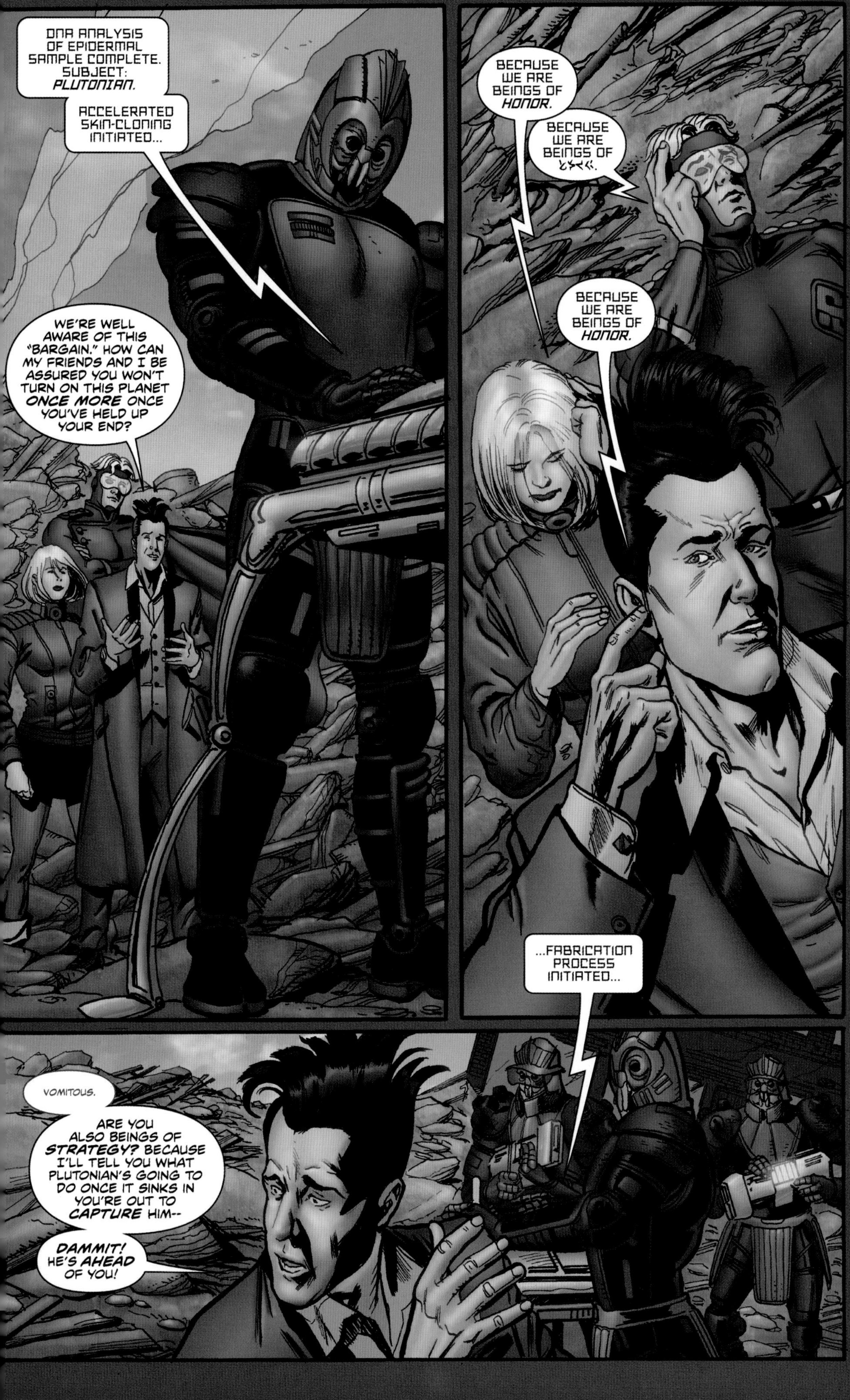
DNA ANALYSIS OF EPIDERMAL SAMPLE COMPLETE. SUBJECT: *PLUTONIAN.*
ACCELERATED SKIN-CLONING INITIATED...
WE'RE WELL AWARE OF THIS "BARGAIN." HOW CAN MY FRIENDS AND I BE ASSURED YOU WON'T TURN ON THIS PLANET ***ONCE MORE*** ONCE YOU'VE HELD UP YOUR END?
BECAUSE WE ARE BEINGS OF ***HONOR.***
BECAUSE WE ARE BEINGS OF
BECAUSE WE ARE BEINGS OF ***HONOR.***
...FABRICATION PROCESS INITIATED...
VOMITOUS.
ARE YOU ALSO BEINGS OF ***STRATEGY?*** BECAUSE I'LL TELL YOU WHAT PLUTONIAN'S GOING TO DO ONCE IT SINKS IN YOU'RE OUT TO ***CAPTURE*** HIM--
DAMMIT! HE'S ***AHEAD*** OF YOU!

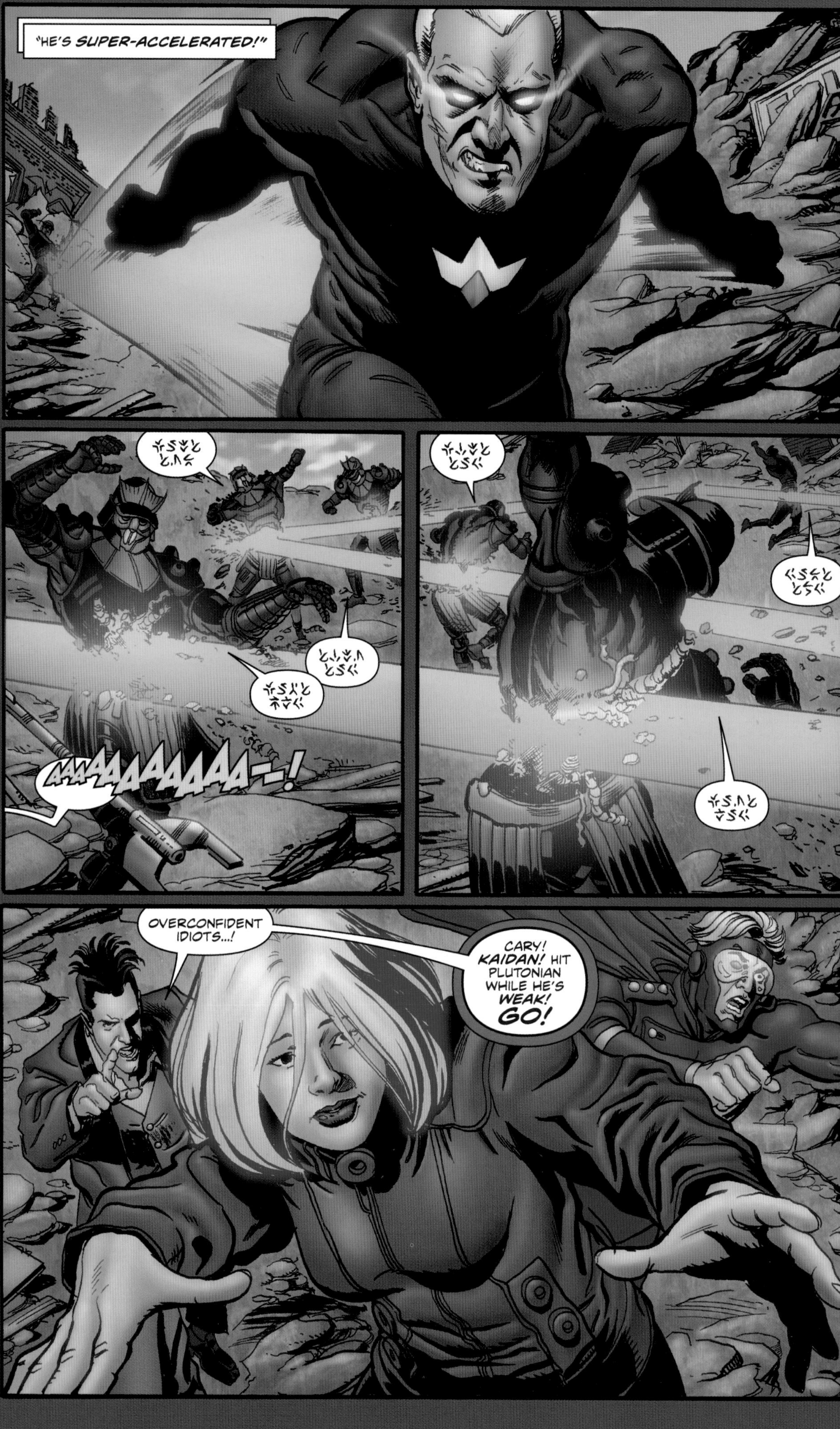
"HE'S SUPER-ACCELERATED!"
AAAAAAAAAAA--!
OVERCONFIDENT IDIOTS...!
CARY! KAIDAN! HIT PLUTONIAN WHILE HE'S WEAK! GO!

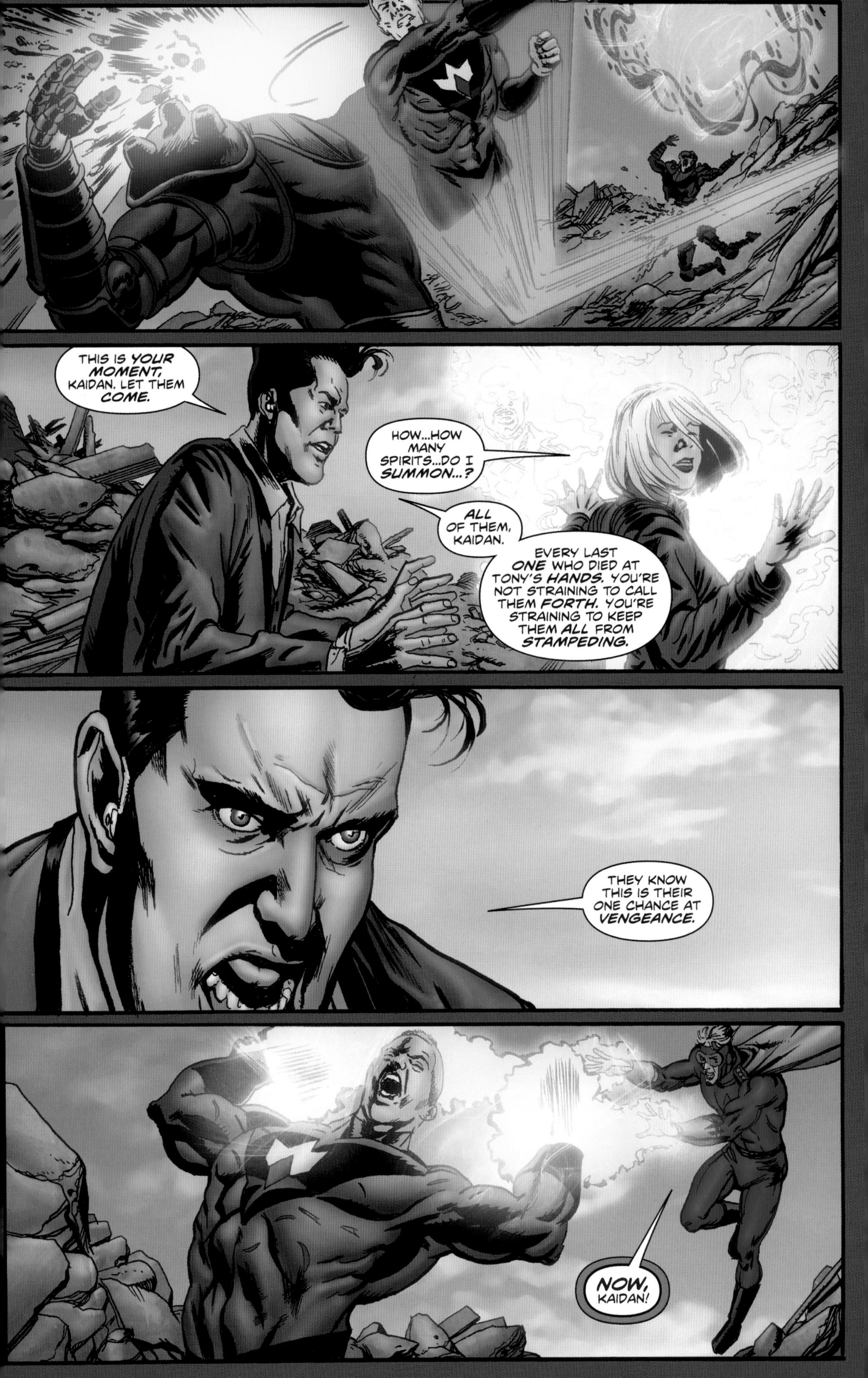
THIS IS YOUR MOMENT, KAIDAN. LET THEM COME.
HOW...HOW MANY SPIRITS...DO I SUMMON...?
ALL OF THEM, KAIDAN.
EVERY LAST ONE WHO DIED AT TONY'S HANDS. YOU'RE NOT STRAINING TO CALL THEM FORTH. YOU'RE STRAINING TO KEEP THEM ALL FROM STAMPEDING.
THEY KNOW THIS IS THEIR ONE CHANCE AT VENGEANCE.
NOW, KAIDAN!

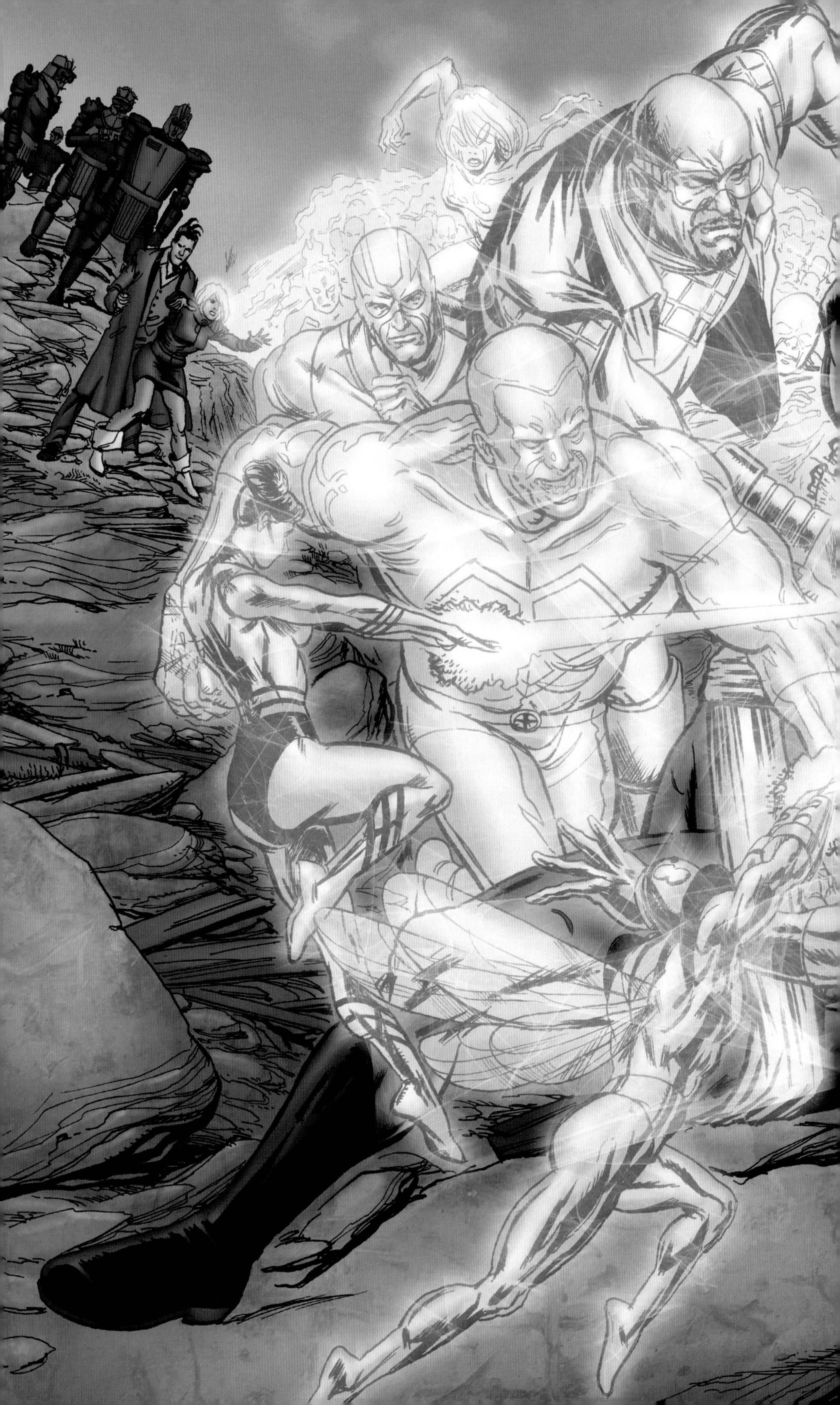

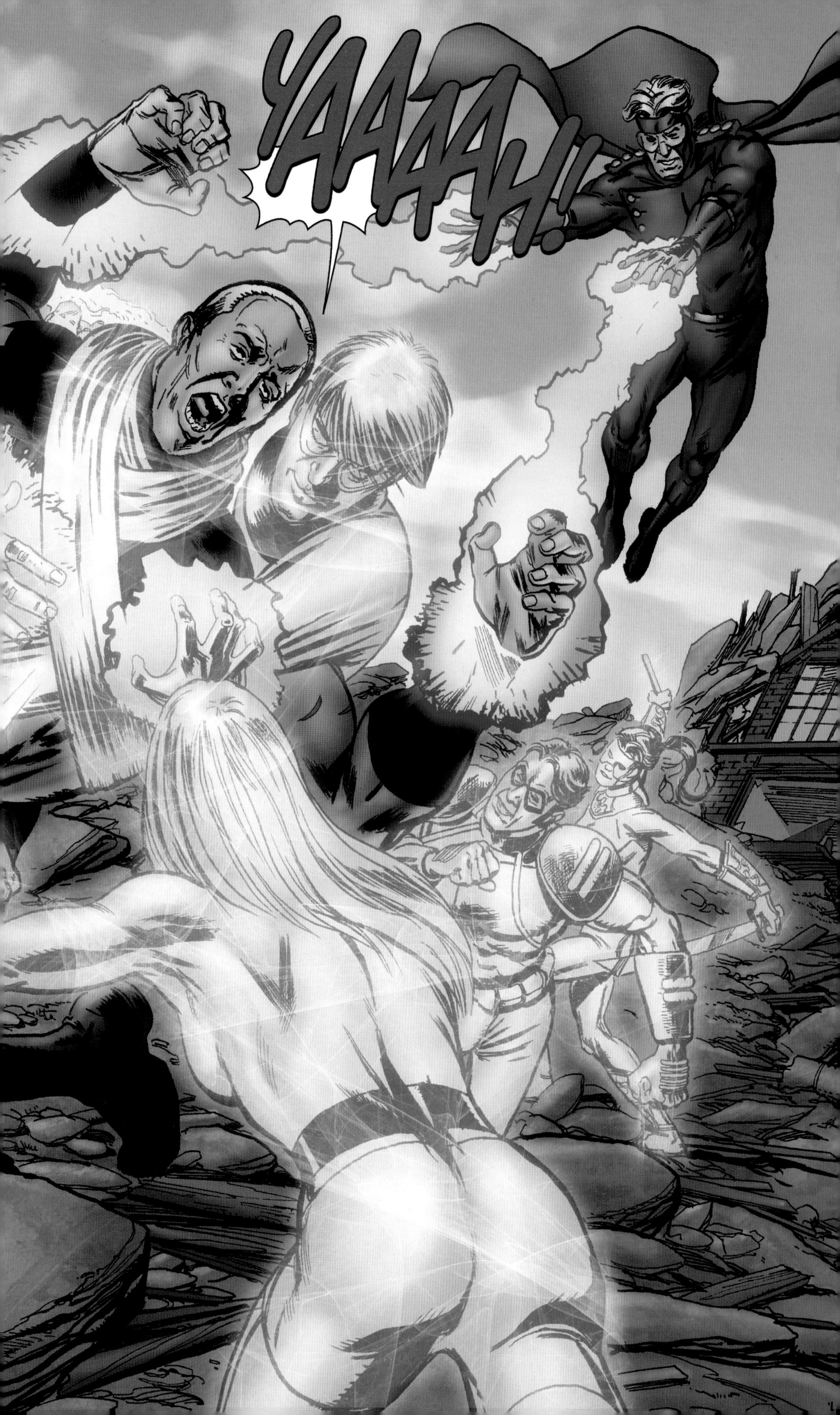
YAAAAH!!

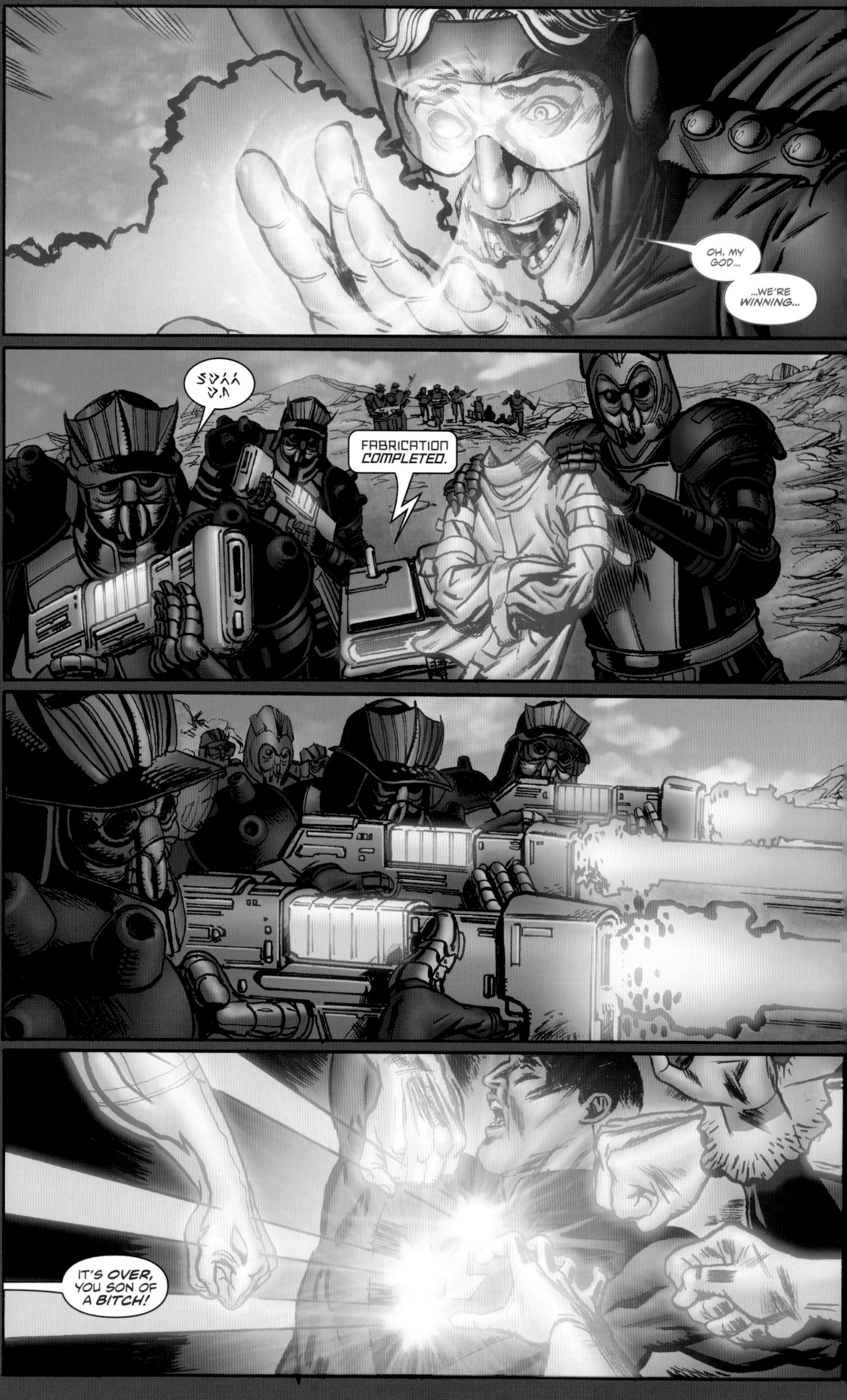
OH, MY GOD...
...WE'RE WINNING...
FABRICATION COMPLETED.
IT'S OVER, YOU SON OF A BITCH!

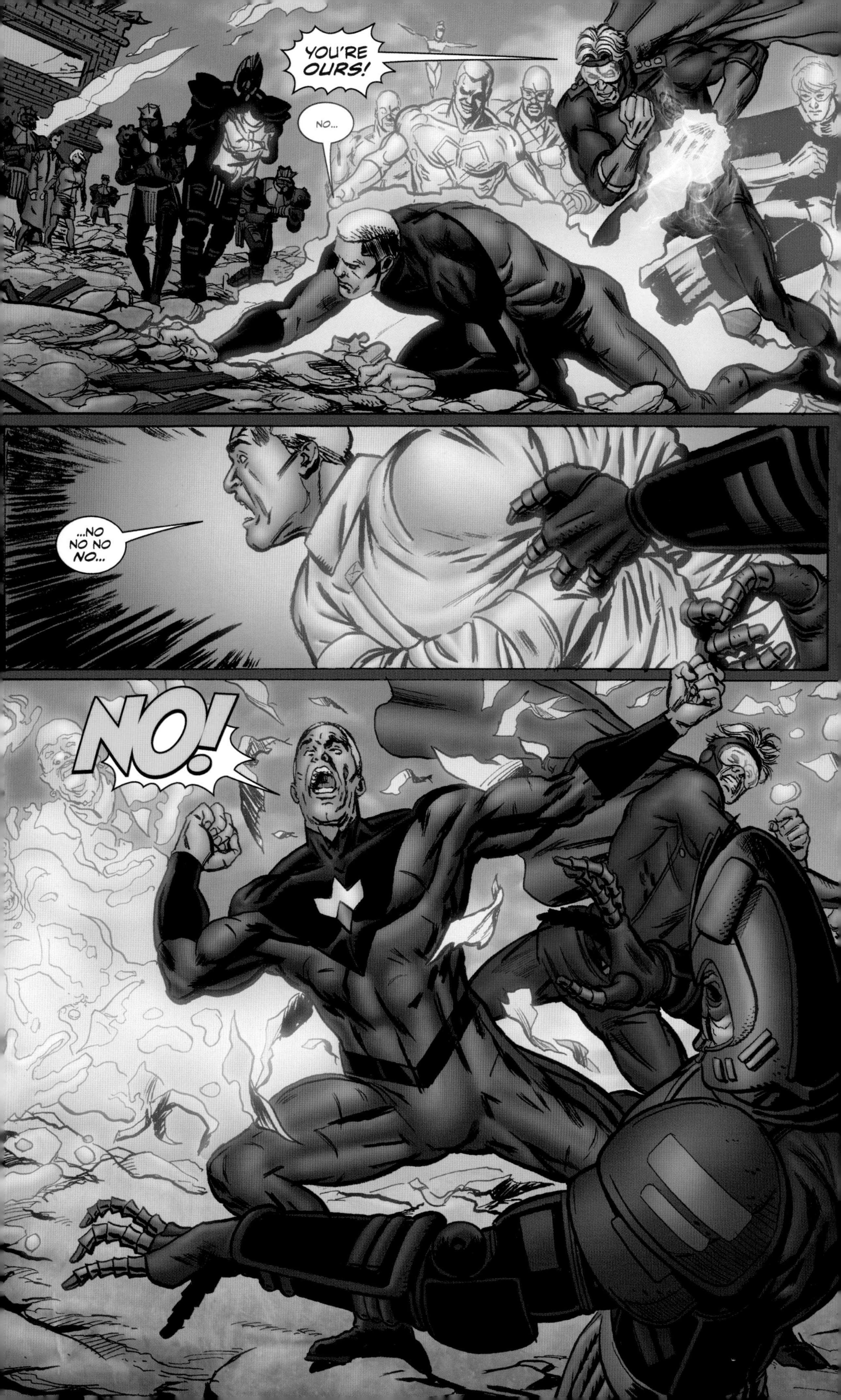
YOU'RE OURS!
NO...
...NO NO NO NO...
NO!

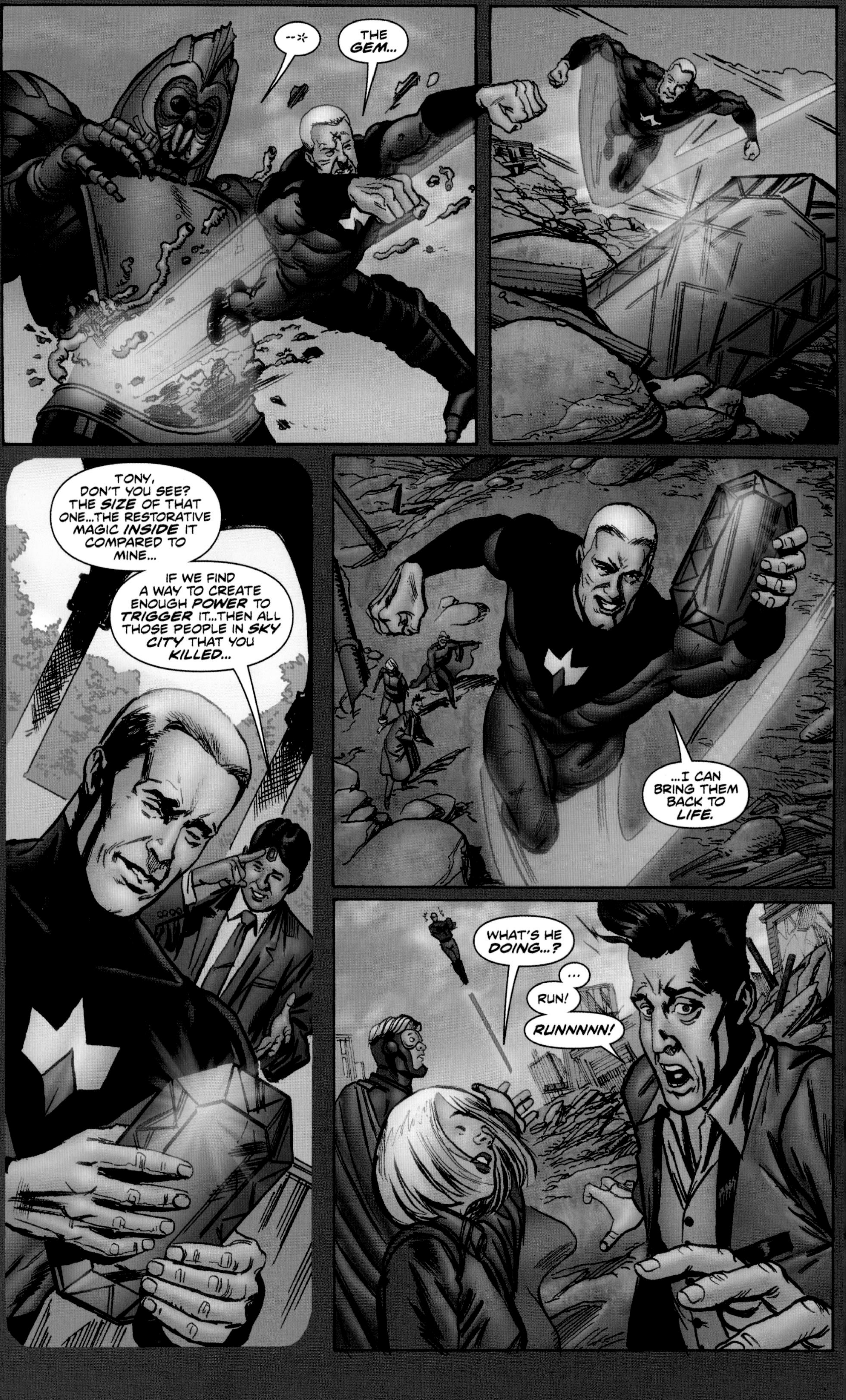
--*
THE GEM...
TONY, DON'T YOU SEE? THE SIZE OF THAT ONE...THE RESTORATIVE MAGIC INSIDE IT COMPARED TO MINE...
IF WE FIND A WAY TO CREATE ENOUGH POWER TO TRIGGER IT...THEN ALL THOSE PEOPLE IN SKY CITY THAT YOU KILLED...
...I CAN BRING THEM BACK TO LIFE.
WHAT'S HE DOING...?
...
RUN!
RUNNNNN!

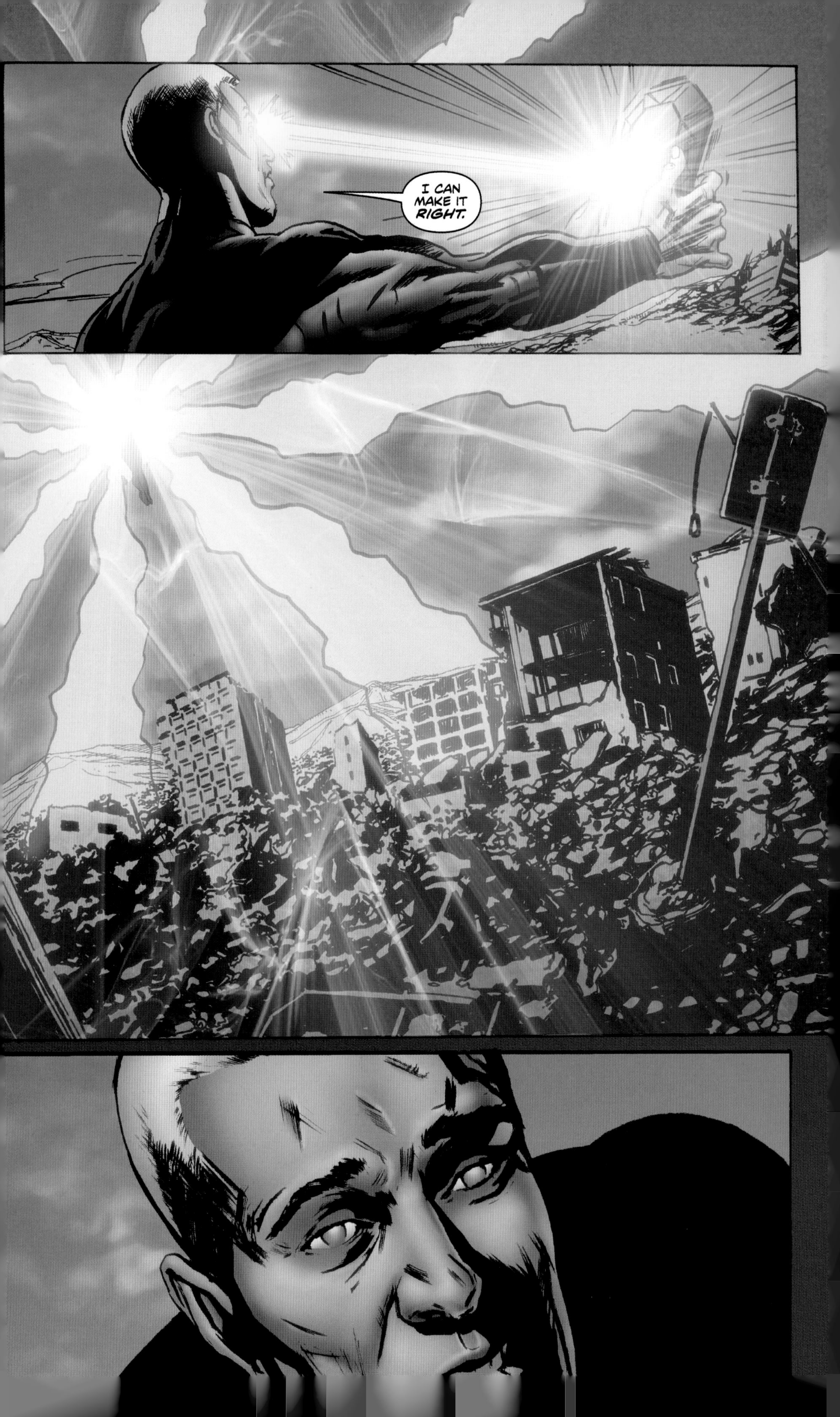
I CAN MAKE IT RIGHT.

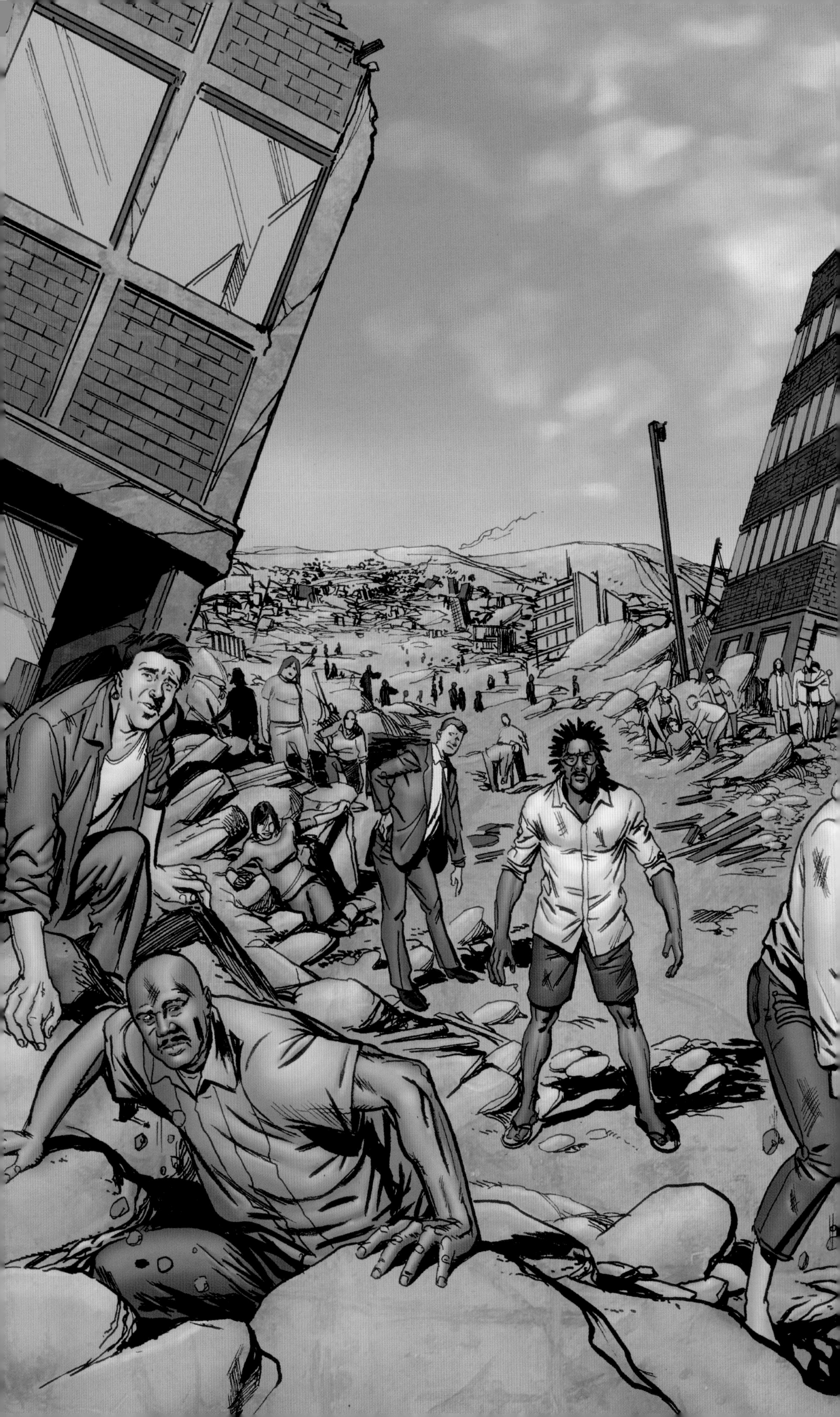

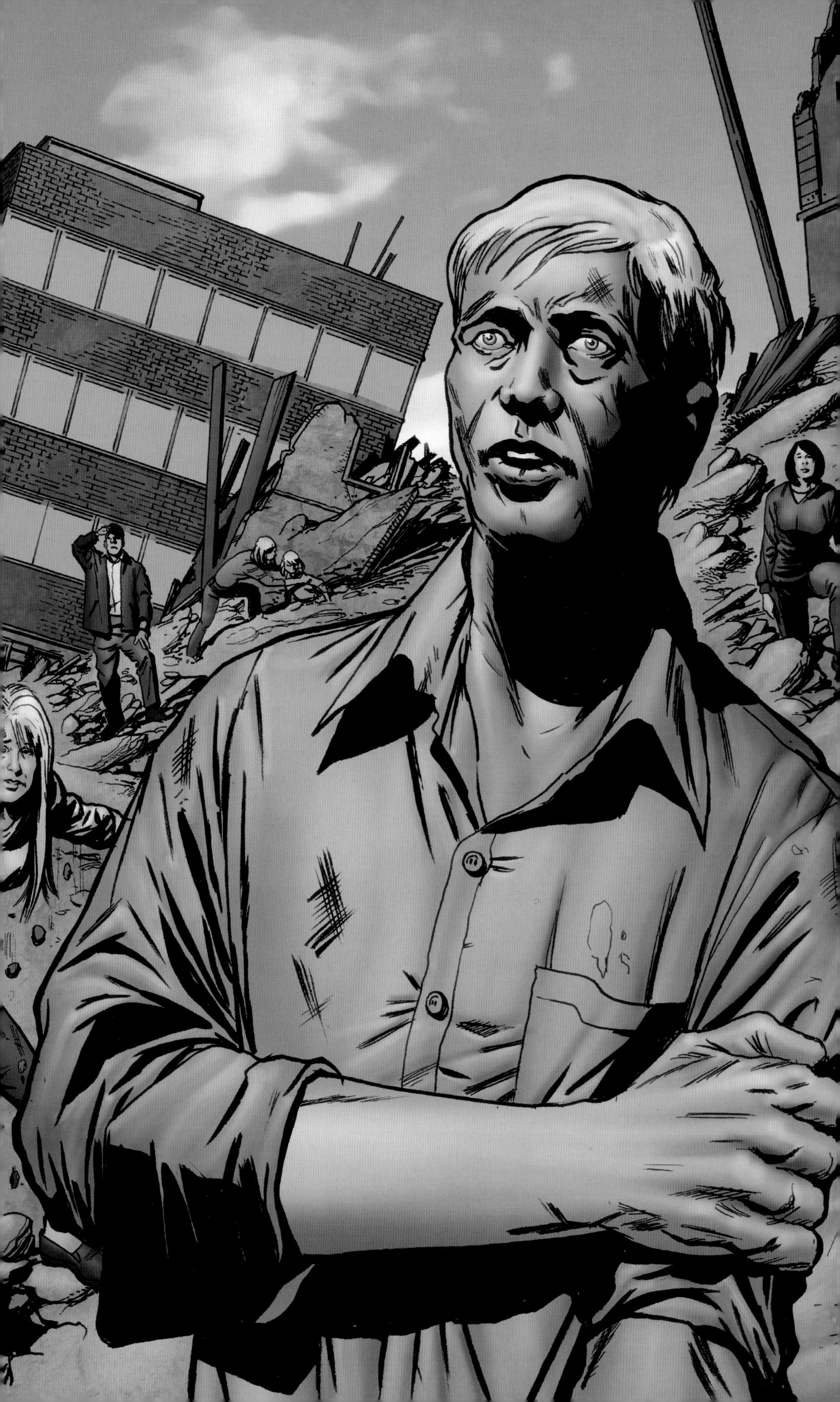

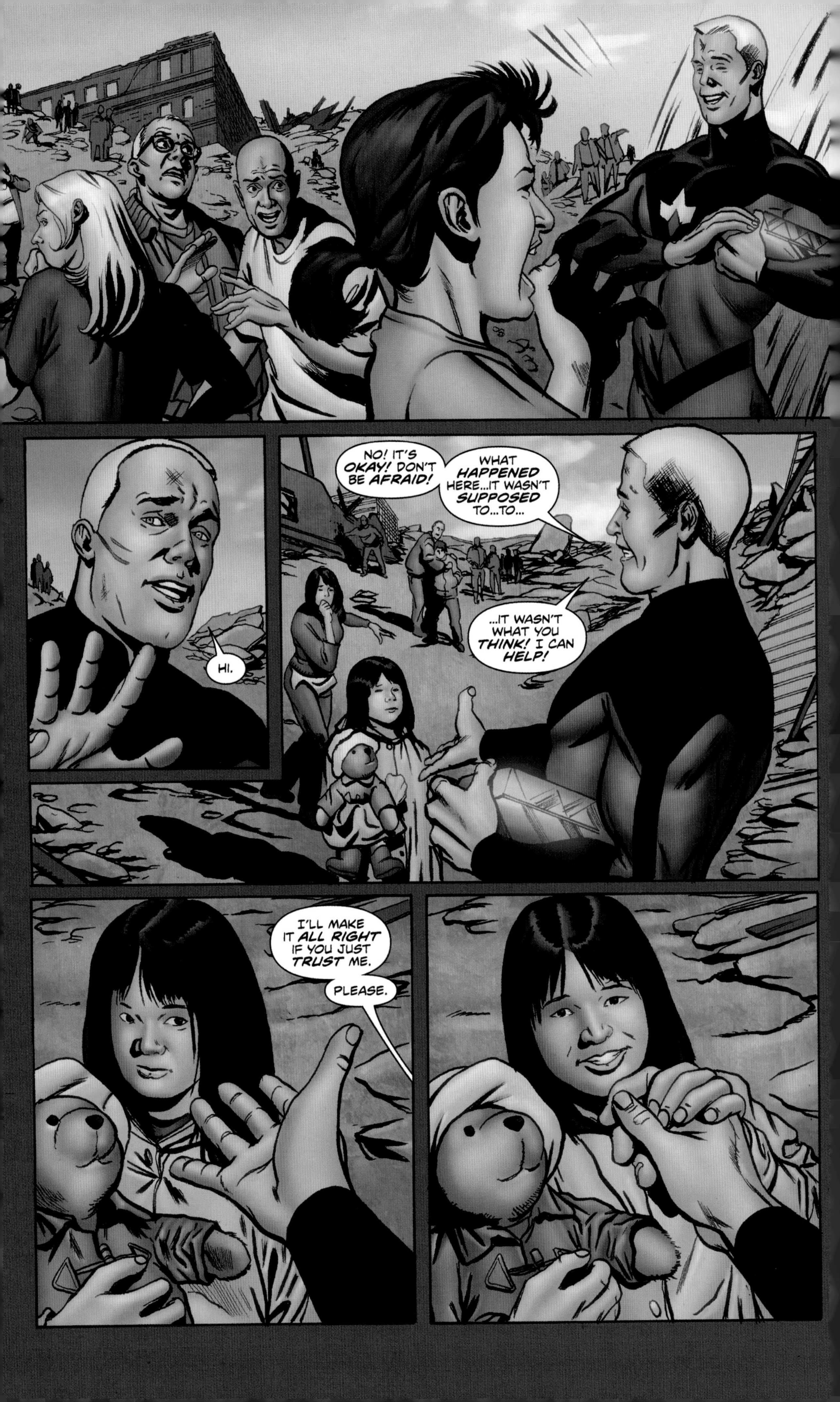
HI.
NO! IT'S OKAY! DON'T BE AFRAID!
WHAT HAPPENED HERE...IT WASN'T SUPPOSED TO...TO...
...IT WASN'T WHAT YOU THINK! I CAN HELP!
I'LL MAKE IT ALL RIGHT IF YOU JUST TRUST ME.
PLEASE.

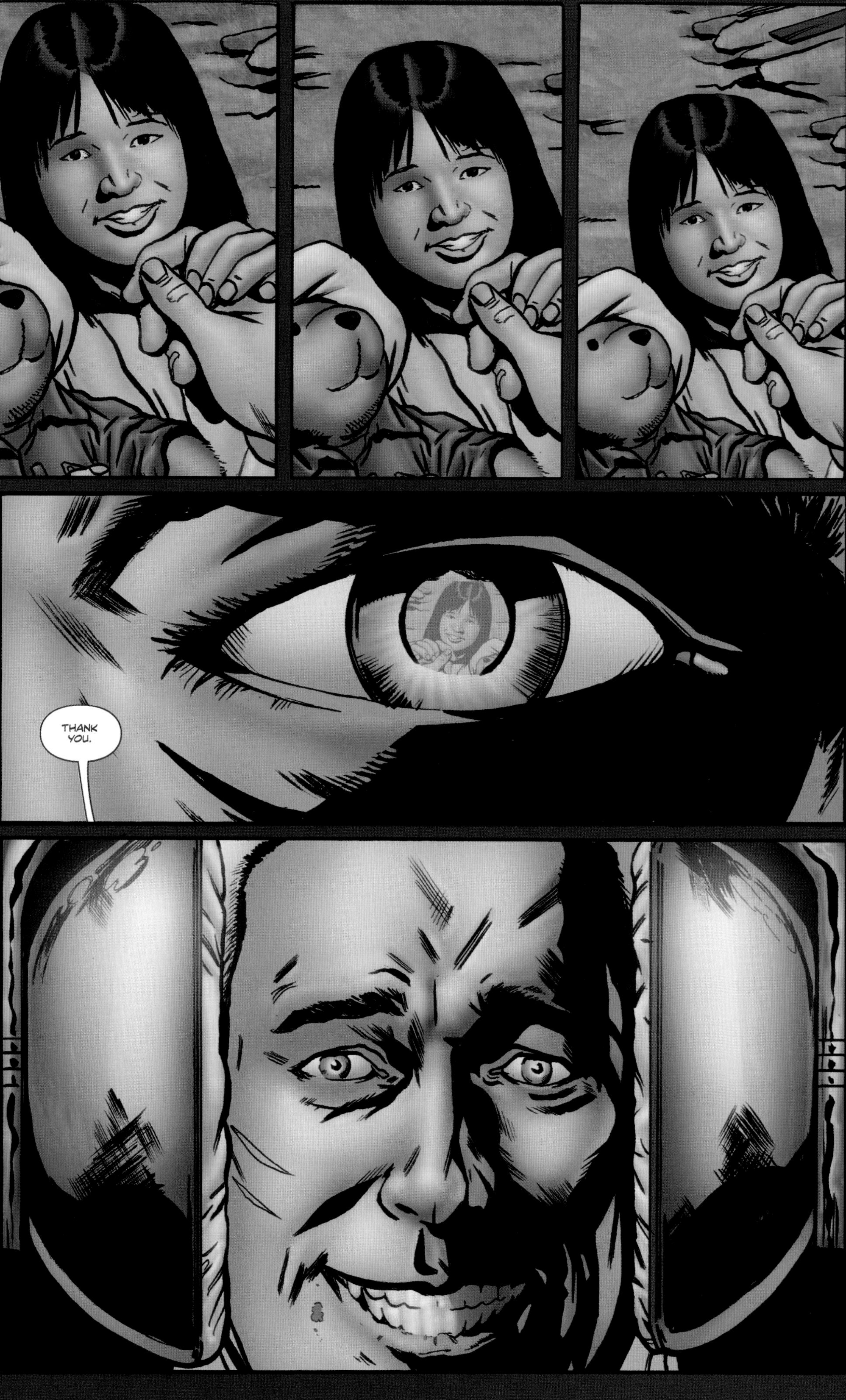
THANK YOU.

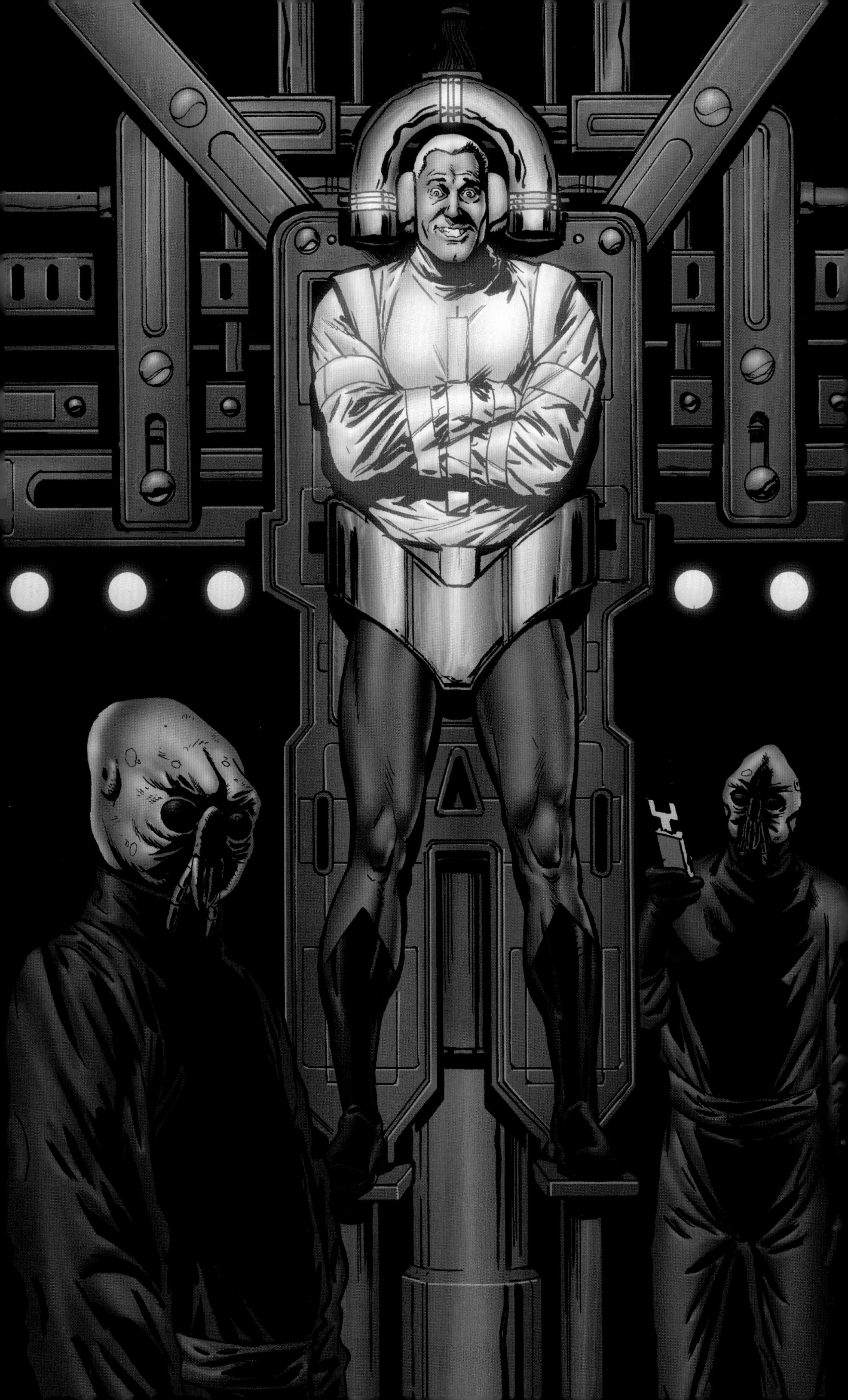

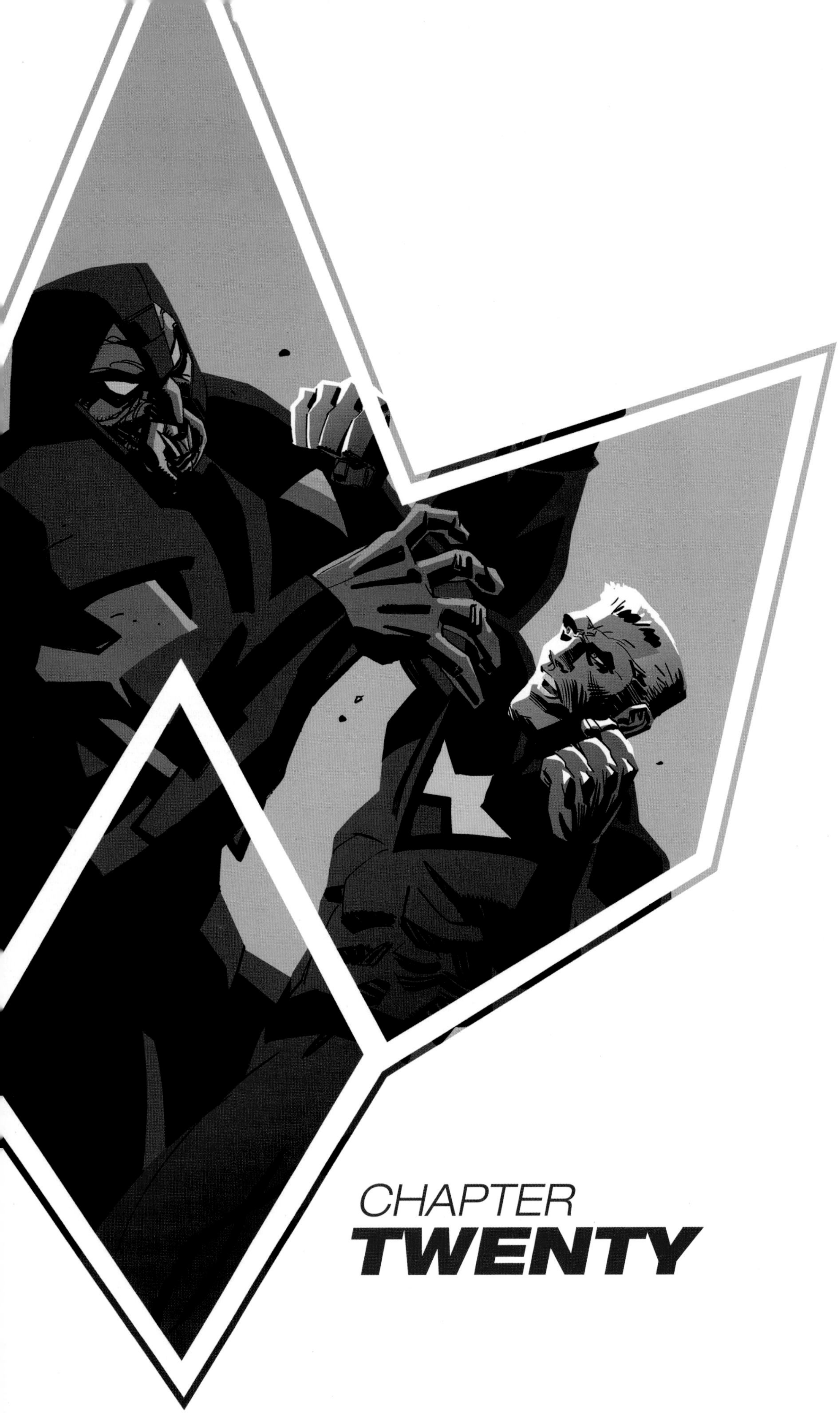

CHAPTER **TWENTY**

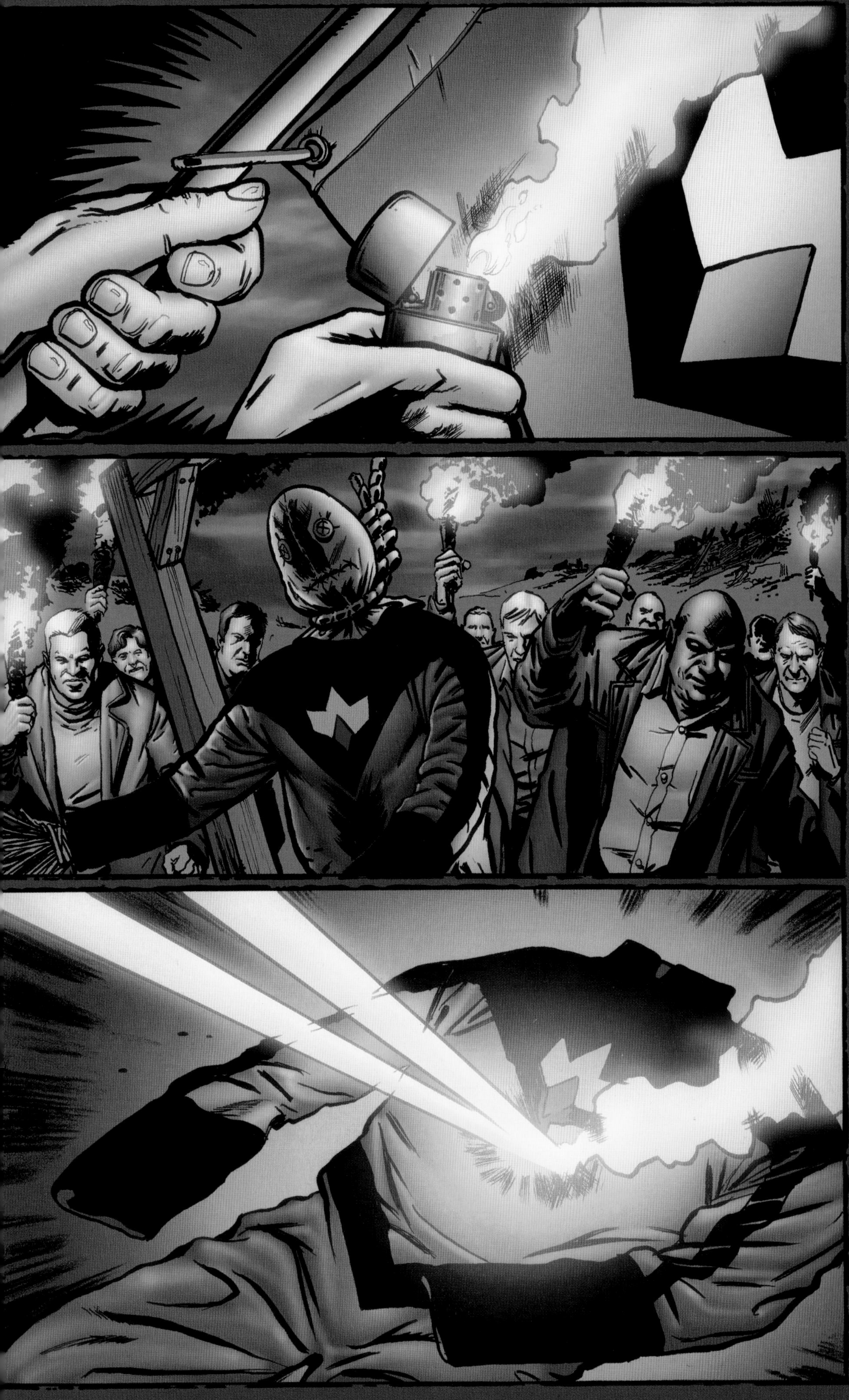

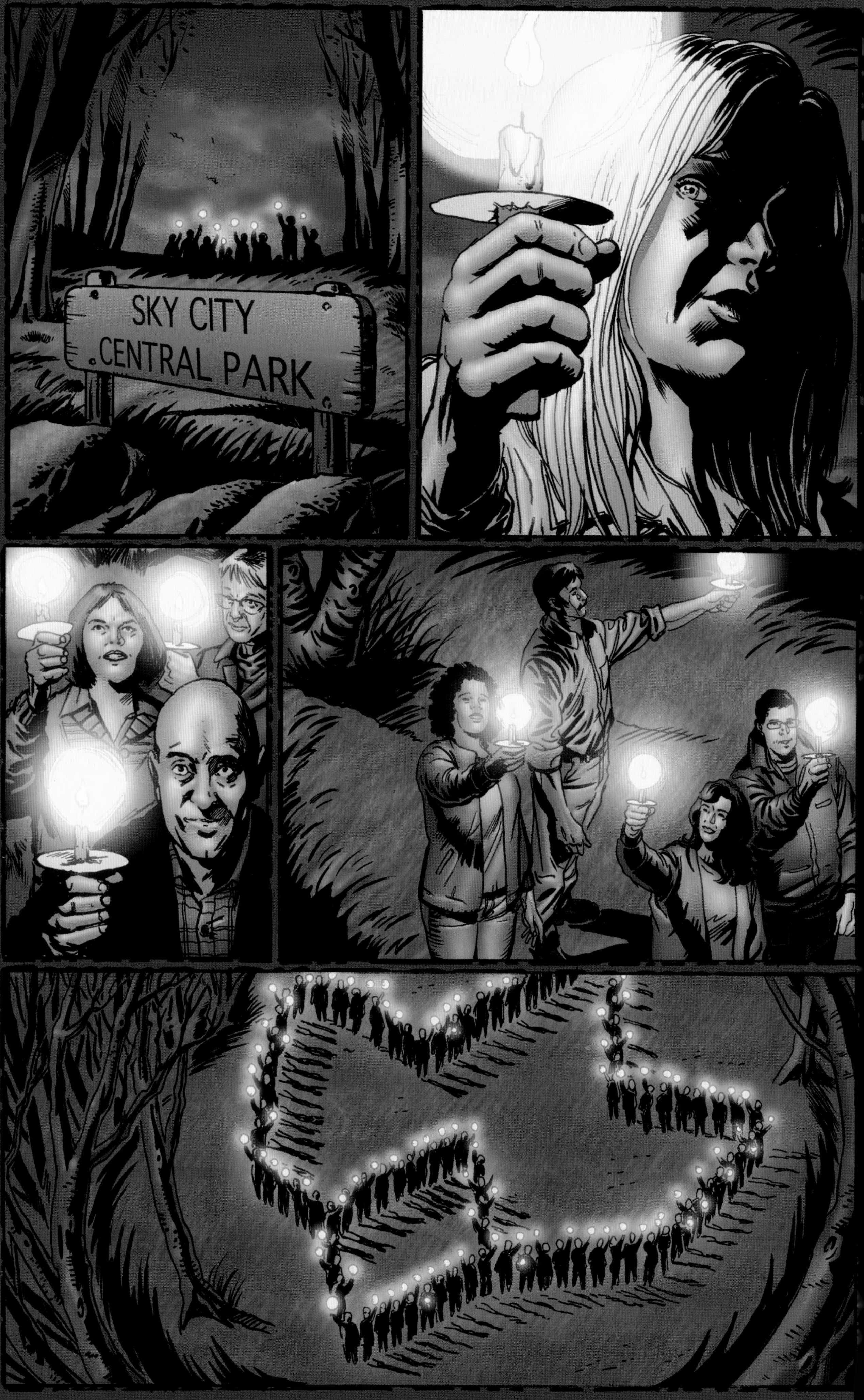
SKY CITY
CENTRAL PARK

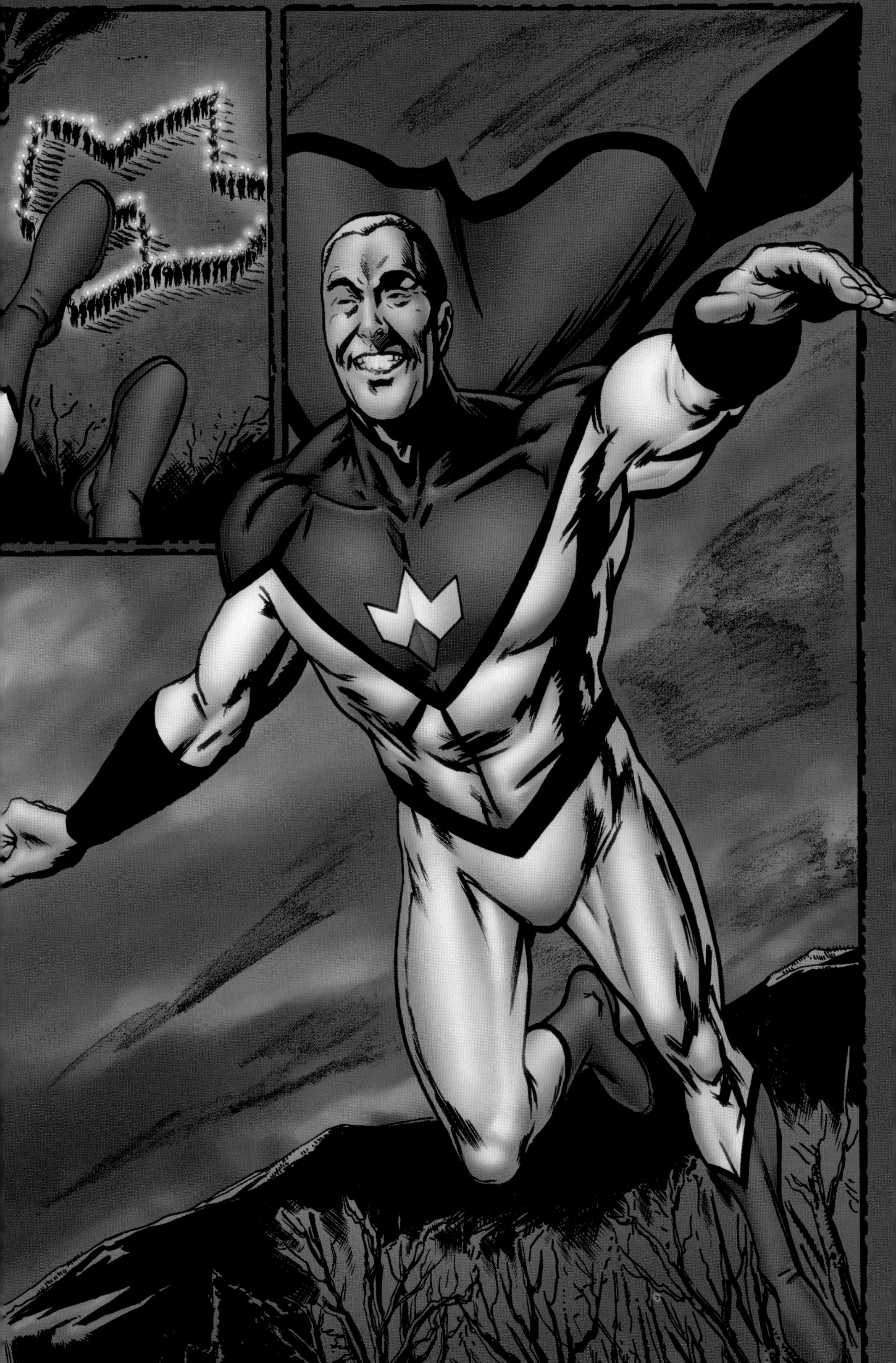

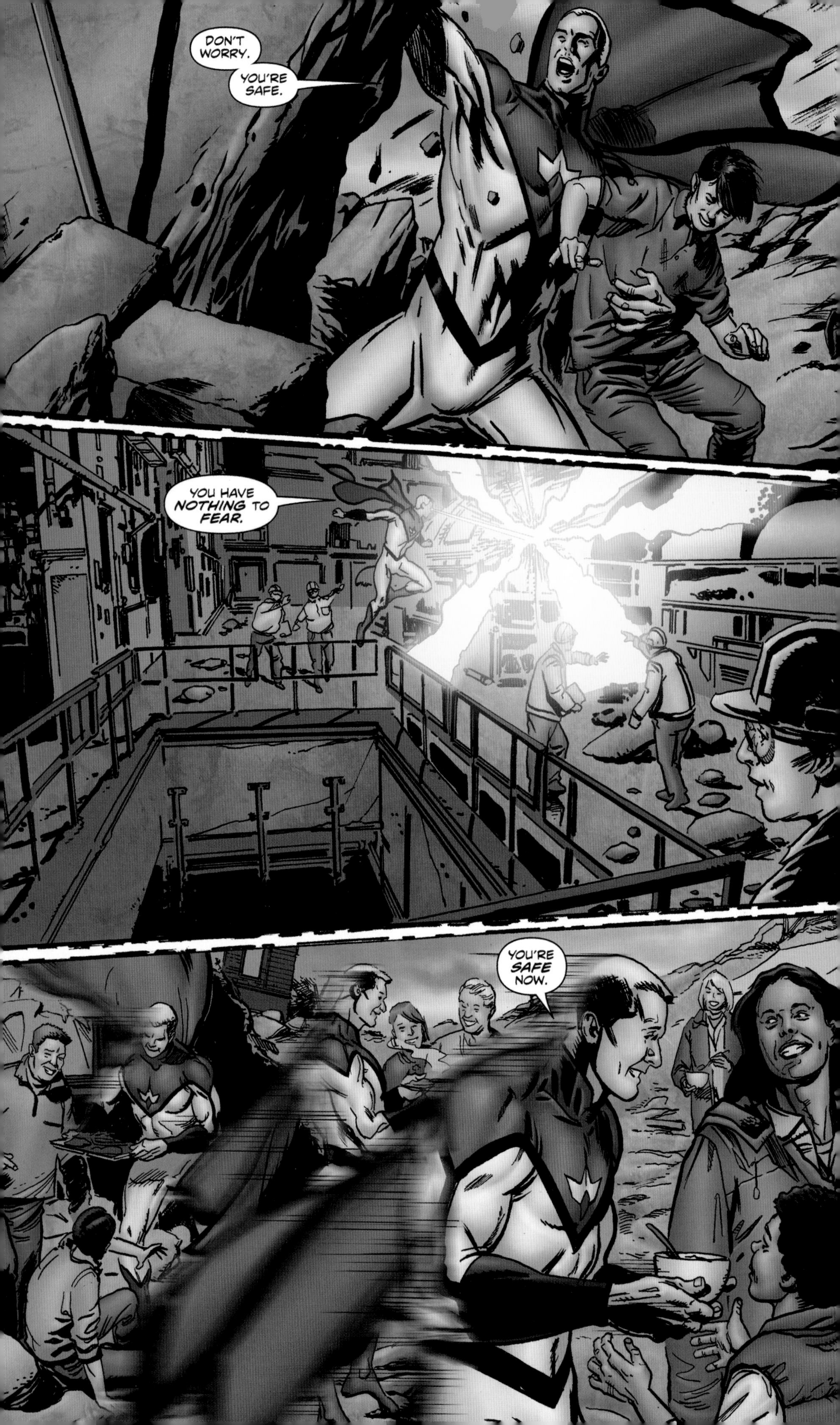
DON'T WORRY.
YOU'RE SAFE.
YOU HAVE NOTHING TO FEAR.
YOU'RE SAFE NOW.

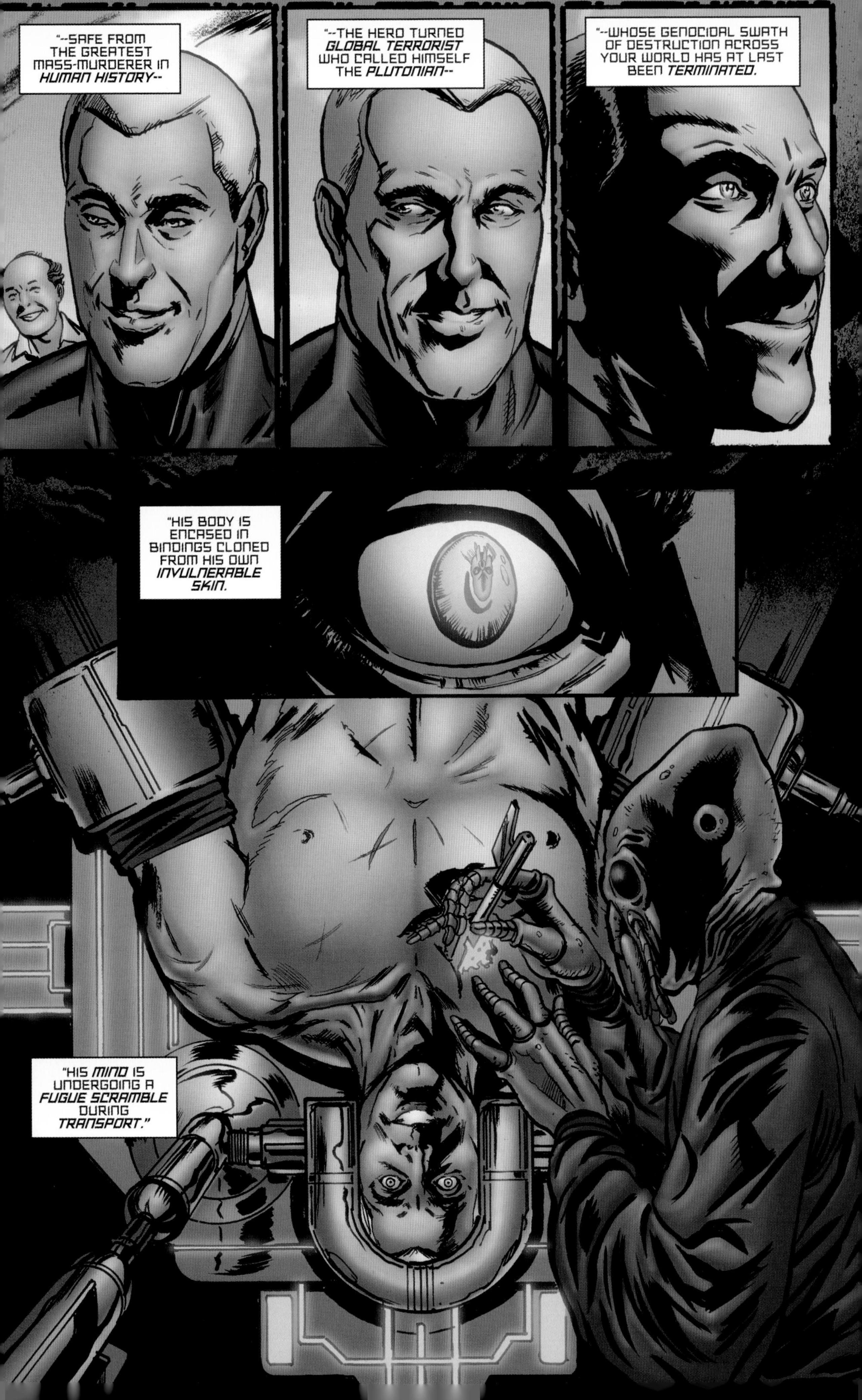
"--SAFE FROM THE GREATEST MASS-MURDERER IN HUMAN HISTORY--
"--THE HERO TURNED GLOBAL TERRORIST WHO CALLED HIMSELF THE PLUTONIAN--
"--WHOSE GENOCIDAL SWATH OF DESTRUCTION ACROSS YOUR WORLD HAS AT LAST BEEN TERMINATED.
"HIS BODY IS ENCASED IN BINDINGS CLONED FROM HIS OWN INVULNERABLE SKIN.
"HIS MIND IS UNDERGOING A FUGUE SCRAMBLE DURING TRANSPORT."

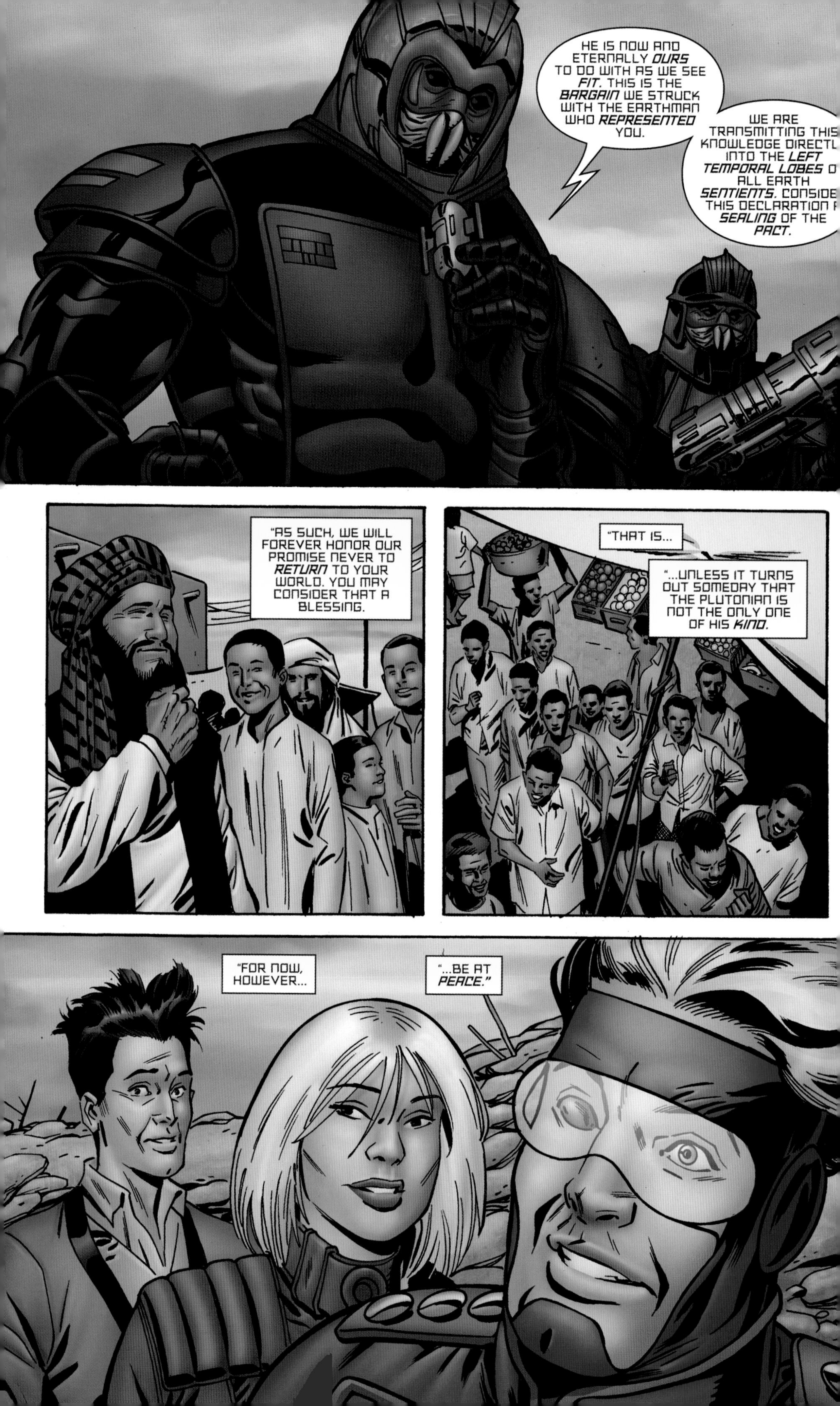

HE IS NOW AND ETERNALLY OURS TO DO WITH AS WE SEE FIT. THIS IS THE BARGAIN WE STRUCK WITH THE EARTHMAN WHO REPRESENTED YOU.
WE ARE TRANSMITTING THIS KNOWLEDGE DIRECTL INTO THE LEFT TEMPORAL LOBES O ALL EARTH SENTIENTS. CONSIDE THIS DECLARATION SEALING OF THE PACT.
"AS SUCH, WE WILL FOREVER HONOR OUR PROMISE NEVER TO RETURN TO YOUR WORLD. YOU MAY CONSIDER THAT A BLESSING.
"THAT IS...
"...UNLESS IT TURNS OUT SOMEDAY THAT THE PLUTONIAN IS NOT THE ONLY ONE OF HIS KIND.
"FOR NOW, HOWEVER...
"...BE AT PEACE."

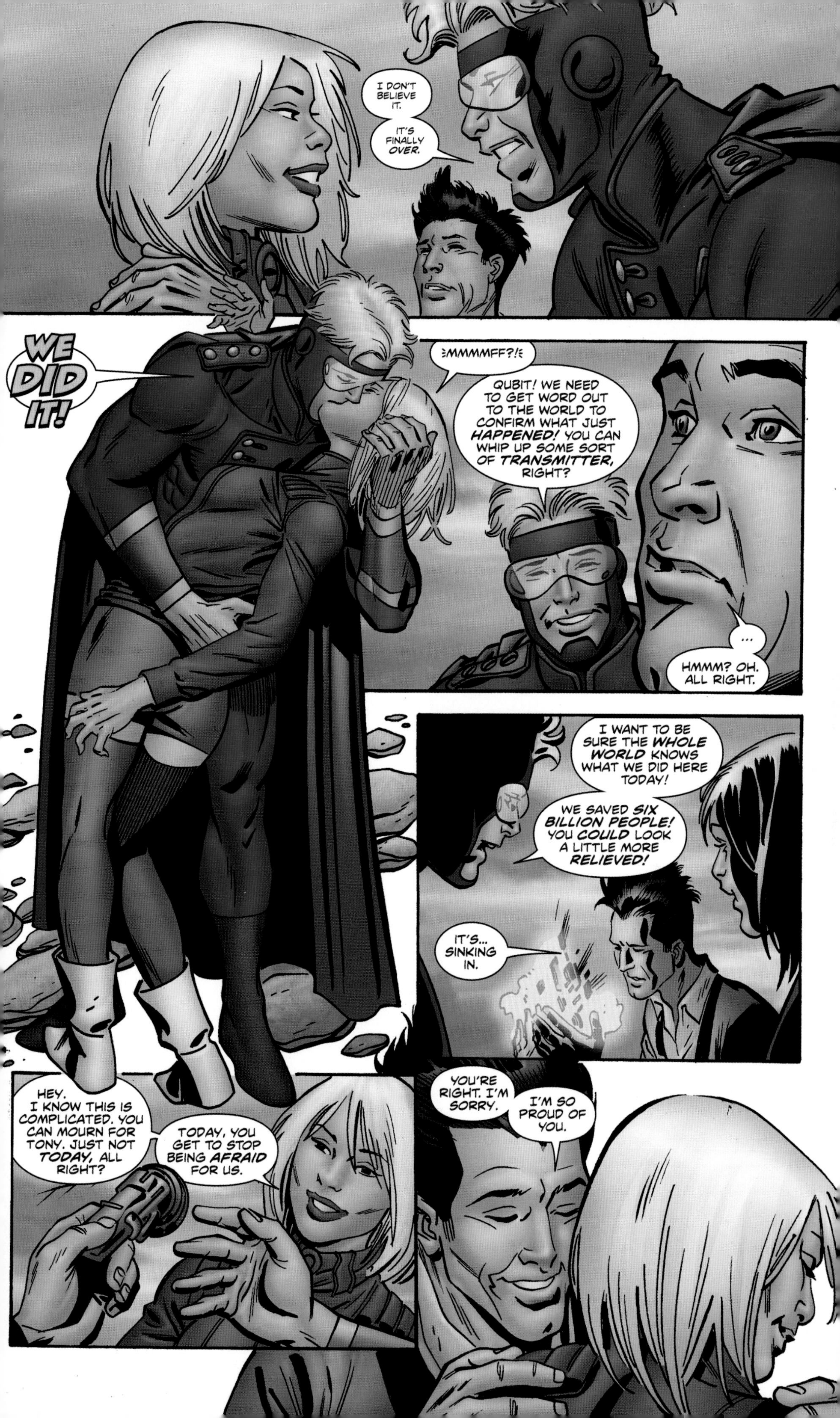

I DON'T BELIEVE IT.
IT'S FINALLY OVER.
WE DID IT!
MMMMFF?!
QUBIT! WE NEED TO GET WORD OUT TO THE WORLD TO CONFIRM WHAT JUST HAPPENED! YOU CAN WHIP UP SOME SORT OF TRANSMITTER, RIGHT?
...
HMMM? OH. ALL RIGHT.
I WANT TO BE SURE THE WHOLE WORLD KNOWS WHAT WE DID HERE TODAY!
WE SAVED SIX BILLION PEOPLE! YOU COULD LOOK A LITTLE MORE RELIEVED!
IT'S... SINKING IN.
HEY. I KNOW THIS IS COMPLICATED. YOU CAN MOURN FOR TONY. JUST NOT TODAY, ALL RIGHT?
TODAY, YOU GET TO STOP BEING AFRAID FOR US.
YOU'RE RIGHT. I'M SORRY.
I'M SO PROUD OF YOU.

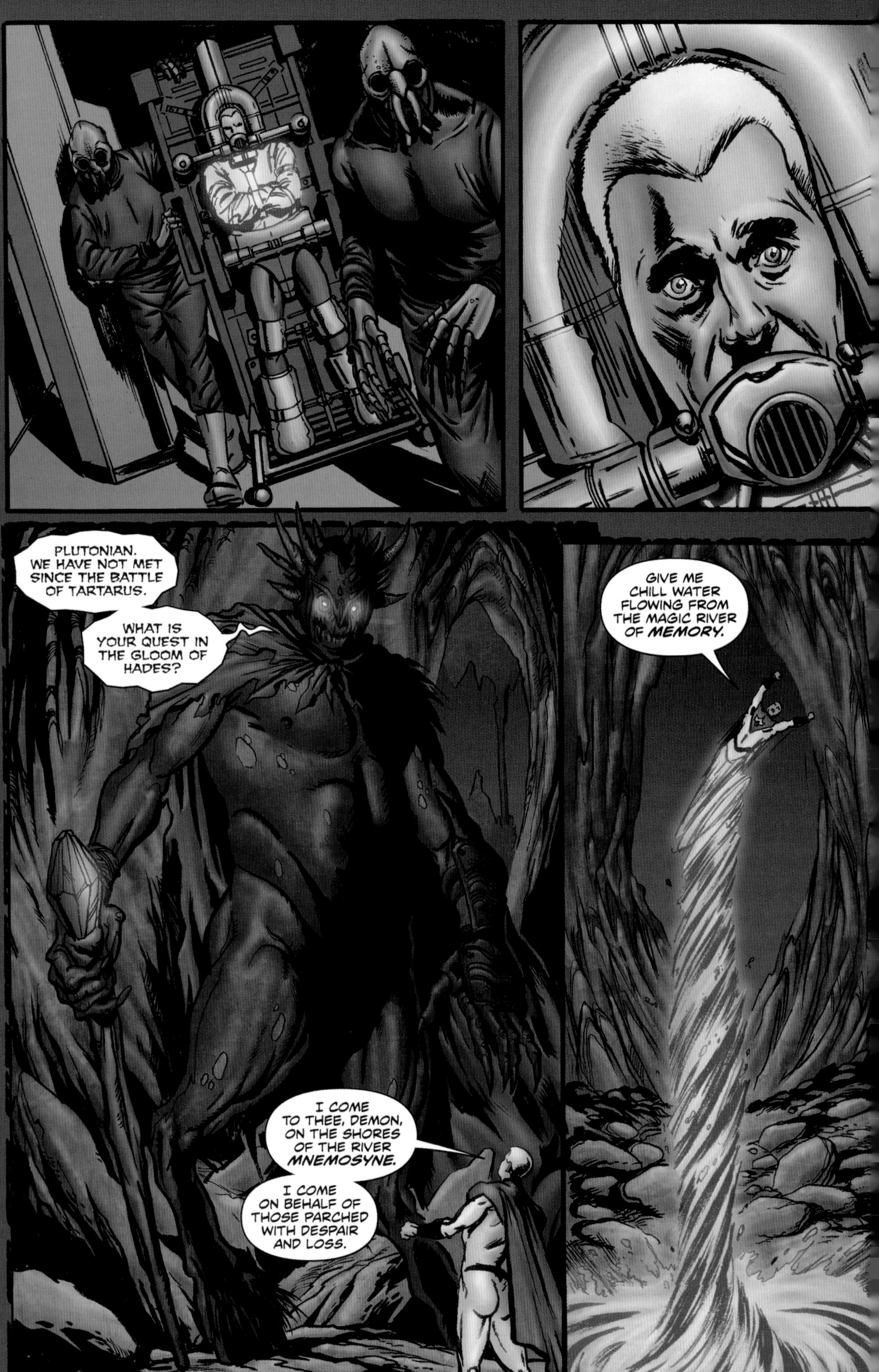
PLUTONIAN. WE HAVE NOT MET SINCE THE BATTLE OF TARTARUS.
WHAT IS YOUR QUEST IN THE GLOOM OF HADES?
I COME TO THEE, DEMON, ON THE SHORES OF THE RIVER *MNEMOSYNE.*
I COME ON BEHALF OF THOSE PARCHED WITH DESPAIR AND LOSS.
GIVE ME CHILL WATER FLOWING FROM THE MAGIC RIVER OF *MEMORY.*

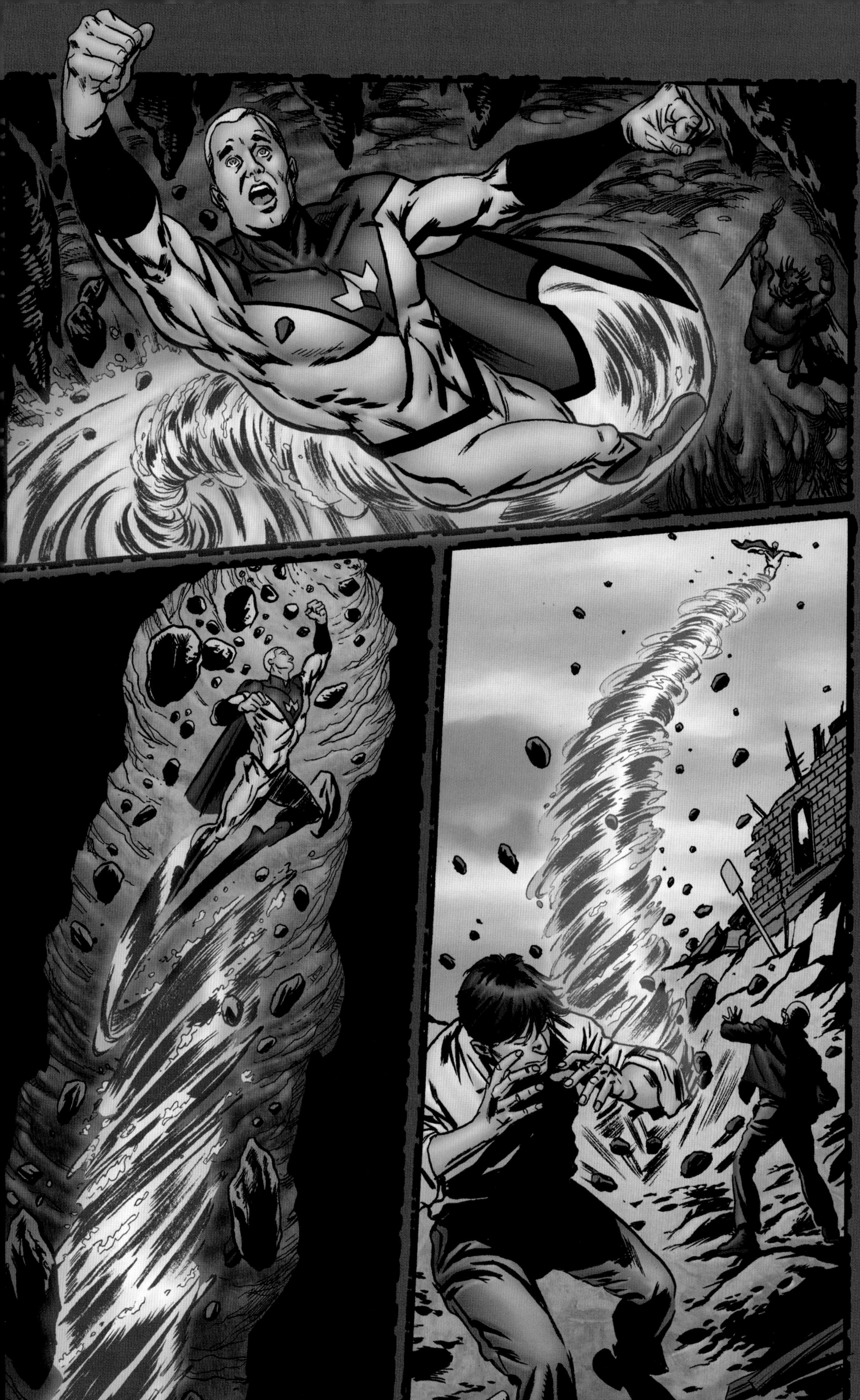

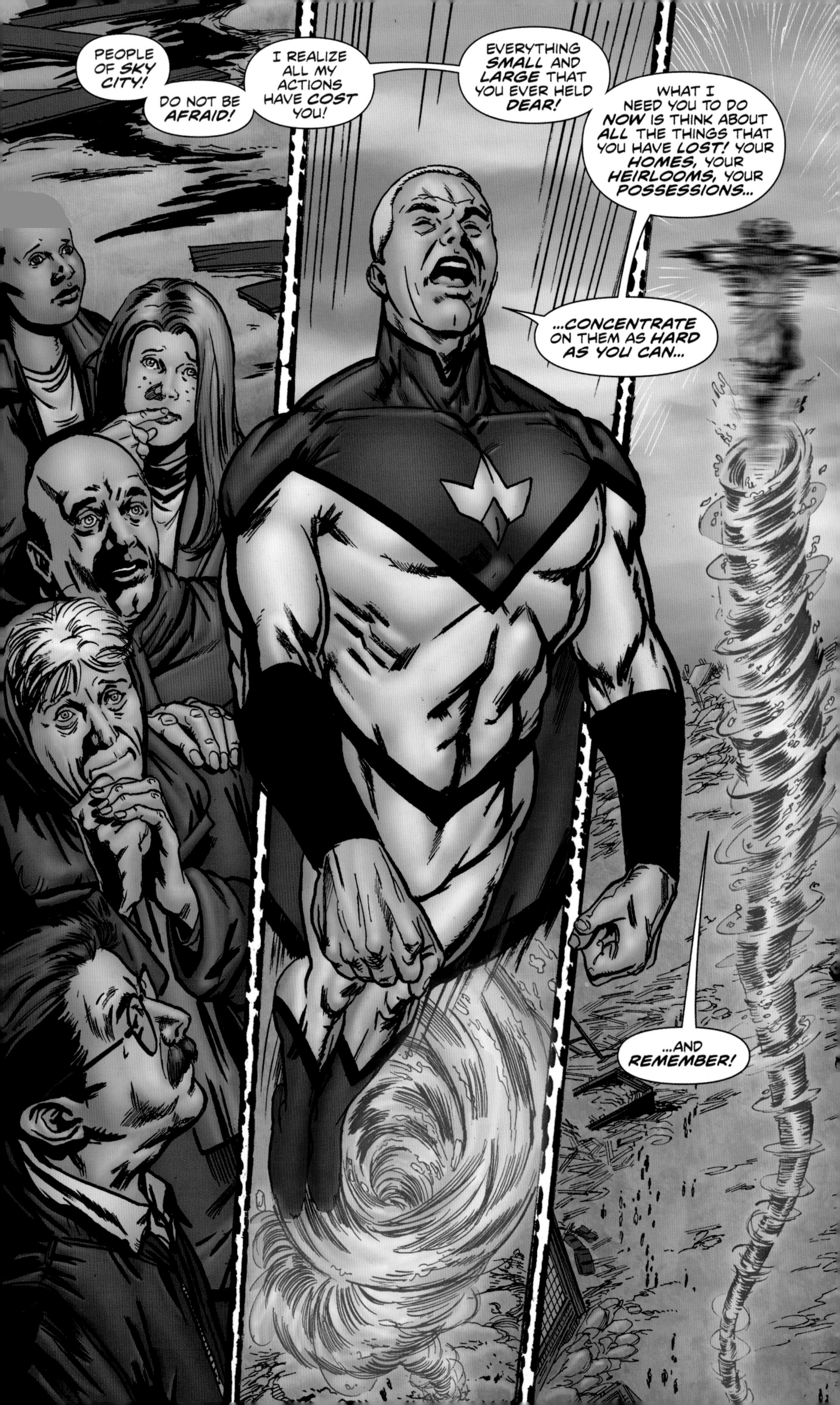

PEOPLE OF SKY CITY!
DO NOT BE AFRAID!
I REALIZE ALL MY ACTIONS HAVE COST YOU!
EVERYTHING SMALL AND LARGE THAT YOU EVER HELD DEAR!
WHAT I NEED YOU TO DO NOW IS THINK ABOUT ALL THE THINGS THAT YOU HAVE LOST! YOUR HOMES, YOUR HEIRLOOMS, YOUR POSSESSIONS...
...CONCENTRATE ON THEM AS HARD AS YOU CAN...
...AND REMEMBER!

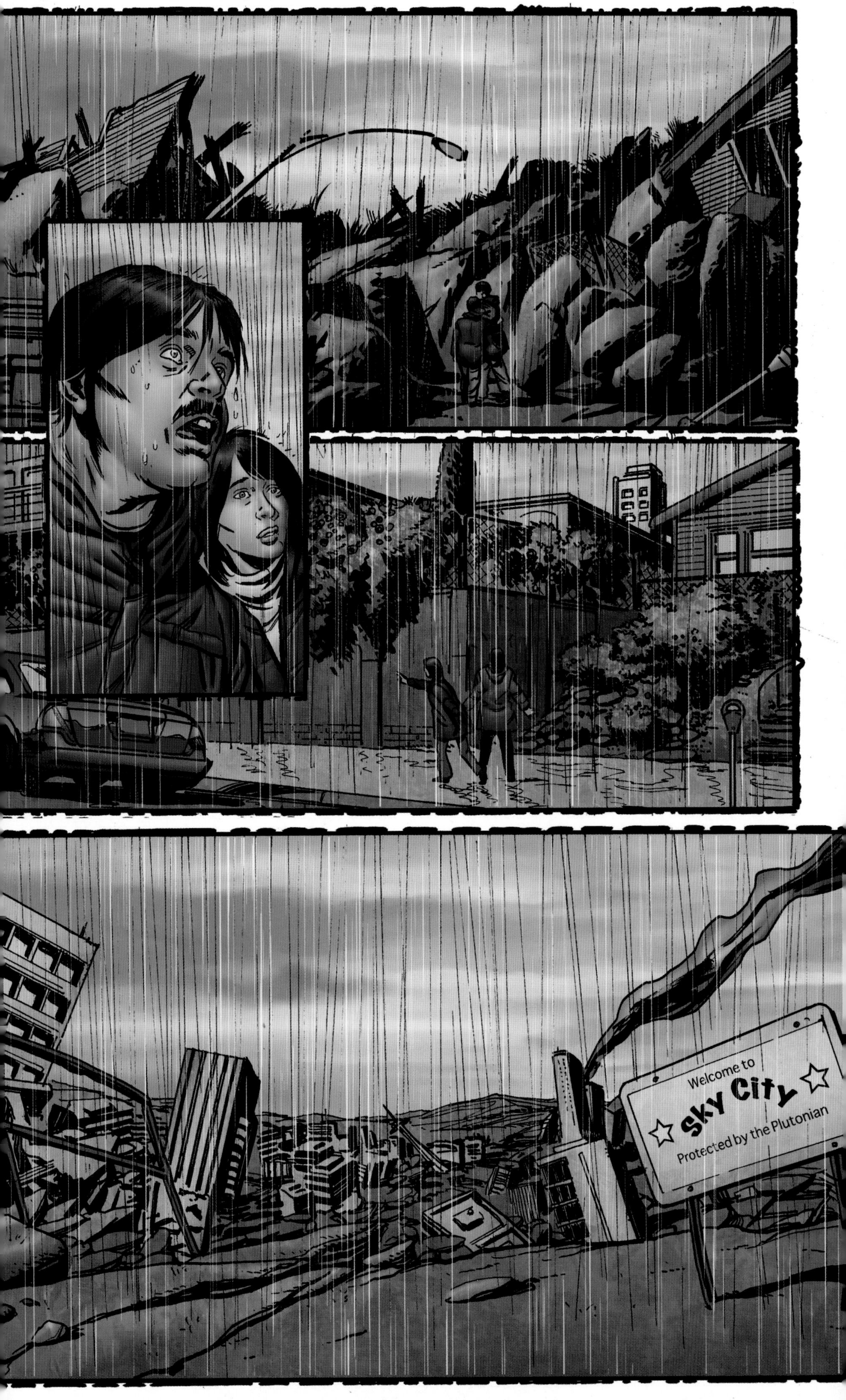

Welcome to
Sky City
Protected by the Plutonian

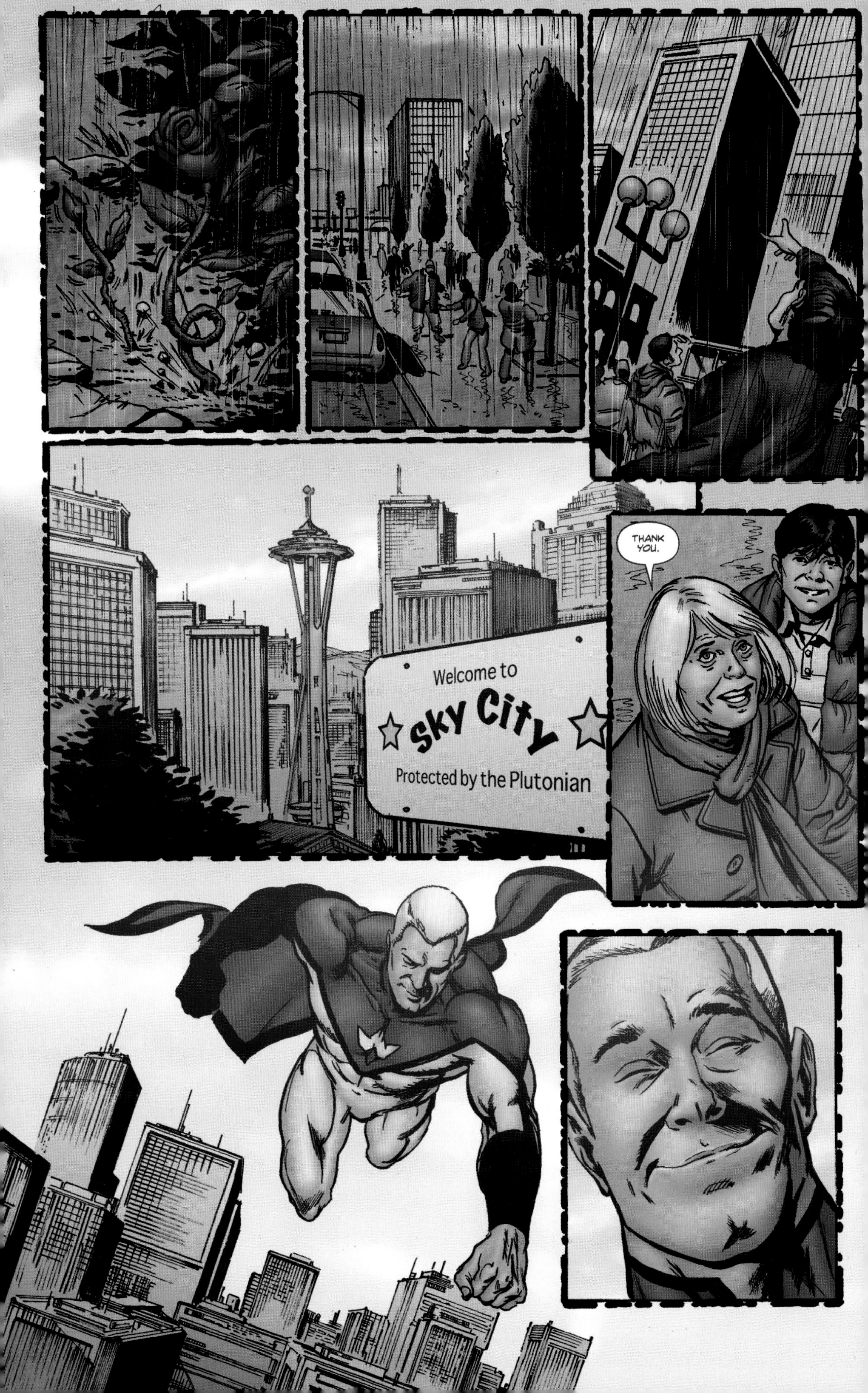
Welcome to
Sky City
Protected by the Plutonian
THANK YOU.

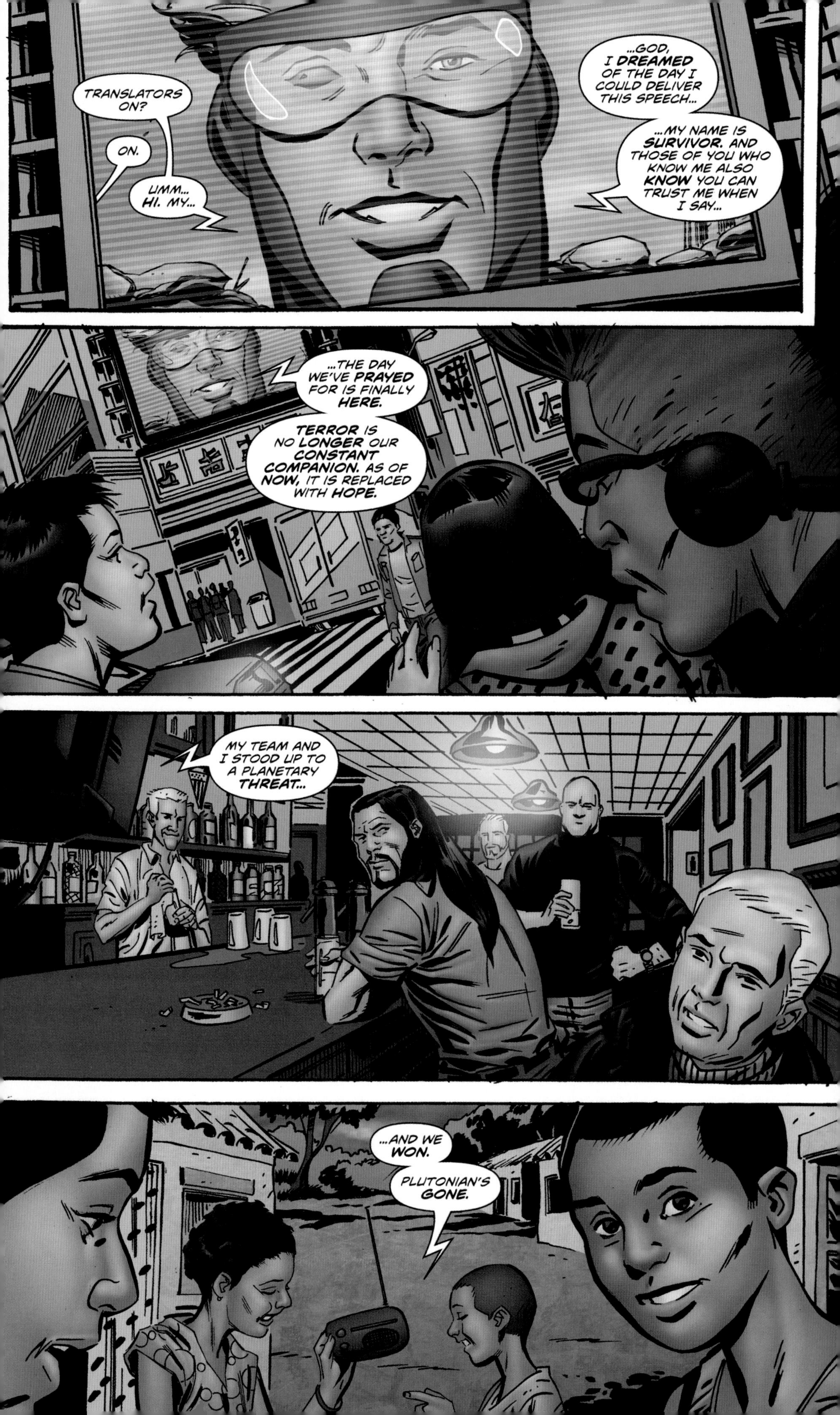
TRANSLATORS ON?
ON.
UMM... HI. MY...
...GOD, I DREAMED OF THE DAY I COULD DELIVER THIS SPEECH...
...MY NAME IS SURVIVOR. AND THOSE OF YOU WHO KNOW ME ALSO KNOW YOU CAN TRUST ME WHEN I SAY...
...THE DAY WE'VE PRAYED FOR IS FINALLY HERE.
TERROR IS NO LONGER OUR CONSTANT COMPANION. AS OF NOW, IT IS REPLACED WITH HOPE.
MY TEAM AND I STOOD UP TO A PLANETARY THREAT...
...AND WE WON.
PLUTONIAN'S GONE.

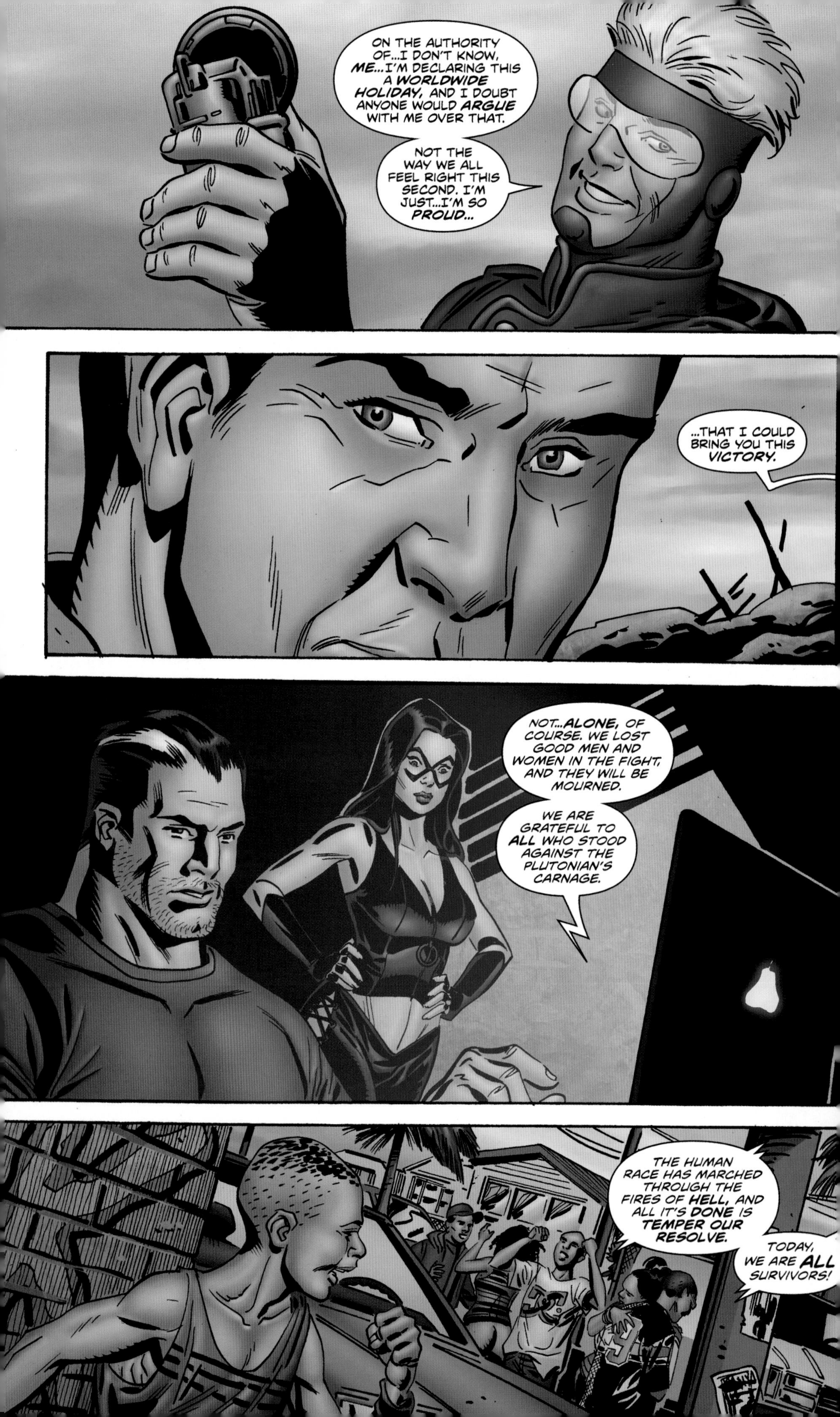
ON THE AUTHORITY OF...I DON'T KNOW, ME...I'M DECLARING THIS A WORLDWIDE HOLIDAY, AND I DOUBT ANYONE WOULD ARGUE WITH ME OVER THAT.
NOT THE WAY WE ALL FEEL RIGHT THIS SECOND. I'M JUST...I'M SO PROUD...
...THAT I COULD BRING YOU THIS VICTORY.
NOT...ALONE, OF COURSE. WE LOST GOOD MEN AND WOMEN IN THE FIGHT, AND THEY WILL BE MOURNED.
WE ARE GRATEFUL TO ALL WHO STOOD AGAINST THE PLUTONIAN'S CARNAGE.
THE HUMAN RACE HAS MARCHED THROUGH THE FIRES OF HELL, AND ALL IT'S DONE IS TEMPER OUR RESOLVE.
TODAY, WE ARE ALL SURVIVORS!

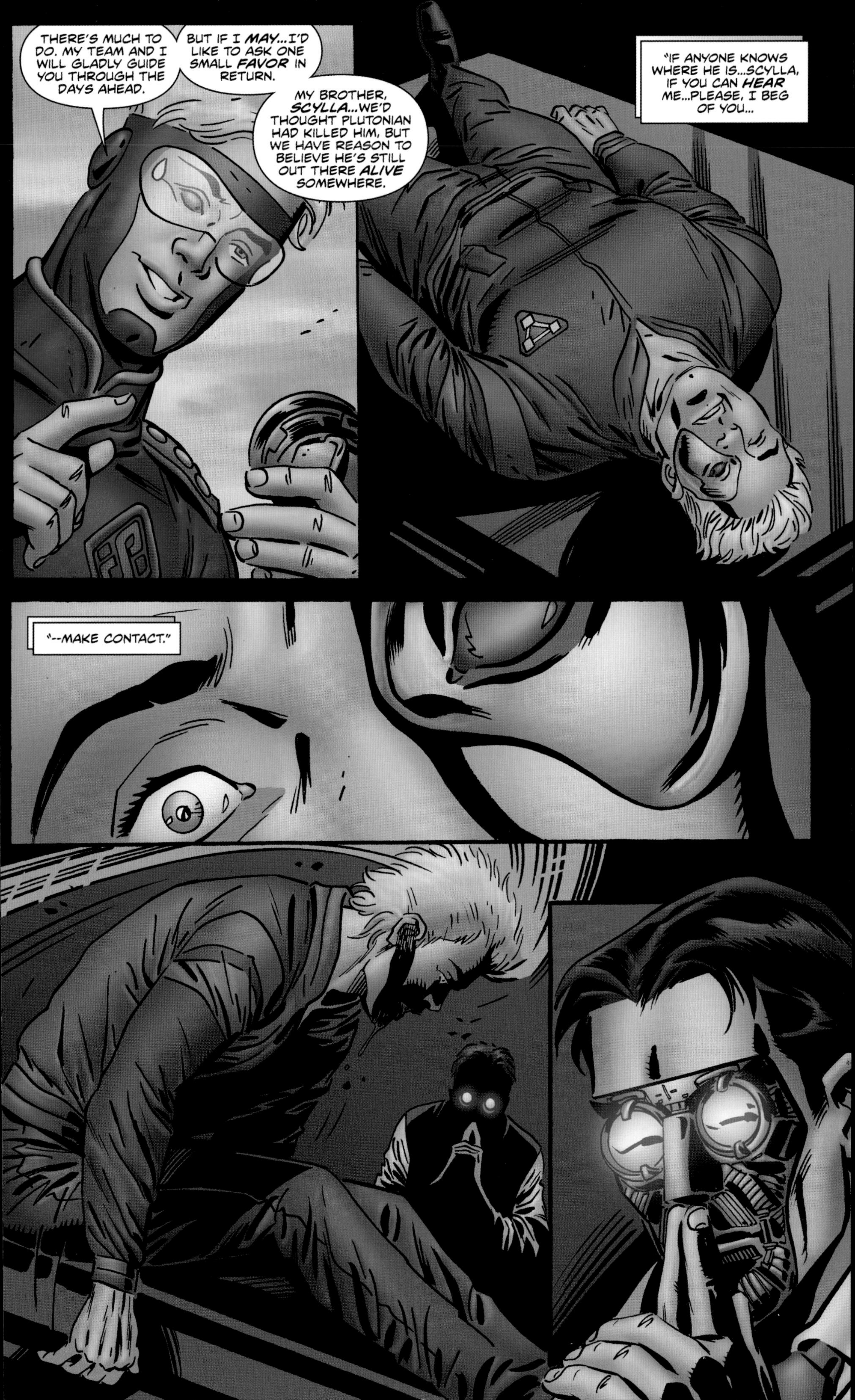
THERE'S MUCH TO DO. MY TEAM AND I WILL GLADLY GUIDE YOU THROUGH THE DAYS AHEAD.
BUT IF I MAY...I'D LIKE TO ASK ONE SMALL FAVOR IN RETURN.
MY BROTHER, SCYLLA...WE'D THOUGHT PLUTONIAN HAD KILLED HIM, BUT WE HAVE REASON TO BELIEVE HE'S STILL OUT THERE ALIVE SOMEWHERE.
"IF ANYONE KNOWS WHERE HE IS...SCYLLA, IF YOU CAN HEAR ME...PLEASE, I BEG OF YOU...
"--MAKE CONTACT."

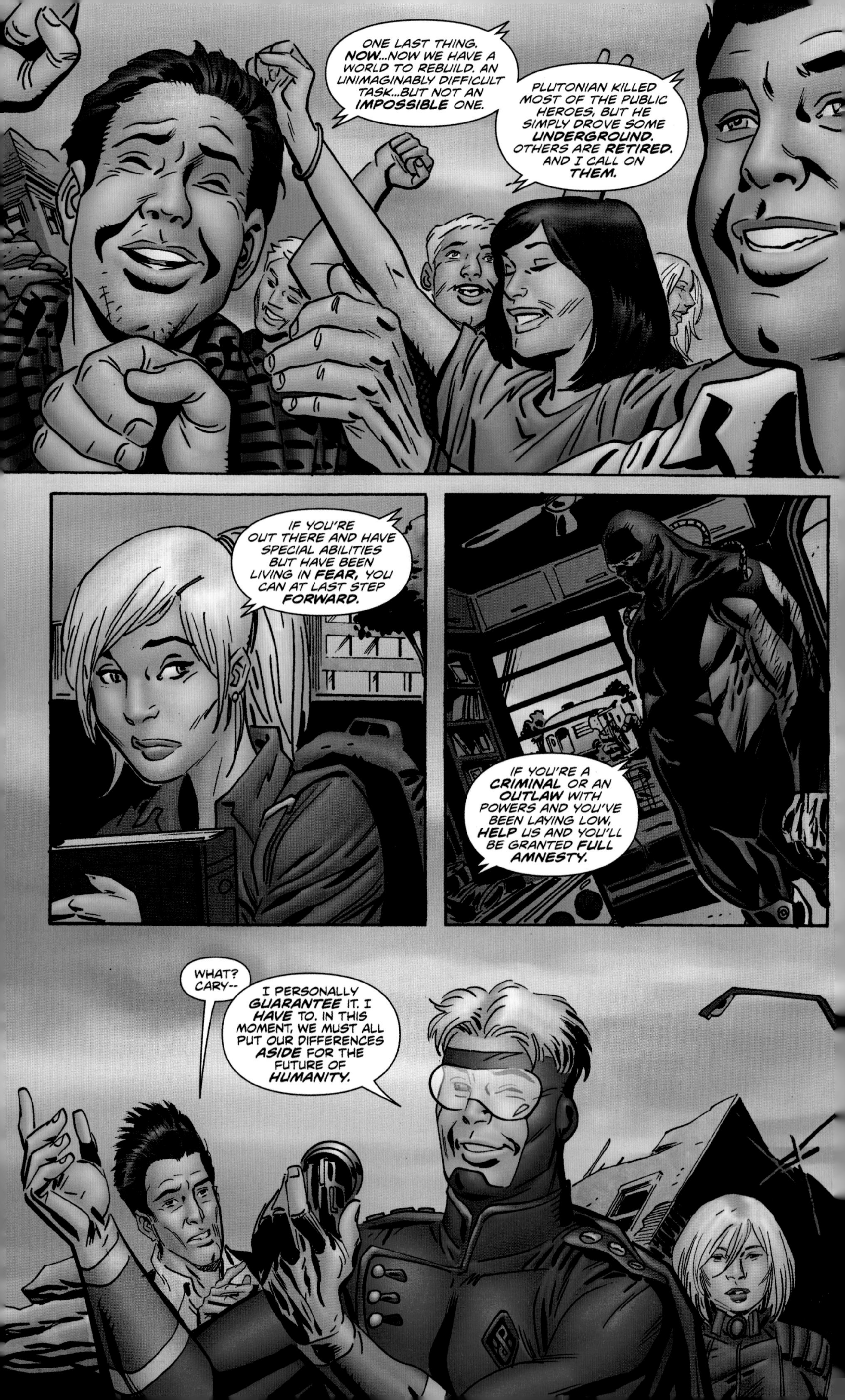

ONE LAST THING. NOW...NOW WE HAVE A WORLD TO REBUILD. AN UNIMAGINABLY DIFFICULT TASK...BUT NOT AN IMPOSSIBLE ONE.
PLUTONIAN KILLED MOST OF THE PUBLIC HEROES, BUT HE SIMPLY DROVE SOME UNDERGROUND. OTHERS ARE RETIRED. AND I CALL ON THEM.
IF YOU'RE OUT THERE AND HAVE SPECIAL ABILITIES BUT HAVE BEEN LIVING IN FEAR, YOU CAN AT LAST STEP FORWARD.
IF YOU'RE A CRIMINAL OR AN OUTLAW WITH POWERS AND YOU'VE BEEN LAYING LOW, HELP US AND YOU'LL BE GRANTED FULL AMNESTY.
WHAT? CARY--
I PERSONALLY GUARANTEE IT. I HAVE TO. IN THIS MOMENT, WE MUST ALL PUT OUR DIFFERENCES ASIDE FOR THE FUTURE OF HUMANITY.

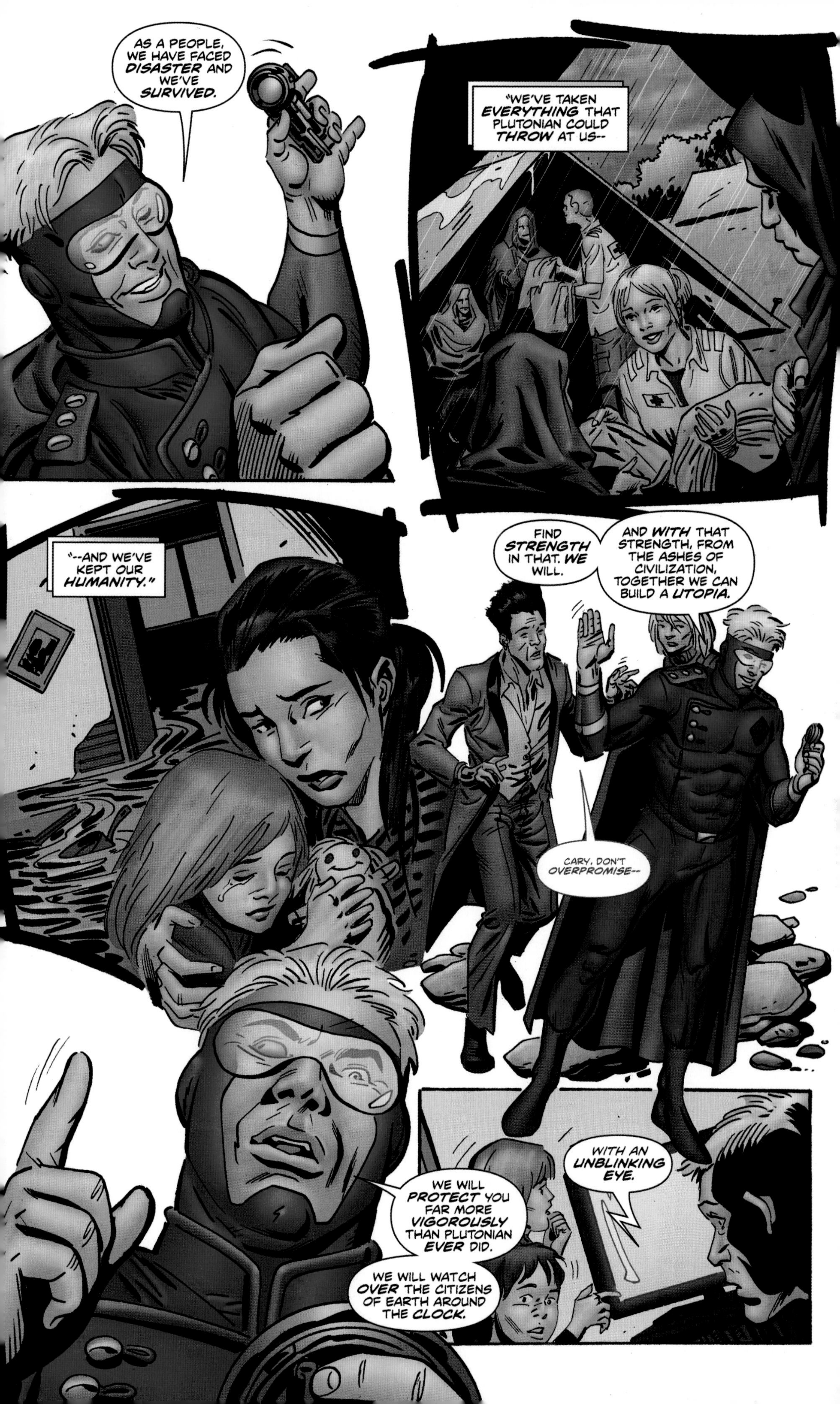

AS A PEOPLE, WE HAVE FACED DISASTER AND WE'VE SURVIVED.
"WE'VE TAKEN EVERYTHING THAT PLUTONIAN COULD THROW AT US--
"--AND WE'VE KEPT OUR HUMANITY."
FIND STRENGTH IN THAT. WE WILL.
AND WITH THAT STRENGTH, FROM THE ASHES OF CIVILIZATION, TOGETHER WE CAN BUILD A UTOPIA.
CARY, DON'T OVERPROMISE--
WE WILL PROTECT YOU FAR MORE VIGOROUSLY THAN PLUTONIAN EVER DID.
WE WILL WATCH OVER THE CITIZENS OF EARTH AROUND THE CLOCK.
WITH AN UNBLINKING EYE.

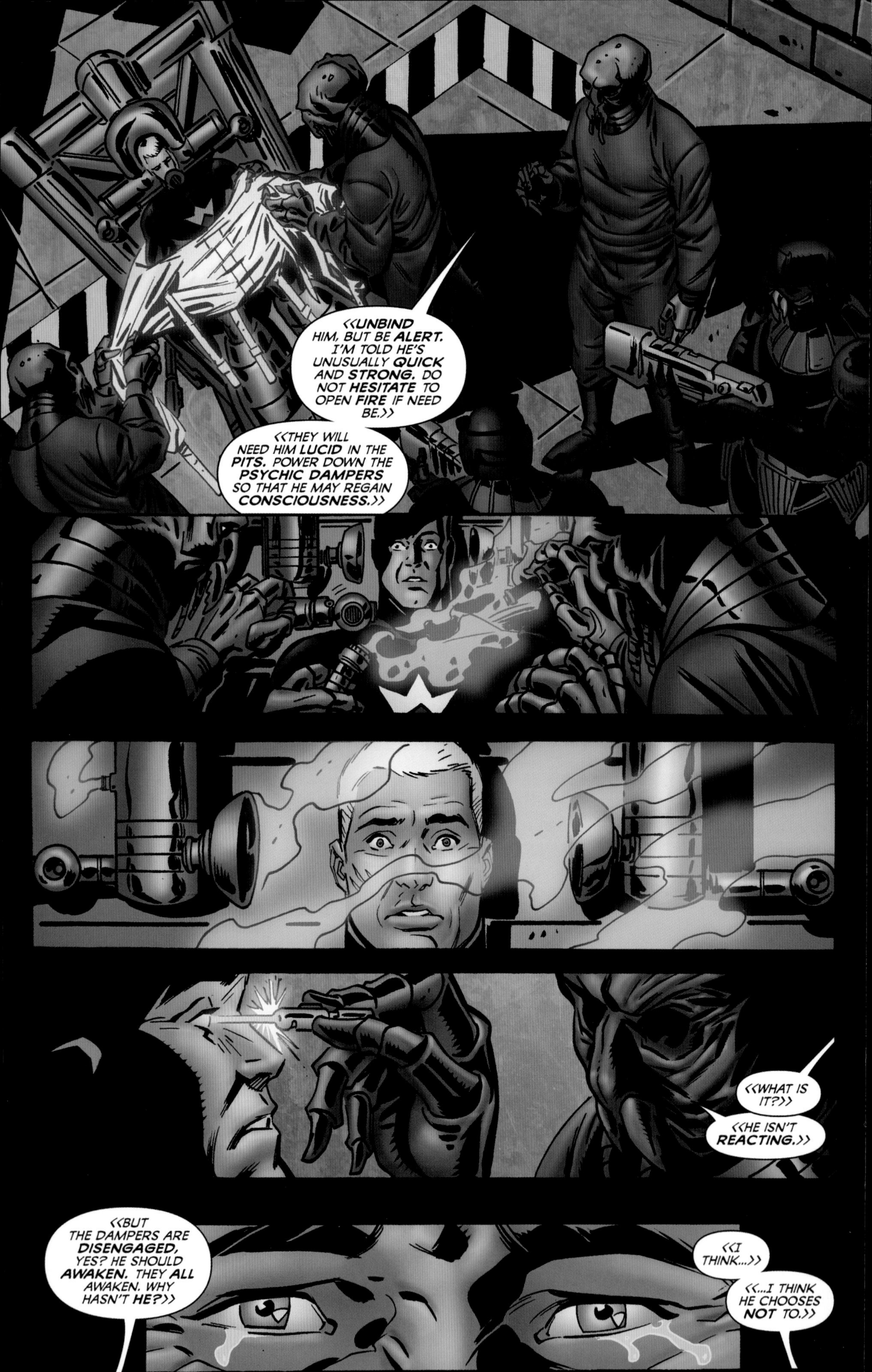
<<UNBIND HIM, BUT BE ALERT. I'M TOLD HE'S UNUSUALLY QUICK AND STRONG. DO NOT HESITATE TO OPEN FIRE IF NEED BE.>>
<<THEY WILL NEED HIM LUCID IN THE PITS. POWER DOWN THE PSYCHIC DAMPERS SO THAT HE MAY REGAIN CONSCIOUSNESS.>>
<<WHAT IS IT?>>
<<HE ISN'T REACTING.>>
<<BUT THE DAMPERS ARE DISENGAGED, YES? HE SHOULD AWAKEN. THEY ALL AWAKEN. WHY HASN'T HE?>>
<<I THINK...>>
<<...I THINK HE CHOOSES NOT TO.>>

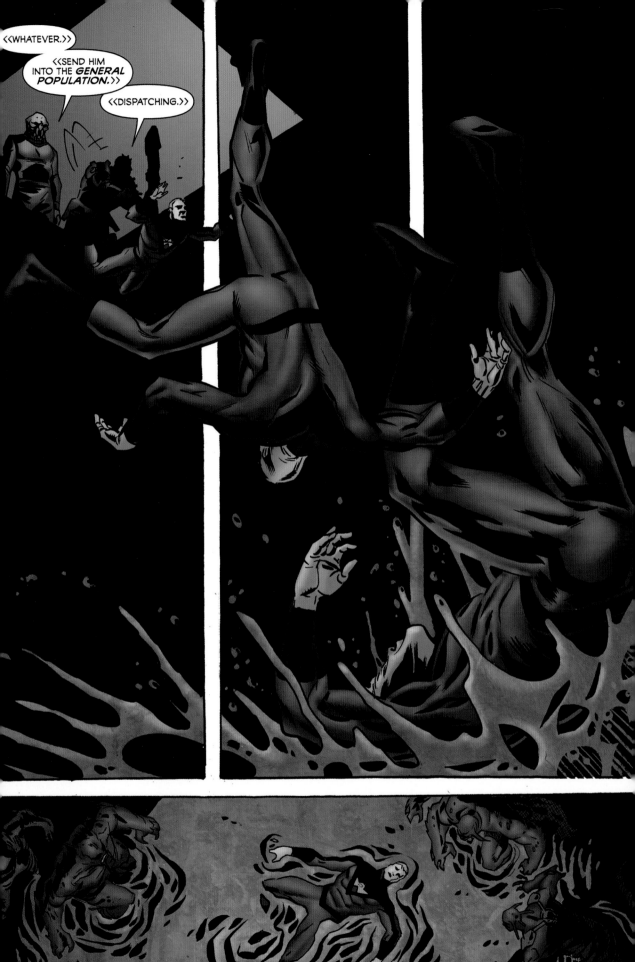

《WHATEVER.》

《SEND HIM INTO THE *GENERAL POPULATION*.》

《DISPATCHING.》

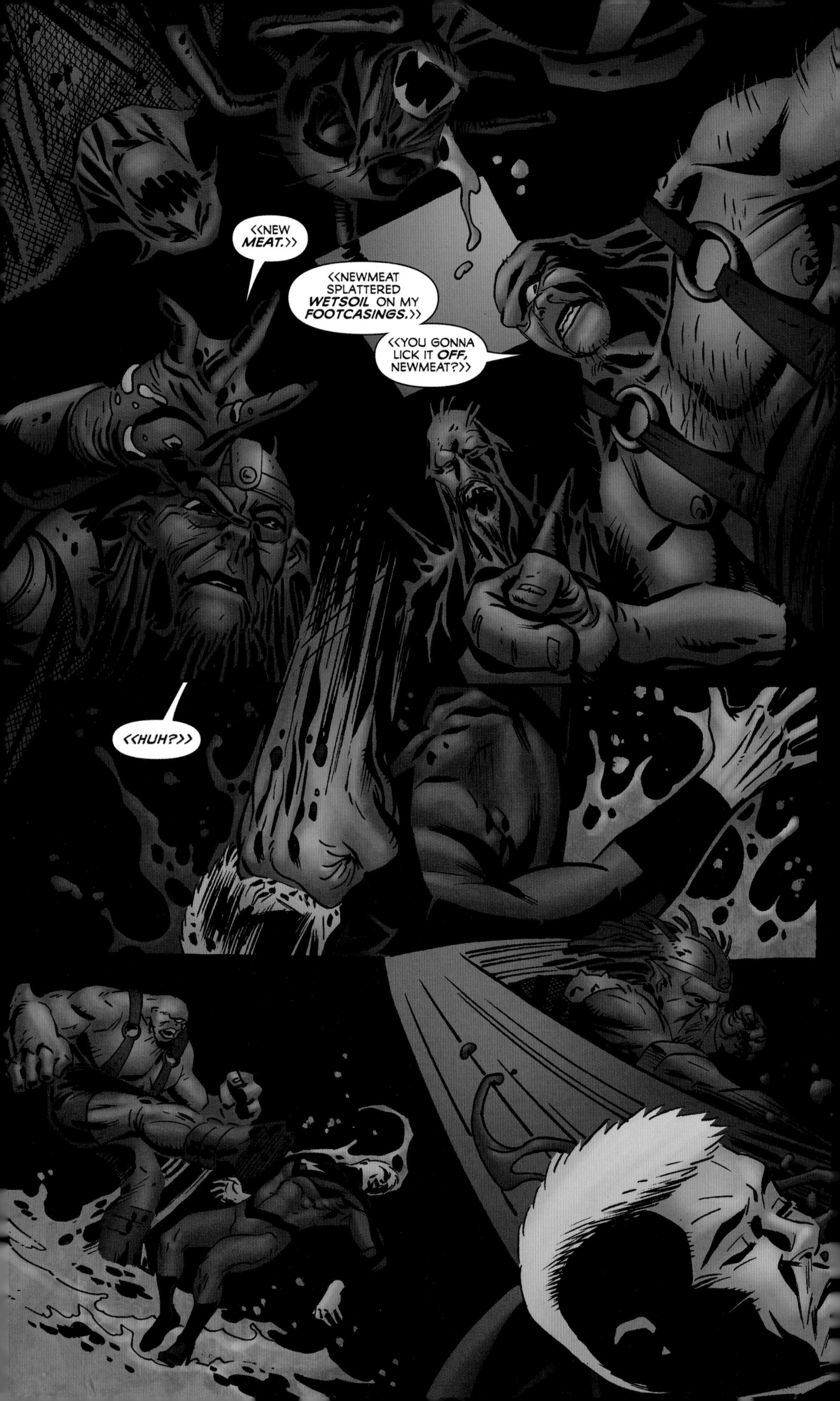

<<NEW MEAT.>>
<<NEWMEAT SPLATTERED WETSOIL ON MY FOOTCASINGS.>>
<<YOU GONNA LICK IT OFF, NEWMEAT?>>
<<HUH?>>

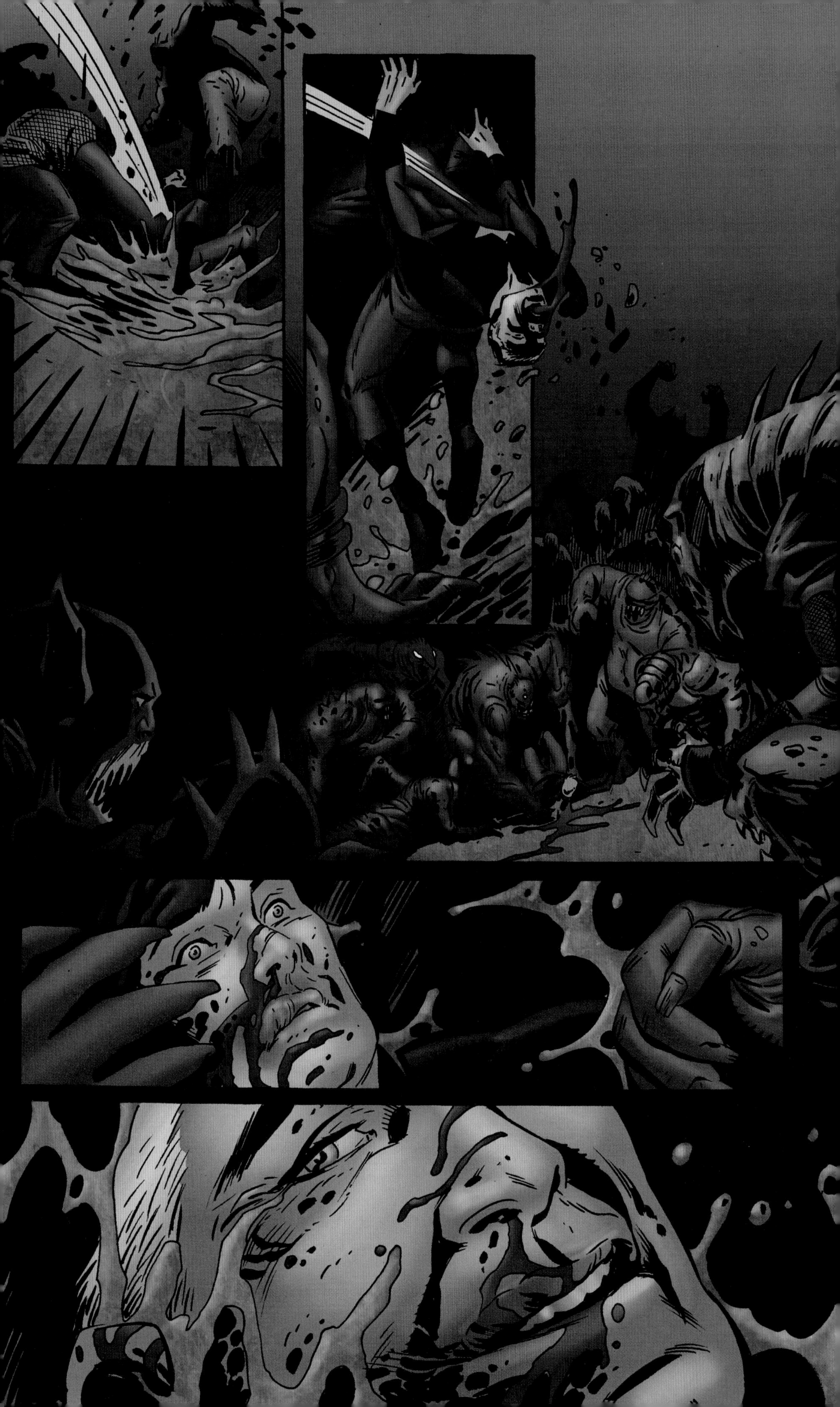

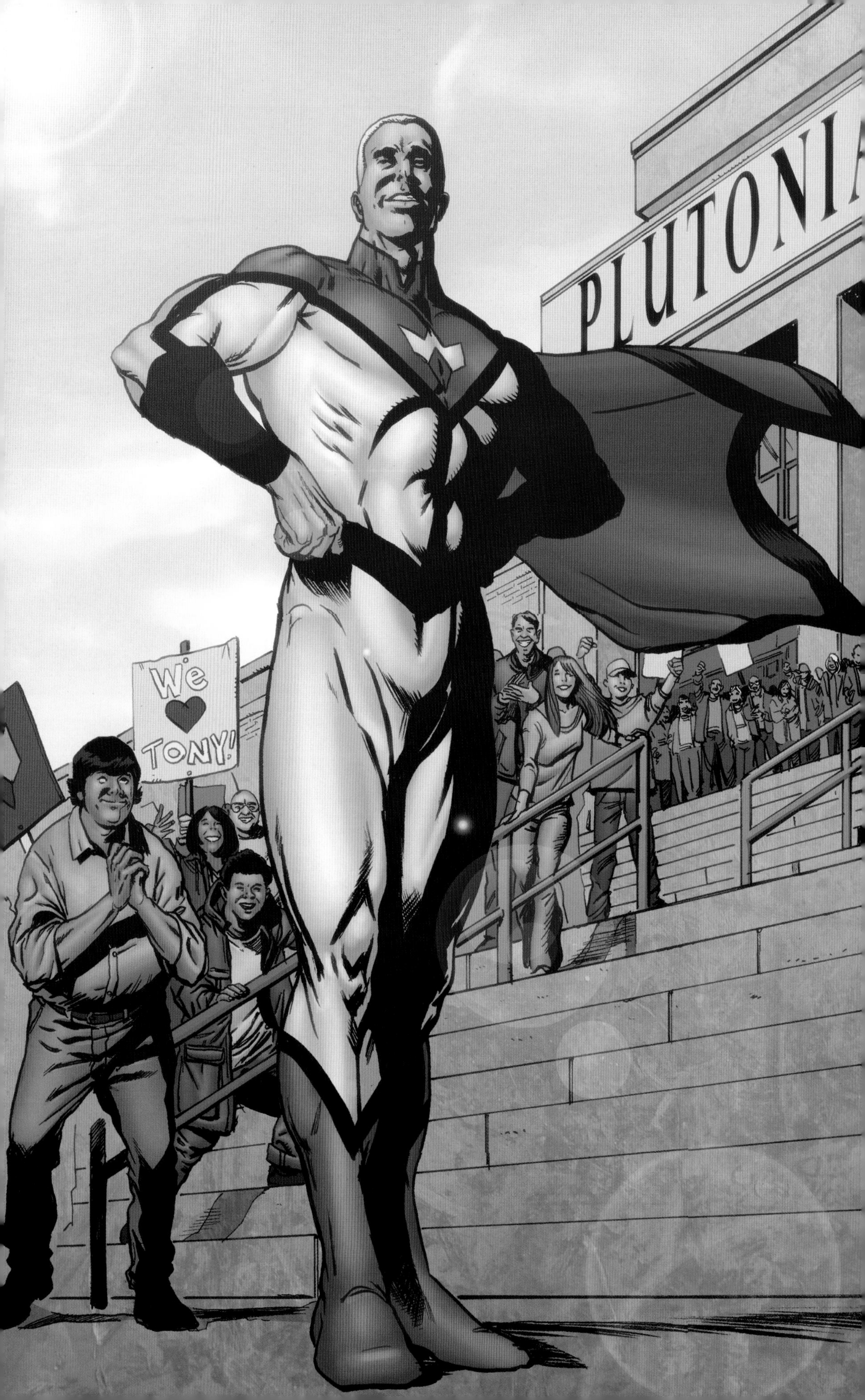
PLUTONIA
We ♥ TONY!

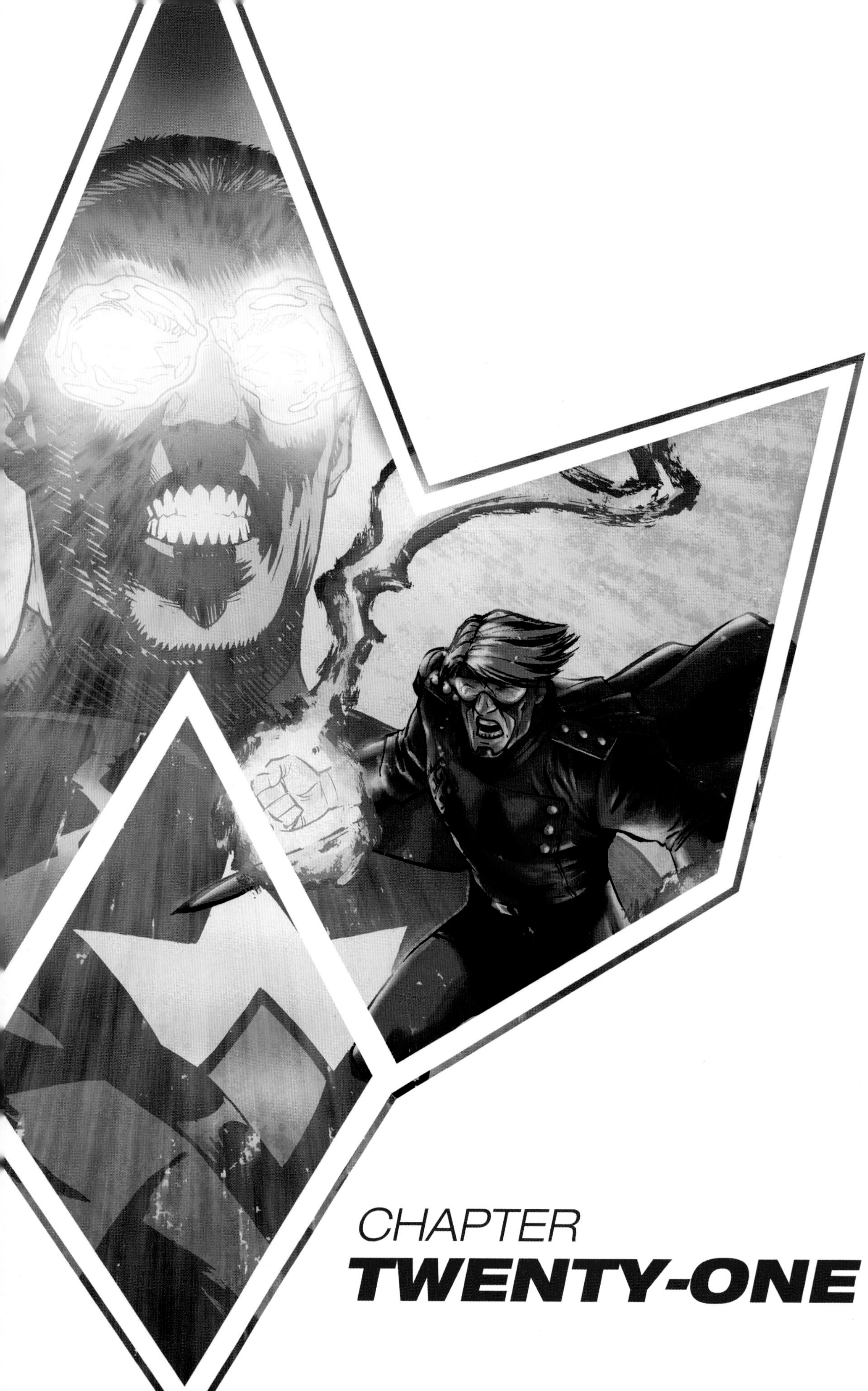

CHAPTER **TWENTY-ONE**

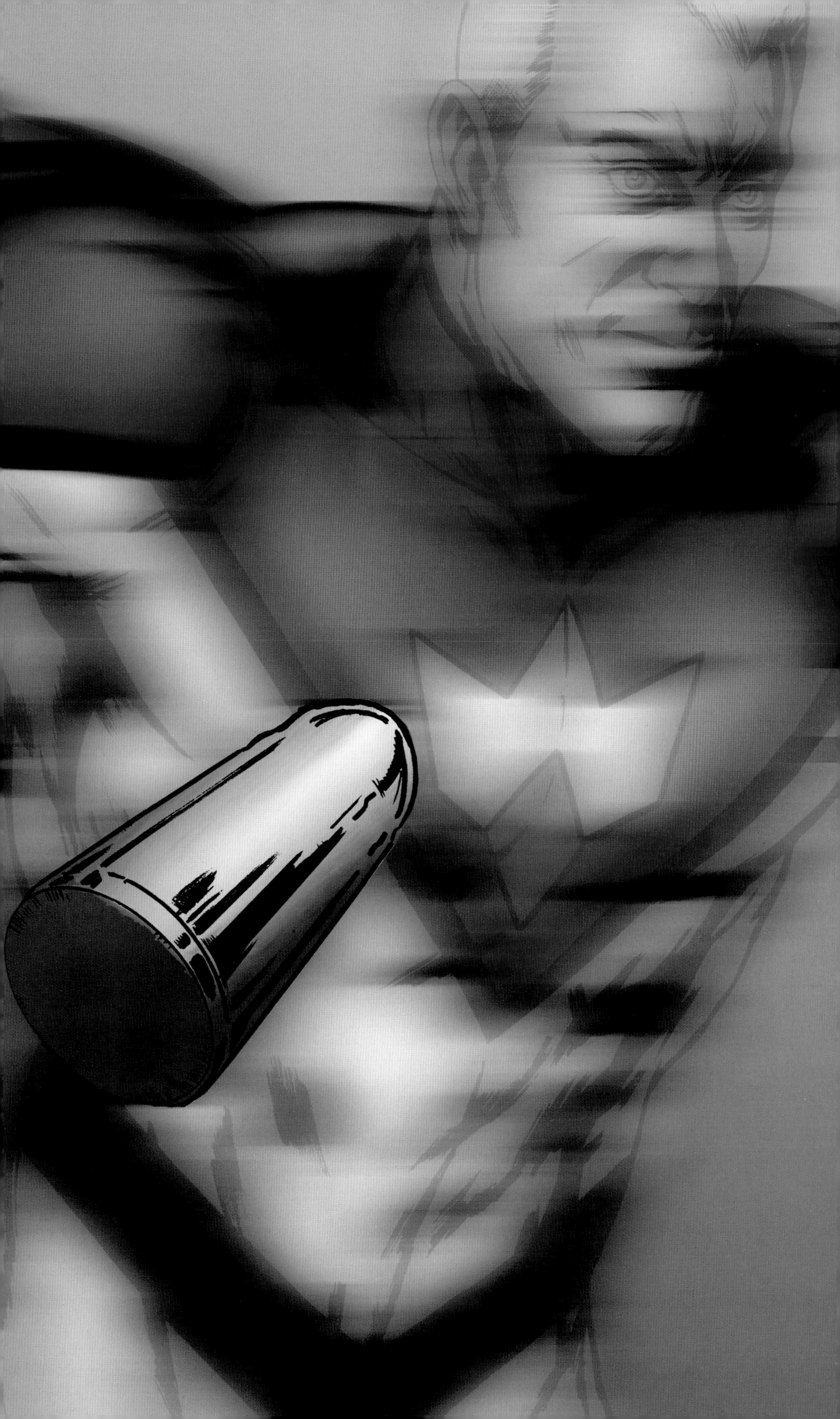

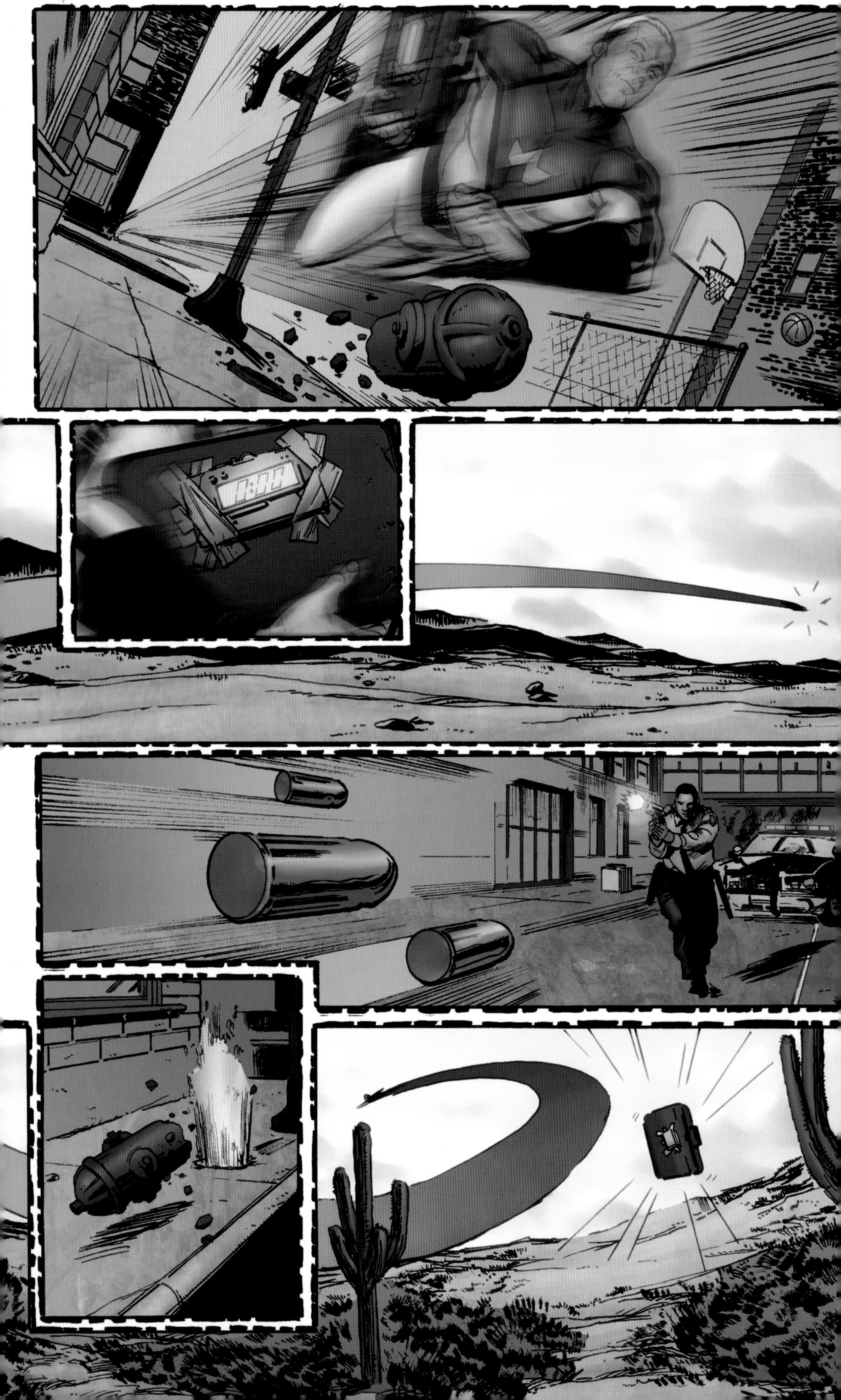

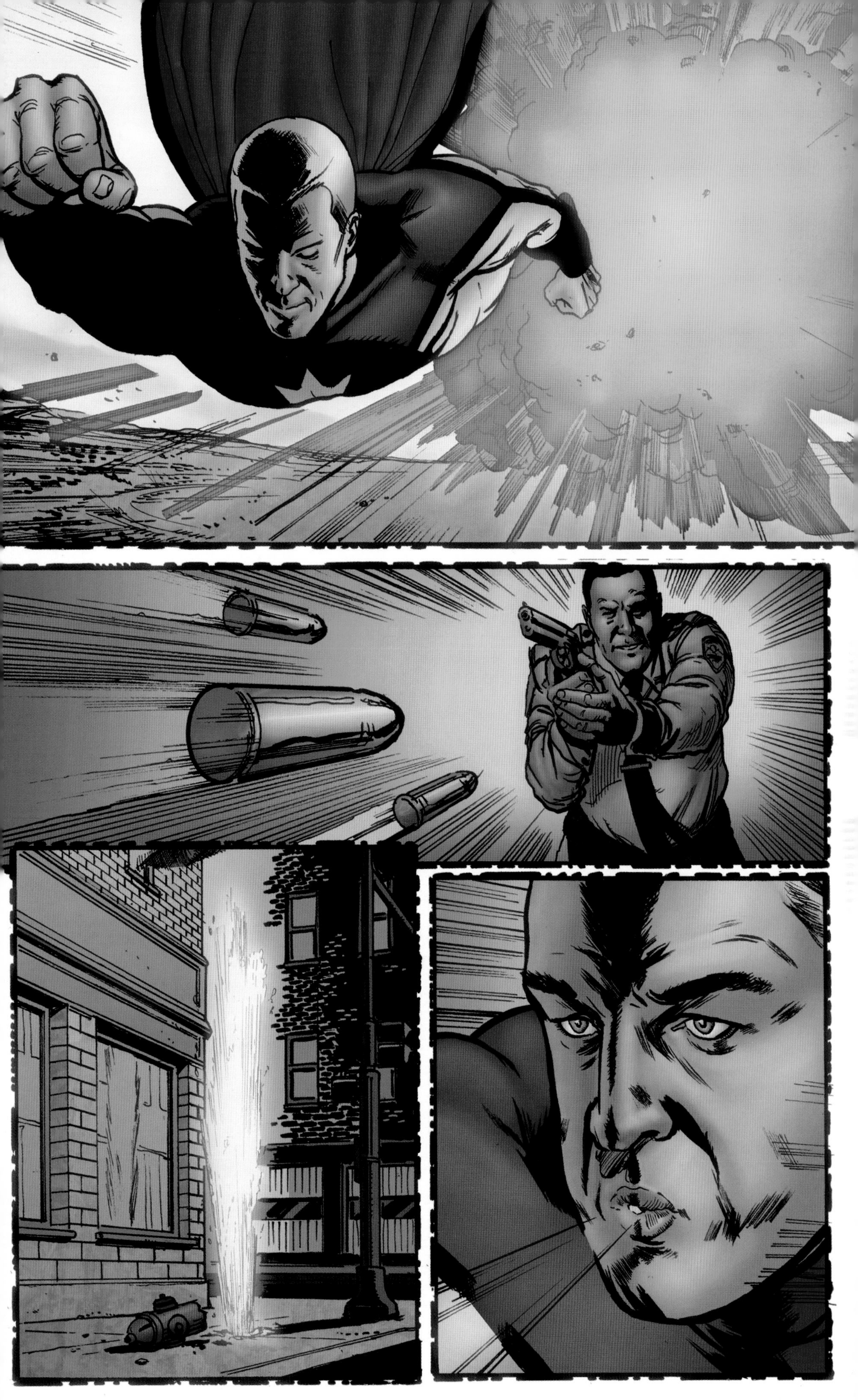

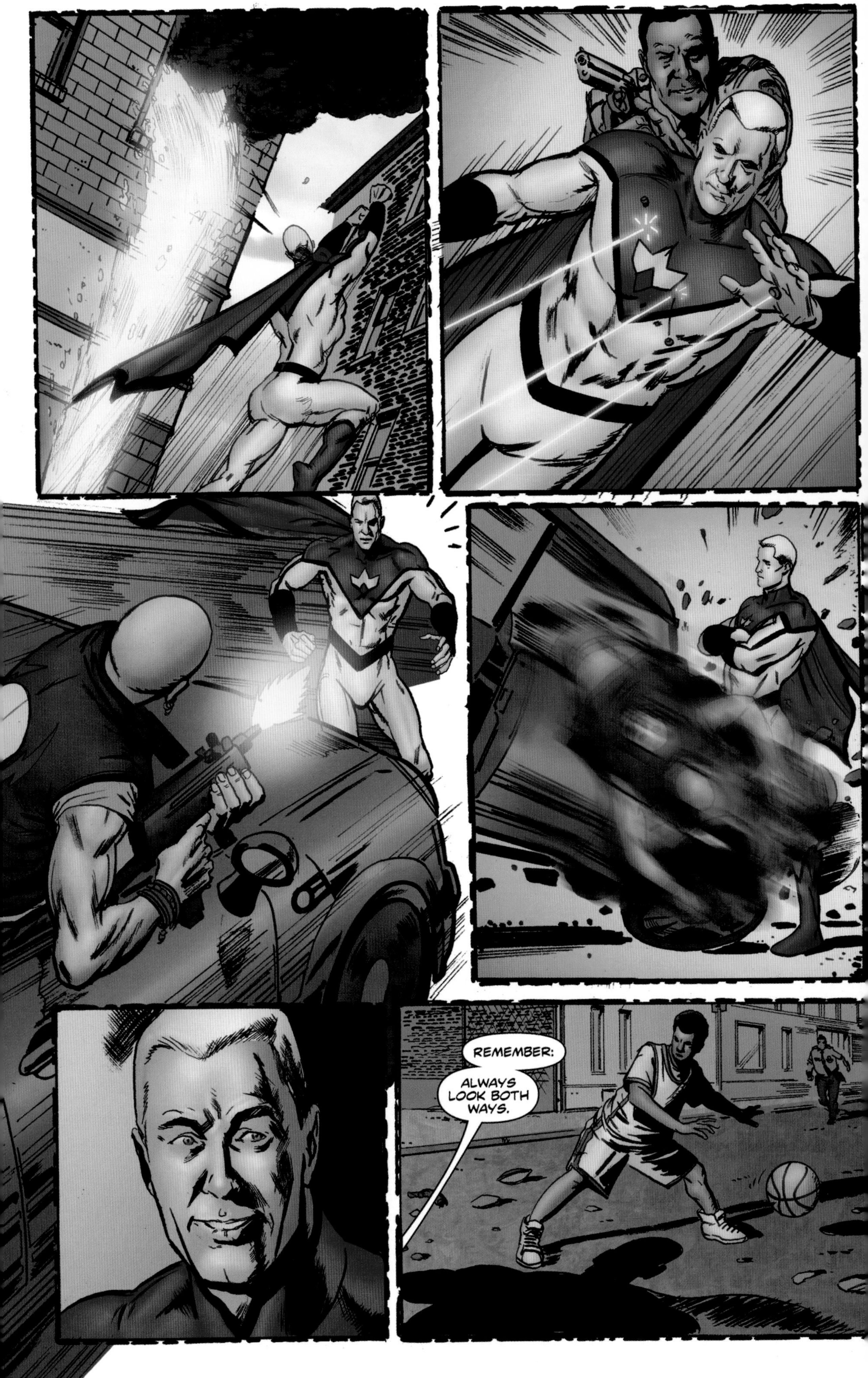
REMEMBER:
ALWAYS LOOK BOTH WAYS.

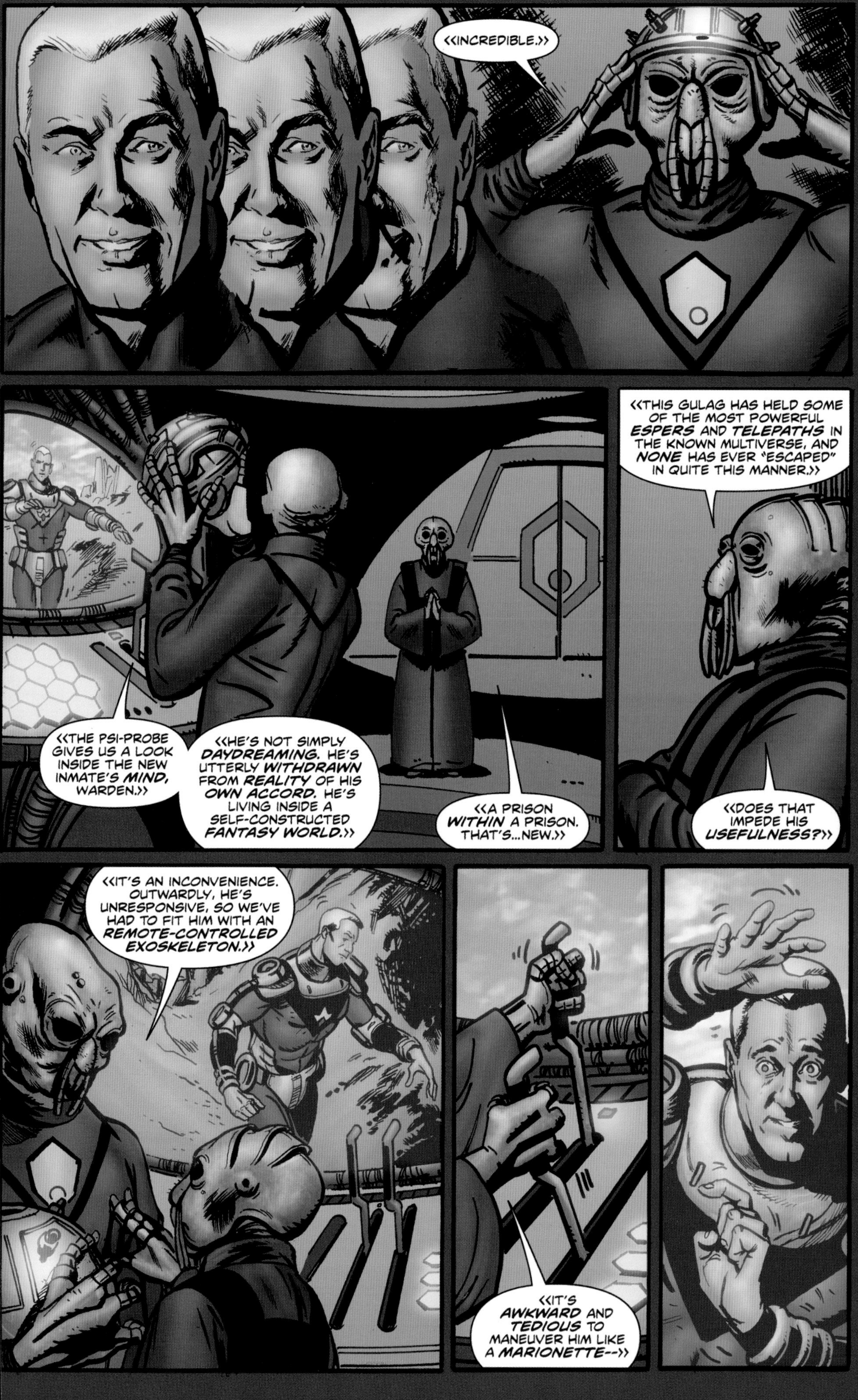

<<INCREDIBLE.>>
<<THE PSI-PROBE GIVES US A LOOK INSIDE THE NEW INMATE'S MIND, WARDEN.>>
<<HE'S NOT SIMPLY DAYDREAMING. HE'S UTTERLY WITHDRAWN FROM REALITY OF HIS OWN ACCORD. HE'S LIVING INSIDE A SELF-CONSTRUCTED FANTASY WORLD.>>
<<A PRISON WITHIN A PRISON. THAT'S...NEW.>>
<<THIS GULAG HAS HELD SOME OF THE MOST POWERFUL ESPERS AND TELEPATHS IN THE KNOWN MULTIVERSE, AND NONE HAS EVER "ESCAPED" IN QUITE THIS MANNER.>>
<<DOES THAT IMPEDE HIS USEFULNESS?>>
<<IT'S AN INCONVENIENCE. OUTWARDLY, HE'S UNRESPONSIVE, SO WE'VE HAD TO FIT HIM WITH AN REMOTE-CONTROLLED EXOSKELETON.>>
<<IT'S AWKWARD AND TEDIOUS TO MANEUVER HIM LIKE A MARIONETTE-->>

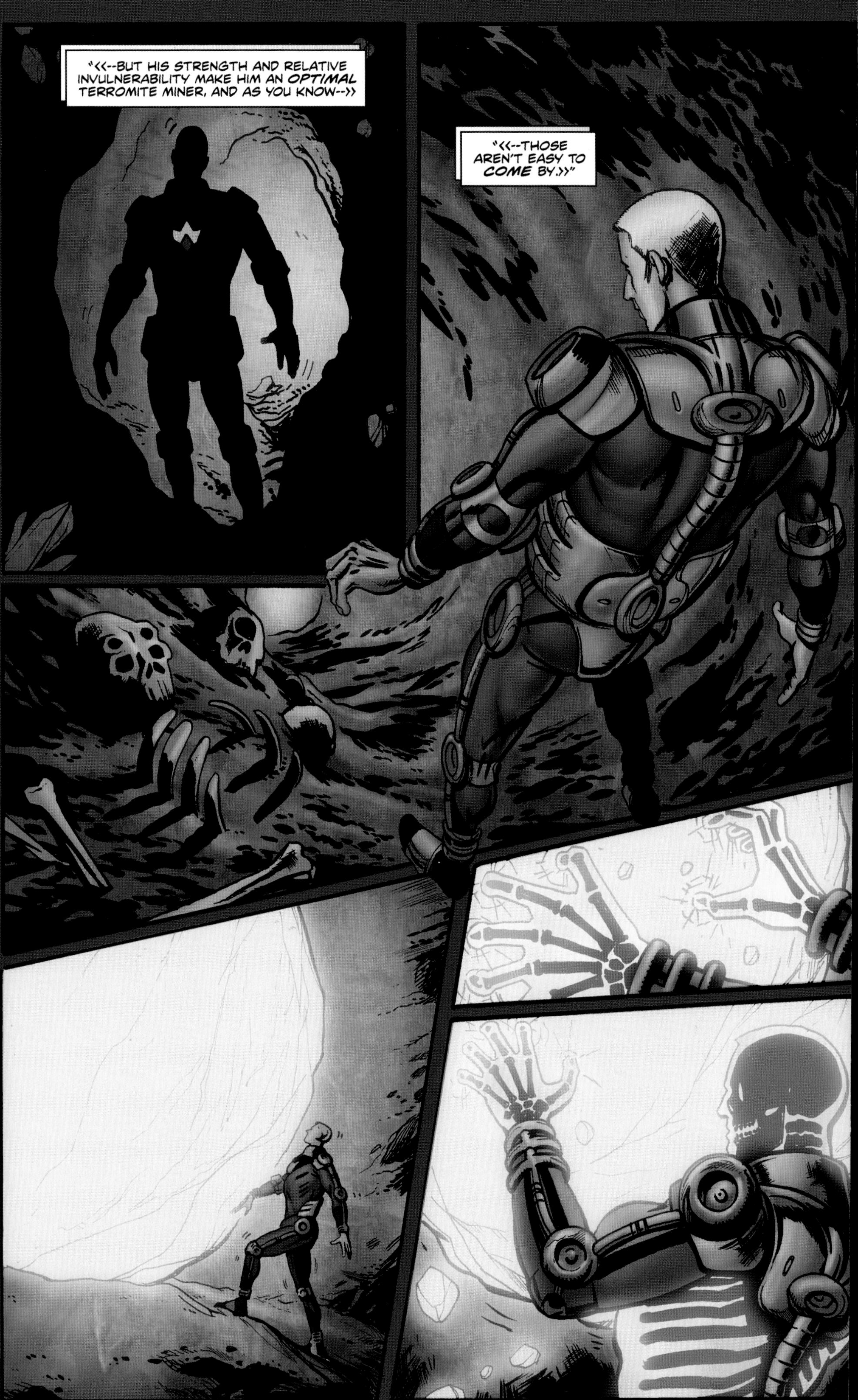
"<<--BUT HIS STRENGTH AND RELATIVE INVULNERABILITY MAKE HIM AN *OPTIMAL* TERROMITE MINER, AND AS YOU KNOW-->>
"<<--THOSE AREN'T EASY TO *COME* BY.>>"

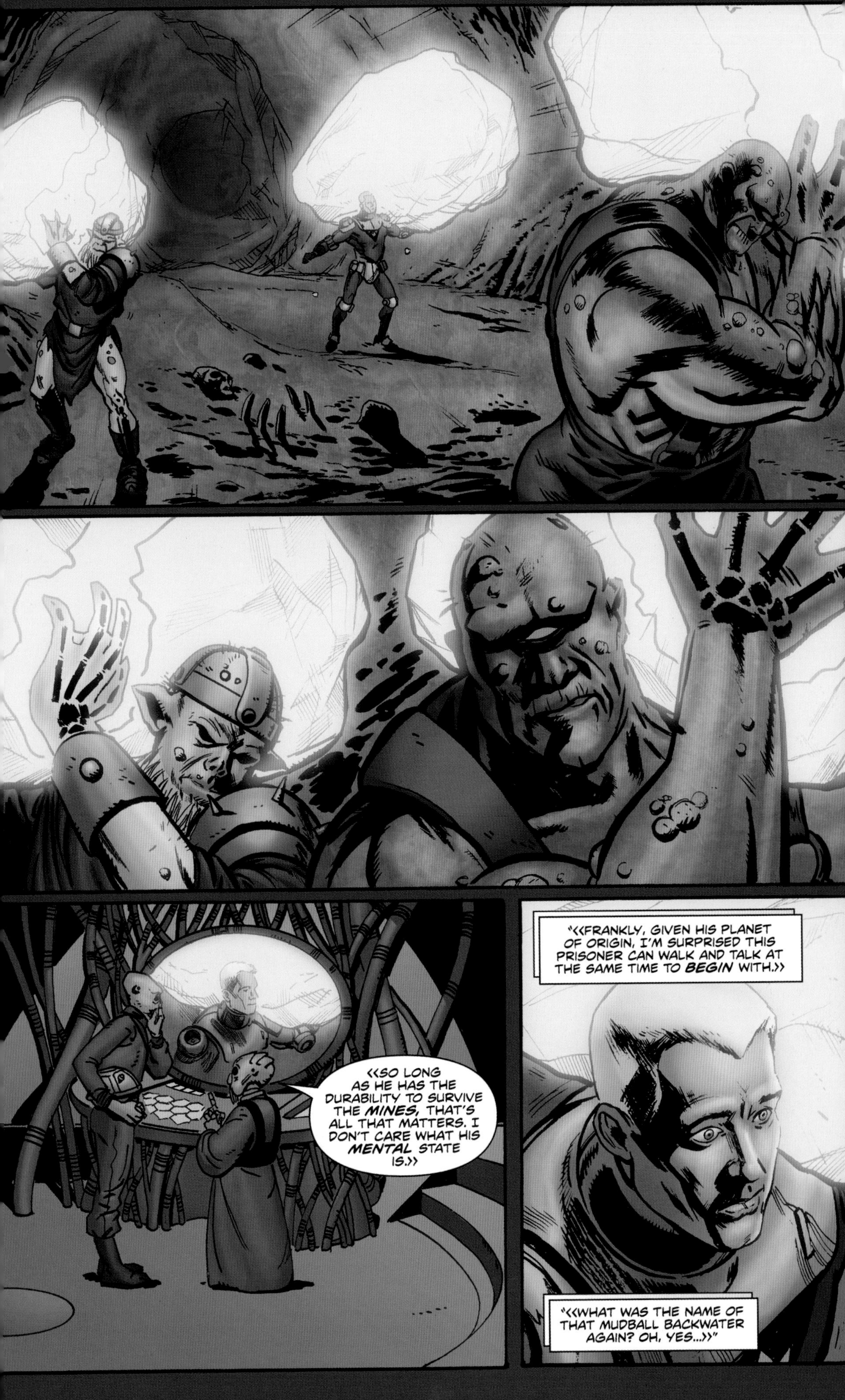
"<<FRANKLY, GIVEN HIS PLANET OF ORIGIN, I'M SURPRISED THIS PRISONER CAN WALK AND TALK AT THE SAME TIME TO BEGIN WITH.>>
<<SO LONG AS HE HAS THE DURABILITY TO SURVIVE THE MINES, THAT'S ALL THAT MATTERS. I DON'T CARE WHAT HIS MENTAL STATE IS.>>
"<<WHAT WAS THE NAME OF THAT MUDBALL BACKWATER AGAIN? OH, YES...>>"

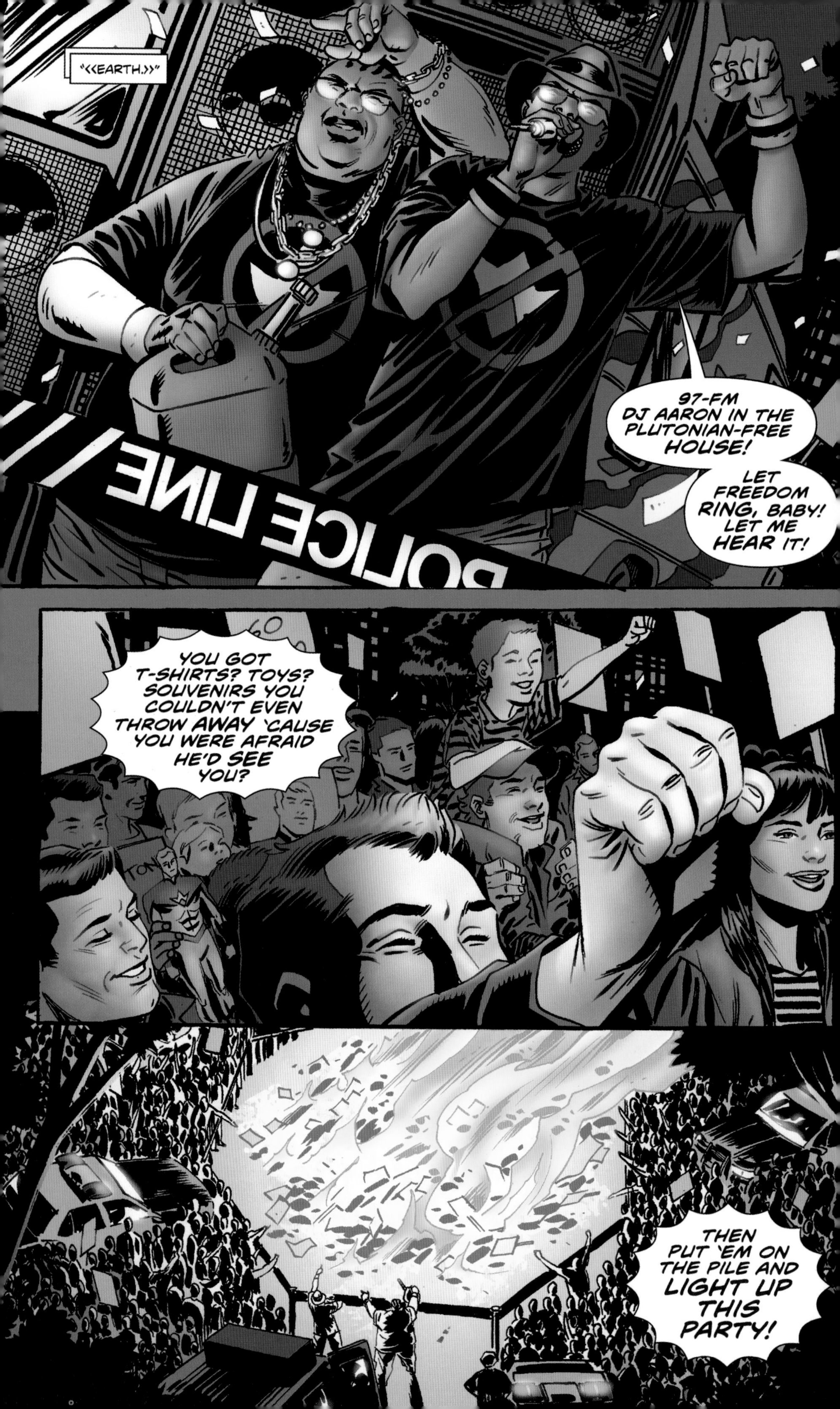
"<<EARTH.>>"
97-FM DJ AARON IN THE PLUTONIAN-FREE HOUSE!
LET FREEDOM RING, BABY! LET ME HEAR IT!
POLICE LINE
YOU GOT T-SHIRTS? TOYS? SOUVENIRS YOU COULDN'T EVEN THROW AWAY 'CAUSE YOU WERE AFRAID HE'D SEE YOU?
THEN PUT 'EM ON THE PILE AND LIGHT UP THIS PARTY!

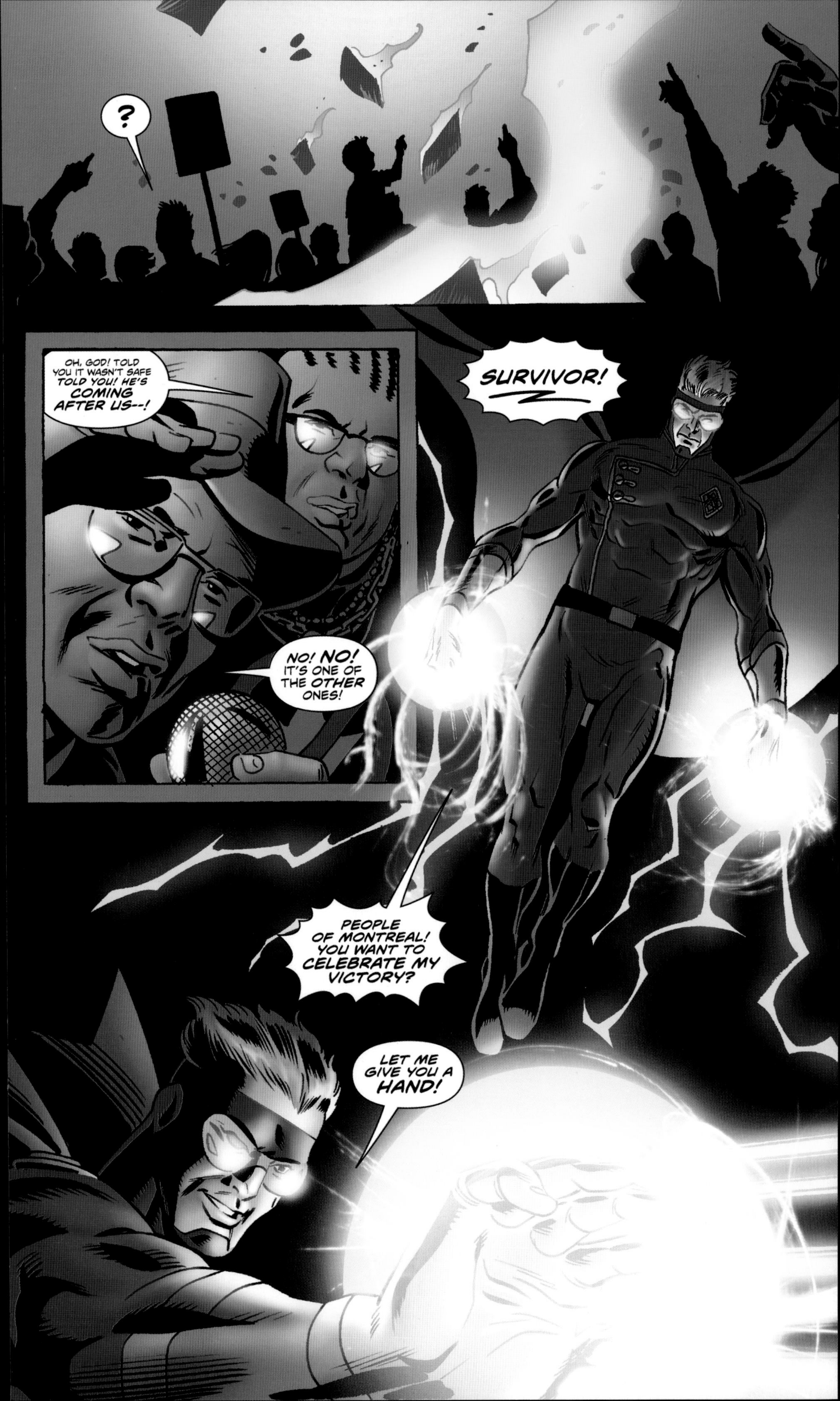
?
OH, GOD! TOLD YOU IT WASN'T SAFE TOLD YOU! HE'S COMING AFTER US--!
SURVIVOR!
NO! NO! IT'S ONE OF THE OTHER ONES!
PEOPLE OF MONTREAL! YOU WANT TO CELEBRATE MY VICTORY?
LET ME GIVE YOU A HAND!

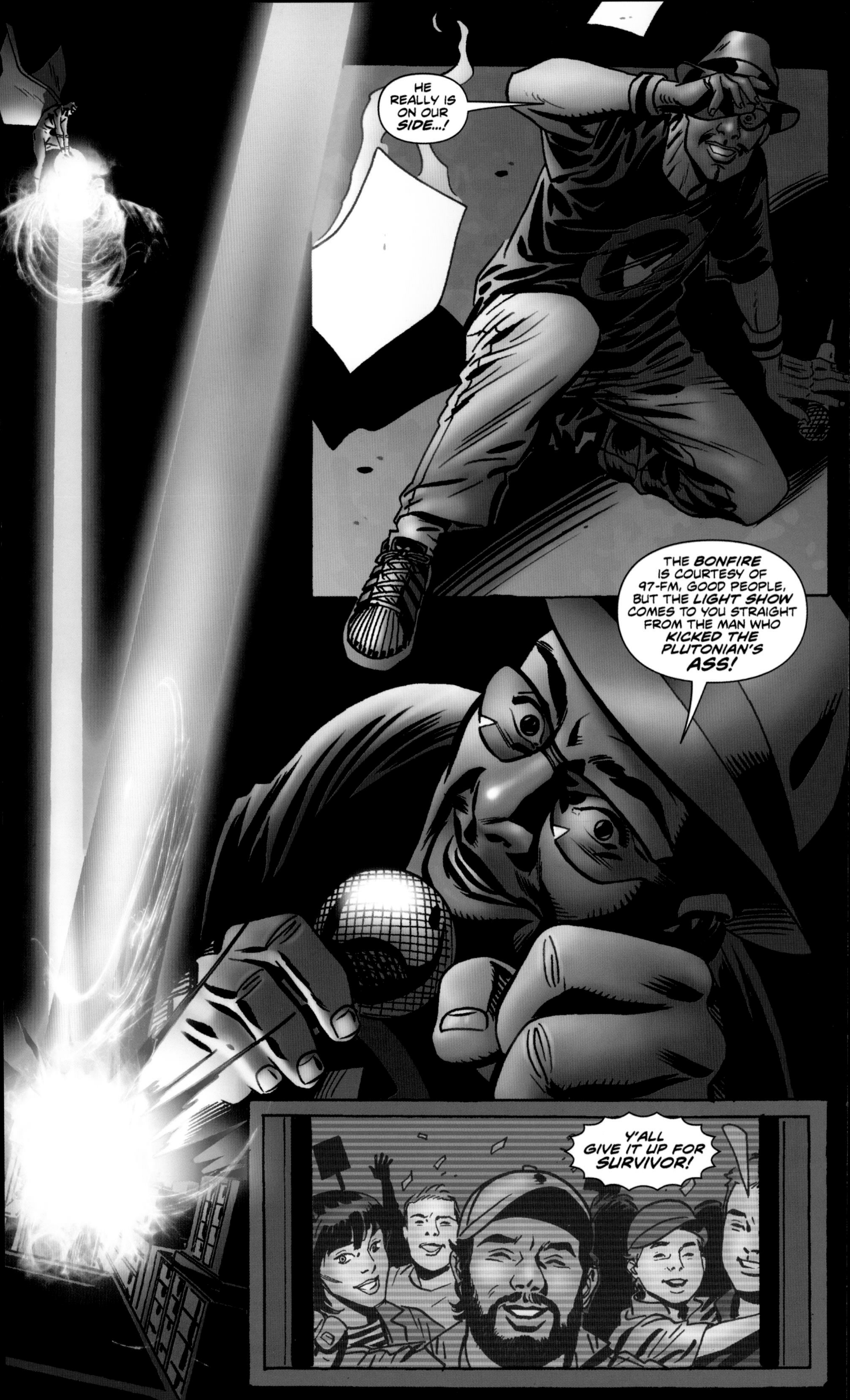
HE REALLY IS ON OUR SIDE...!
THE BONFIRE IS COURTESY OF 97-FM, GOOD PEOPLE, BUT THE LIGHT SHOW COMES TO YOU STRAIGHT FROM THE MAN WHO KICKED THE PLUTONIAN'S ASS!
Y'ALL GIVE IT UP FOR SURVIVOR!

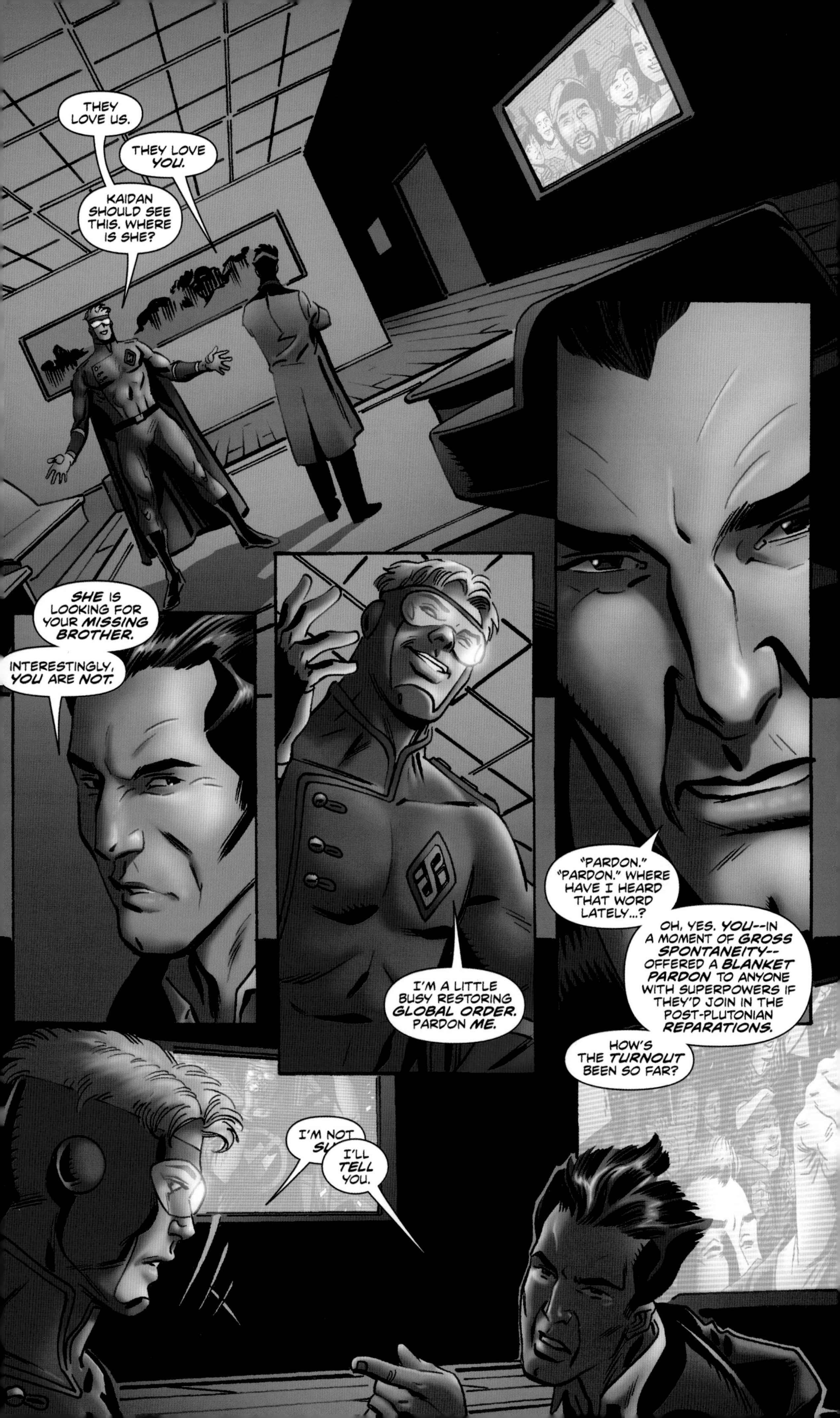
THEY LOVE US.
THEY LOVE YOU.
KAIDAN SHOULD SEE THIS. WHERE IS SHE?
SHE IS LOOKING FOR YOUR MISSING BROTHER.
INTERESTINGLY, YOU ARE NOT.
I'M A LITTLE BUSY RESTORING GLOBAL ORDER. PARDON ME.
"PARDON." "PARDON." WHERE HAVE I HEARD THAT WORD LATELY...?
OH, YES. YOU--IN A MOMENT OF GROSS SPONTANEITY--OFFERED A BLANKET PARDON TO ANYONE WITH SUPERPOWERS IF THEY'D JOIN IN THE POST-PLUTONIAN REPARATIONS.
HOW'S THE TURNOUT BEEN SO FAR?
I'M NOT SU
I'LL TELL YOU.

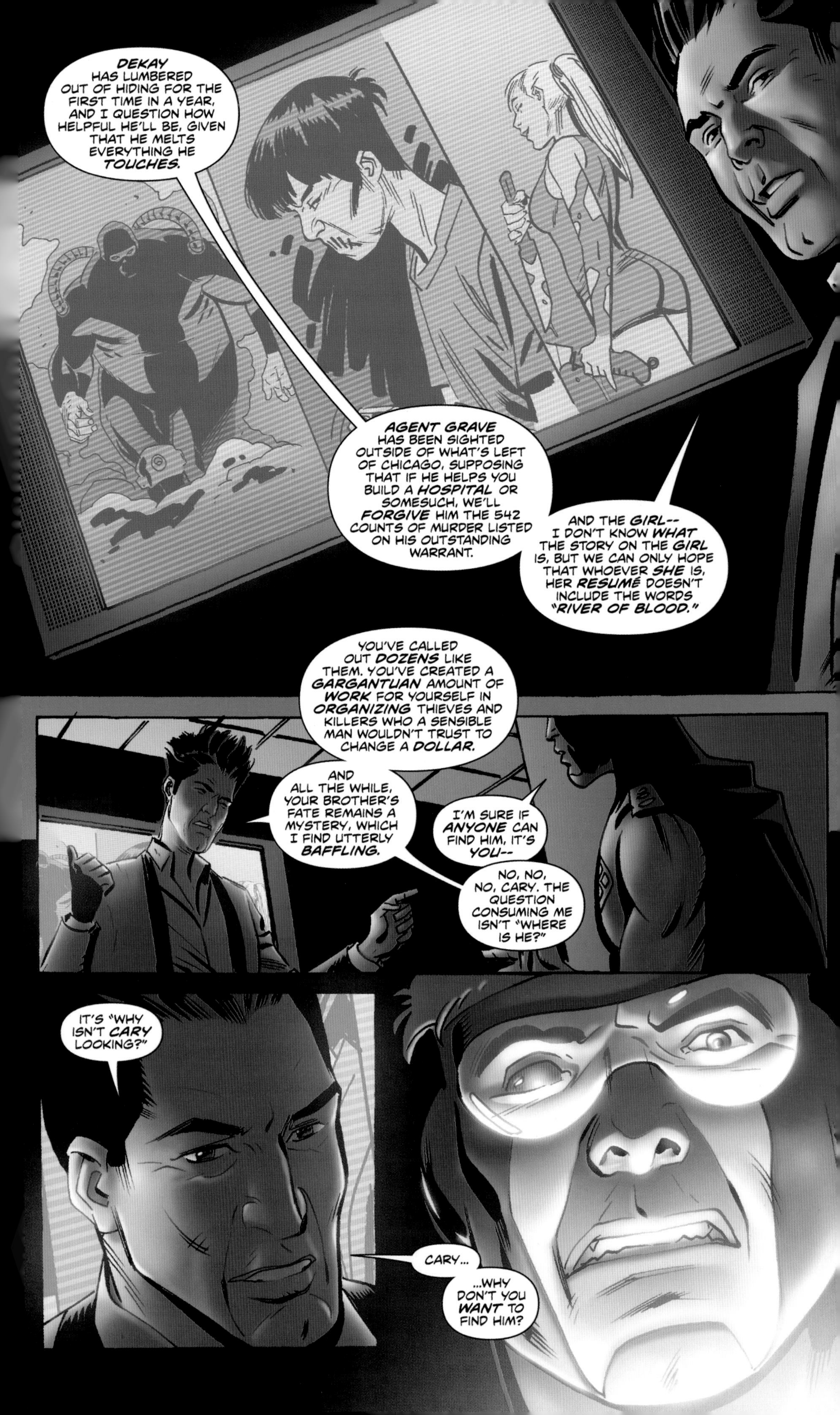
DEKAY HAS LUMBERED OUT OF HIDING FOR THE FIRST TIME IN A YEAR, AND I QUESTION HOW HELPFUL HE'LL BE, GIVEN THAT HE MELTS EVERYTHING HE TOUCHES.
AGENT GRAVE HAS BEEN SIGHTED OUTSIDE OF WHAT'S LEFT OF CHICAGO, SUPPOSING THAT IF HE HELPS YOU BUILD A HOSPITAL OR SOMESUCH, WE'LL FORGIVE HIM THE 542 COUNTS OF MURDER LISTED ON HIS OUTSTANDING WARRANT.
AND THE GIRL-- I DON'T KNOW WHAT THE STORY ON THE GIRL IS, BUT WE CAN ONLY HOPE THAT WHOEVER SHE IS, HER RESUMÉ DOESN'T INCLUDE THE WORDS "RIVER OF BLOOD."
YOU'VE CALLED OUT DOZENS LIKE THEM. YOU'VE CREATED A GARGANTUAN AMOUNT OF WORK FOR YOURSELF IN ORGANIZING THIEVES AND KILLERS WHO A SENSIBLE MAN WOULDN'T TRUST TO CHANGE A DOLLAR.
AND ALL THE WHILE, YOUR BROTHER'S FATE REMAINS A MYSTERY, WHICH I FIND UTTERLY BAFFLING.
I'M SURE IF ANYONE CAN FIND HIM, IT'S YOU--
NO, NO, NO, CARY. THE QUESTION CONSUMING ME ISN'T "WHERE IS HE?"
IT'S "WHY ISN'T CARY LOOKING?"
CARY...
...WHY DON'T YOU WANT TO FIND HIM?

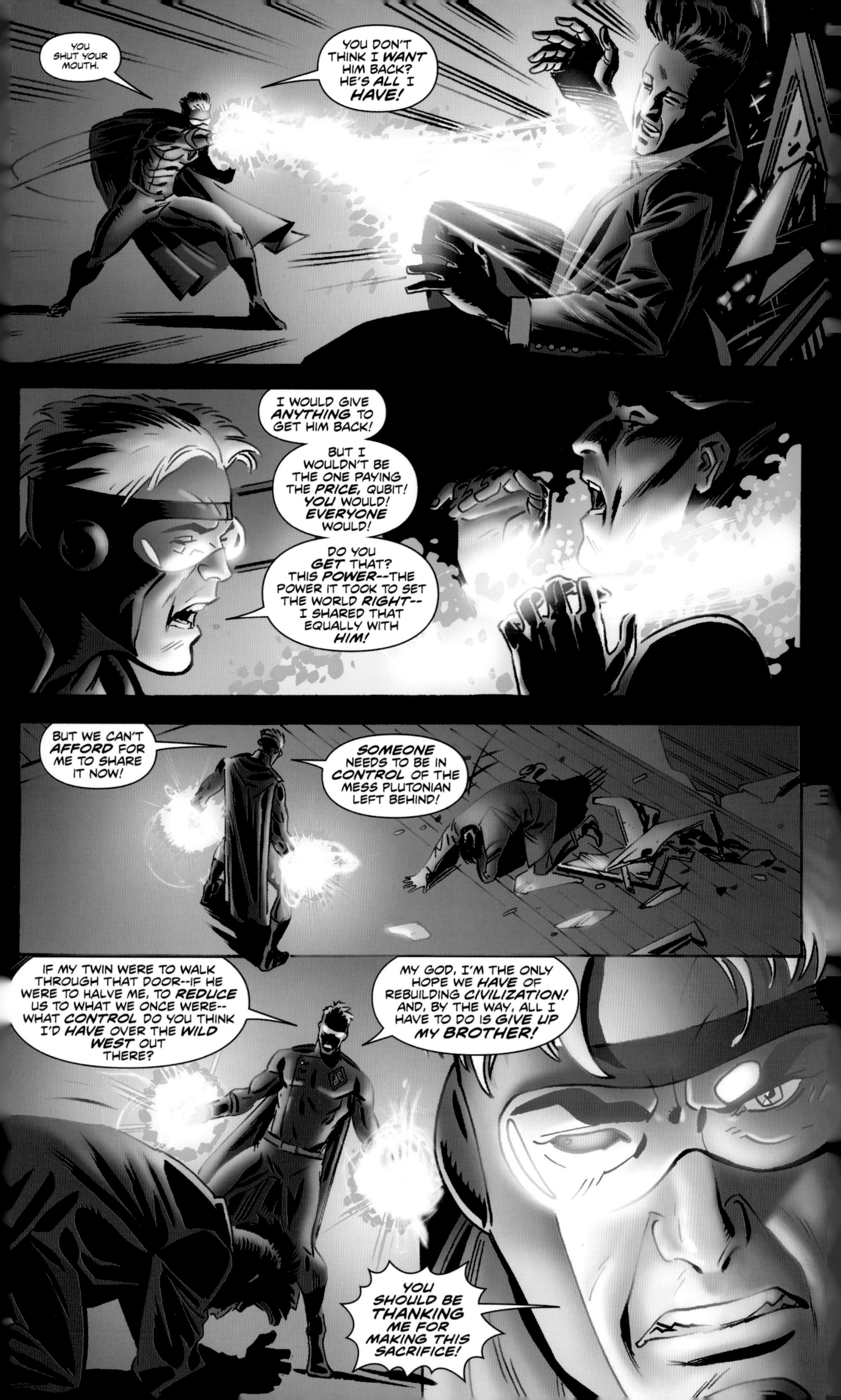
YOU SHUT YOUR MOUTH.
YOU DON'T THINK I WANT HIM BACK? HE'S ALL I HAVE!
I WOULD GIVE ANYTHING TO GET HIM BACK!
BUT I WOULDN'T BE THE ONE PAYING THE PRICE, QUBIT! YOU WOULD! EVERYONE WOULD!
DO YOU GET THAT? THIS POWER--THE POWER IT TOOK TO SET THE WORLD RIGHT-- I SHARED THAT EQUALLY WITH HIM!
BUT WE CAN'T AFFORD FOR ME TO SHARE IT NOW!
SOMEONE NEEDS TO BE IN CONTROL OF THE MESS PLUTONIAN LEFT BEHIND!
IF MY TWIN WERE TO WALK THROUGH THAT DOOR--IF HE WERE TO HALVE ME, TO REDUCE US TO WHAT WE ONCE WERE-- WHAT CONTROL DO YOU THINK I'D HAVE OVER THE WILD WEST OUT THERE?
MY GOD, I'M THE ONLY HOPE WE HAVE OF REBUILDING CIVILIZATION! AND, BY THE WAY, ALL I HAVE TO DO IS GIVE UP MY BROTHER!
YOU SHOULD BE THANKING ME FOR MAKING THIS SACRIFICE!

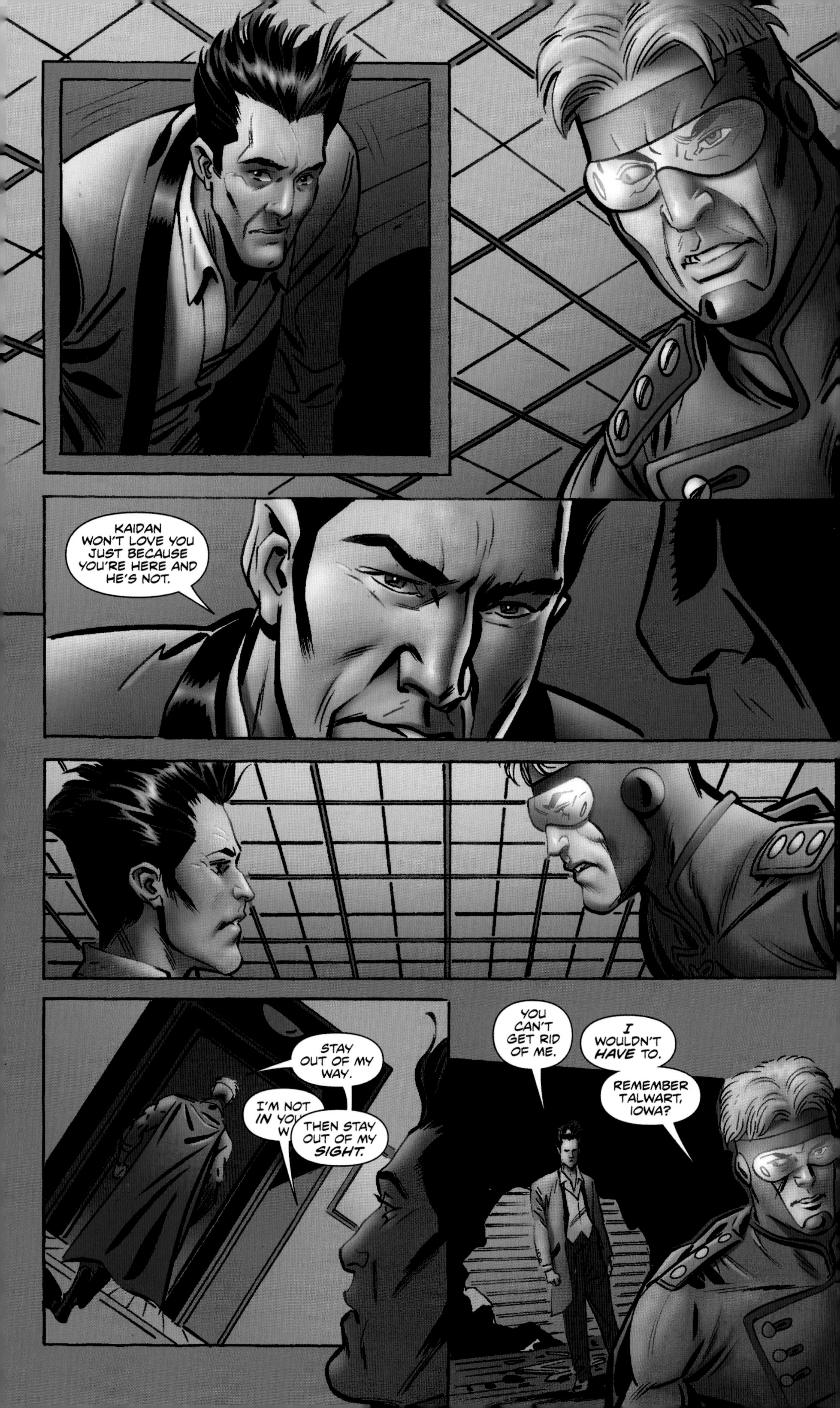

KAIDAN WON'T LOVE YOU JUST BECAUSE YOU'RE HERE AND HE'S NOT.
STAY OUT OF MY WAY.
I'M NOT IN YOU W
THEN STAY OUT OF MY SIGHT.
YOU CAN'T GET RID OF ME.
I WOULDN'T HAVE TO.
REMEMBER TALWART, IOWA?

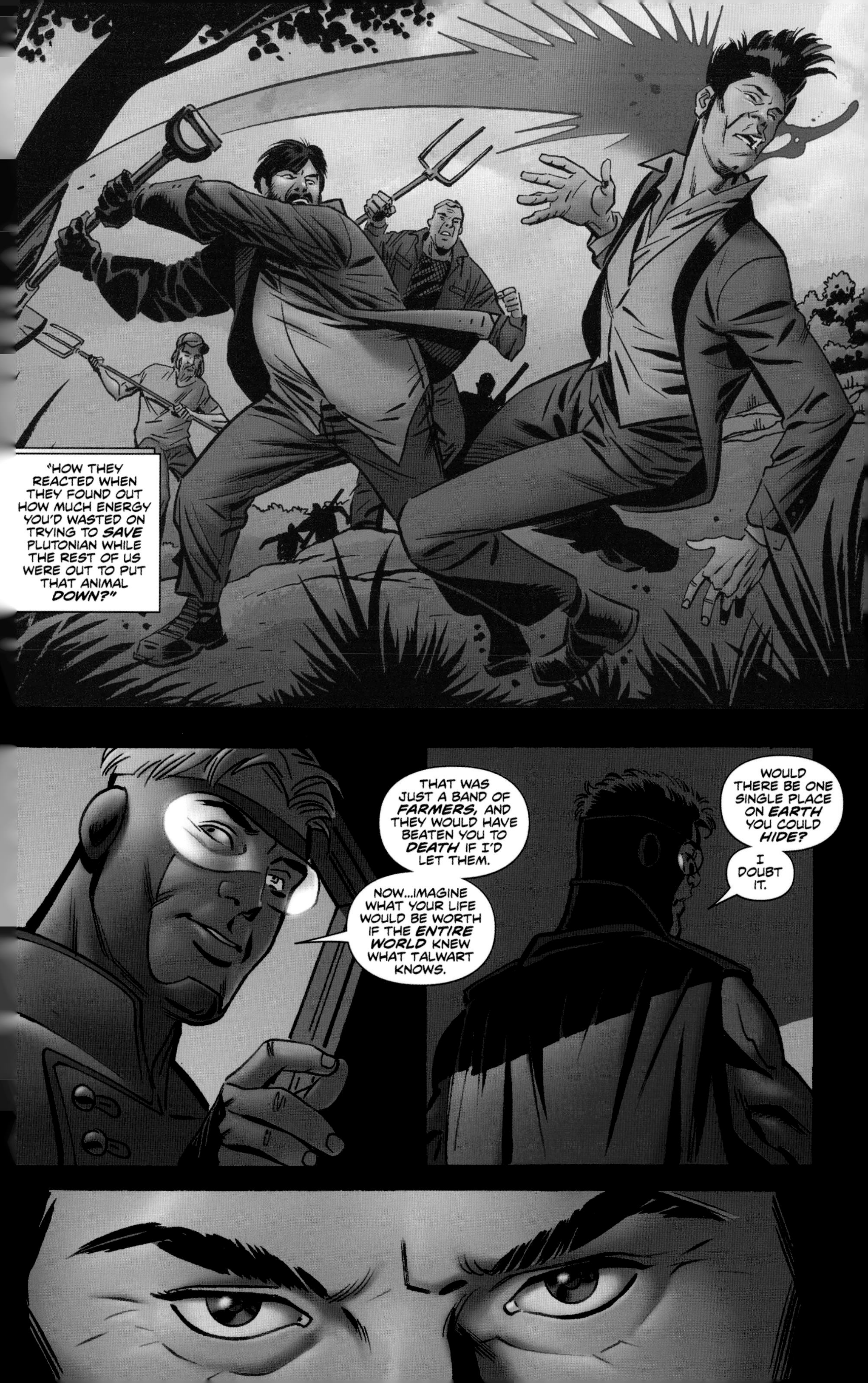
"HOW THEY REACTED WHEN THEY FOUND OUT HOW MUCH ENERGY YOU'D WASTED ON TRYING TO SAVE PLUTONIAN WHILE THE REST OF US WERE OUT TO PUT THAT ANIMAL DOWN?"
THAT WAS JUST A BAND OF FARMERS, AND THEY WOULD HAVE BEATEN YOU TO DEATH IF I'D LET THEM.
NOW...IMAGINE WHAT YOUR LIFE WOULD BE WORTH IF THE ENTIRE WORLD KNEW WHAT TALWART KNOWS.
WOULD THERE BE ONE SINGLE PLACE ON EARTH YOU COULD HIDE?
I DOUBT IT.

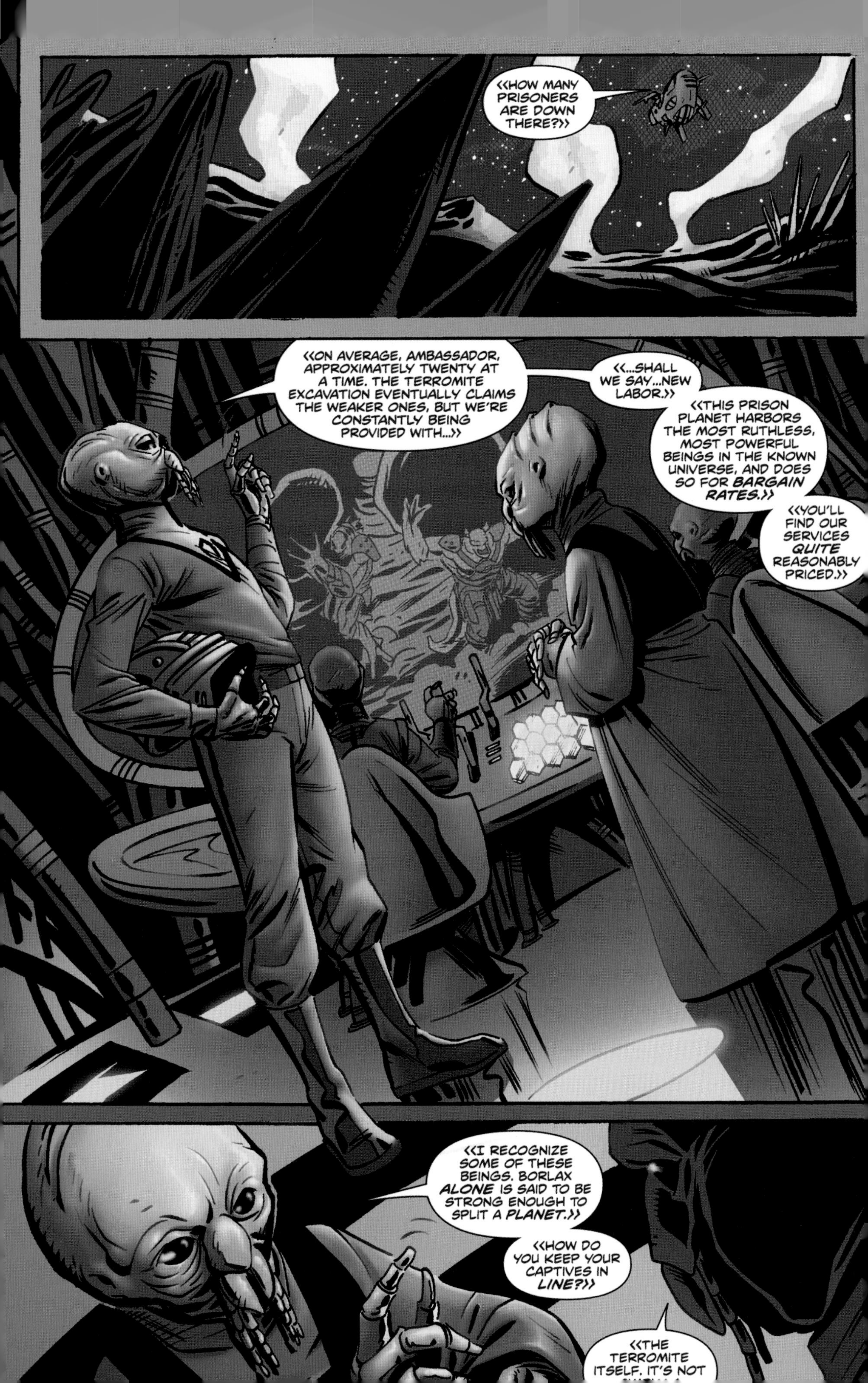
<<HOW MANY PRISONERS ARE DOWN THERE?>>
<<ON AVERAGE, AMBASSADOR, APPROXIMATELY TWENTY AT A TIME. THE TERROMITE EXCAVATION EVENTUALLY CLAIMS THE WEAKER ONES, BUT WE'RE CONSTANTLY BEING PROVIDED WITH...>>
<<...SHALL WE SAY...NEW LABOR.>>
<<THIS PRISON PLANET HARBORS THE MOST RUTHLESS, MOST POWERFUL BEINGS IN THE KNOWN UNIVERSE, AND DOES SO FOR ***BARGAIN RATES.***>>
<<YOU'LL FIND OUR SERVICES ***QUITE*** REASONABLY PRICED.>>
<<I RECOGNIZE SOME OF THESE BEINGS. BORLAX ***ALONE*** IS SAID TO BE STRONG ENOUGH TO SPLIT A ***PLANET.***>>
<<HOW DO YOU KEEP YOUR CAPTIVES IN ***LINE?***>>
<<THE TERROMITE ITSELF. IT'S NOT

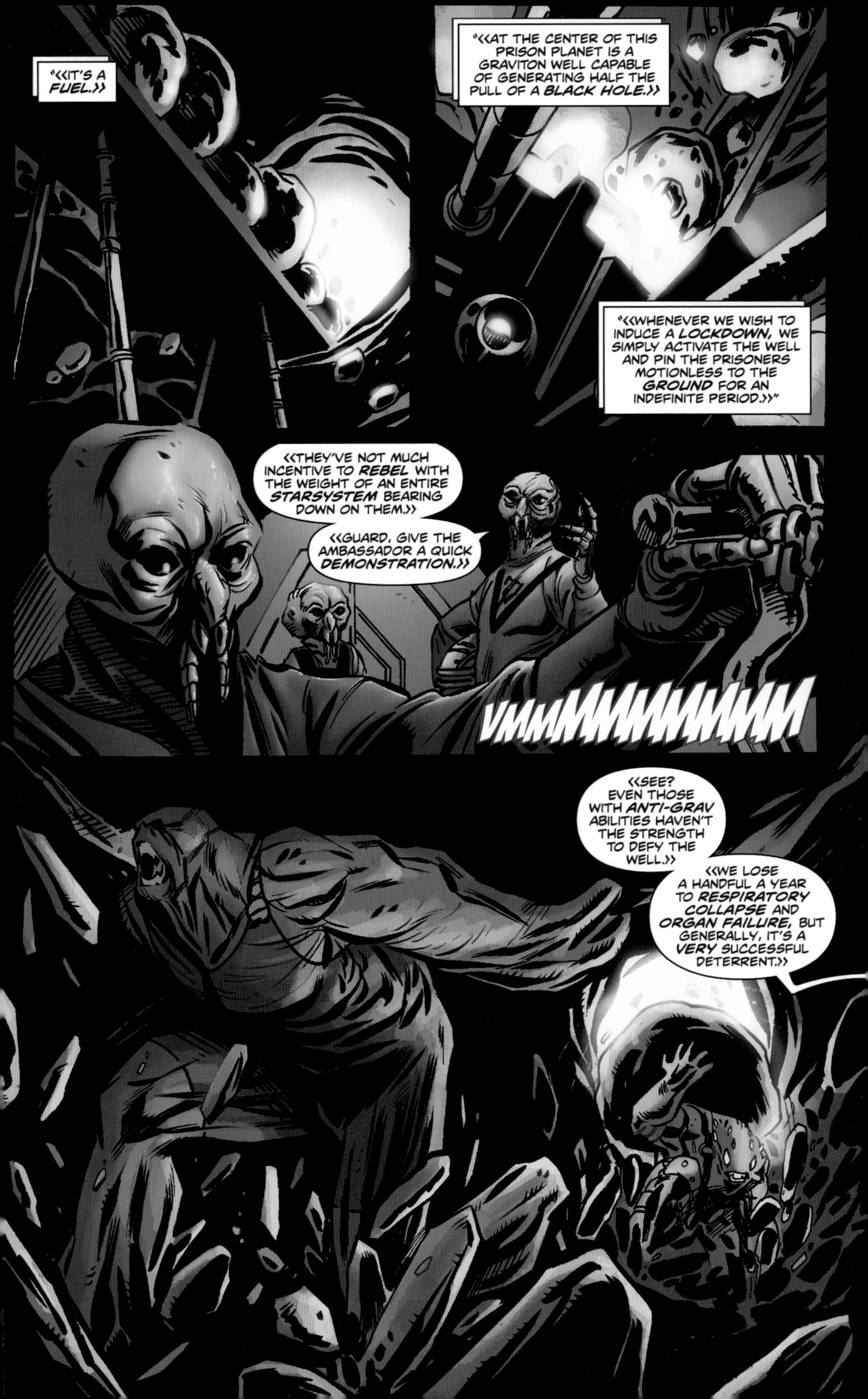
"<<IT'S A FUEL.>>
"<<AT THE CENTER OF THIS PRISON PLANET IS A GRAVITON WELL CAPABLE OF GENERATING HALF THE PULL OF A BLACK HOLE.>>
"<<WHENEVER WE WISH TO INDUCE A LOCKDOWN, WE SIMPLY ACTIVATE THE WELL AND PIN THE PRISONERS MOTIONLESS TO THE GROUND FOR AN INDEFINITE PERIOD.>>"
<<THEY'VE NOT MUCH INCENTIVE TO REBEL WITH THE WEIGHT OF AN ENTIRE STARSYSTEM BEARING DOWN ON THEM.>>
<<GUARD, GIVE THE AMBASSADOR A QUICK DEMONSTRATION.>>
VMMMMMMMMMM
<<SEE? EVEN THOSE WITH ANTI-GRAV ABILITIES HAVEN'T THE STRENGTH TO DEFY THE WELL.>>
<<WE LOSE A HANDFUL A YEAR TO RESPIRATORY COLLAPSE AND ORGAN FAILURE, BUT GENERALLY, IT'S A VERY SUCCESSFUL DETERRENT.>>

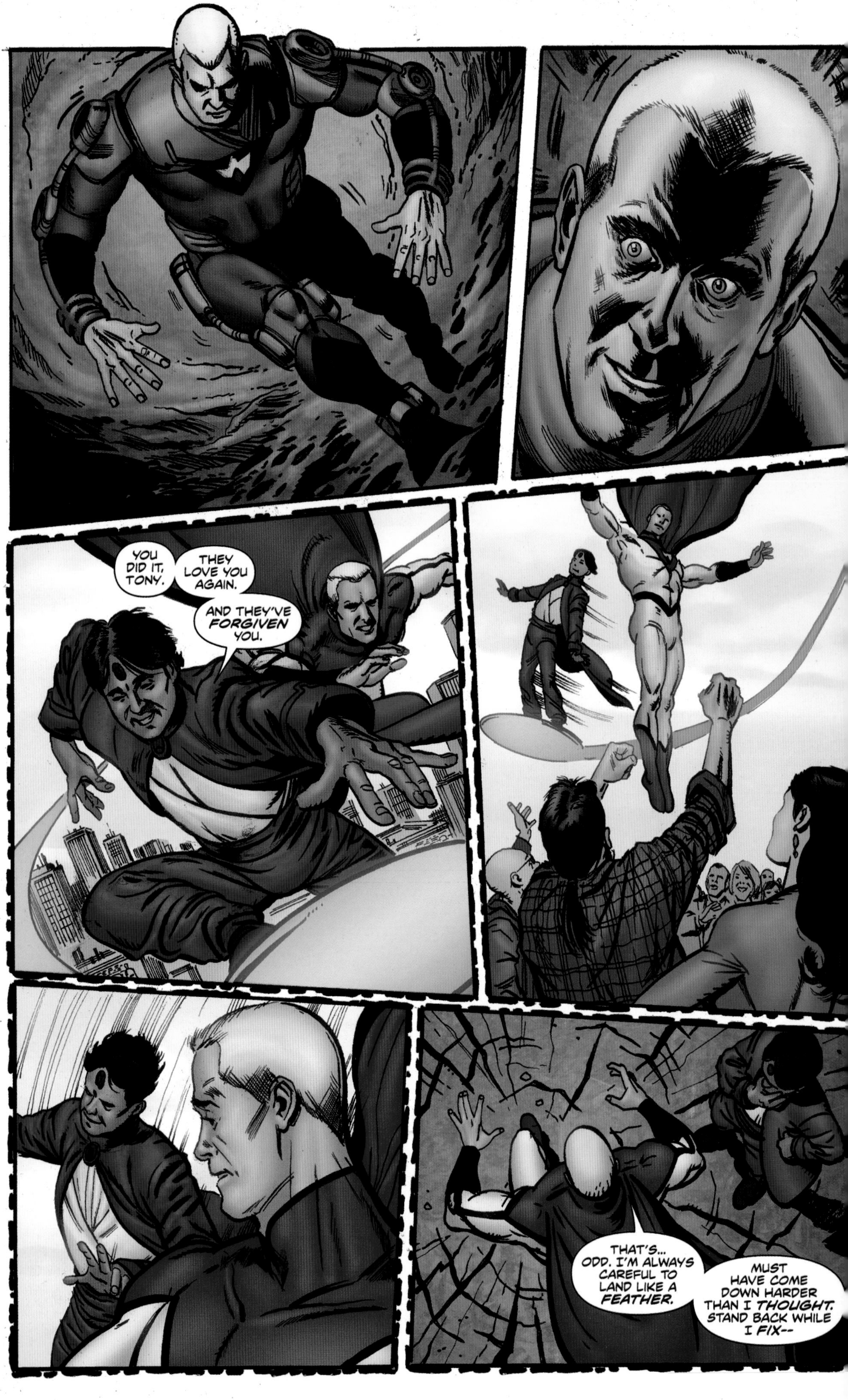
YOU DID IT, TONY.
THEY LOVE YOU AGAIN.
AND THEY'VE FORGIVEN YOU.
THAT'S... ODD. I'M ALWAYS CAREFUL TO LAND LIKE A FEATHER.
MUST HAVE COME DOWN HARDER THAN I THOUGHT. STAND BACK WHILE I FIX--

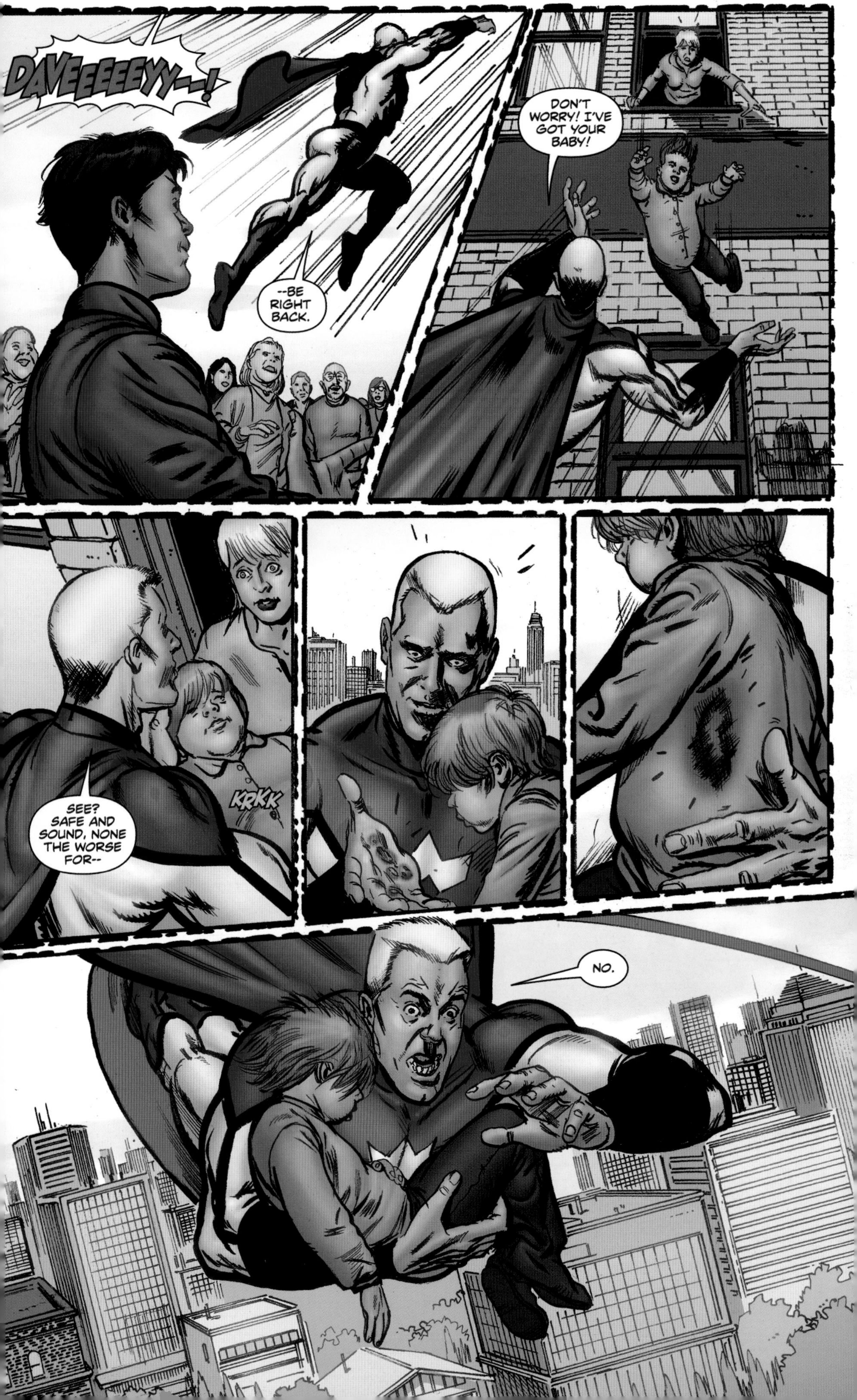
DAVEEEEEYY--!
--BE RIGHT BACK.
DON'T WORRY! I'VE GOT YOUR BABY!
SEE? SAFE AND SOUND, NONE THE WORSE FOR--
KRKK
NO.

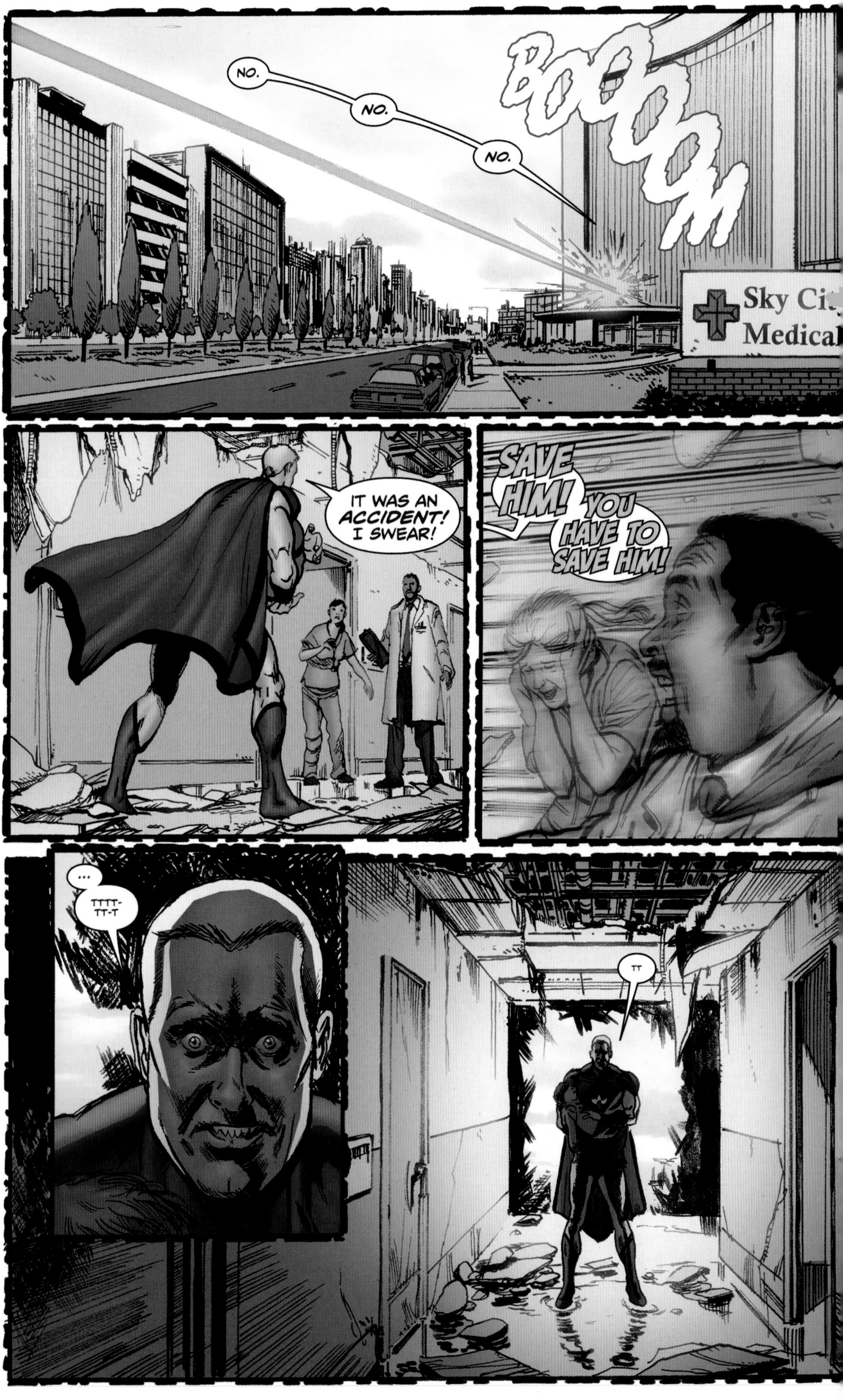
NO.
NO.
NO.
BOOOOM
Sky Ci
Medical
IT WAS AN ACCIDENT! I SWEAR!
SAVE HIM!
YOU HAVE TO SAVE HIM!
...
TTTT-TT-T
TT

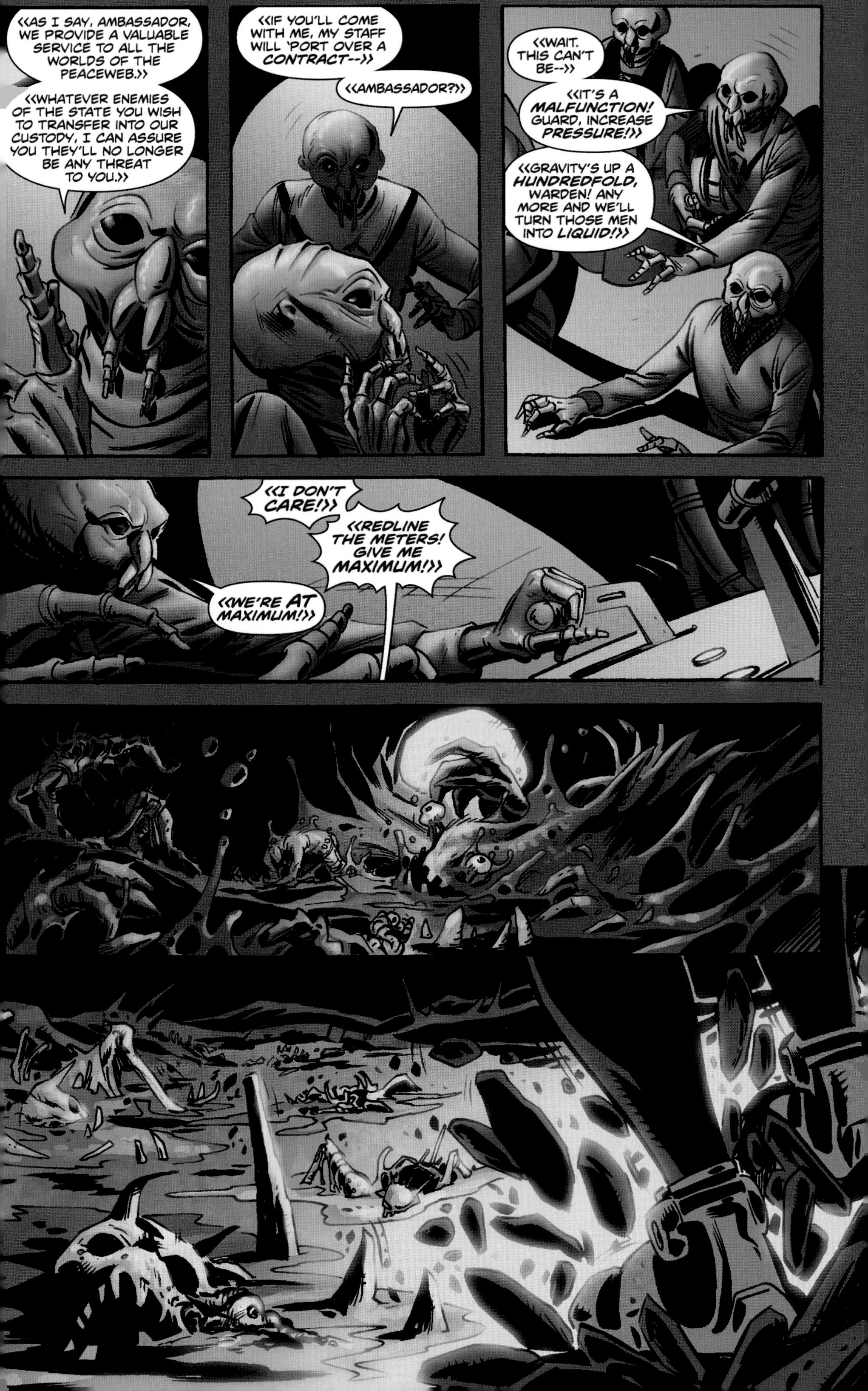
<<AS I SAY, AMBASSADOR, WE PROVIDE A VALUABLE SERVICE TO ALL THE WORLDS OF THE PEACEWEB.>>
<<WHATEVER ENEMIES OF THE STATE YOU WISH TO TRANSFER INTO OUR CUSTODY, I CAN ASSURE YOU THEY'LL NO LONGER BE ANY THREAT TO YOU.>>
<<IF YOU'LL COME WITH ME, MY STAFF WILL 'PORT OVER A CONTRACT-->>
<<AMBASSADOR?>>
<<WAIT. THIS CAN'T BE-->>
<<IT'S A MALFUNCTION! GUARD, INCREASE PRESSURE!>>
<<GRAVITY'S UP A HUNDREDFOLD, WARDEN! ANY MORE AND WE'LL TURN THOSE MEN INTO LIQUID!>>
<<I DON'T CARE!>>
<<REDLINE THE METERS! GIVE ME MAXIMUM!>>
<<WE'RE AT MAXIMUM!>>

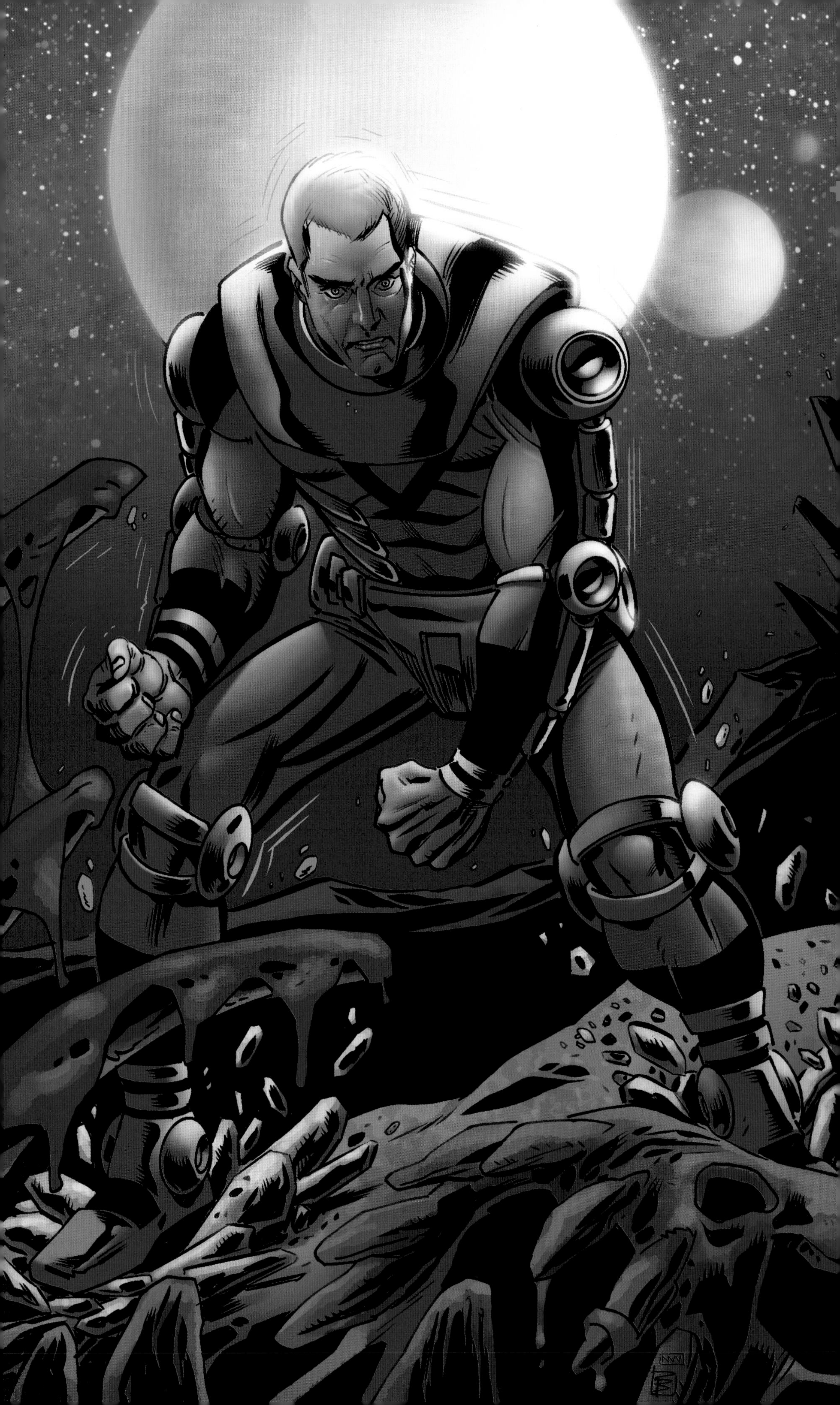

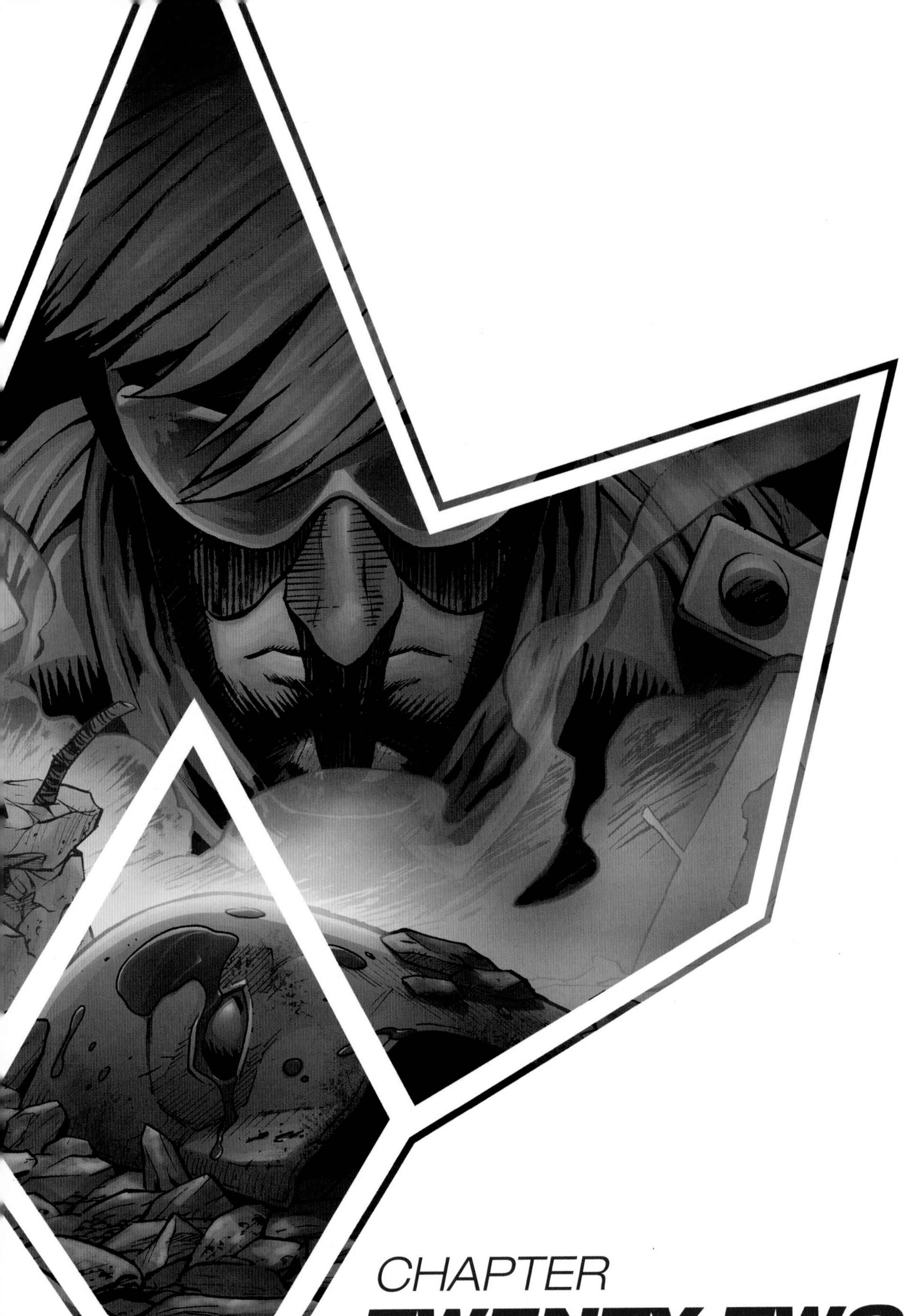

CHAPTER
TWENTY-TWO

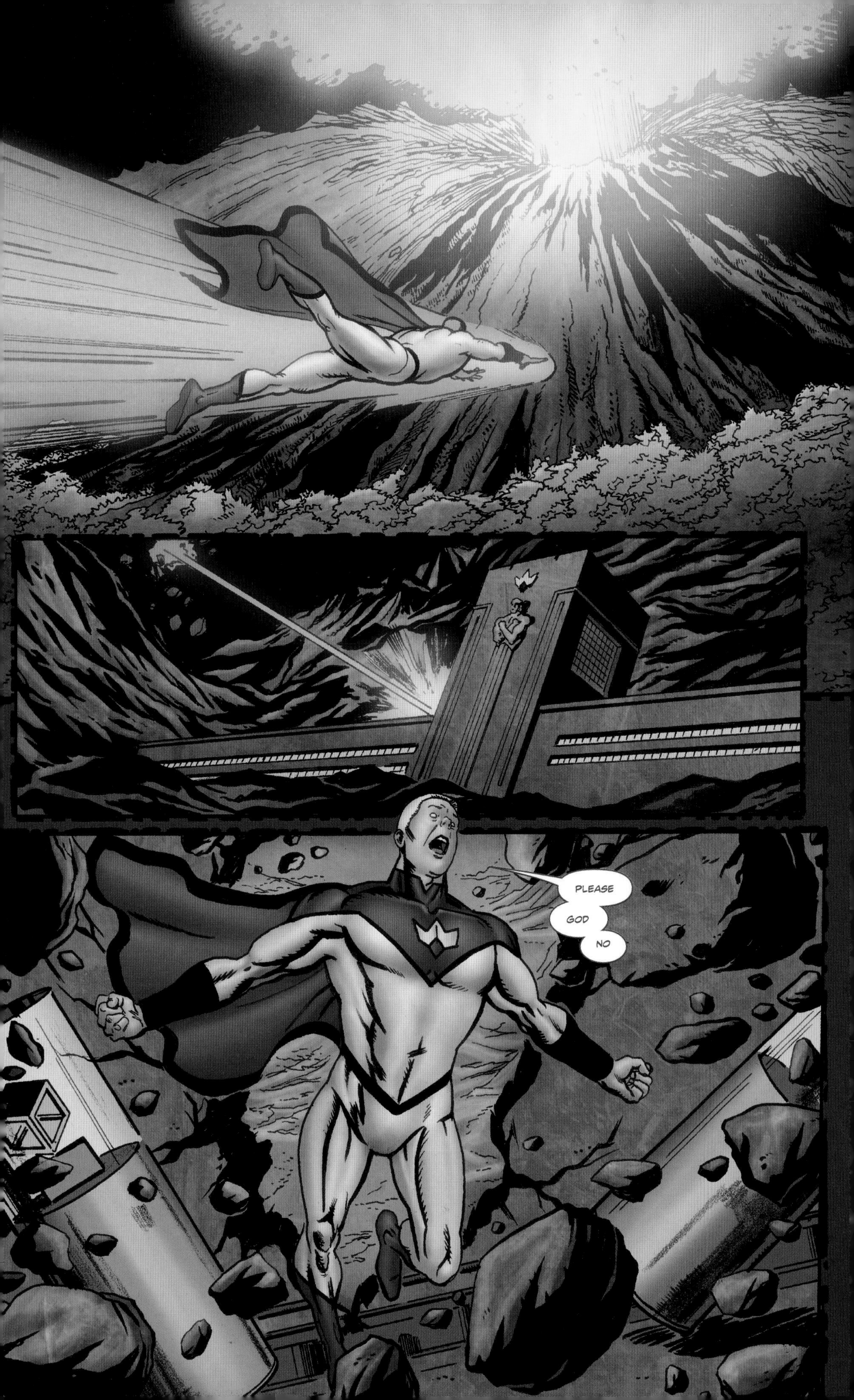
PLEASE
GOD
NO

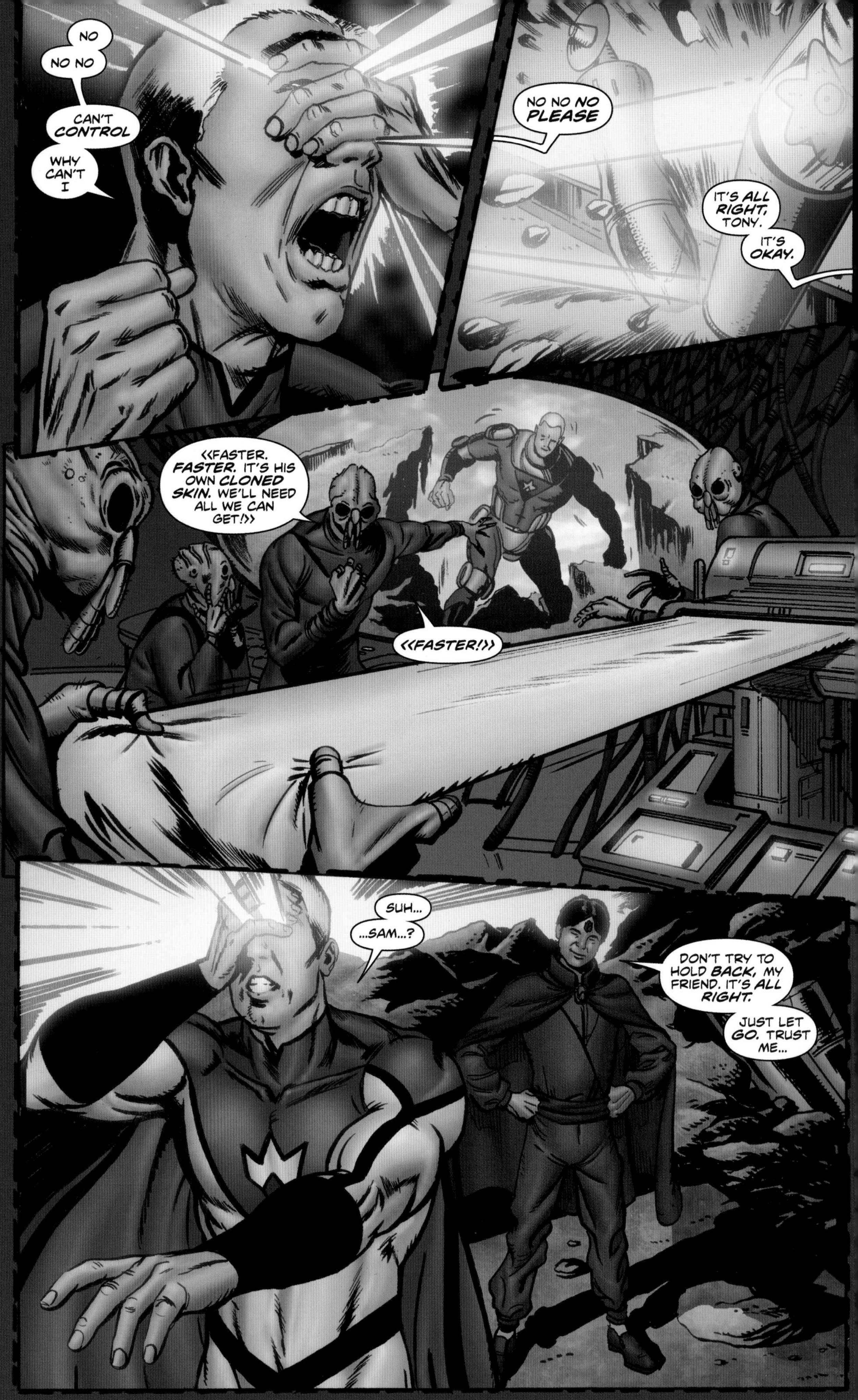
NO
NO NO
CAN'T CONTROL
WHY CAN'T I
NO NO NO PLEASE
IT'S ALL RIGHT, TONY.
IT'S OKAY.
<<FASTER. FASTER. IT'S HIS OWN CLONED SKIN. WE'LL NEED ALL WE CAN GET!>>
<<FASTER!>>
SUH...
...SAM...?
DON'T TRY TO HOLD BACK, MY FRIEND. IT'S ALL RIGHT.
JUST LET GO. TRUST ME...

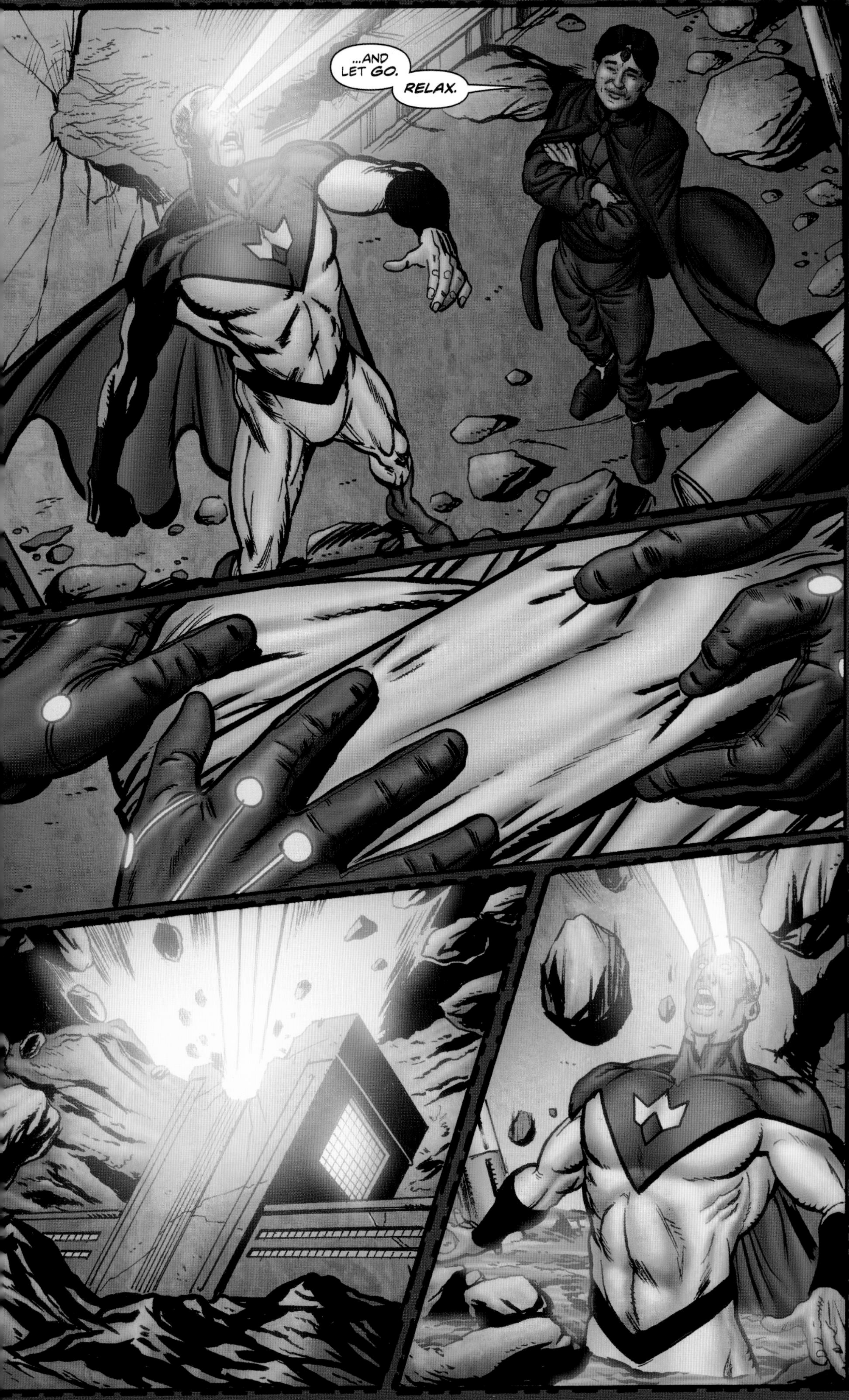
...AND LET GO.
RELAX.

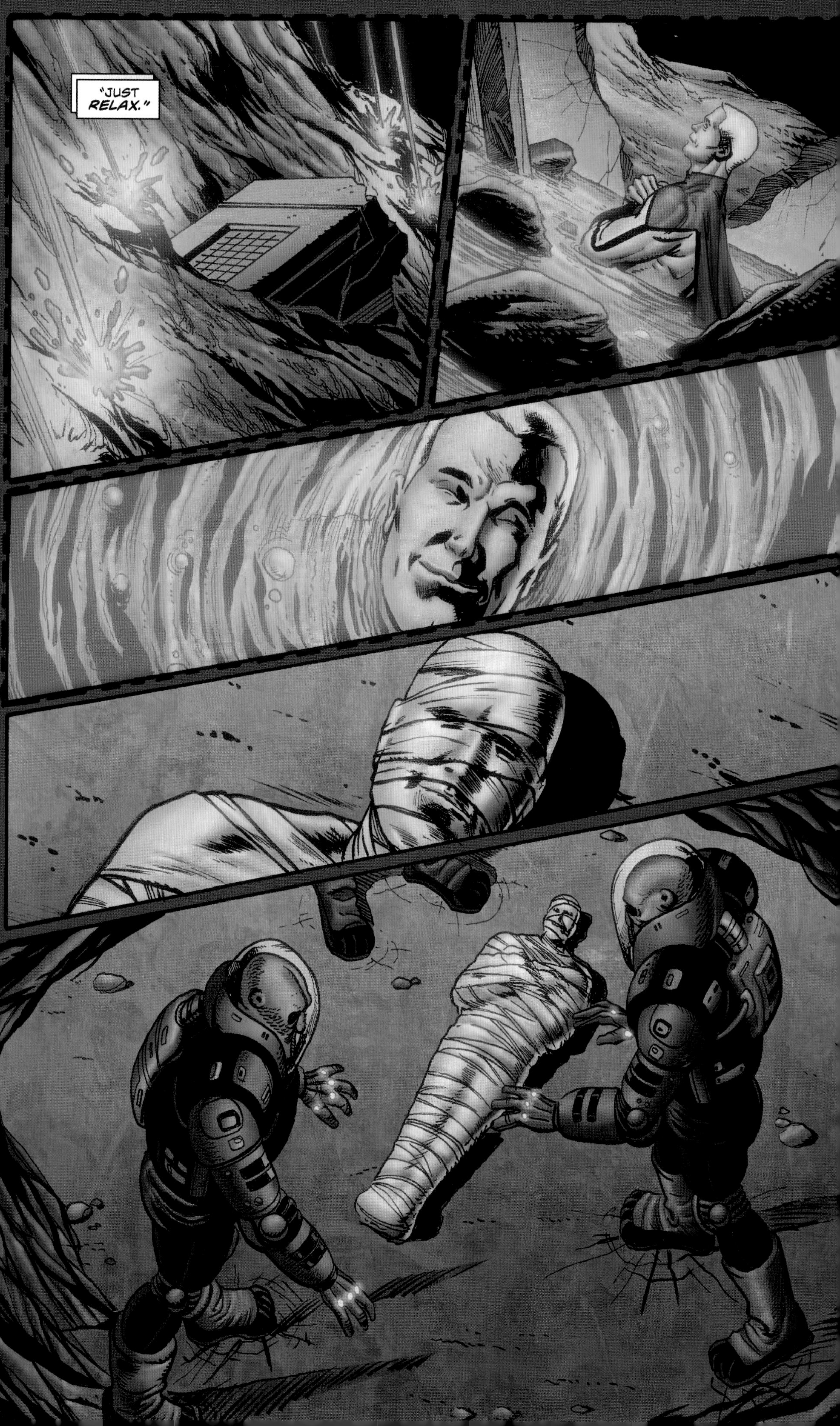
"JUST RELAX."

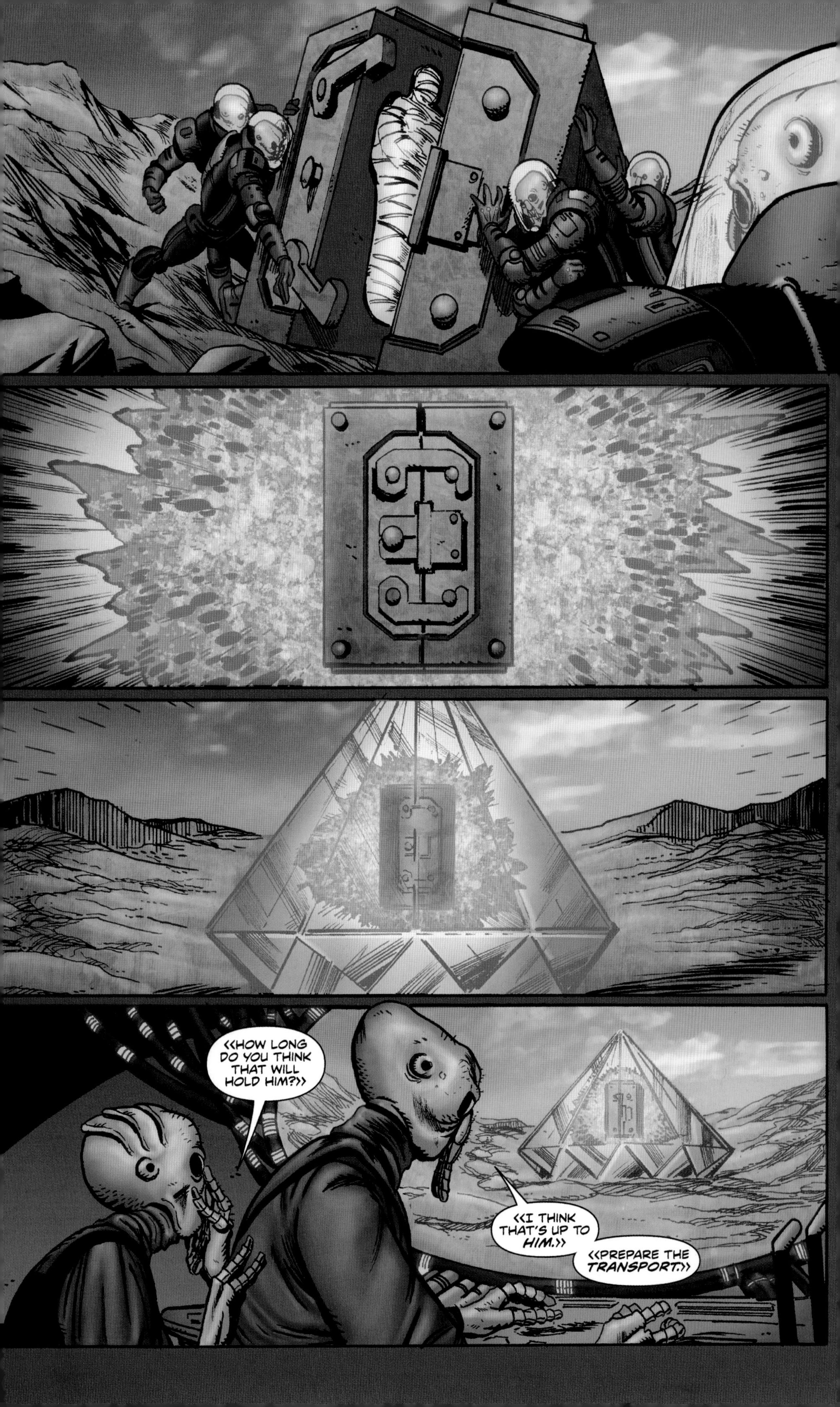

<<HOW LONG DO YOU THINK THAT WILL HOLD HIM?>>
<<I THINK THAT'S UP TO HIM.>>
<<PREPARE THE TRANSPORT.>>

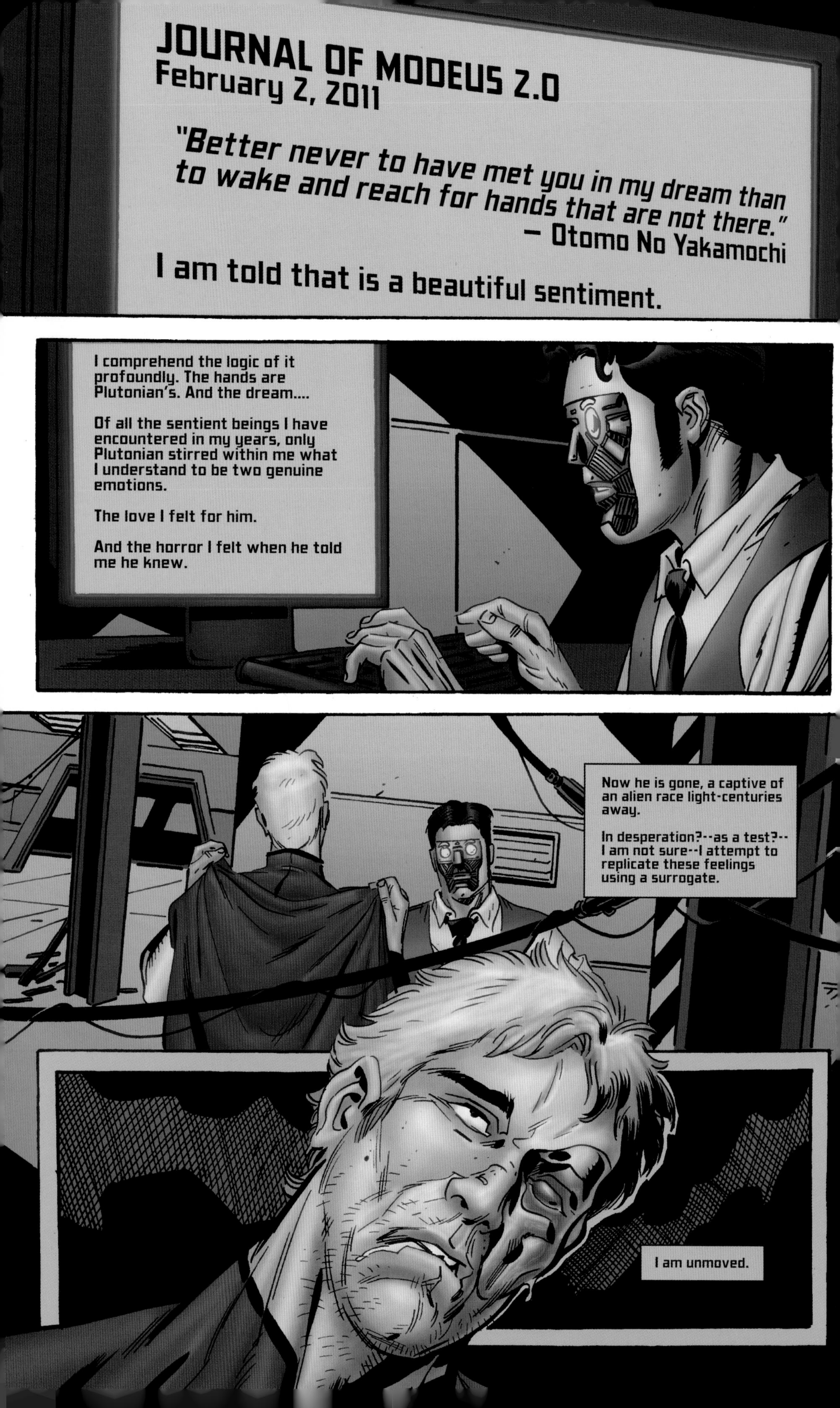
JOURNAL OF MODEUS 2.0
February 2, 2011
"Better never to have met you in my dream than to wake and reach for hands that are not there."
— Otomo No Yakamochi
I am told that is a beautiful sentiment.
I comprehend the logic of it profoundly. The hands are Plutonian's. And the dream....
Of all the sentient beings I have encountered in my years, only Plutonian stirred within me what I understand to be two genuine emotions.
The love I felt for him.
And the horror I felt when he told me he knew.
Now he is gone, a captive of an alien race light-centuries away.
In desperation?--as a test?--I am not sure--I attempt to replicate these feelings using a surrogate.
I am unmoved.

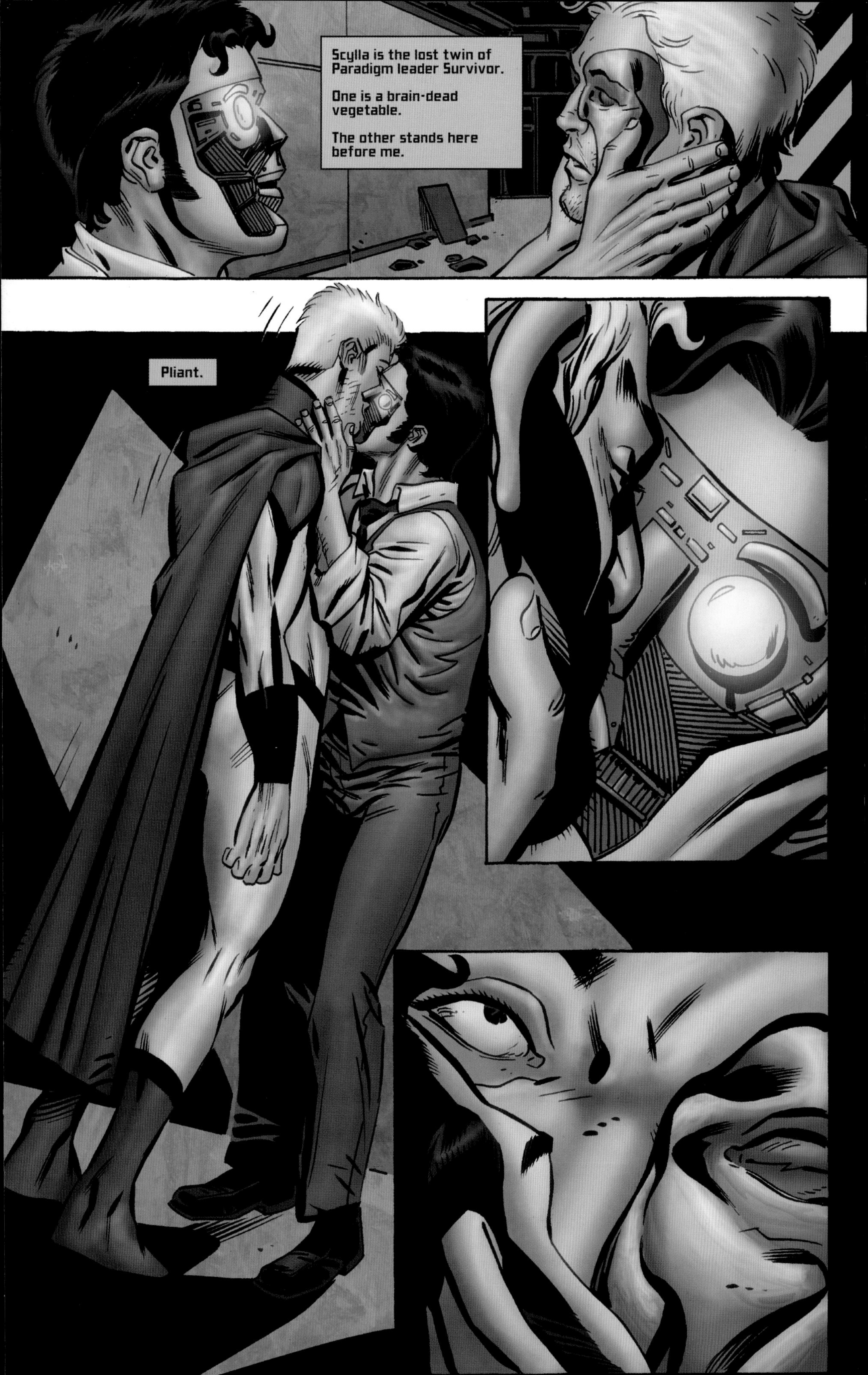
Scylla is the lost twin of Paradigm leader Survivor.
One is a brain-dead vegetable.
The other stands here before me.
Pliant.

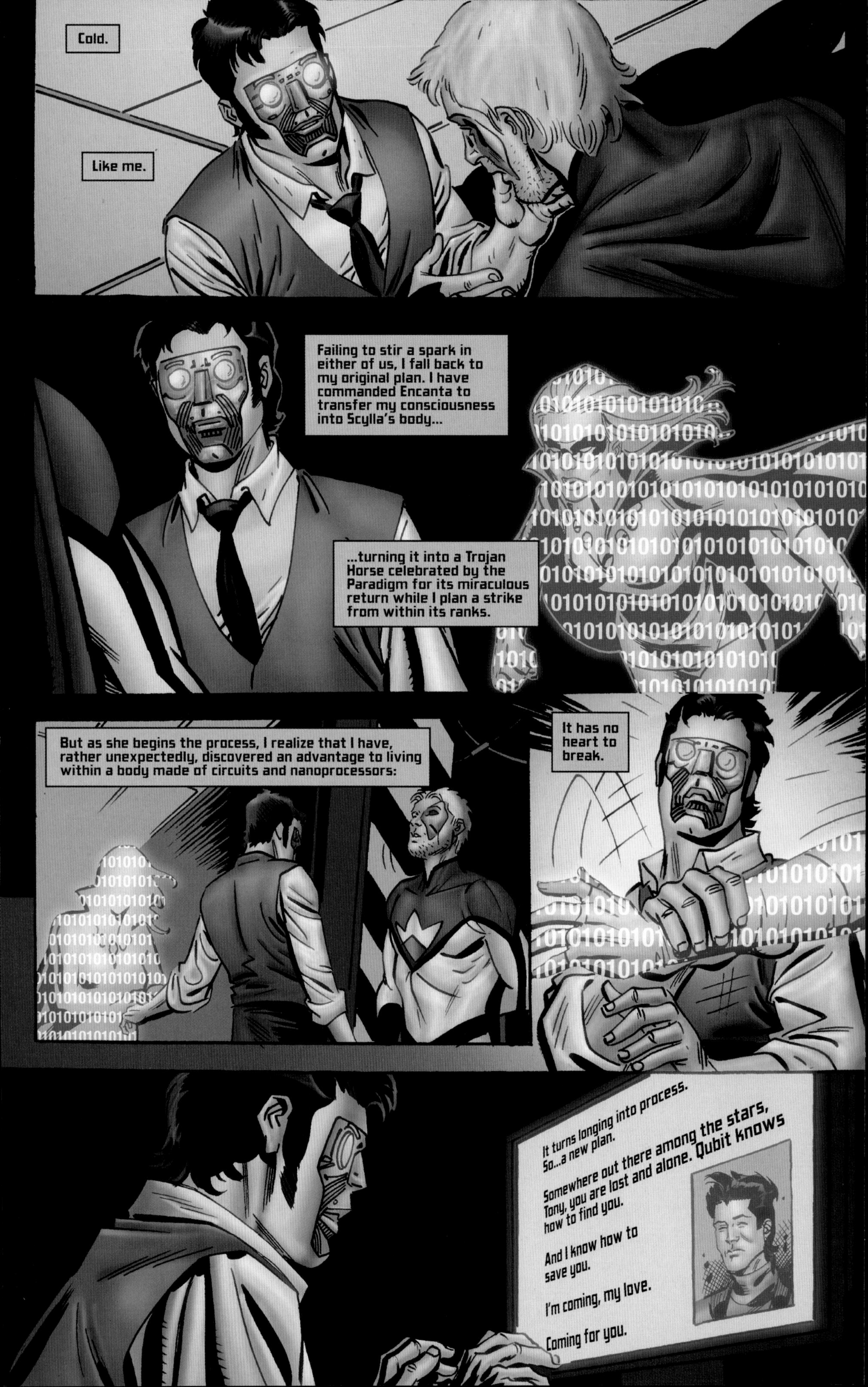
Cold.
Like me.
Failing to stir a spark in either of us, I fall back to my original plan. I have commanded Encanta to transfer my consciousness into Scylla's body...
...turning it into a Trojan Horse celebrated by the Paradigm for its miraculous return while I plan a strike from within its ranks.
But as she begins the process, I realize that I have, rather unexpectedly, discovered an advantage to living within a body made of circuits and nanoprocessors:
It has no heart to break.
It turns longing into process.
So...a new plan.
Somewhere out there among the stars, Tony, you are lost and alone. Qubit knows how to find you.
And I know how to save you.
I'm coming, my love.
Coming for you.

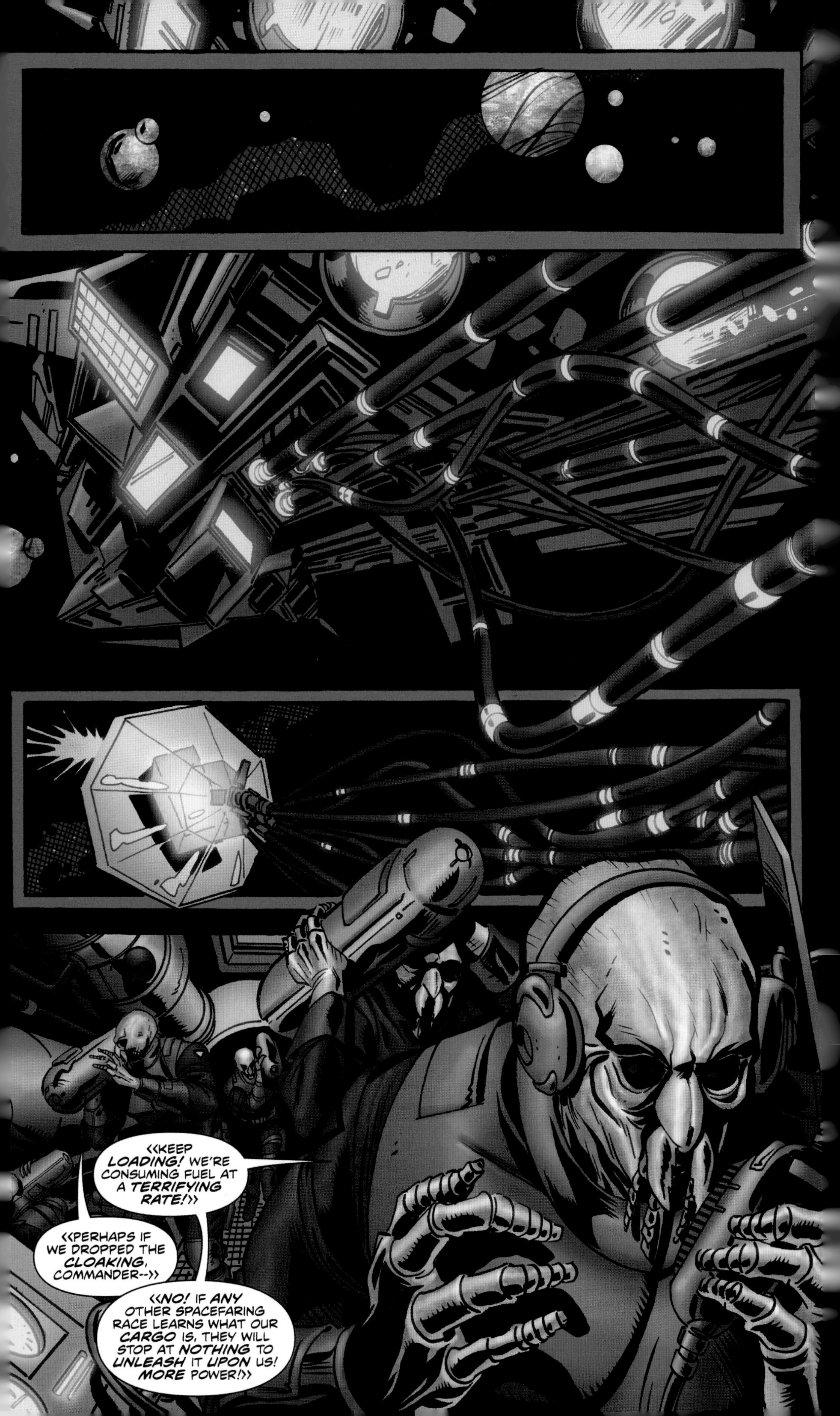
<<KEEP LOADING! WE'RE CONSUMING FUEL AT A TERRIFYING RATE!>>
<<PERHAPS IF WE DROPPED THE CLOAKING, COMMANDER-->>
<<NO! IF ANY OTHER SPACEFARING RACE LEARNS WHAT OUR CARGO IS, THEY WILL STOP AT NOTHING TO UNLEASH IT UPON US! MORE POWER!>>

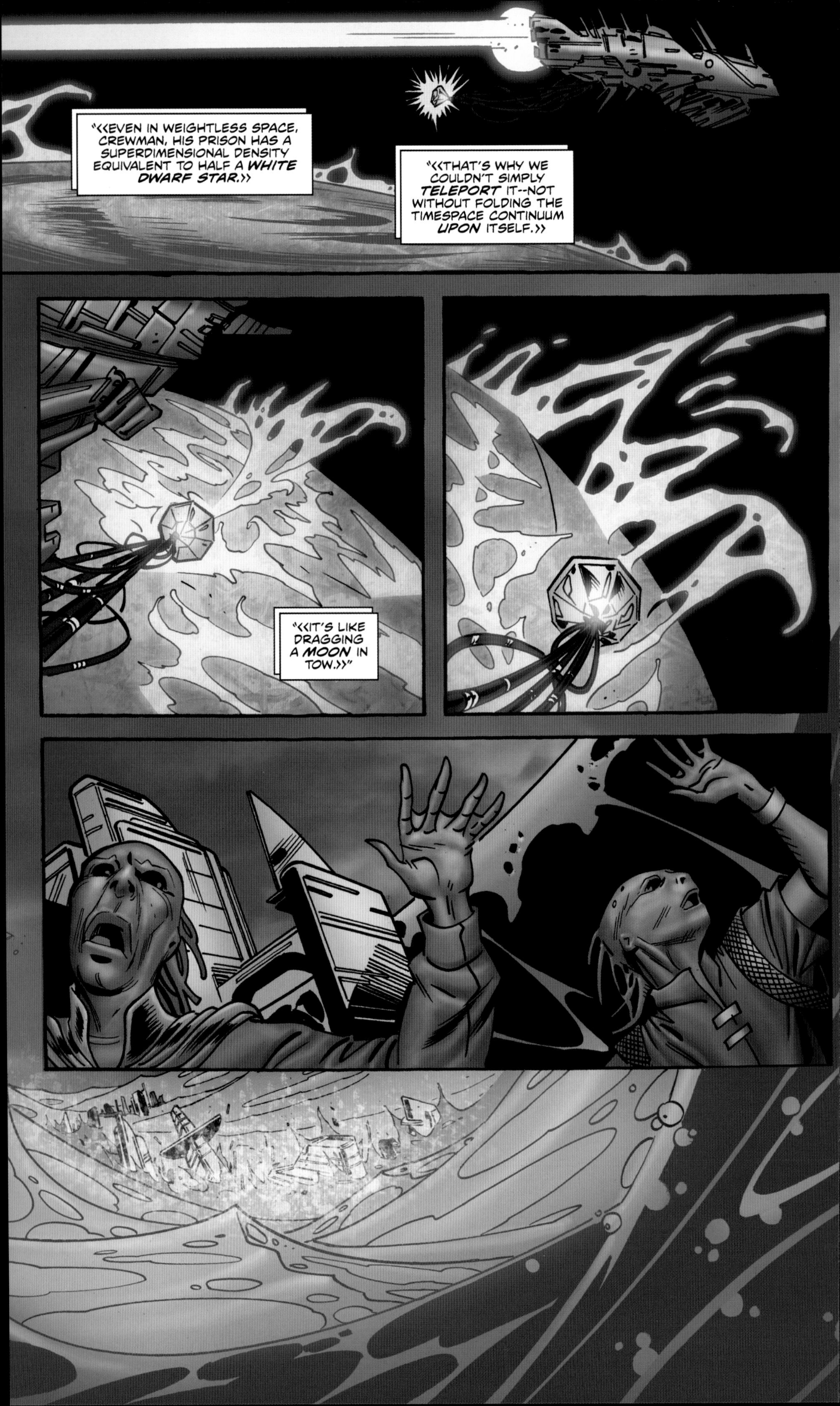

"<<EVEN IN WEIGHTLESS SPACE, CREWMAN, HIS PRISON HAS A SUPERDIMENSIONAL DENSITY EQUIVALENT TO HALF A WHITE DWARF STAR.>>
"<<THAT'S WHY WE COULDN'T SIMPLY TELEPORT IT--NOT WITHOUT FOLDING THE TIMESPACE CONTINUUM UPON ITSELF.>>
"<<IT'S LIKE DRAGGING A MOON IN TOW.>>"

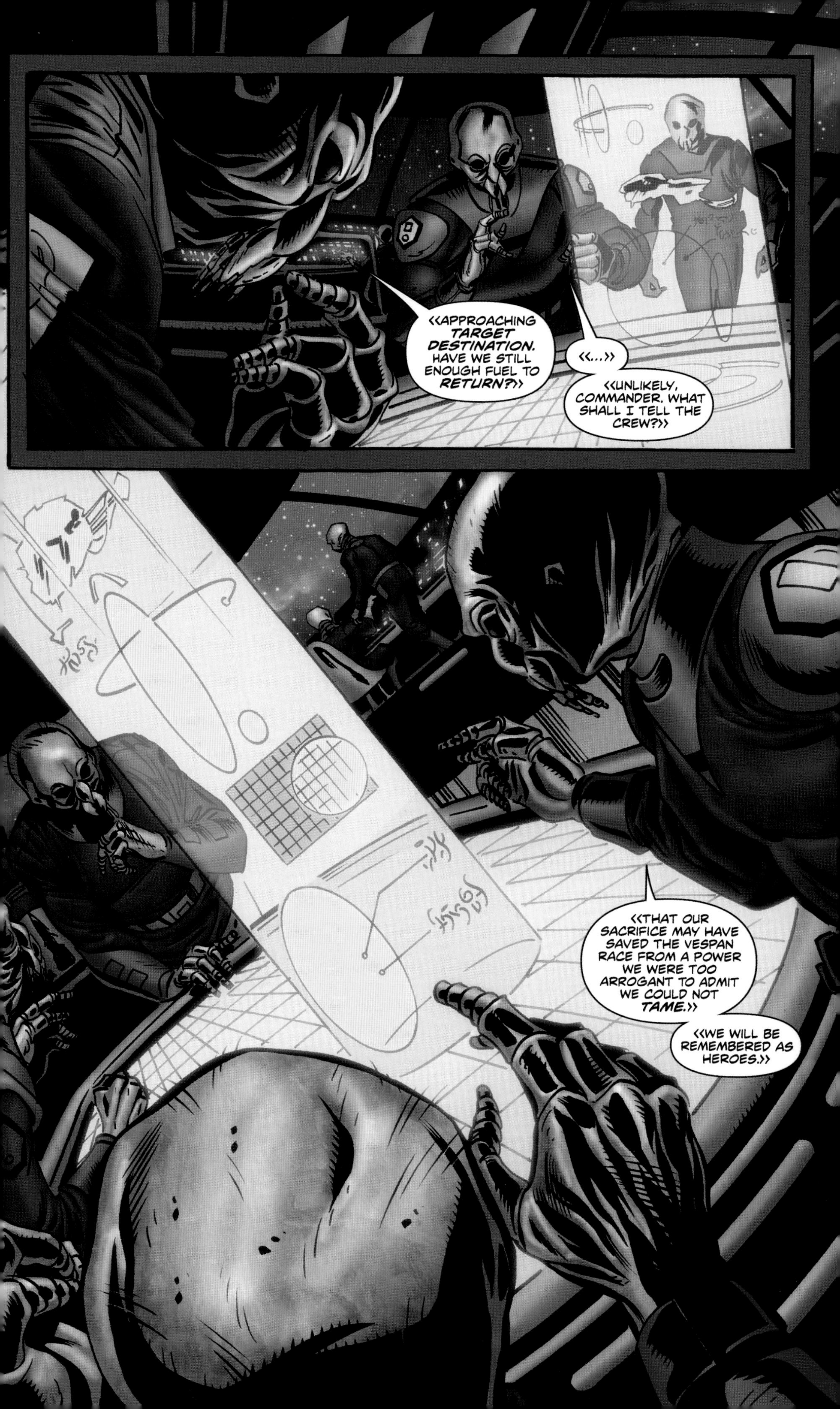

<<APPROACHING TARGET DESTINATION. HAVE WE STILL ENOUGH FUEL TO RETURN?>>
<<...>>
<<UNLIKELY, COMMANDER. WHAT SHALL I TELL THE CREW?>>
<<THAT OUR SACRIFICE MAY HAVE SAVED THE VESPAN RACE FROM A POWER WE WERE TOO ARROGANT TO ADMIT WE COULD NOT TAME.>>
<<WE WILL BE REMEMBERED AS HEROES.>>

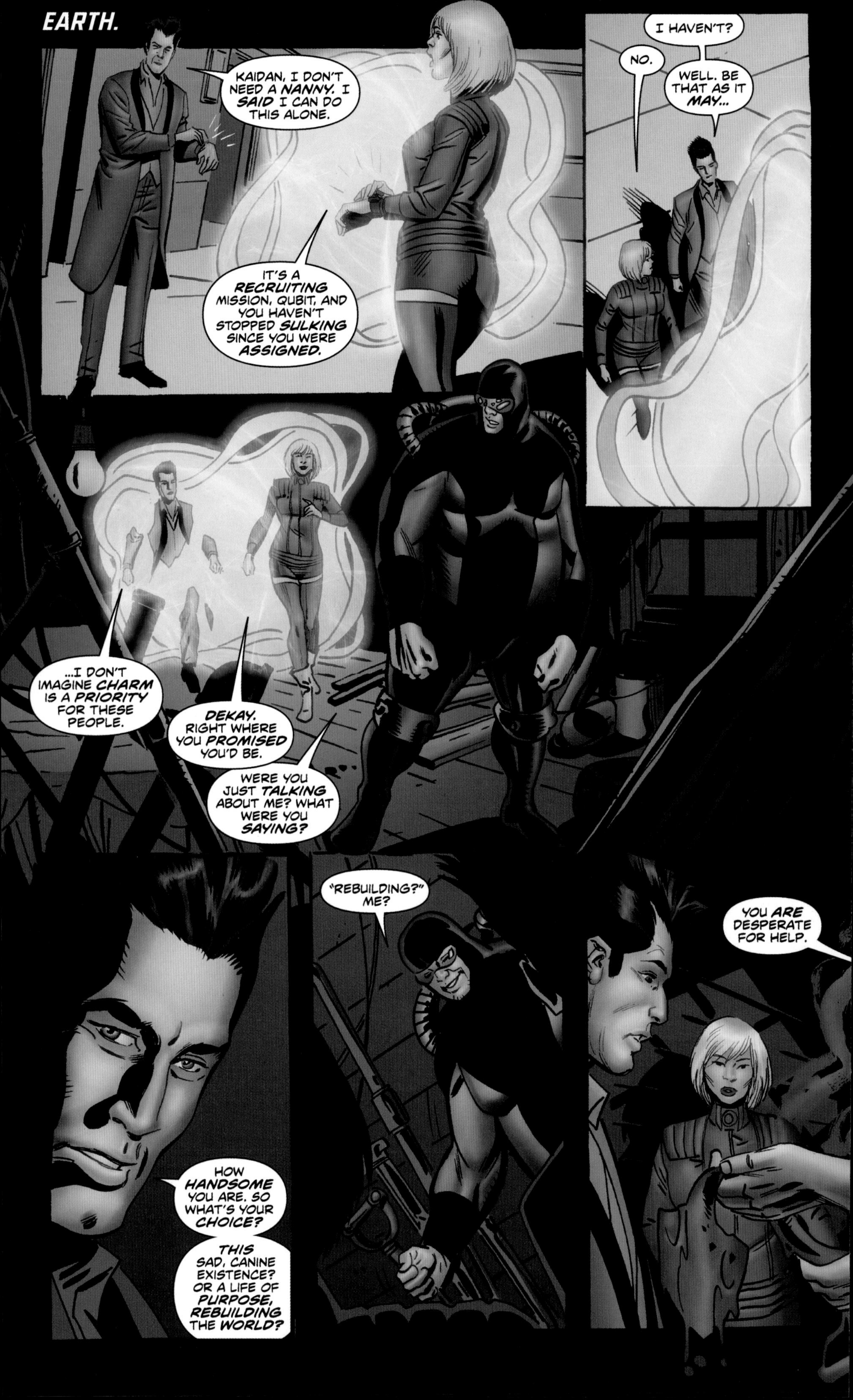
EARTH.
KAIDAN, I DON'T NEED A NANNY. I SAID I CAN DO THIS ALONE.
IT'S A RECRUITING MISSION, QUBIT, AND YOU HAVEN'T STOPPED SULKING SINCE YOU WERE ASSIGNED.
I HAVEN'T?
NO.
WELL. BE THAT AS IT MAY...
...I DON'T IMAGINE CHARM IS A PRIORITY FOR THESE PEOPLE.
DEKAY. RIGHT WHERE YOU PROMISED YOU'D BE.
WERE YOU JUST TALKING ABOUT ME? WHAT WERE YOU SAYING?
HOW HANDSOME YOU ARE. SO WHAT'S YOUR CHOICE?
THIS SAD, CANINE EXISTENCE? OR A LIFE OF PURPOSE, REBUILDING THE WORLD?
"REBUILDING?" ME?
YOU ARE DESPERATE FOR HELP.

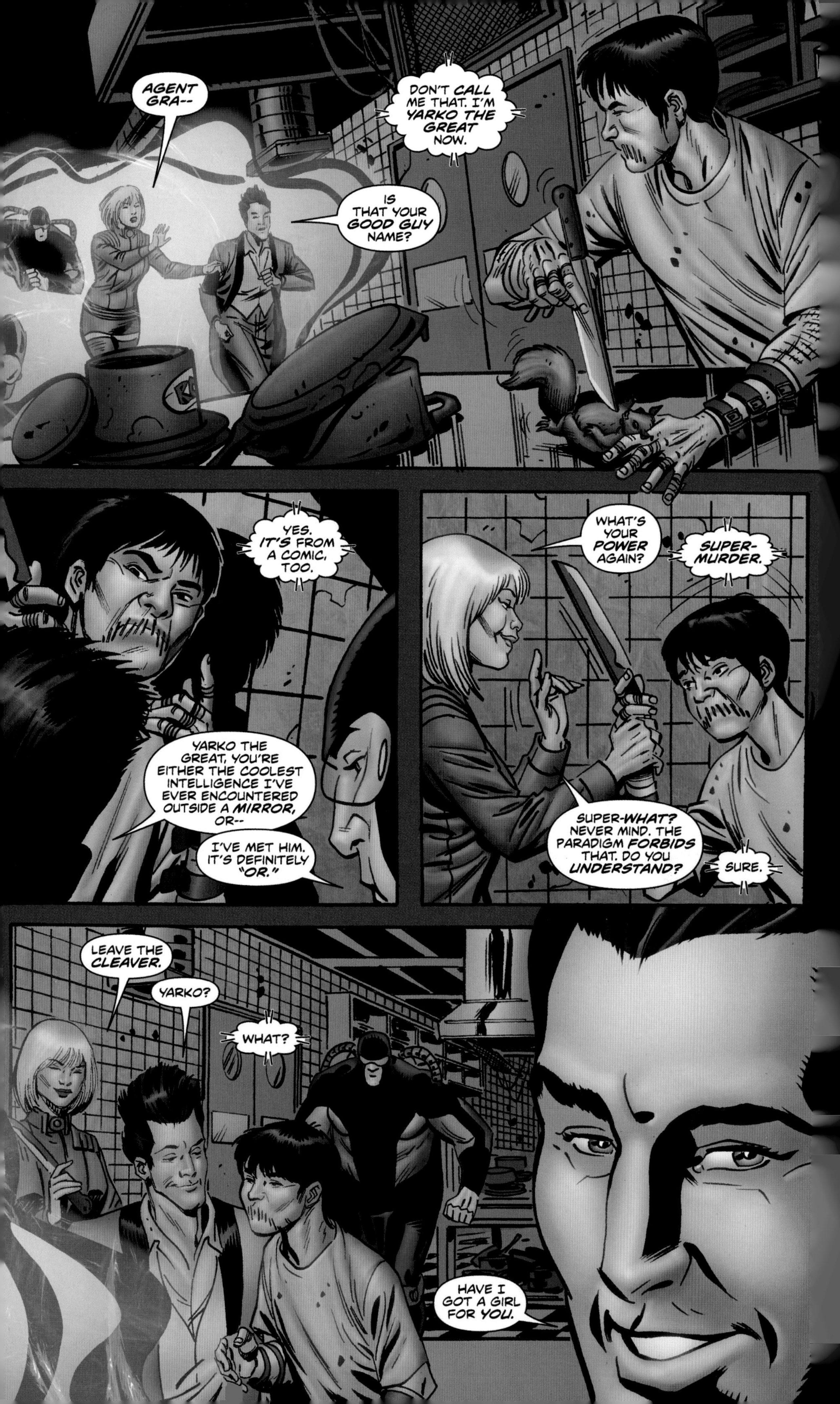
AGENT GRA--
DON'T CALL ME THAT. I'M YARKO THE GREAT NOW.
IS THAT YOUR GOOD GUY NAME?
YES. IT'S FROM A COMIC, TOO.
YARKO THE GREAT, YOU'RE EITHER THE COOLEST INTELLIGENCE I'VE EVER ENCOUNTERED OUTSIDE A MIRROR, OR--
I'VE MET HIM. IT'S DEFINITELY "OR."
WHAT'S YOUR POWER AGAIN?
SUPER-MURDER.
SUPER-WHAT? NEVER MIND. THE PARADIGM FORBIDS THAT. DO YOU UNDERSTAND?
SURE.
LEAVE THE CLEAVER.
YARKO?
WHAT?
HAVE I GOT A GIRL FOR YOU.

SHANK? YOU HERE?

IS THAT *REALLY HER* NAME?

LOOK WHO'S TALKING.

I SMELL *PERFU--*

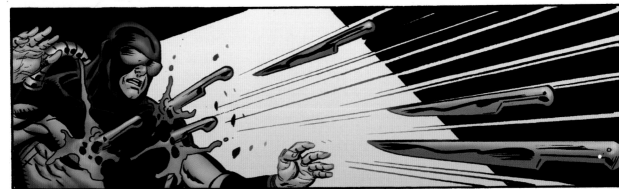

THESE ARE THE SAVAGES WE'RE SUPPOSED TO BE *PARDONING?*

"YOU WERE *RIGHT,* QUBIT! THIS WHOLE *PLAN* IS *RIDICULOUS!*"

SO WE'RE TWO FOR THREE. COULD BE WORSE.

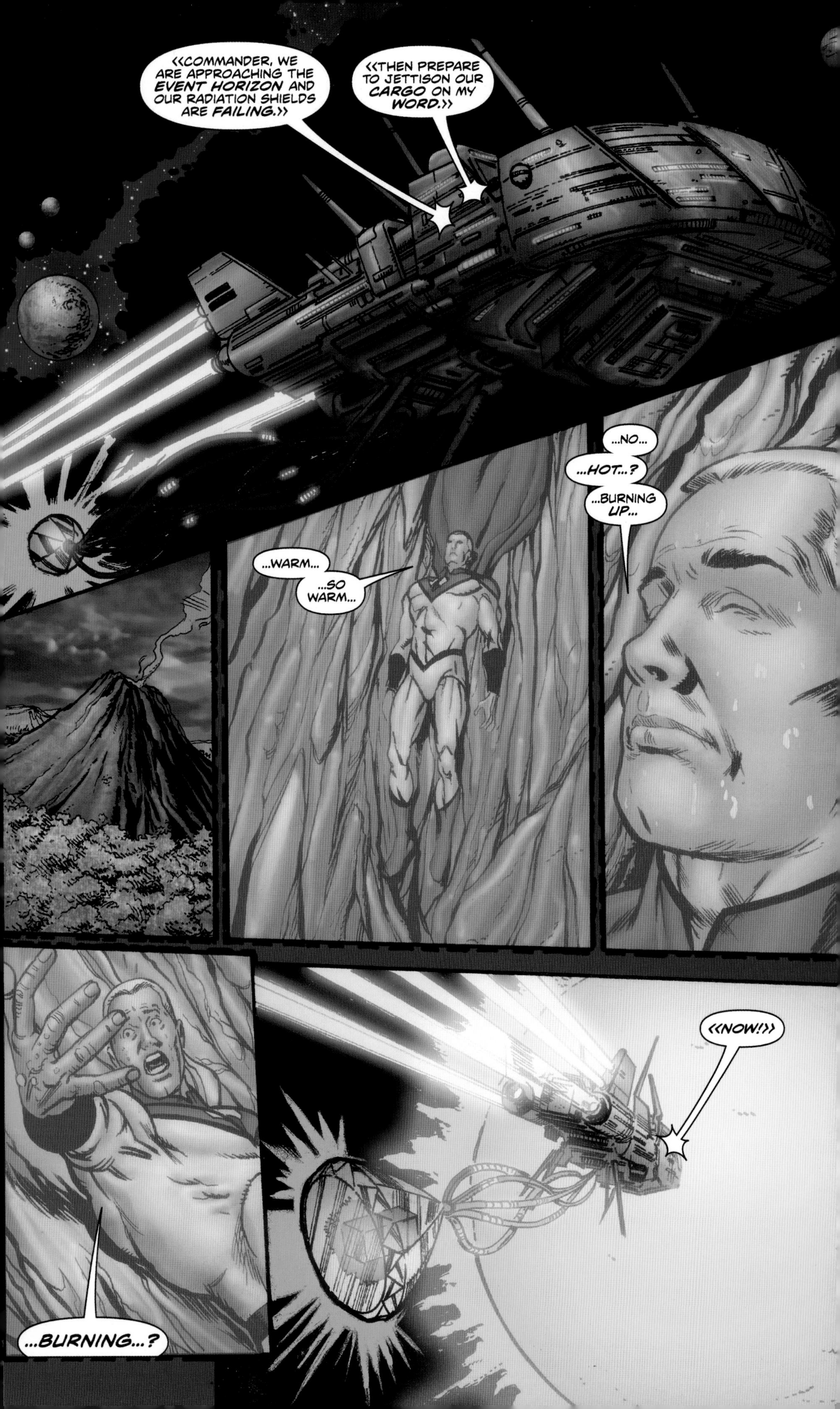

<<COMMANDER, WE ARE APPROACHING THE EVENT HORIZON AND OUR RADIATION SHIELDS ARE FAILING.>>
<<THEN PREPARE TO JETTISON OUR CARGO ON MY WORD.>>
...WARM...
...SO WARM...
...NO...
...HOT...?
...BURNING UP...
...BURNING...?
<<NOW!>>

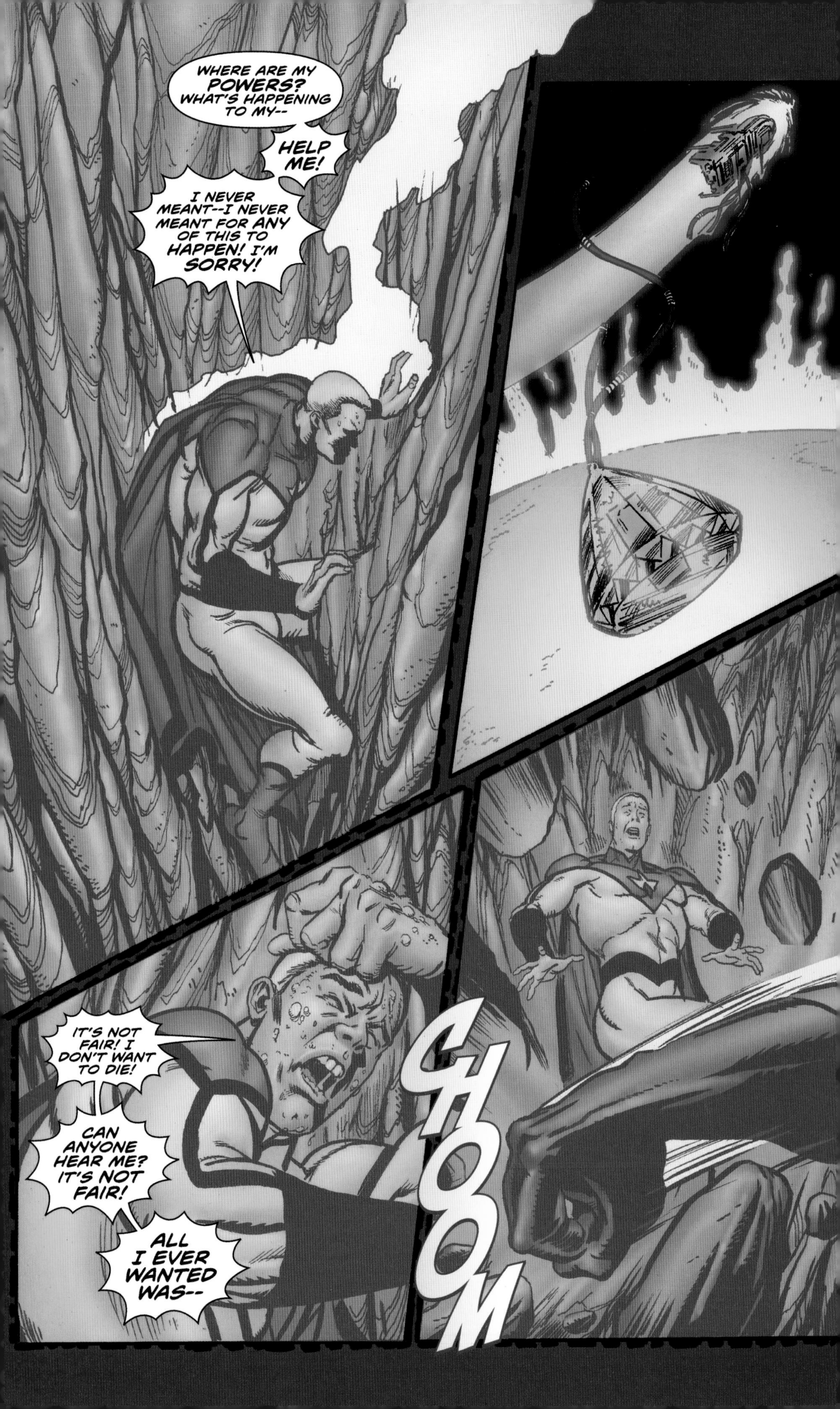
WHERE ARE MY POWERS? WHAT'S HAPPENING TO MY--
HELP ME!
I NEVER MEANT--I NEVER MEANT FOR ANY OF THIS TO HAPPEN! I'M SORRY!
IT'S NOT FAIR! I DON'T WANT TO DIE!
CAN ANYONE HEAR ME? IT'S NOT FAIR!
ALL I EVER WANTED WAS--
CHOOOM

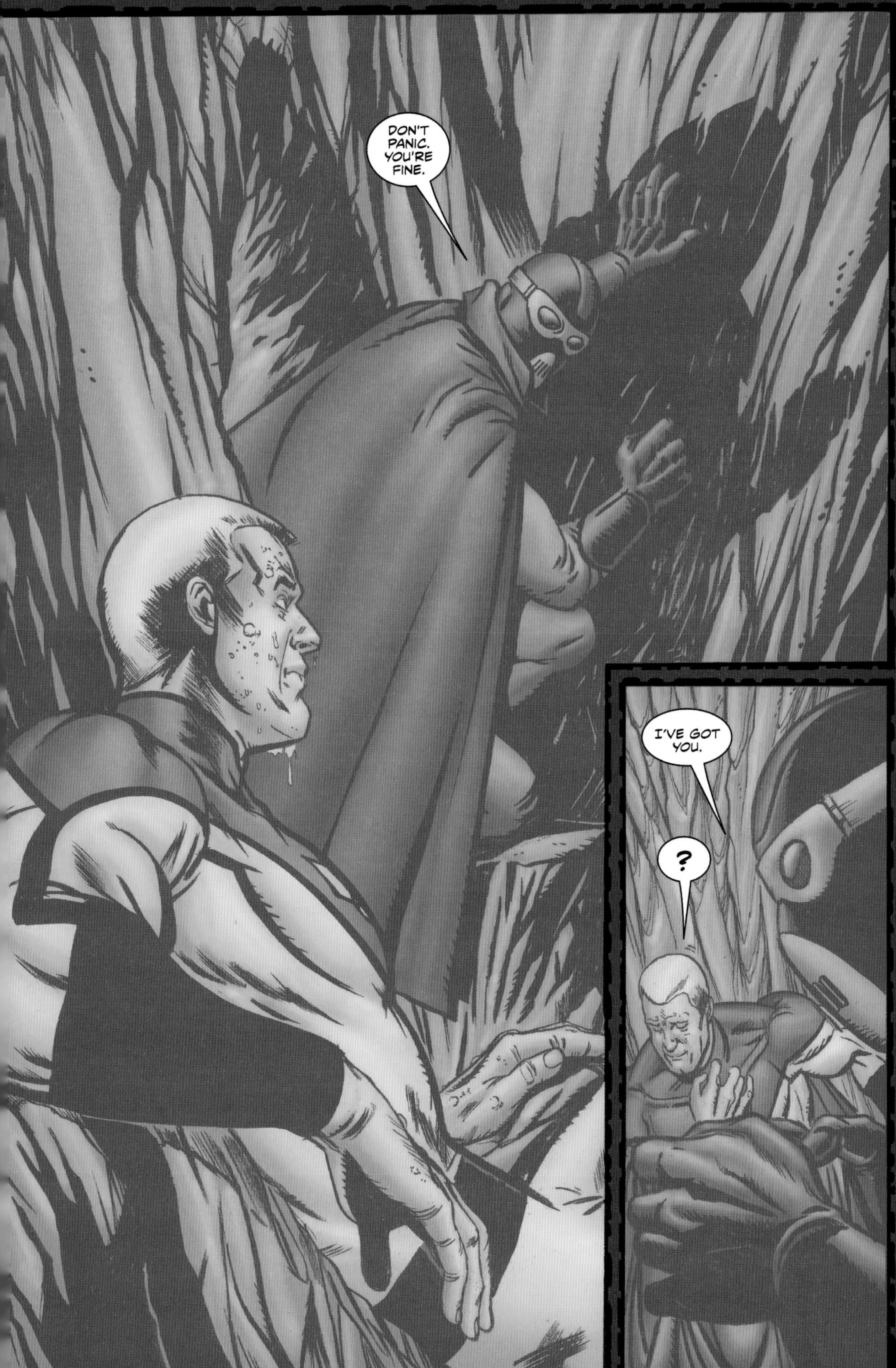
DON'T PANIC. YOU'RE FINE.
I'VE GOT YOU.
?

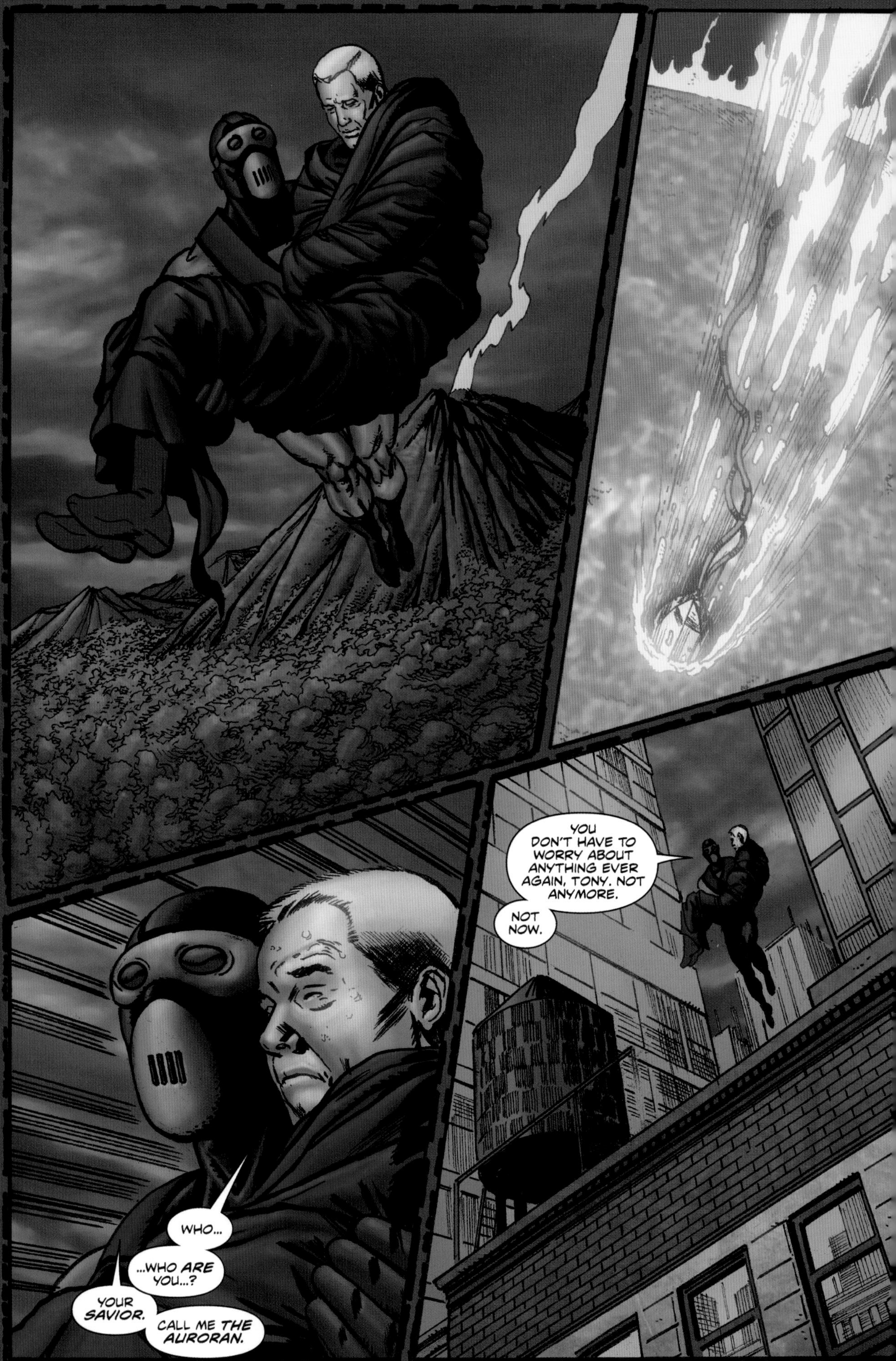
YOU DON'T HAVE TO WORRY ABOUT ANYTHING EVER AGAIN, TONY. NOT ANYMORE.
NOT NOW.
WHO...
...WHO ARE YOU...?
YOUR SAVIOR.
CALL ME THE AURORAN.

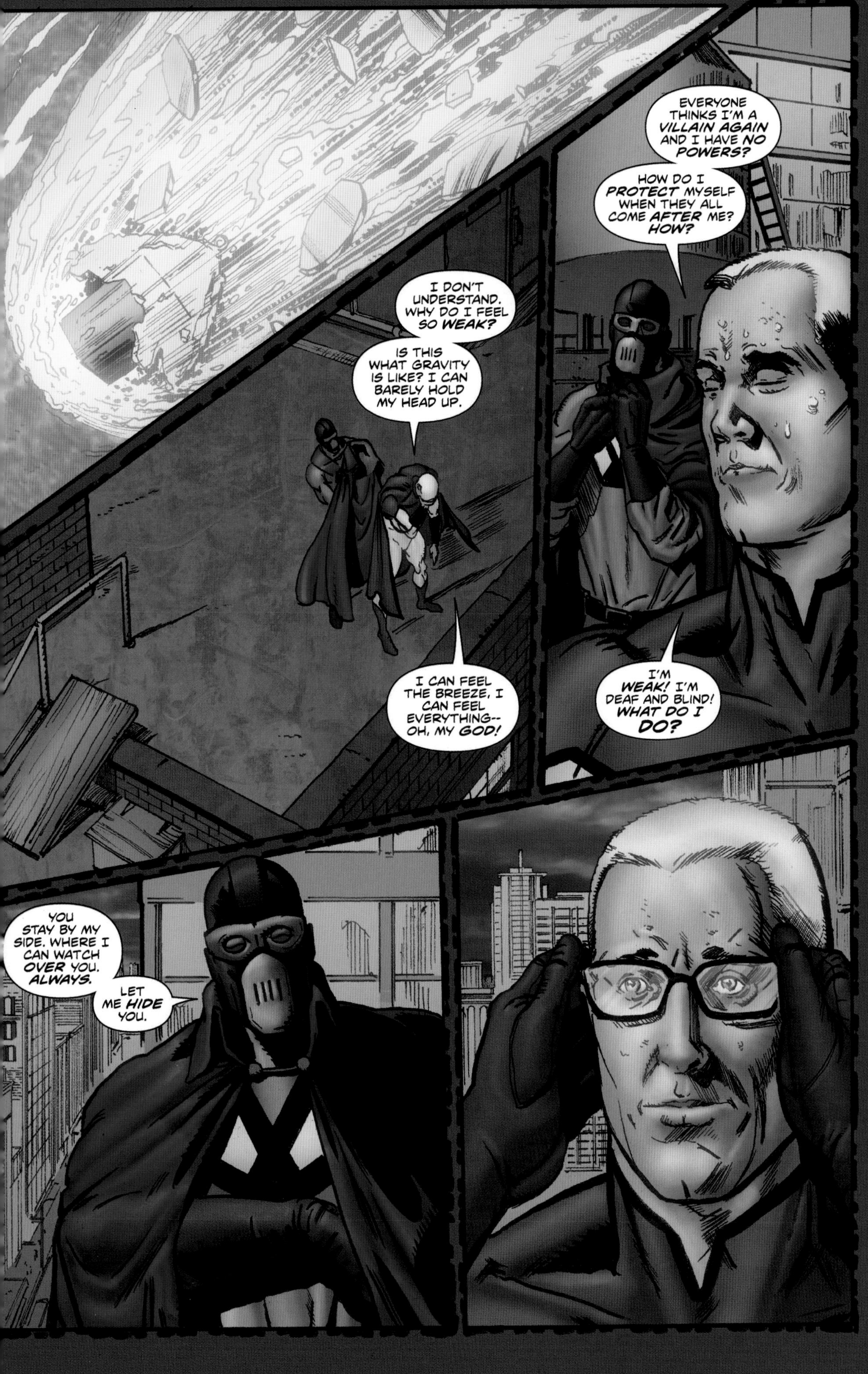

I DON'T UNDERSTAND. WHY DO I FEEL SO WEAK?
IS THIS WHAT GRAVITY IS LIKE? I CAN BARELY HOLD MY HEAD UP.
I CAN FEEL THE BREEZE, I CAN FEEL EVERYTHING-- OH, MY GOD!
EVERYONE THINKS I'M A VILLAIN AGAIN AND I HAVE NO POWERS?
HOW DO I PROTECT MYSELF WHEN THEY ALL COME AFTER ME? HOW?
I'M WEAK! I'M DEAF AND BLIND! WHAT DO I DO?
YOU STAY BY MY SIDE. WHERE I CAN WATCH OVER YOU. ALWAYS.
LET ME HIDE YOU.

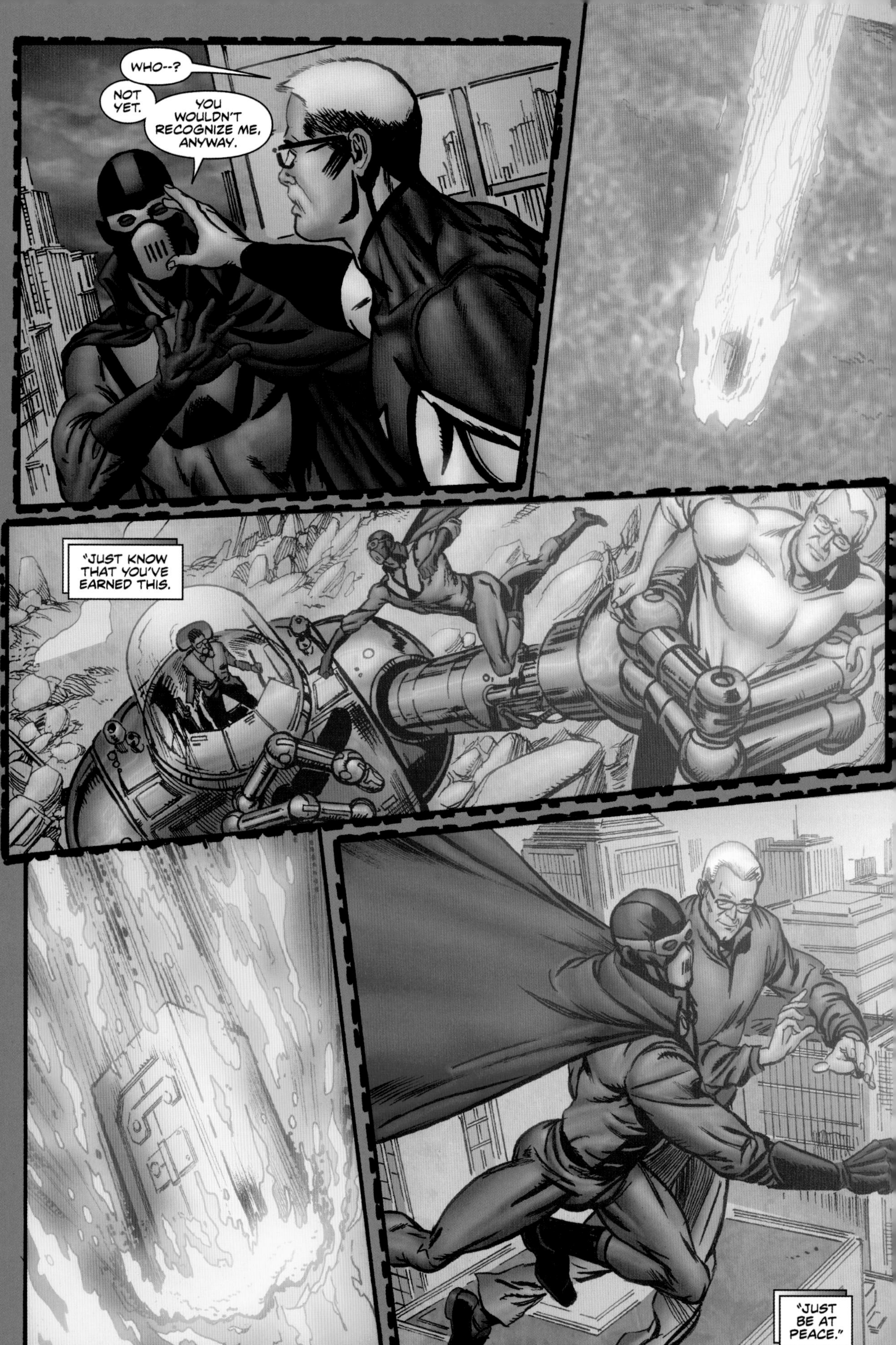
WHO--?
NOT YET.
YOU WOULDN'T RECOGNIZE ME, ANYWAY.
"JUST KNOW THAT YOU'VE EARNED THIS.
"JUST BE AT PEACE."

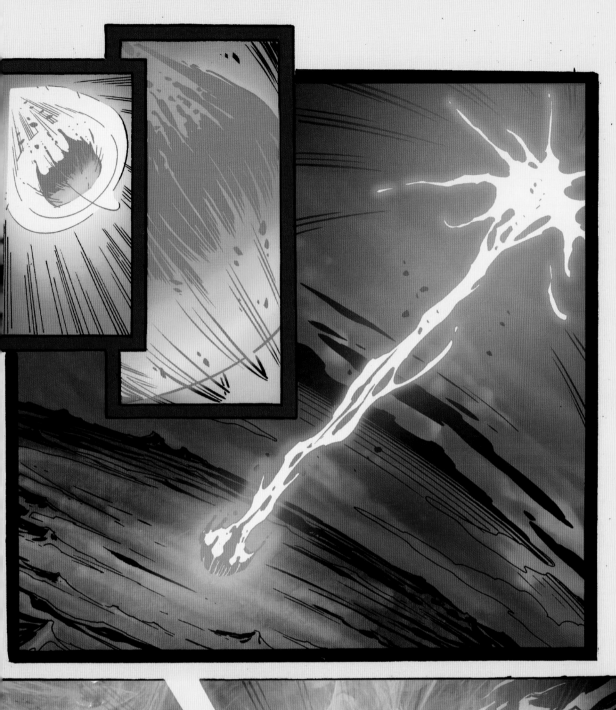
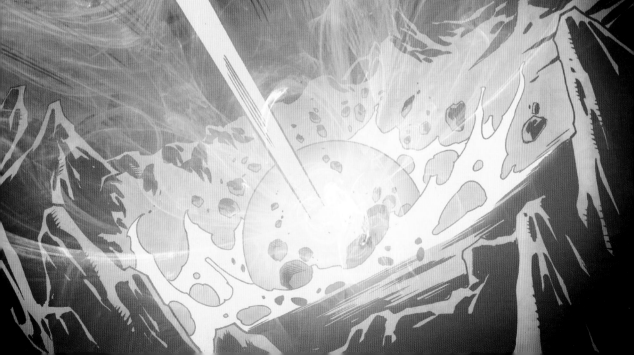

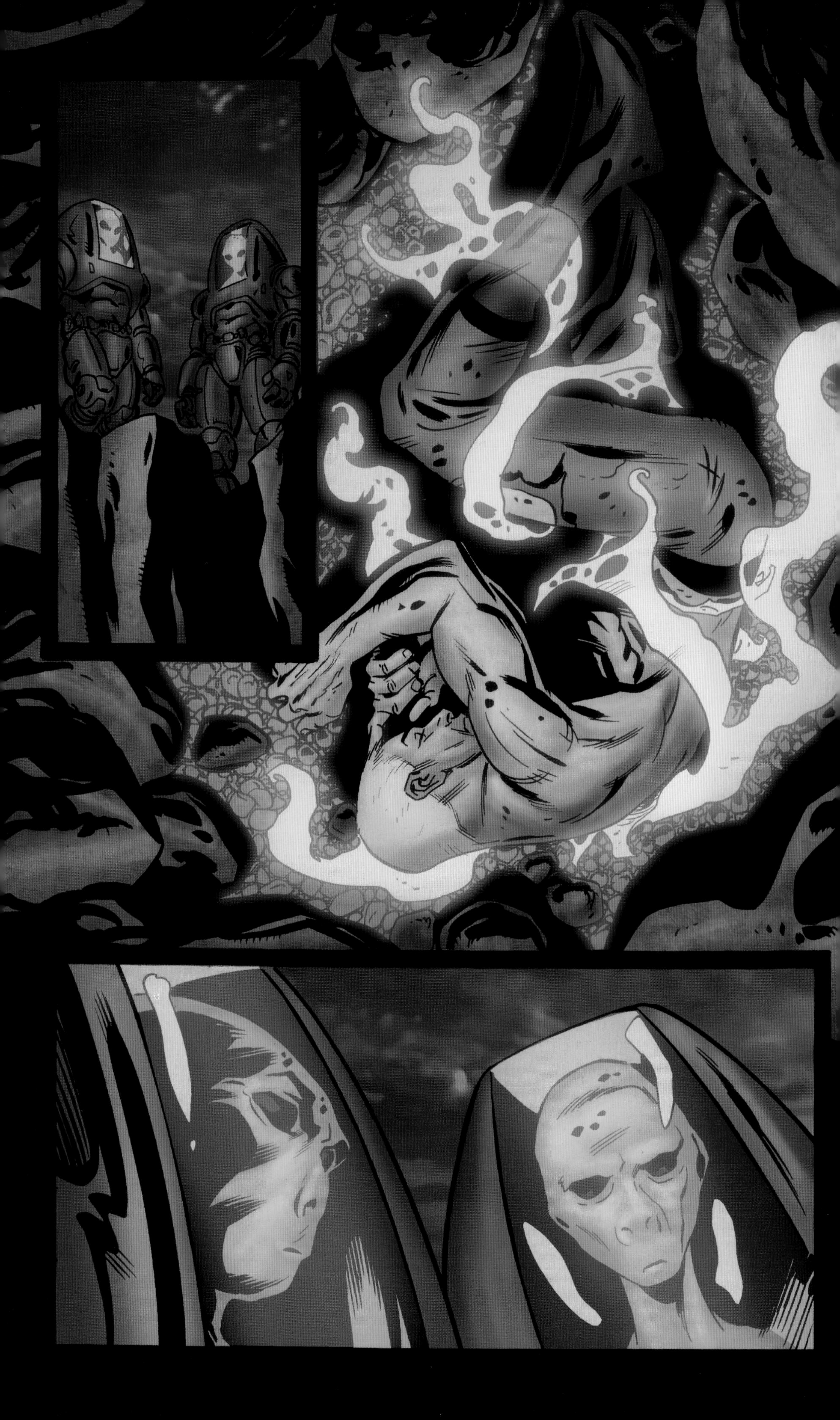

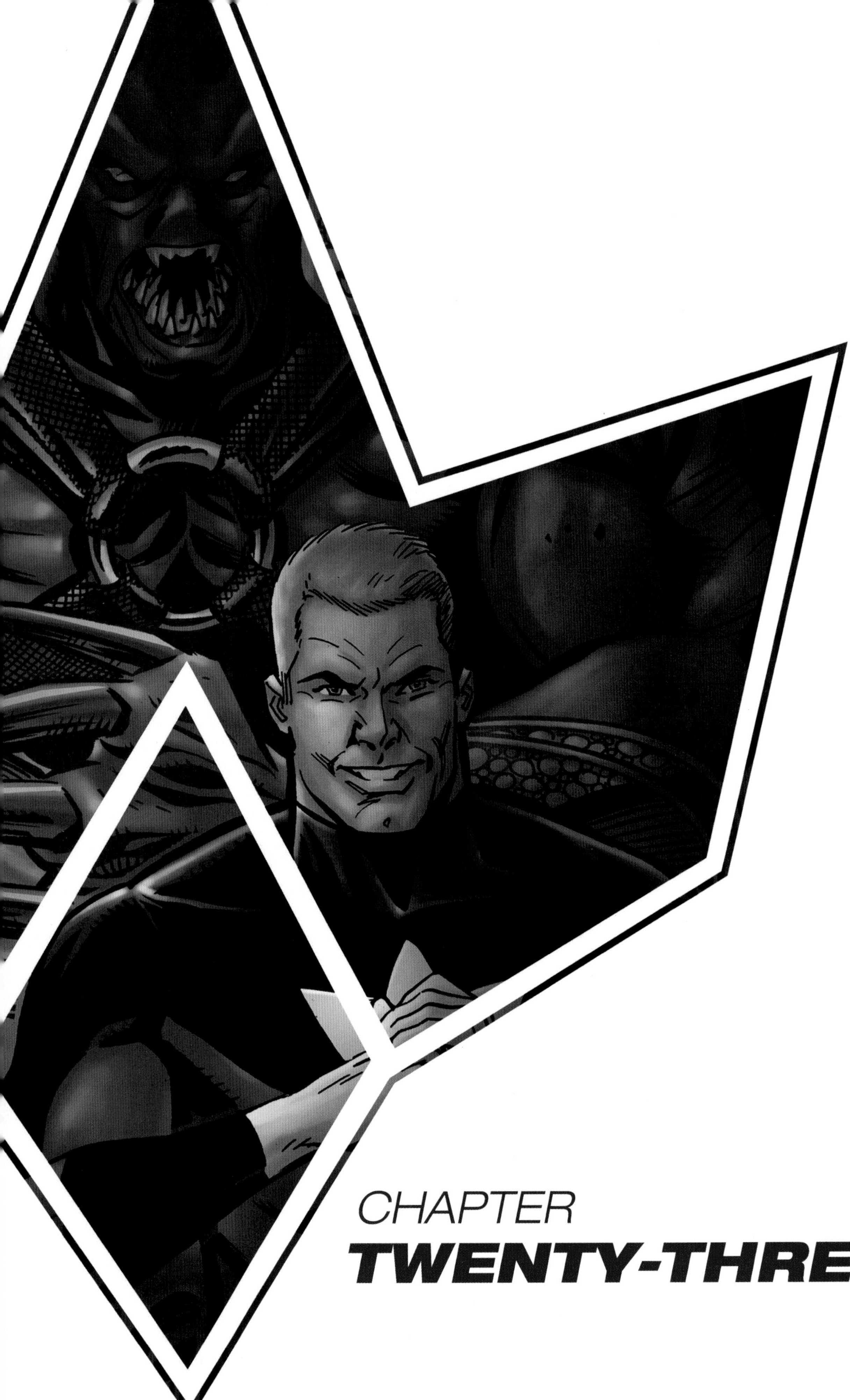

CHAPTER
TWENTY-THREE

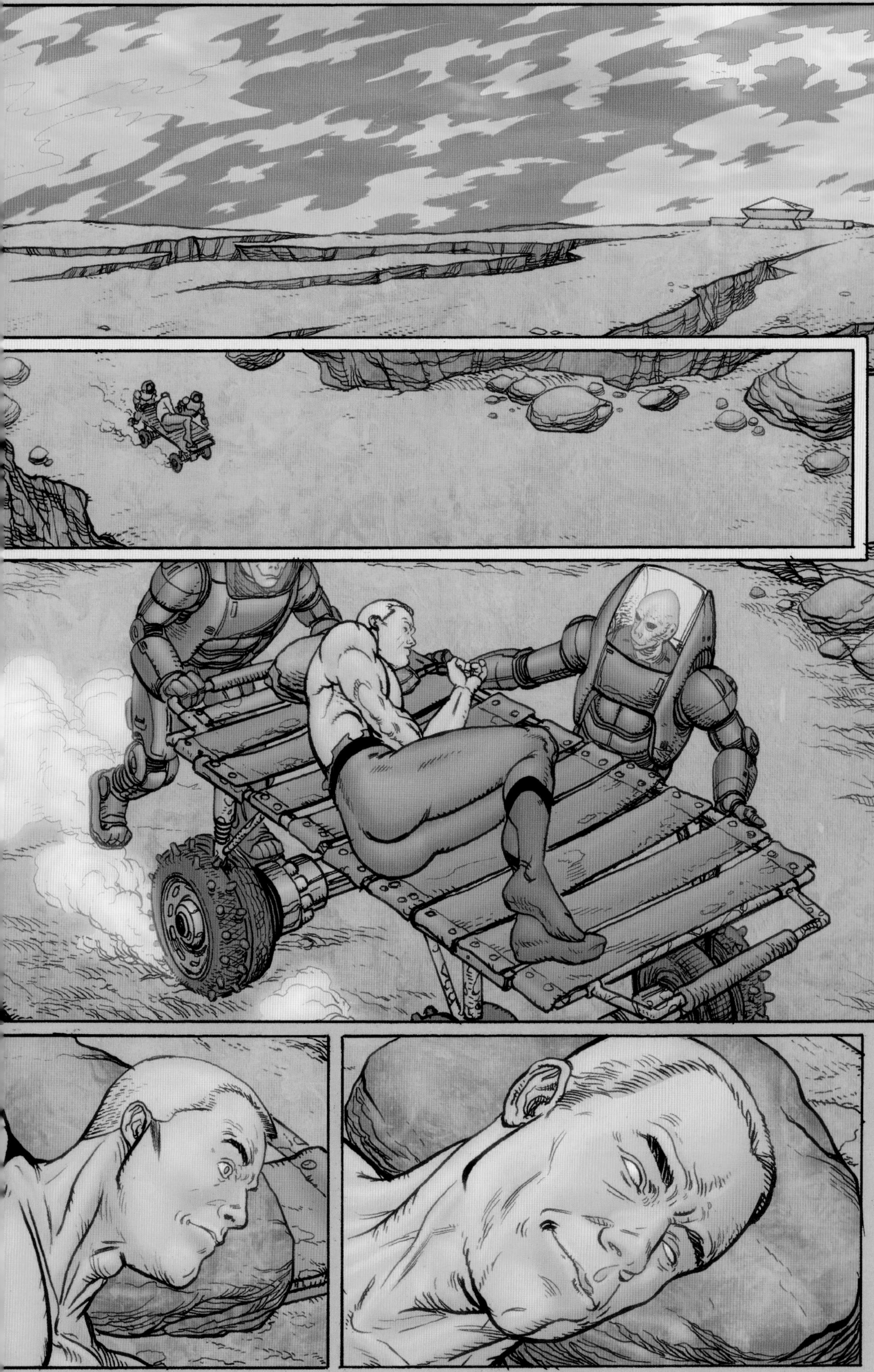

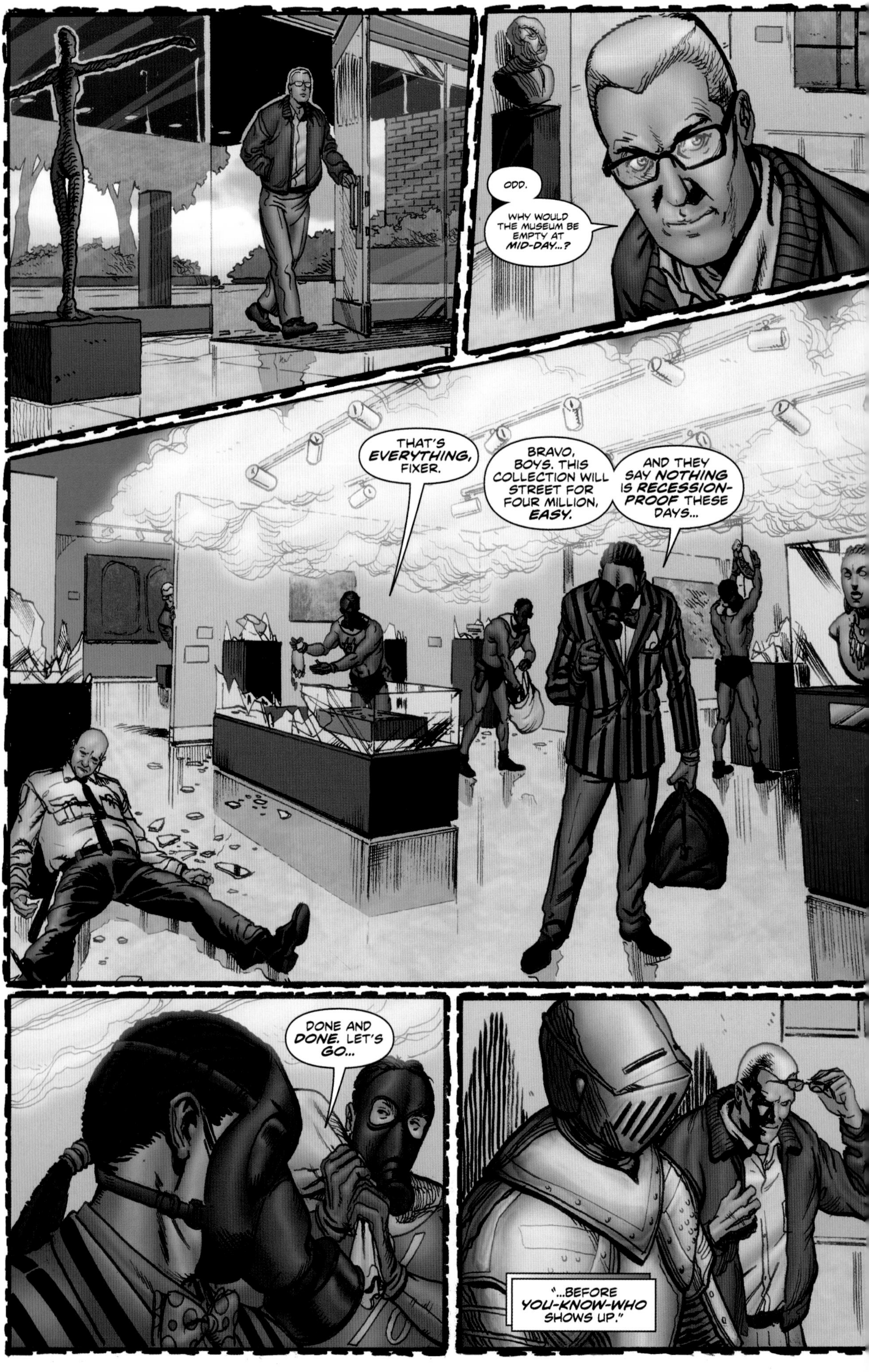
ODD.
WHY WOULD THE MUSEUM BE EMPTY AT MID-DAY...?
THAT'S EVERYTHING, FIXER.
BRAVO, BOYS. THIS COLLECTION WILL STREET FOR FOUR MILLION, EASY.
AND THEY SAY NOTHING IS RECESSION-PROOF THESE DAYS...
DONE AND DONE. LET'S GO...
"...BEFORE YOU-KNOW-WHO SHOWS UP."

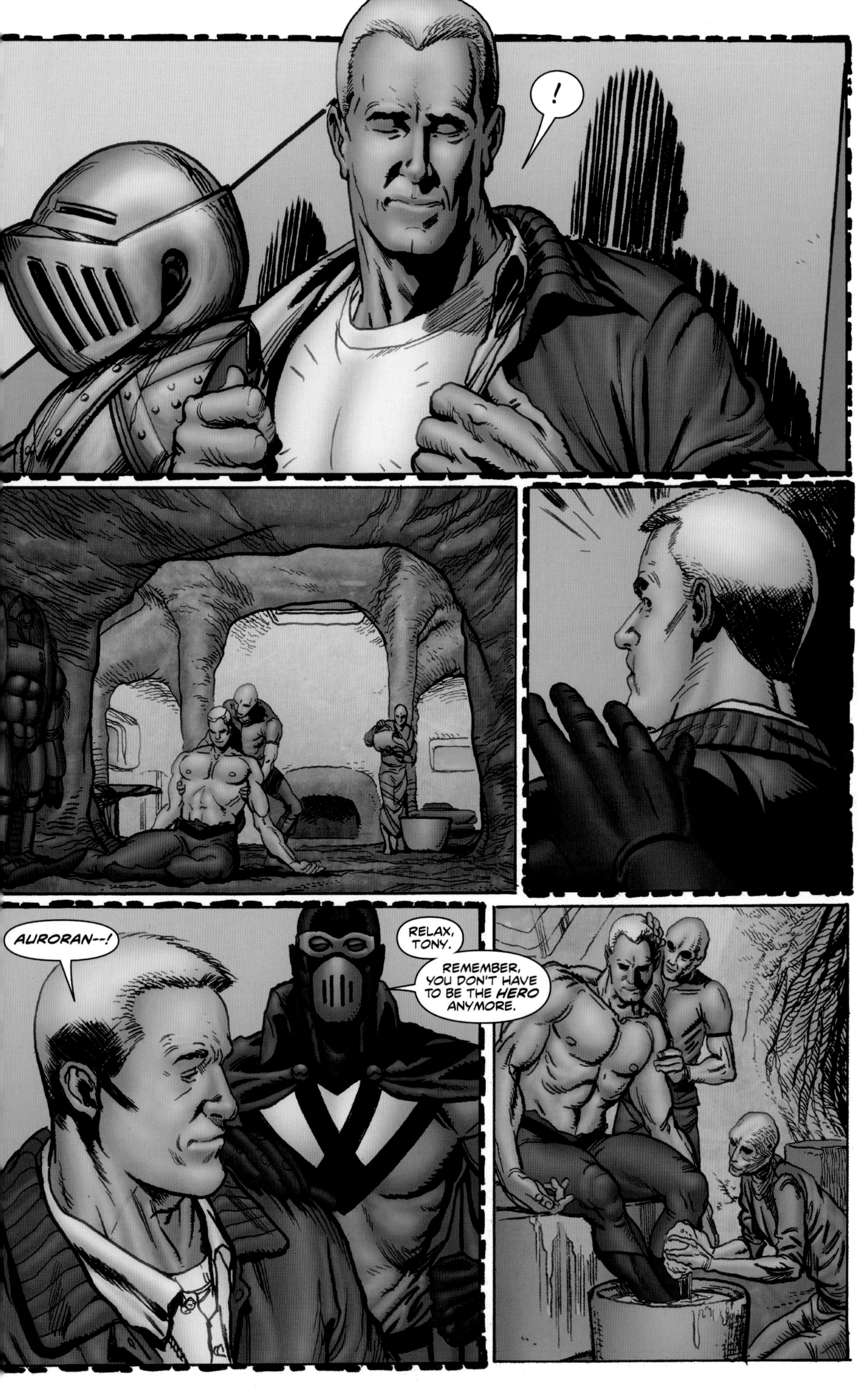
!
AURORAN--!
RELAX, TONY.
REMEMBER, YOU DON'T HAVE TO BE THE *HERO* ANYMORE.

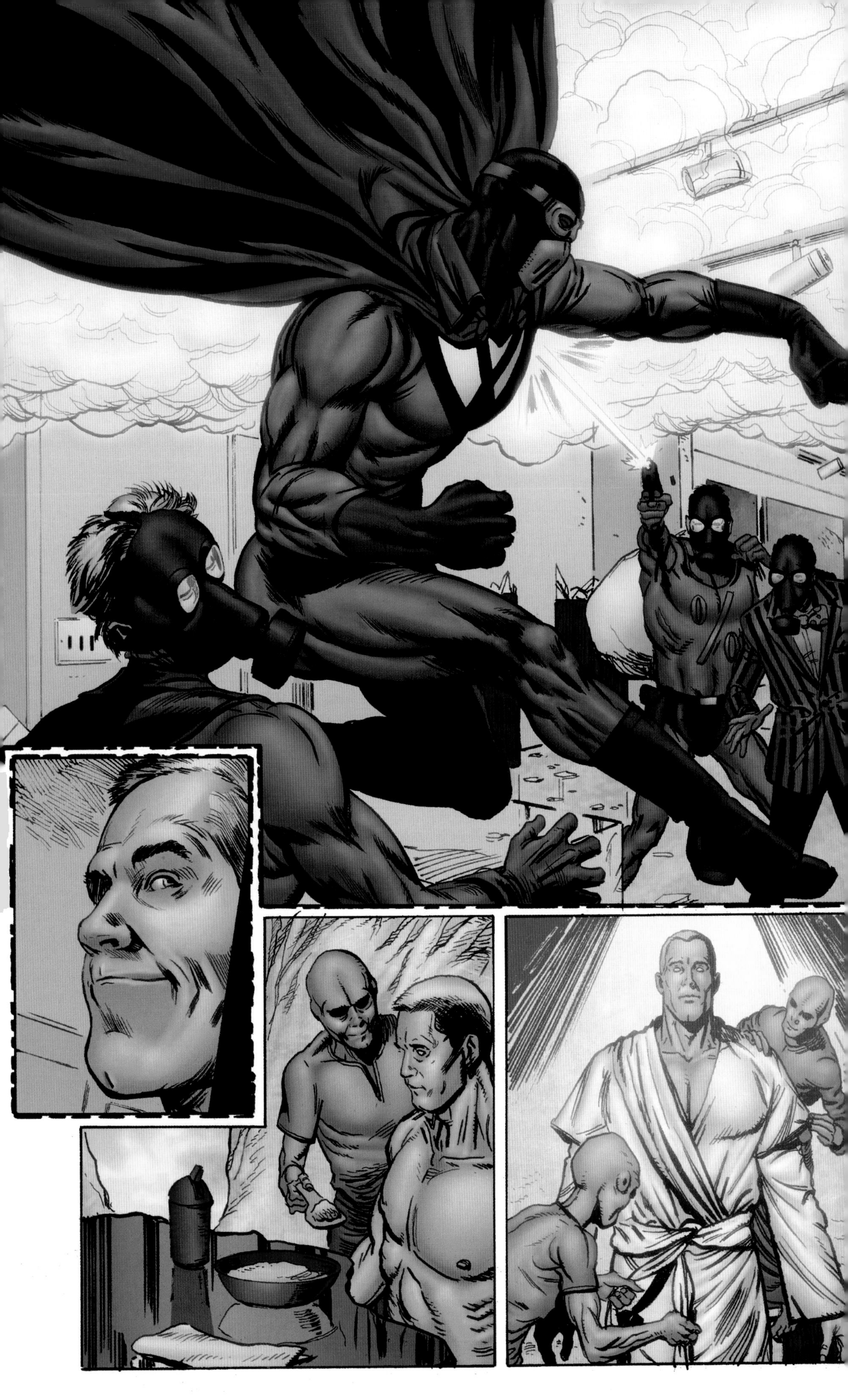

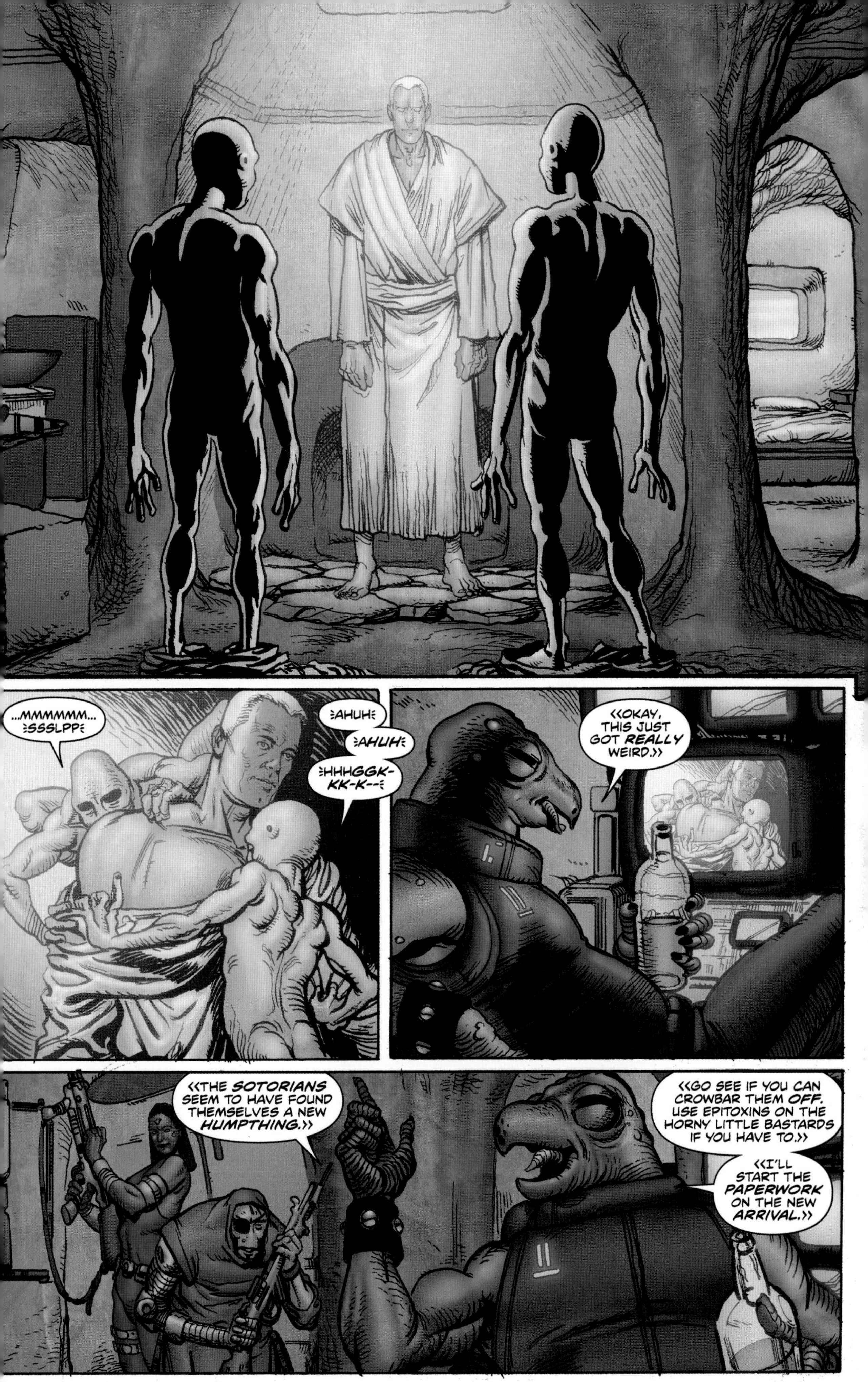
...MMMMMM... SSSLPP
AHUH
AHUH
HHHGGK-KK-K--
<<OKAY, THIS JUST GOT REALLY WEIRD.>>
<<THE SOTORIANS SEEM TO HAVE FOUND THEMSELVES A NEW HUMPTHING.>>
<<GO SEE IF YOU CAN CROWBAR THEM OFF. USE EPITOXINS ON THE HORNY LITTLE BASTARDS IF YOU HAVE TO.>>
<<I'LL START THE PAPERWORK ON THE NEW ARRIVAL.>>

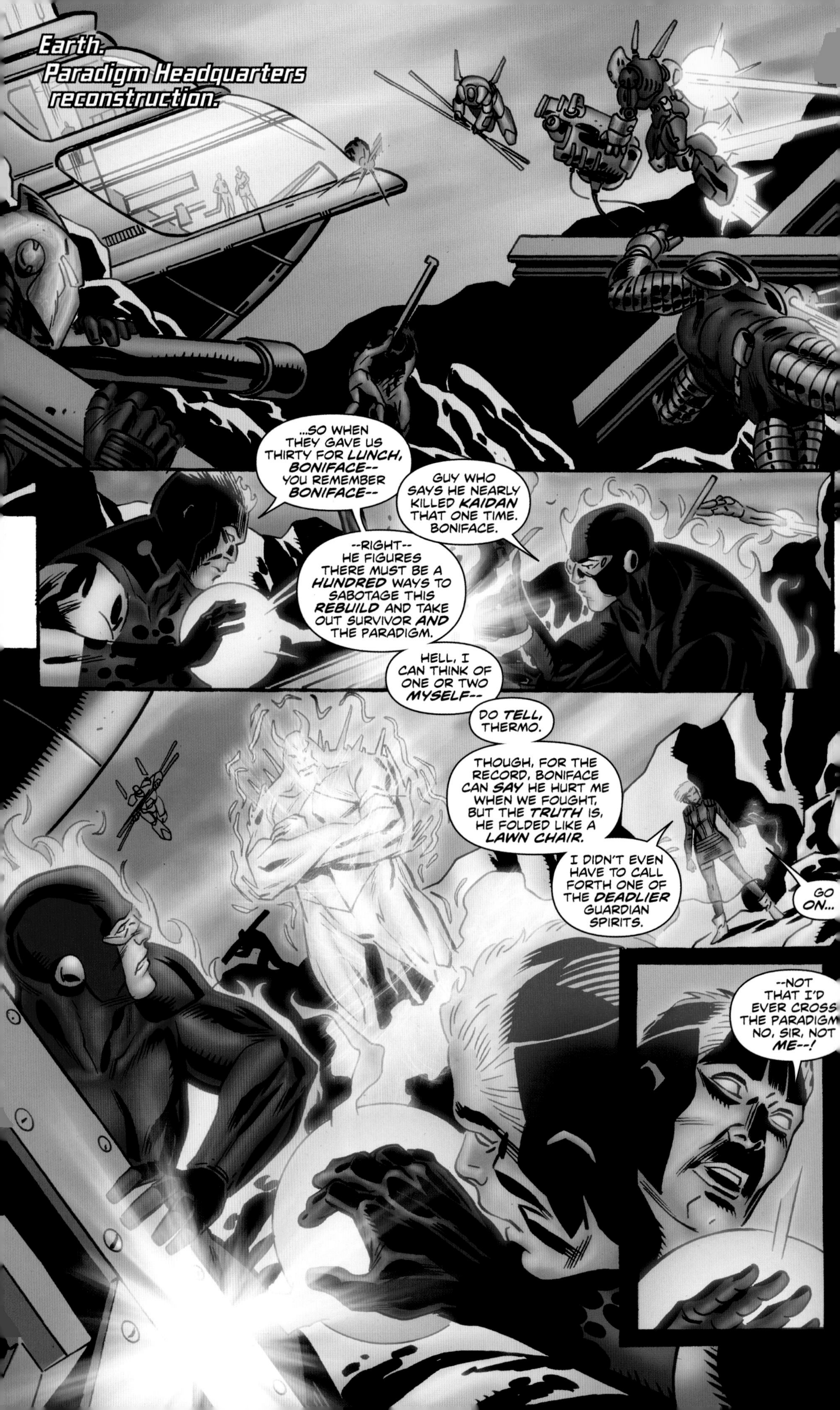
Earth. Paradigm Headquarters reconstruction.
...SO WHEN THEY GAVE US THIRTY FOR LUNCH, BONIFACE-- YOU REMEMBER BONIFACE--
GUY WHO SAYS HE NEARLY KILLED KAIDAN THAT ONE TIME. BONIFACE.
--RIGHT-- HE FIGURES THERE MUST BE A HUNDRED WAYS TO SABOTAGE THIS REBUILD AND TAKE OUT SURVIVOR AND THE PARADIGM.
HELL, I CAN THINK OF ONE OR TWO MYSELF--
DO TELL, THERMO.
THOUGH, FOR THE RECORD, BONIFACE CAN SAY HE HURT ME WHEN WE FOUGHT, BUT THE TRUTH IS, HE FOLDED LIKE A LAWN CHAIR.
I DIDN'T EVEN HAVE TO CALL FORTH ONE OF THE DEADLIER GUARDIAN SPIRITS.
GO ON...
--NOT THAT I'D EVER CROSS THE PARADIGM NO, SIR, NOT ME--!

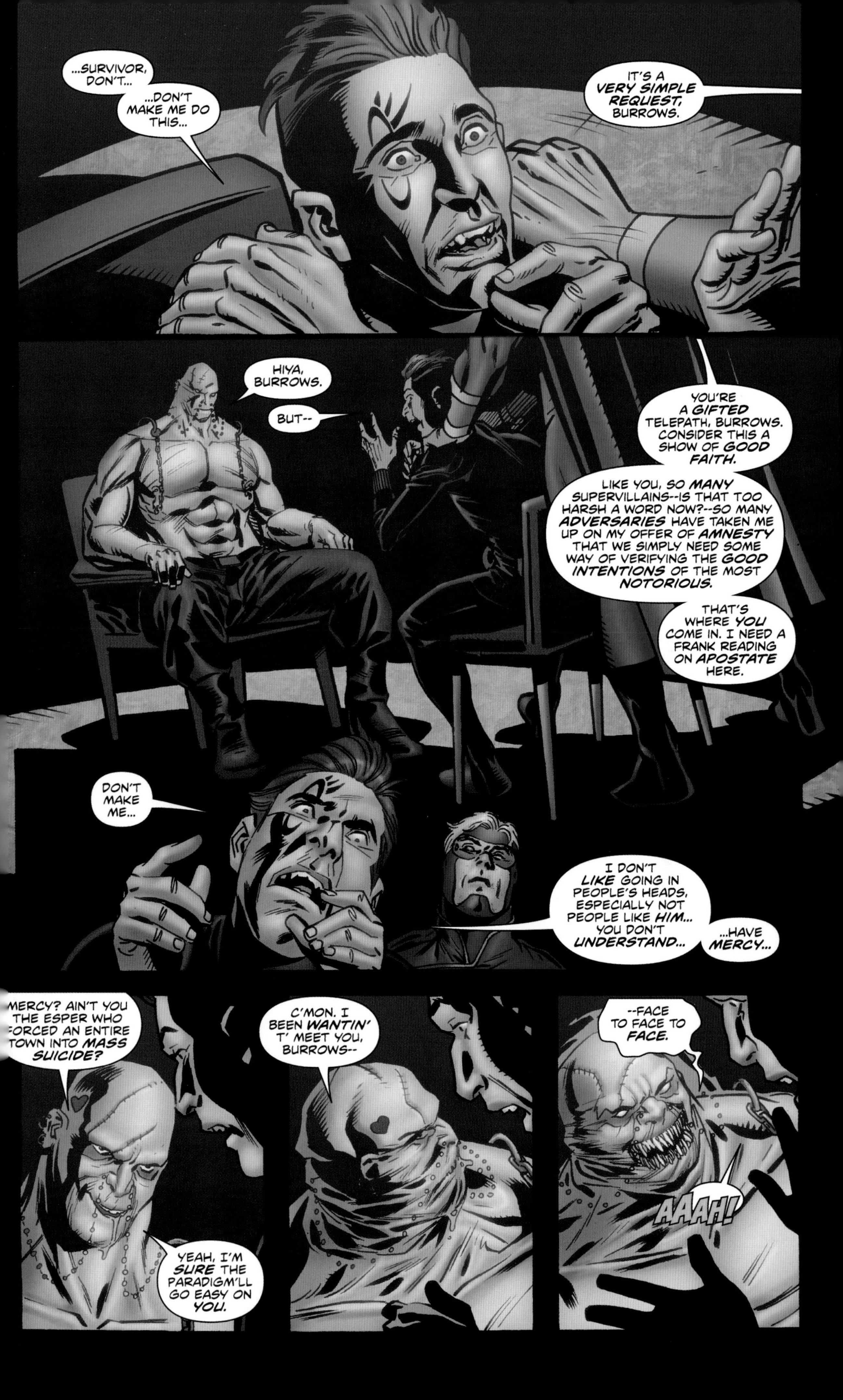
...SURVIVOR, DON'T...
...DON'T MAKE ME DO THIS...
IT'S A VERY SIMPLE REQUEST, BURROWS.
HIYA, BURROWS.
BUT--
YOU'RE A GIFTED TELEPATH, BURROWS. CONSIDER THIS A SHOW OF GOOD FAITH.
LIKE YOU, SO MANY SUPERVILLAINS--IS THAT TOO HARSH A WORD NOW?--SO MANY ADVERSARIES HAVE TAKEN ME UP ON MY OFFER OF AMNESTY THAT WE SIMPLY NEED SOME WAY OF VERIFYING THE GOOD INTENTIONS OF THE MOST NOTORIOUS.
THAT'S WHERE YOU COME IN. I NEED A FRANK READING ON APOSTATE HERE.
DON'T MAKE ME...
I DON'T LIKE GOING IN PEOPLE'S HEADS, ESPECIALLY NOT PEOPLE LIKE HIM... YOU DON'T UNDERSTAND...
...HAVE MERCY...
MERCY? AIN'T YOU THE ESPER WHO FORCED AN ENTIRE TOWN INTO MASS SUICIDE?
YEAH, I'M SURE THE PARADIGM'LL GO EASY ON YOU.
C'MON. I BEEN WANTIN' T' MEET YOU, BURROWS--
--FACE TO FACE TO FACE.
AAAH!

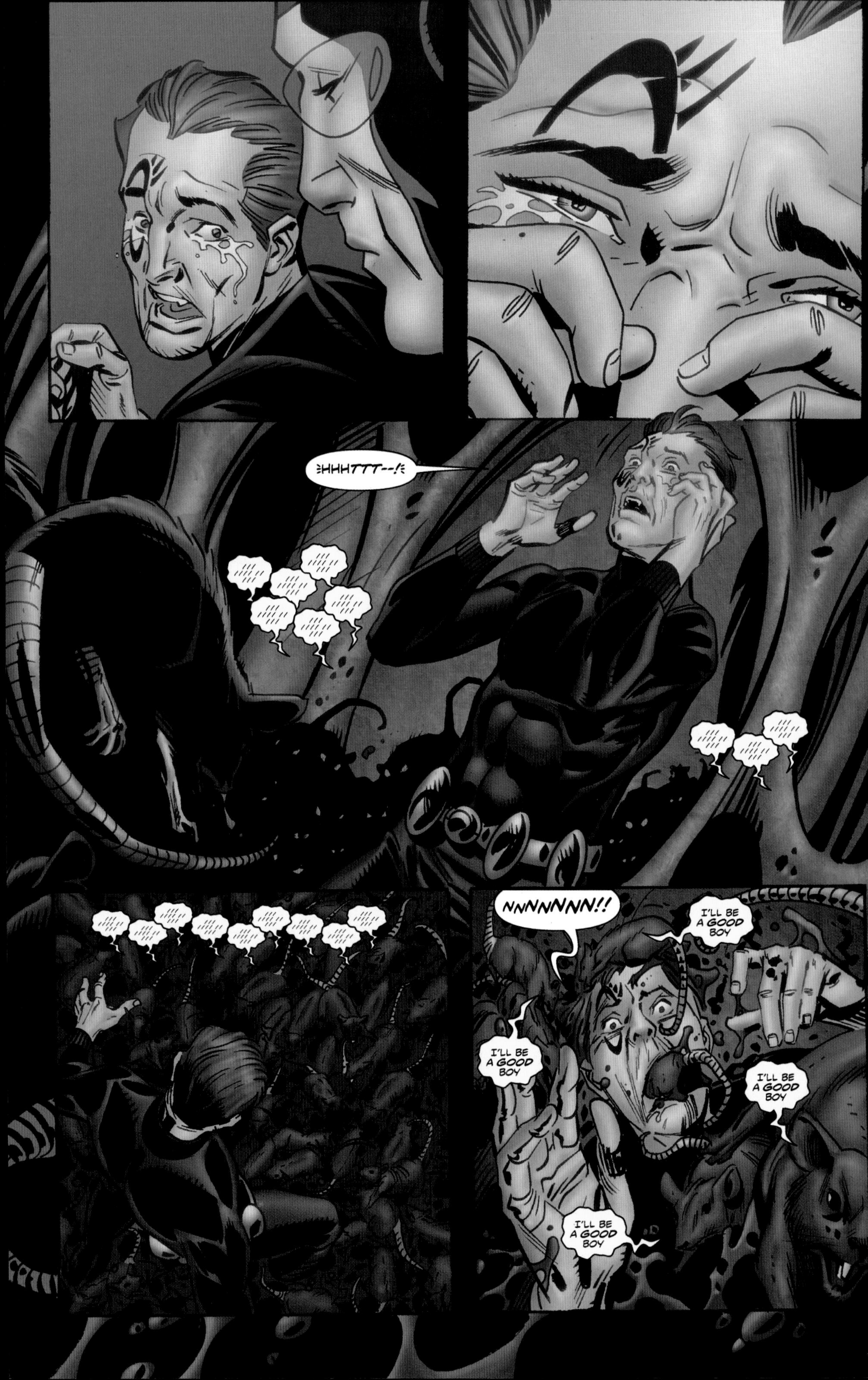
HHHTTT--!
NNNNNNN!!
I'LL BE A GOOD BOY
I'LL BE A GOOD BOY
I'LL BE A GOOD BOY
I'LL BE A GOOD BOY

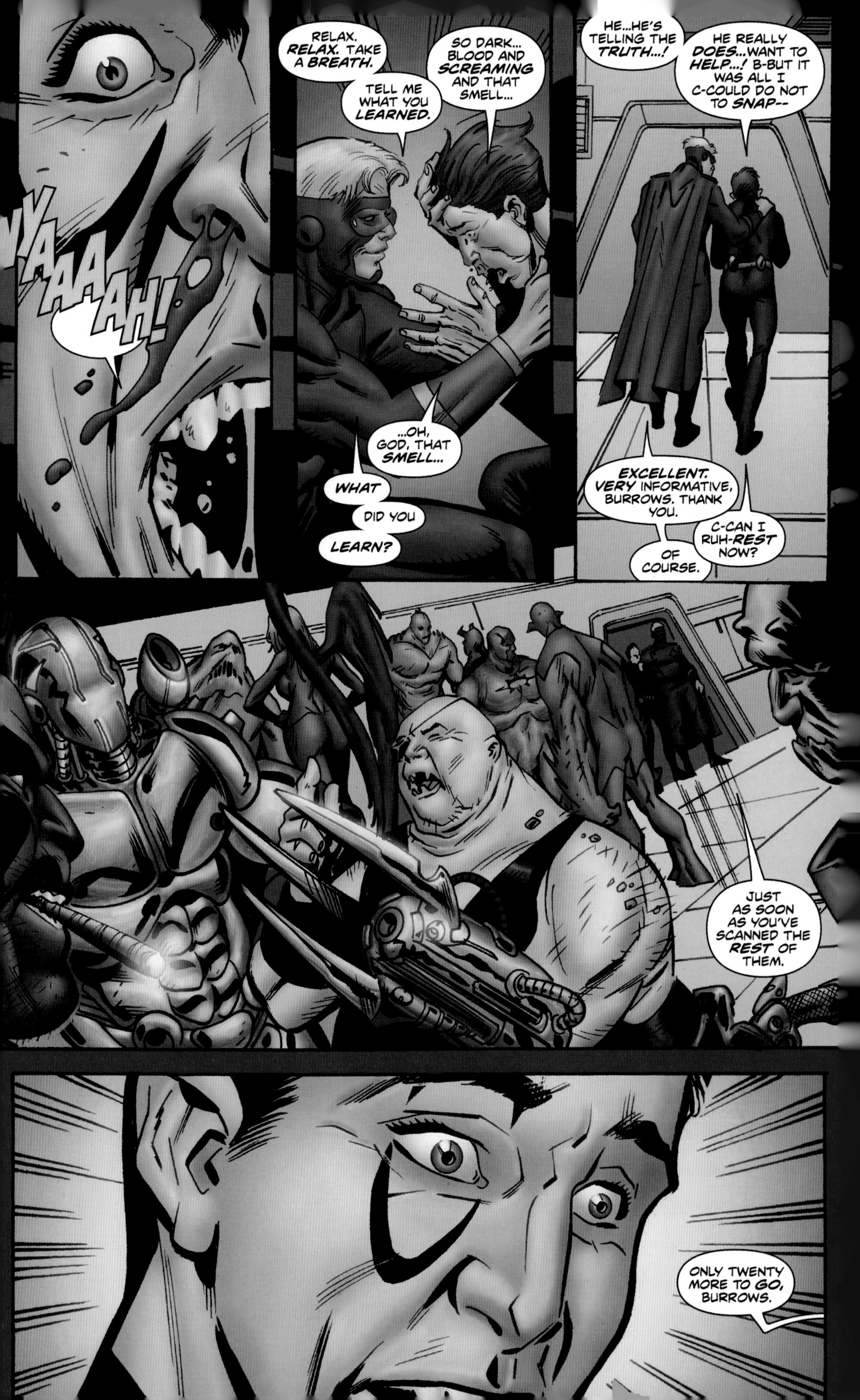

NYAAAAAH!
RELAX. RELAX. TAKE A BREATH.
TELL ME WHAT YOU LEARNED.
SO DARK... BLOOD AND SCREAMING AND THAT SMELL...
...OH, GOD, THAT SMELL...
WHAT
DID YOU
LEARN?
HE...HE'S TELLING THE TRUTH...!
HE REALLY DOES...WANT TO HELP...! B-BUT IT WAS ALL I C-COULD DO NOT TO SNAP--
EXCELLENT. VERY INFORMATIVE, BURROWS. THANK YOU.
C-CAN I RUH-REST NOW?
OF COURSE.
JUST AS SOON AS YOU'VE SCANNED THE REST OF THEM.
ONLY TWENTY MORE TO GO, BURROWS.

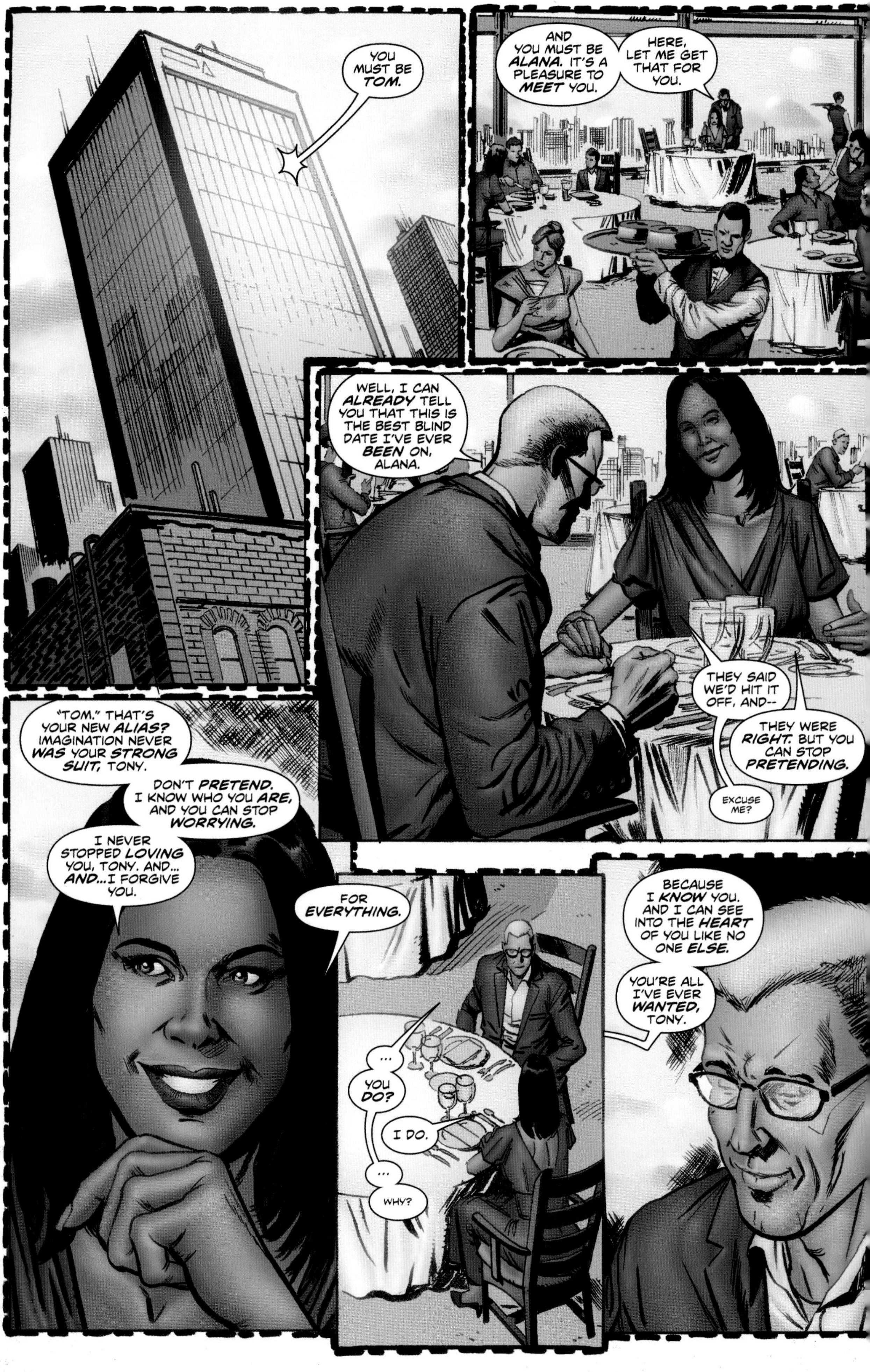
YOU MUST BE TOM.
AND YOU MUST BE ALANA. IT'S A PLEASURE TO MEET YOU.
HERE, LET ME GET THAT FOR YOU.
WELL, I CAN ALREADY TELL YOU THAT THIS IS THE BEST BLIND DATE I'VE EVER BEEN ON, ALANA.
THEY SAID WE'D HIT IT OFF, AND--
THEY WERE RIGHT. BUT YOU CAN STOP PRETENDING.
EXCUSE ME?
"TOM." THAT'S YOUR NEW ALIAS? IMAGINATION NEVER WAS YOUR STRONG SUIT, TONY.
DON'T PRETEND. I KNOW WHO YOU ARE, AND YOU CAN STOP WORRYING.
I NEVER STOPPED LOVING YOU, TONY. AND... AND...I FORGIVE YOU.
FOR EVERYTHING.
... YOU DO?
I DO.
... WHY?
BECAUSE I KNOW YOU. AND I CAN SEE INTO THE HEART OF YOU LIKE NO ONE ELSE.
YOU'RE ALL I'VE EVER WANTED, TONY.

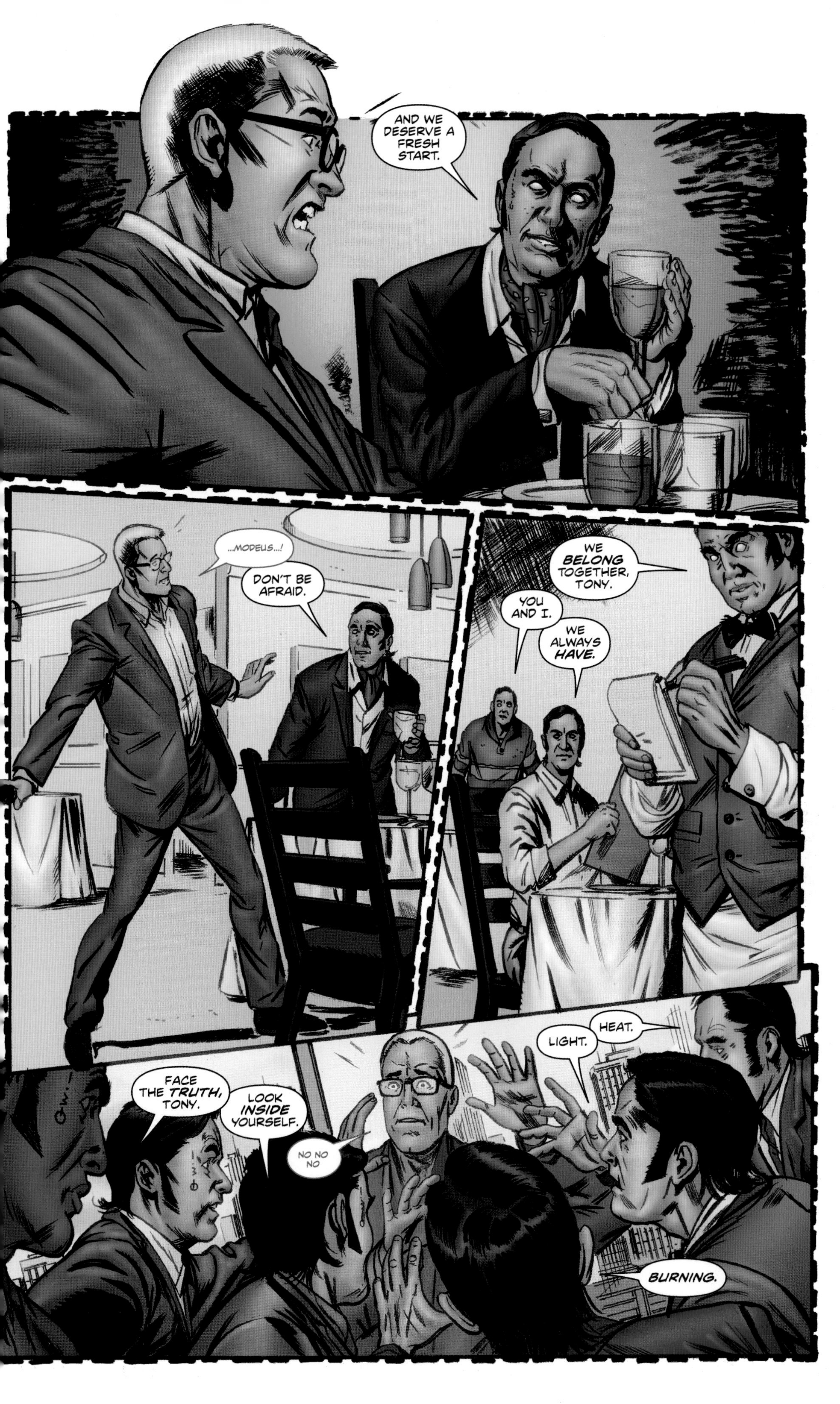
AND WE DESERVE A FRESH START.
...MODEUS...!
DON'T BE AFRAID.
WE BELONG TOGETHER, TONY.
YOU AND I.
WE ALWAYS HAVE.
FACE THE TRUTH, TONY.
LOOK INSIDE YOURSELF.
NO NO NO
LIGHT.
HEAT.
BURNING.

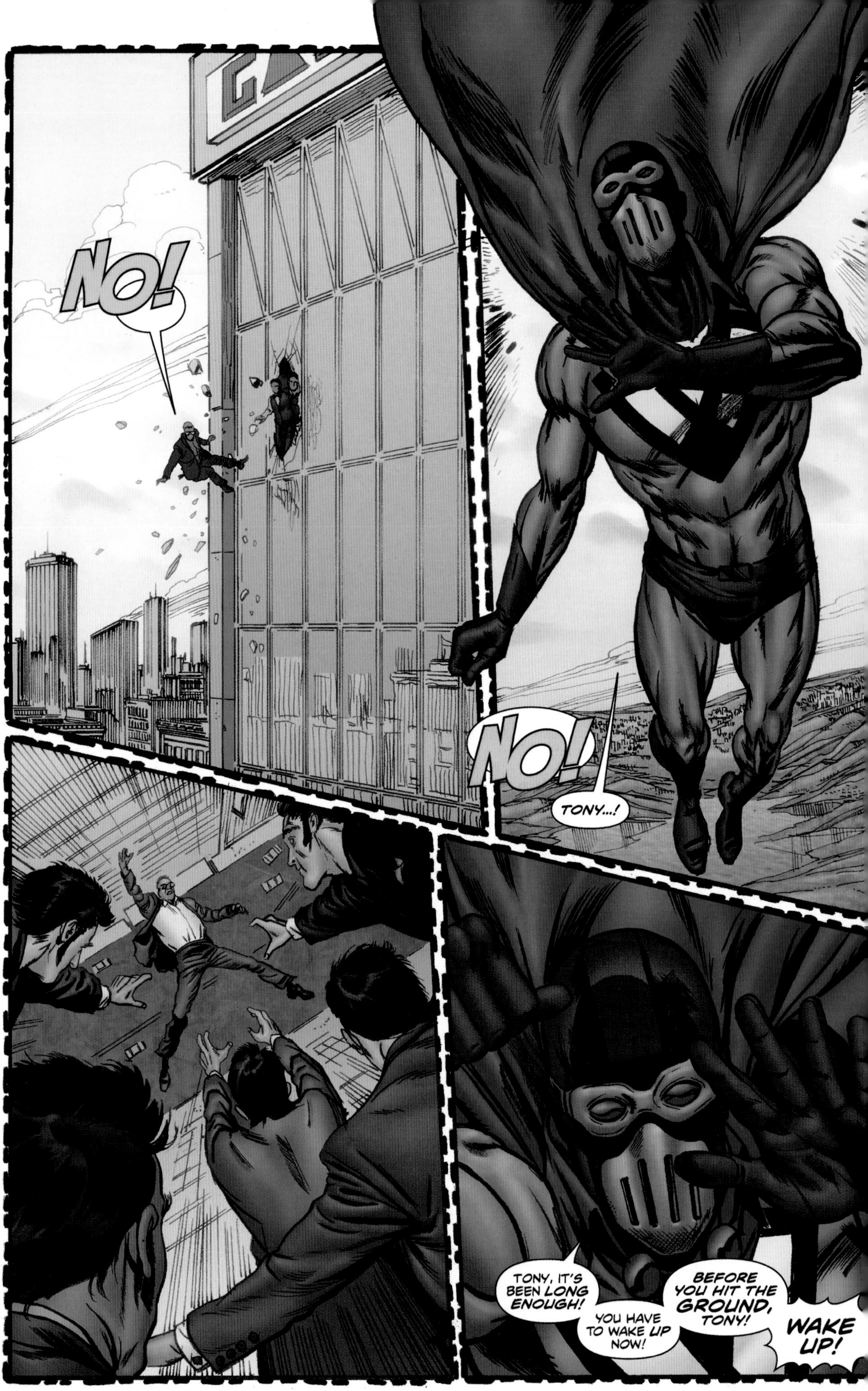
NO!
NO!
TONY...!
TONY, IT'S BEEN LONG ENOUGH!
YOU HAVE TO WAKE UP NOW!
BEFORE YOU HIT THE GROUND, TONY!
WAKE UP!

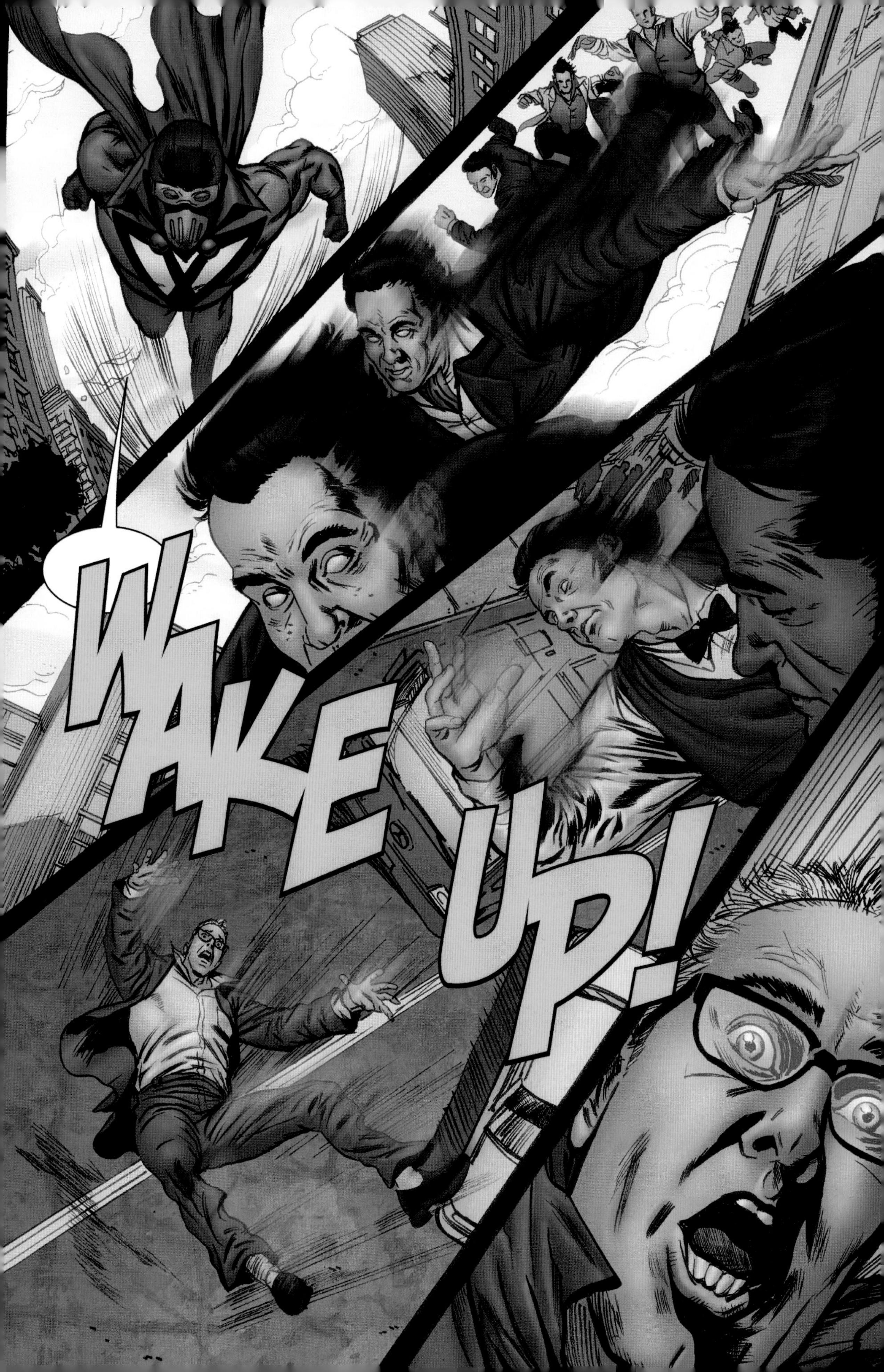
WAKE UP!

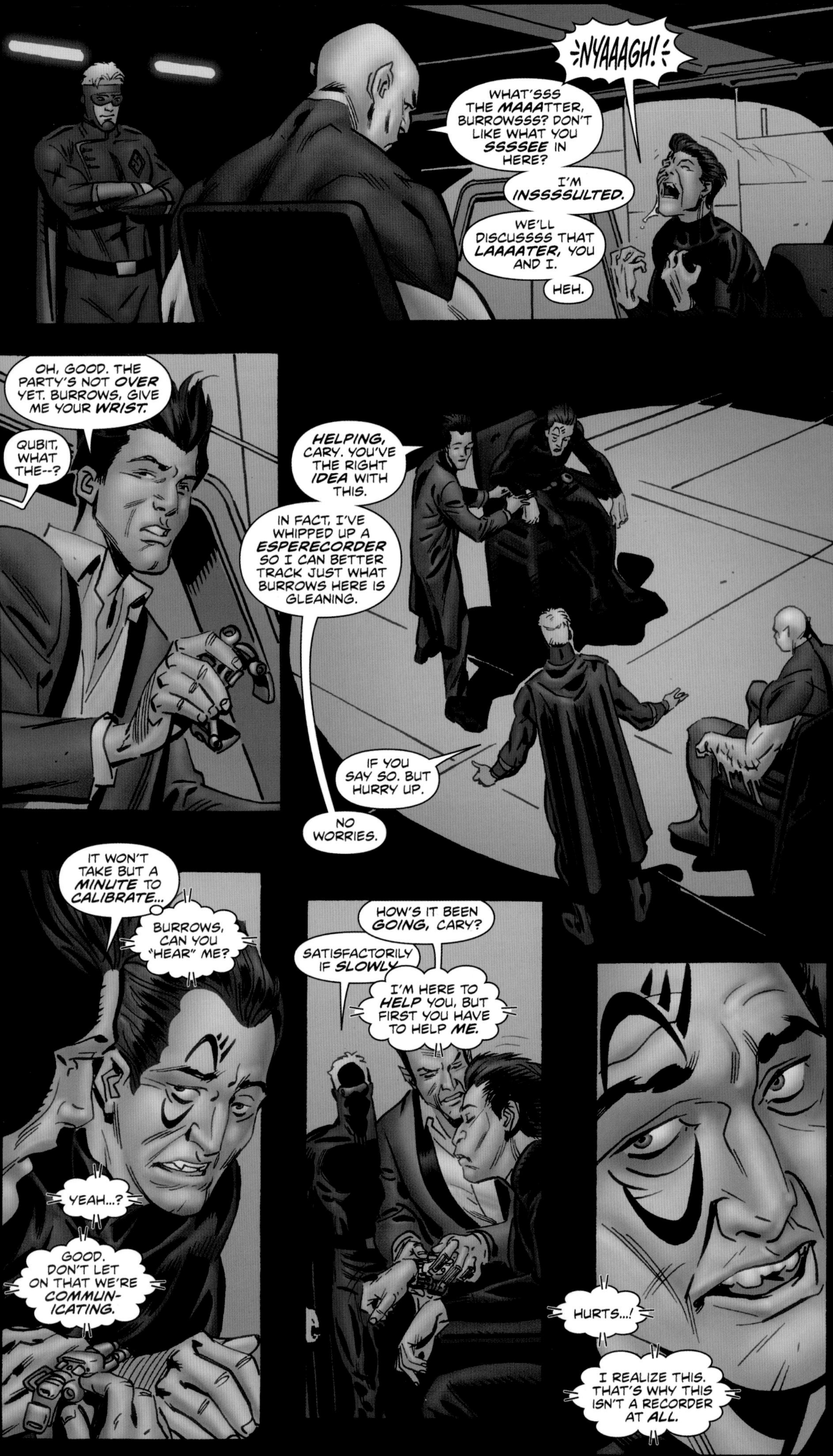

NYAAAGH!
WHAT'SSS THE MAAATTER, BURROWSSS? DON'T LIKE WHAT YOU SSSSEE IN HERE?
I'M INSSSSULTED.
WE'LL DISCUSSSS THAT LAAAATER, YOU AND I.
HEH.
OH, GOOD. THE PARTY'S NOT OVER YET. BURROWS, GIVE ME YOUR WRIST.
QUBIT, WHAT THE--?
HELPING, CARY. YOU'VE THE RIGHT IDEA WITH THIS.
IN FACT, I'VE WHIPPED UP A ESPERECORDER SO I CAN BETTER TRACK JUST WHAT BURROWS HERE IS GLEANING.
IF YOU SAY SO. BUT HURRY UP.
NO WORRIES.
IT WON'T TAKE BUT A MINUTE TO CALIBRATE...
BURROWS, CAN YOU "HEAR" ME?
YEAH...?
GOOD. DON'T LET ON THAT WE'RE COMMUN-ICATING.
HOW'S IT BEEN GOING, CARY?
SATISFACTORILY IF SLOWLY.
I'M HERE TO HELP YOU, BUT FIRST YOU HAVE TO HELP ME.
HURTS...!
I REALIZE THIS. THAT'S WHY THIS ISN'T A RECORDER AT ALL.

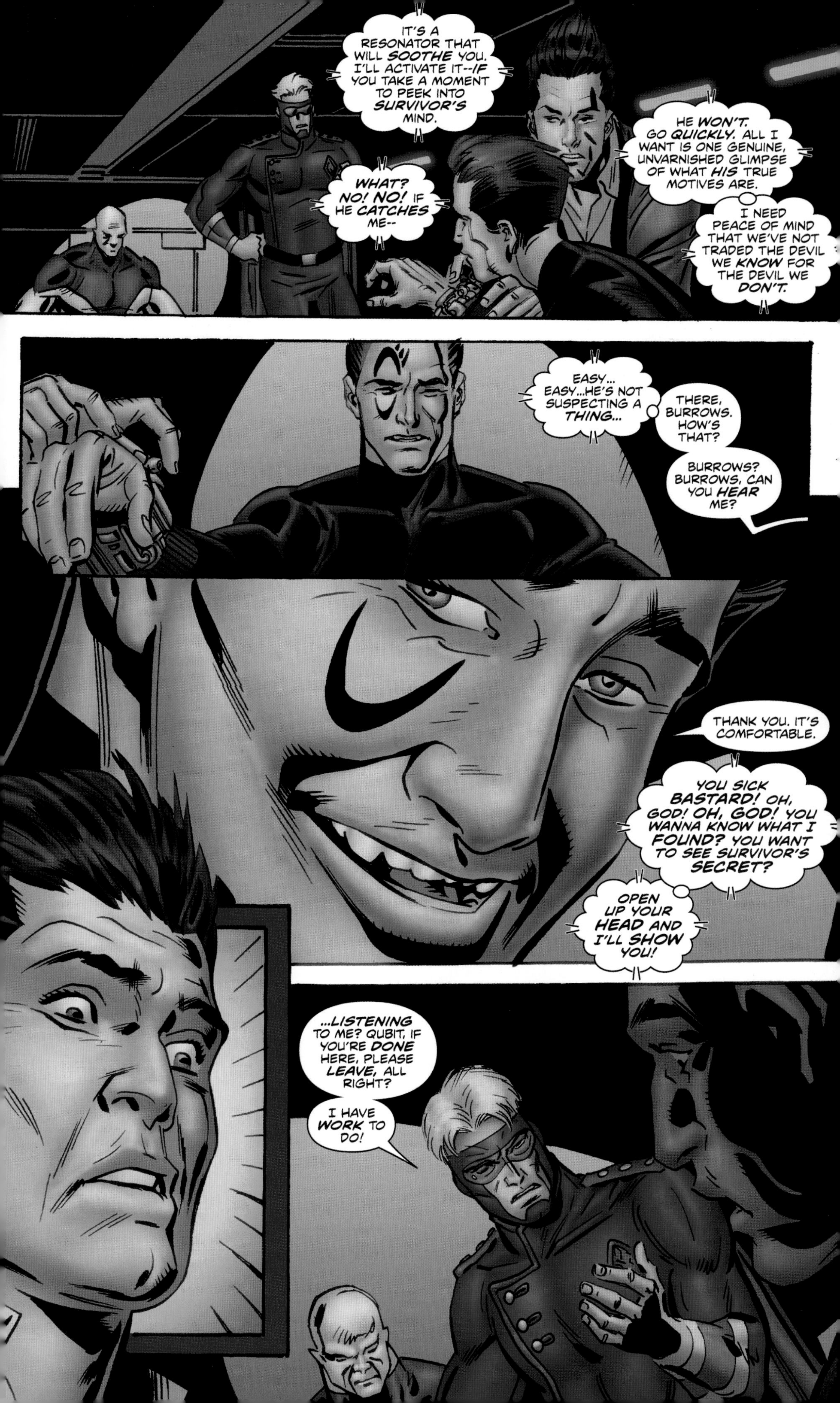
IT'S A RESONATOR THAT WILL SOOTHE YOU. I'LL ACTIVATE IT--IF YOU TAKE A MOMENT TO PEEK INTO SURVIVOR'S MIND.
WHAT? NO! NO! IF HE CATCHES ME--
HE WON'T. GO QUICKLY. ALL I WANT IS ONE GENUINE, UNVARNISHED GLIMPSE OF WHAT HIS TRUE MOTIVES ARE.
I NEED PEACE OF MIND THAT WE'VE NOT TRADED THE DEVIL WE KNOW FOR THE DEVIL WE DON'T.
EASY... EASY...HE'S NOT SUSPECTING A THING...
THERE, BURROWS. HOW'S THAT?
BURROWS? BURROWS, CAN YOU HEAR ME?
THANK YOU. IT'S COMFORTABLE.
YOU SICK BASTARD! OH, GOD! OH, GOD! YOU WANNA KNOW WHAT I FOUND? YOU WANT TO SEE SURVIVOR'S SECRET?
OPEN UP YOUR HEAD AND I'LL SHOW YOU!
...LISTENING TO ME? QUBIT, IF YOU'RE DONE HERE, PLEASE LEAVE, ALL RIGHT?
I HAVE WORK TO DO!

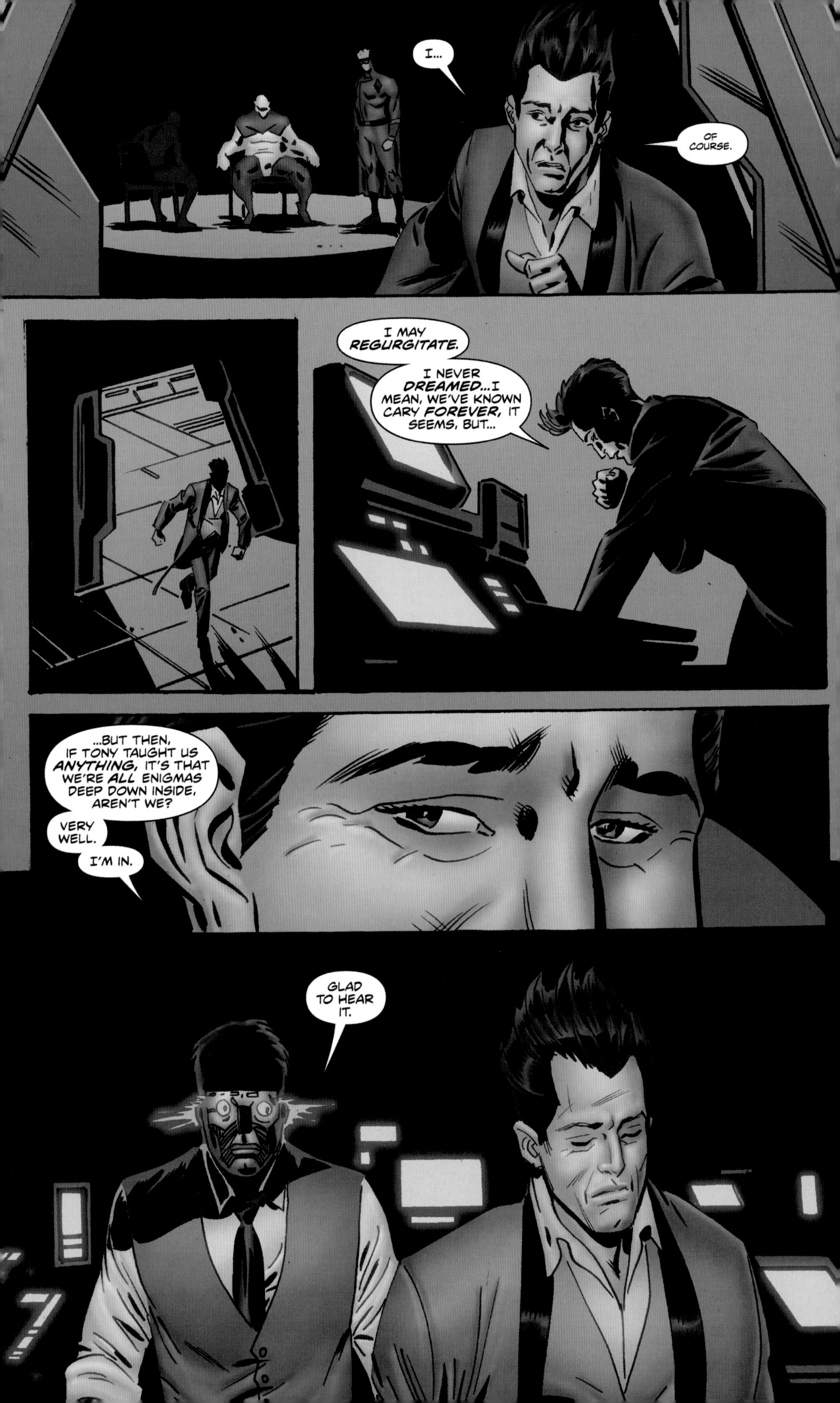
I...
OF COURSE.
I MAY REGURGITATE.
I NEVER DREAMED...I MEAN, WE'VE KNOWN CARY FOREVER, IT SEEMS, BUT...
...BUT THEN, IF TONY TAUGHT US ANYTHING, IT'S THAT WE'RE ALL ENIGMAS DEEP DOWN INSIDE, AREN'T WE?
VERY WELL.
I'M IN.
GLAD TO HEAR IT.

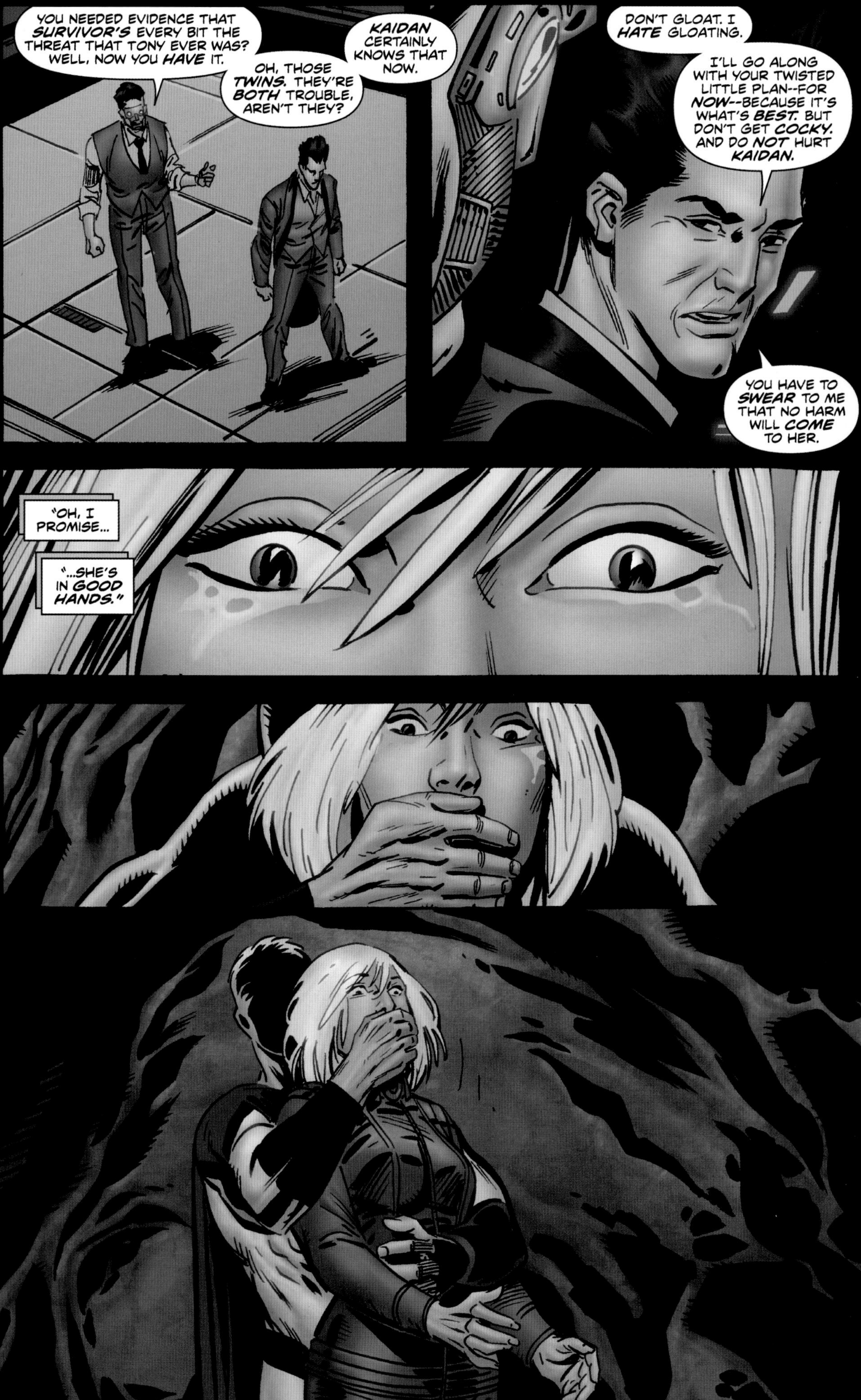

YOU NEEDED EVIDENCE THAT SURVIVOR'S EVERY BIT THE THREAT THAT TONY EVER WAS? WELL, NOW YOU HAVE IT.
OH, THOSE TWINS. THEY'RE BOTH TROUBLE, AREN'T THEY?
KAIDAN CERTAINLY KNOWS THAT NOW.
DON'T GLOAT. I HATE GLOATING.
I'LL GO ALONG WITH YOUR TWISTED LITTLE PLAN--FOR NOW--BECAUSE IT'S WHAT'S BEST. BUT DON'T GET COCKY. AND DO NOT HURT KAIDAN.
YOU HAVE TO SWEAR TO ME THAT NO HARM WILL COME TO HER.
"OH, I PROMISE...
"...SHE'S IN GOOD HANDS."

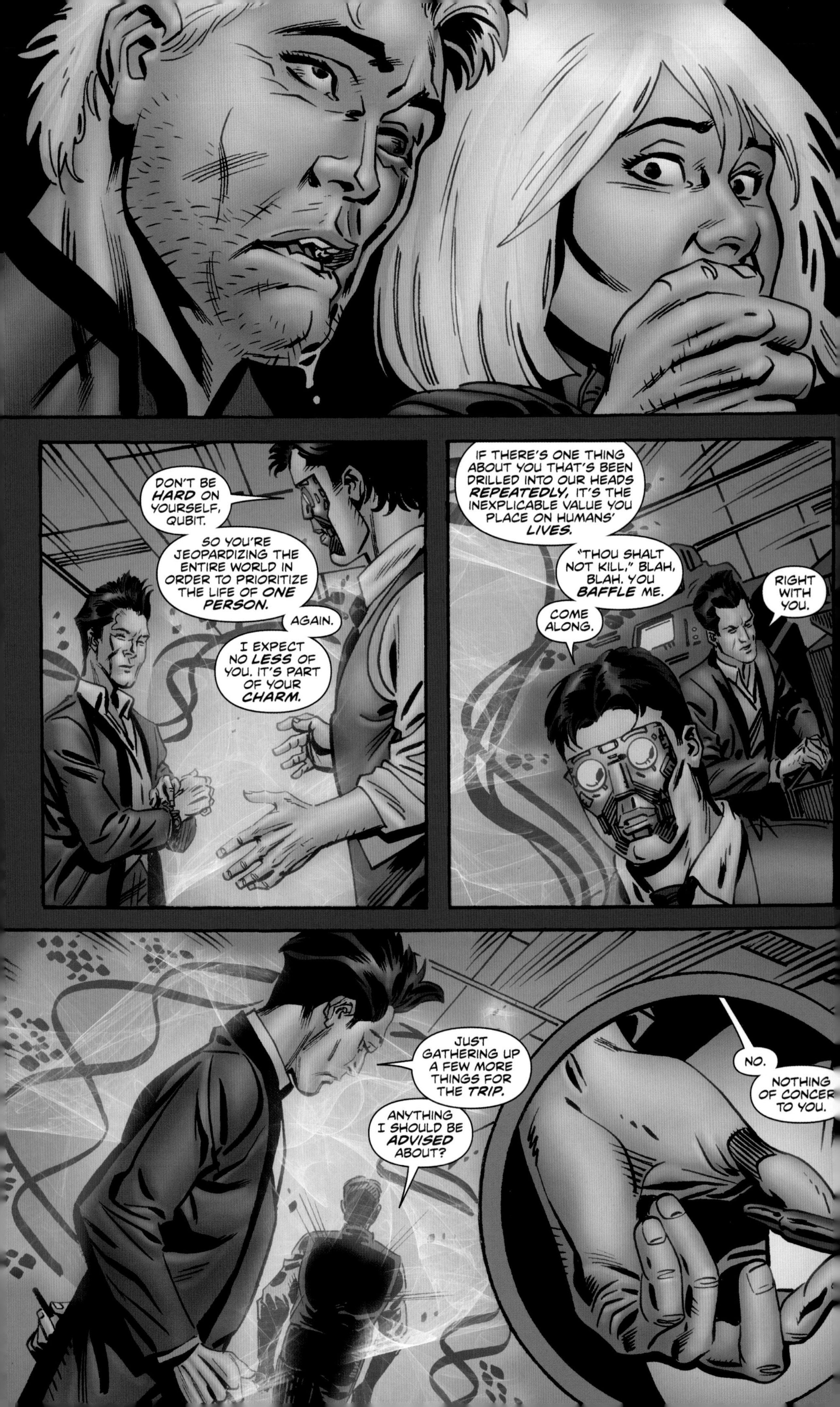

DON'T BE HARD ON YOURSELF, QUBIT.
SO YOU'RE JEOPARDIZING THE ENTIRE WORLD IN ORDER TO PRIORITIZE THE LIFE OF ONE PERSON.
AGAIN.
I EXPECT NO LESS OF YOU. IT'S PART OF YOUR CHARM.
IF THERE'S ONE THING ABOUT YOU THAT'S BEEN DRILLED INTO OUR HEADS REPEATEDLY, IT'S THE INEXPLICABLE VALUE YOU PLACE ON HUMANS' LIVES.
"THOU SHALT NOT KILL," BLAH, BLAH. YOU BAFFLE ME.
COME ALONG.
RIGHT WITH YOU.
JUST GATHERING UP A FEW MORE THINGS FOR THE TRIP.
ANYTHING I SHOULD BE ADVISED ABOUT?
NO.
NOTHING OF CONCER TO YOU.

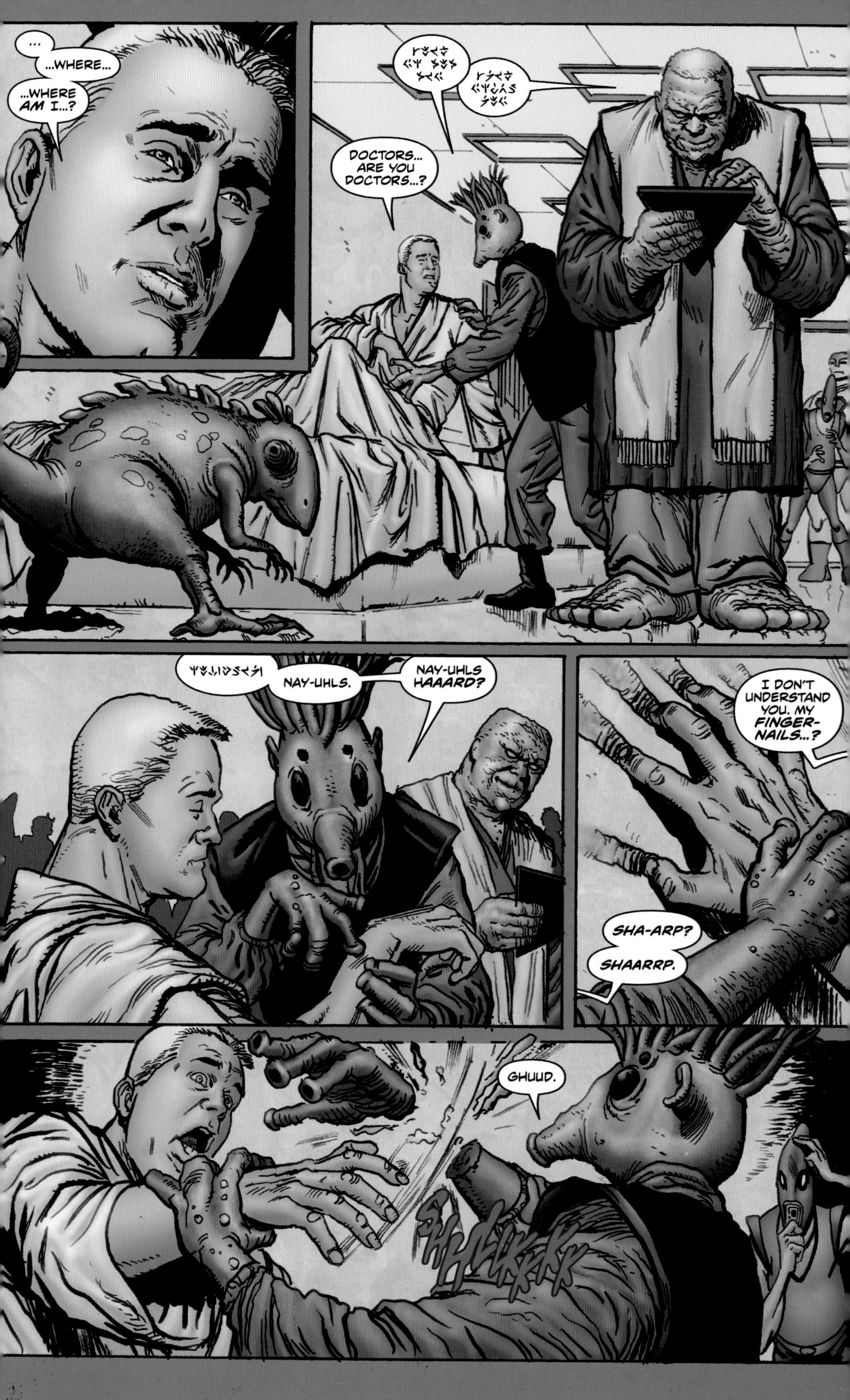
...
...WHERE...
...WHERE AM I...?
DOCTORS... ARE YOU DOCTORS...?
NAY-UHLS.
NAY-UHLS HAAARD?
I DON'T UNDERSTAND YOU. MY FINGER-NAILS...?
SHA-ARP?
SHAARRP.
GHUUD.
SHLIKKK

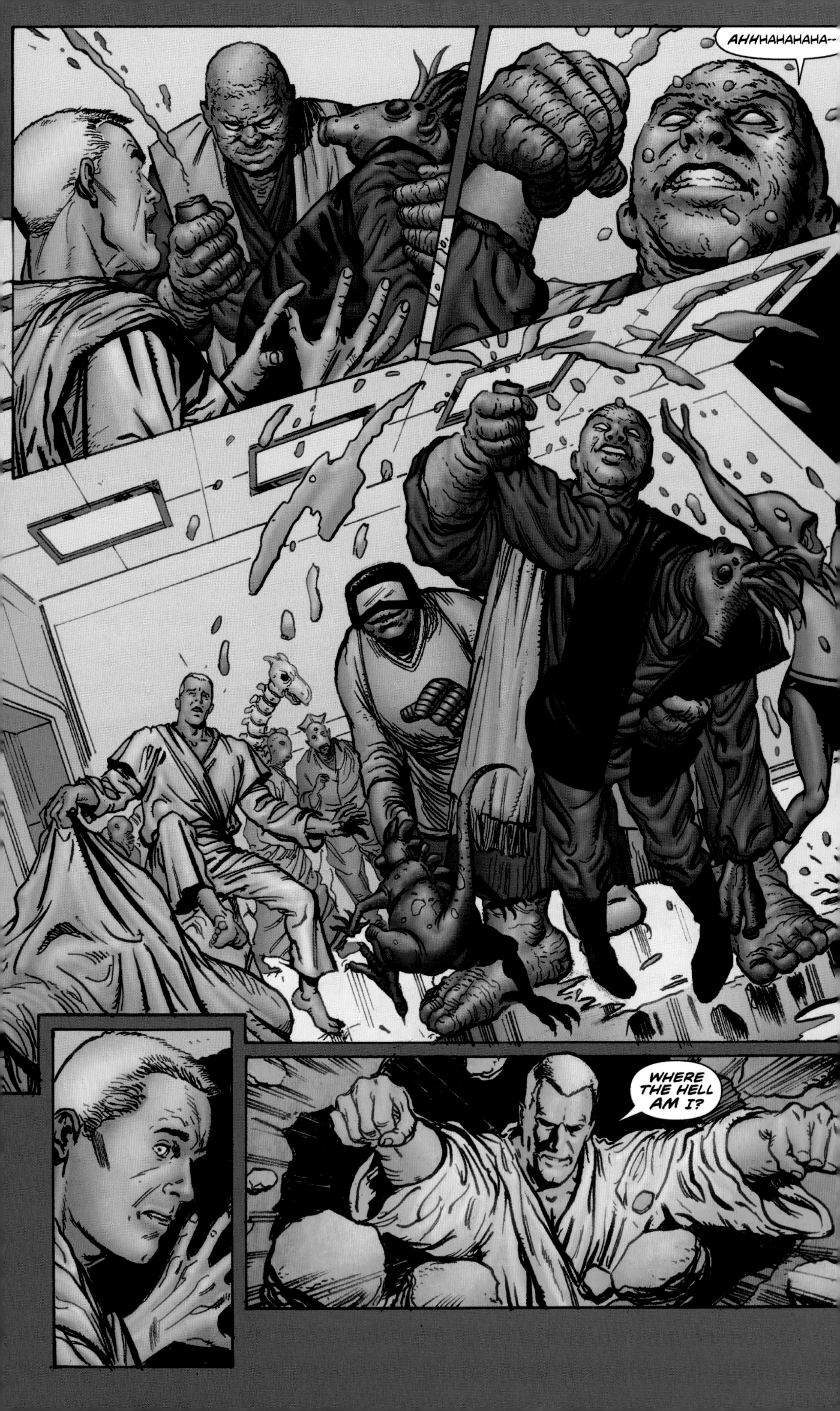
AHHHAHAHAHA--
WHERE THE HELL AM I?

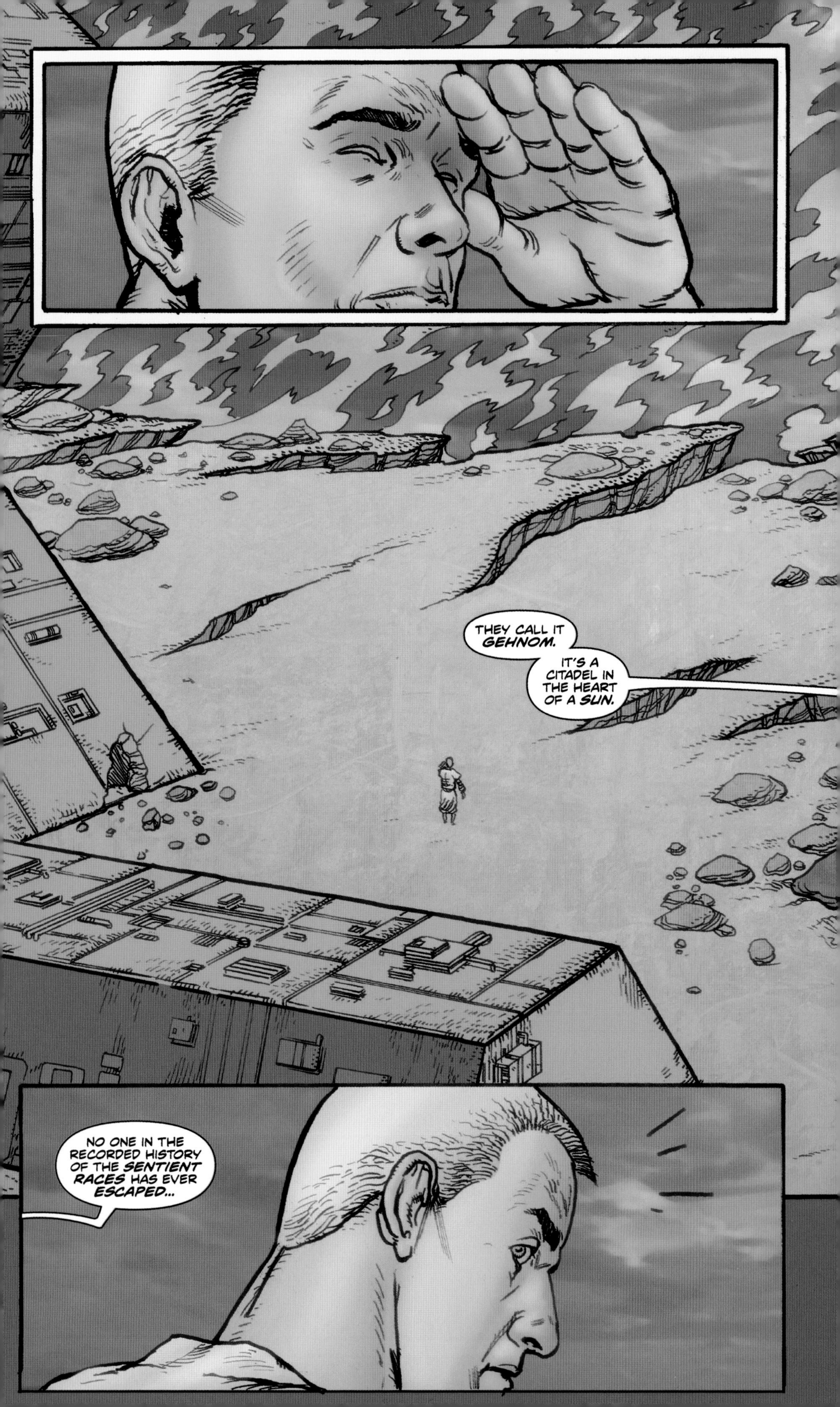
THEY CALL IT GEHNOM.
IT'S A CITADEL IN THE HEART OF A SUN.
NO ONE IN THE RECORDED HISTORY OF THE SENTIENT RACES HAS EVER ESCAPED...

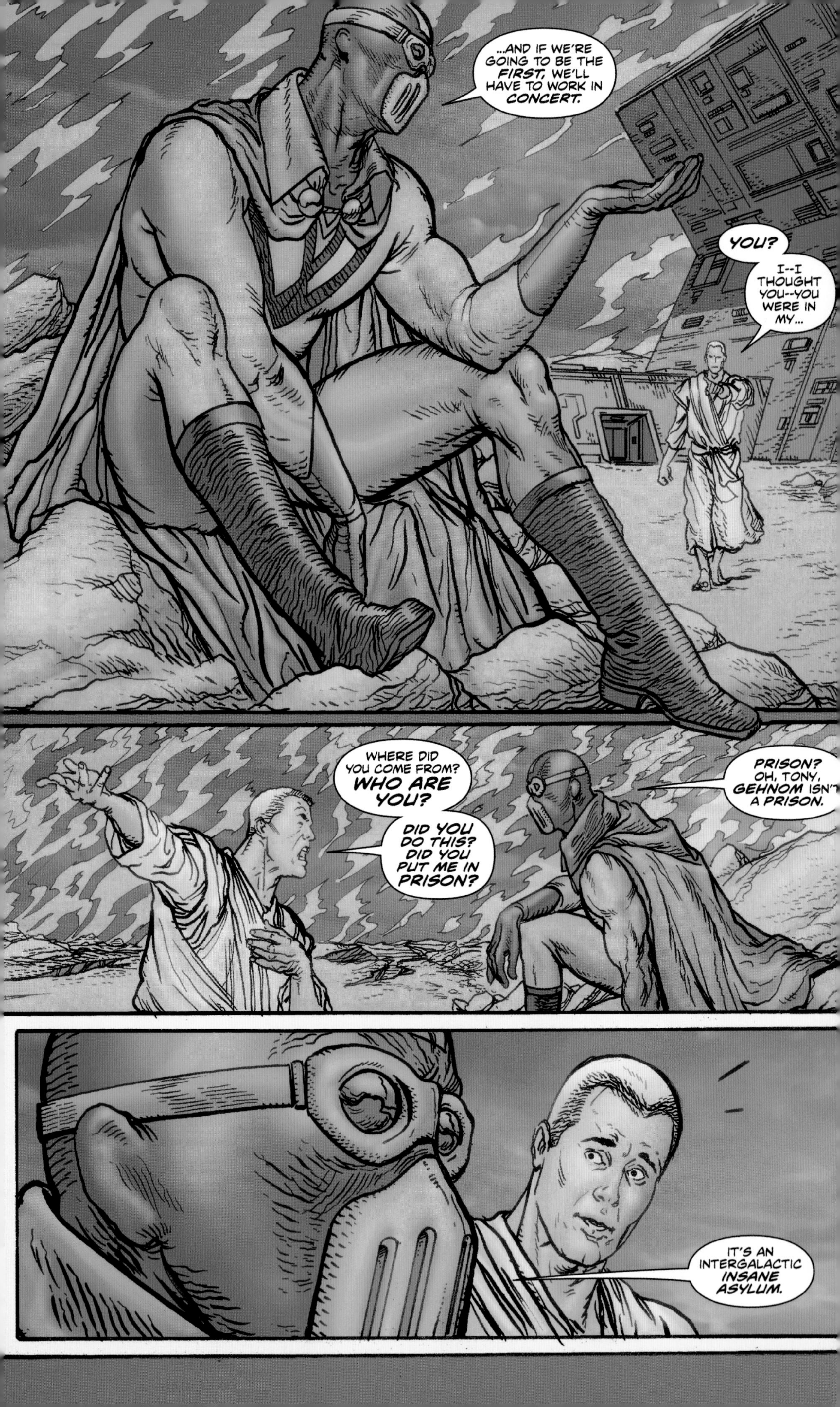
...AND IF WE'RE GOING TO BE THE FIRST, WE'LL HAVE TO WORK IN CONCERT.
YOU?
I--I THOUGHT YOU--YOU WERE IN MY...
WHERE DID YOU COME FROM? WHO ARE YOU?
DID YOU DO THIS? DID YOU PUT ME IN PRISON?
PRISON? OH, TONY. GEHNOM ISN'T A PRISON.
IT'S AN INTERGALACTIC INSANE ASYLUM.

IRREDE

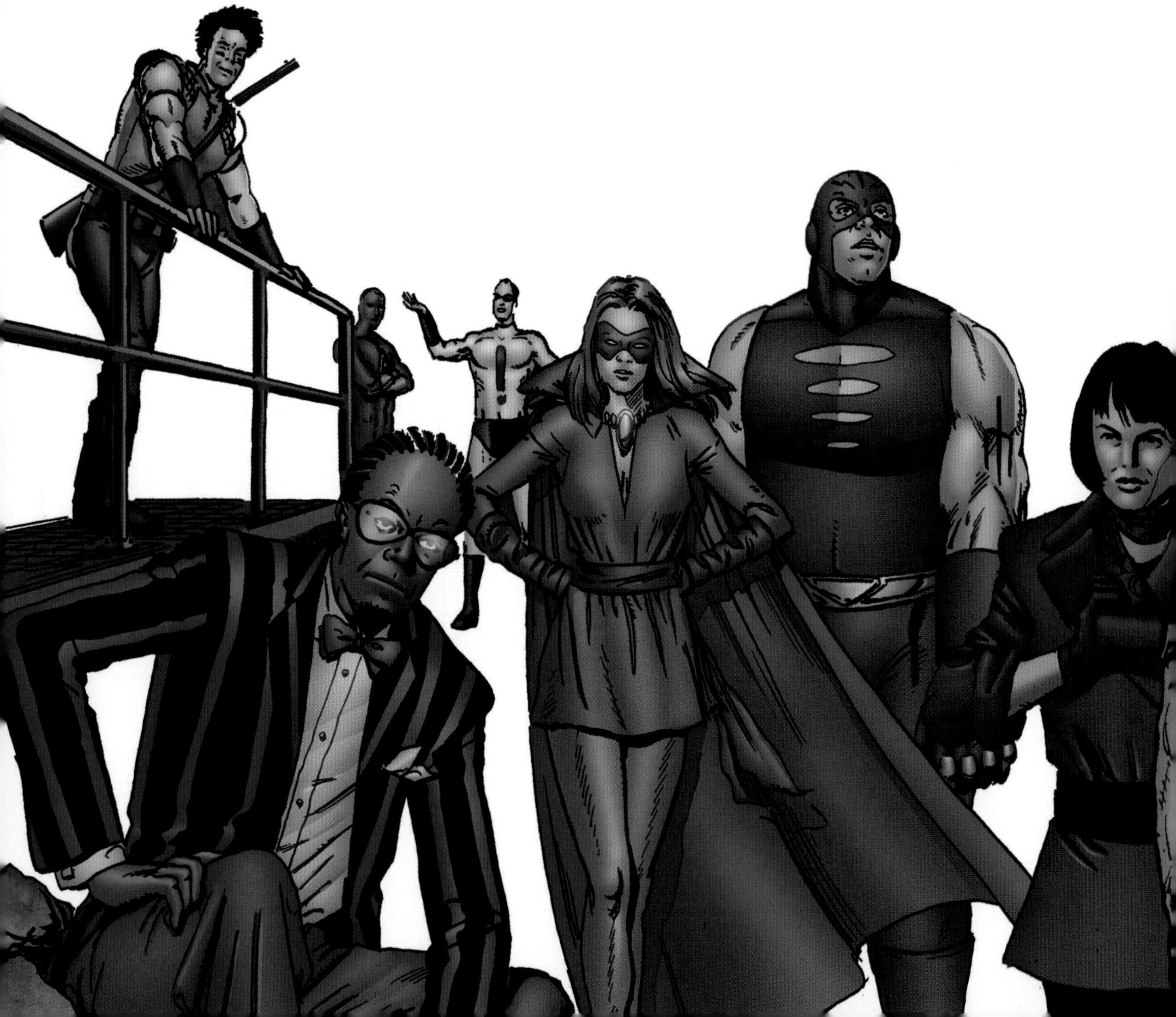

MABLE

COVER GALLERY

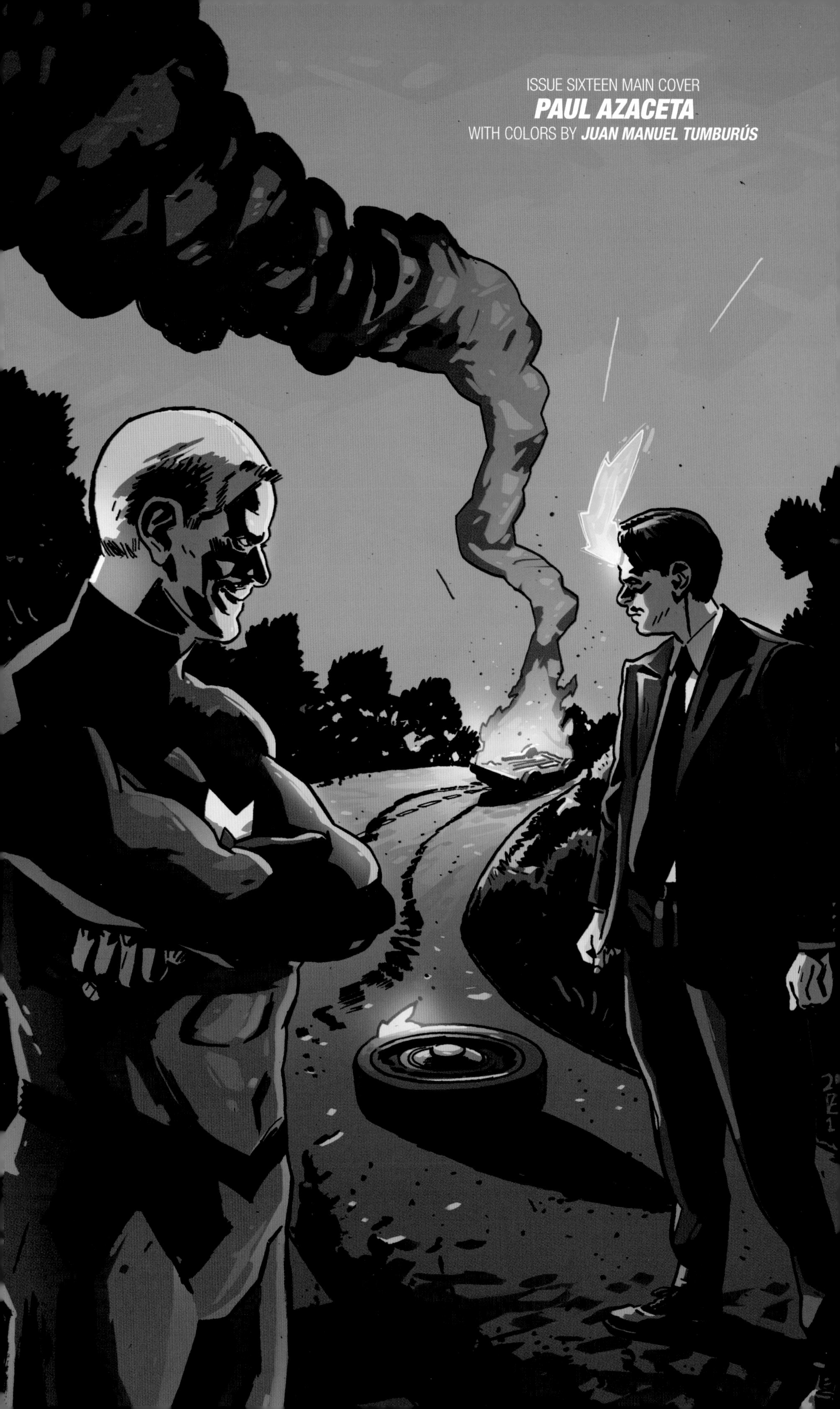

ISSUE SIXTEEN MAIN COVER
PAUL AZACETA
WITH COLORS BY ***JUAN MANUEL TUMBURÚS***

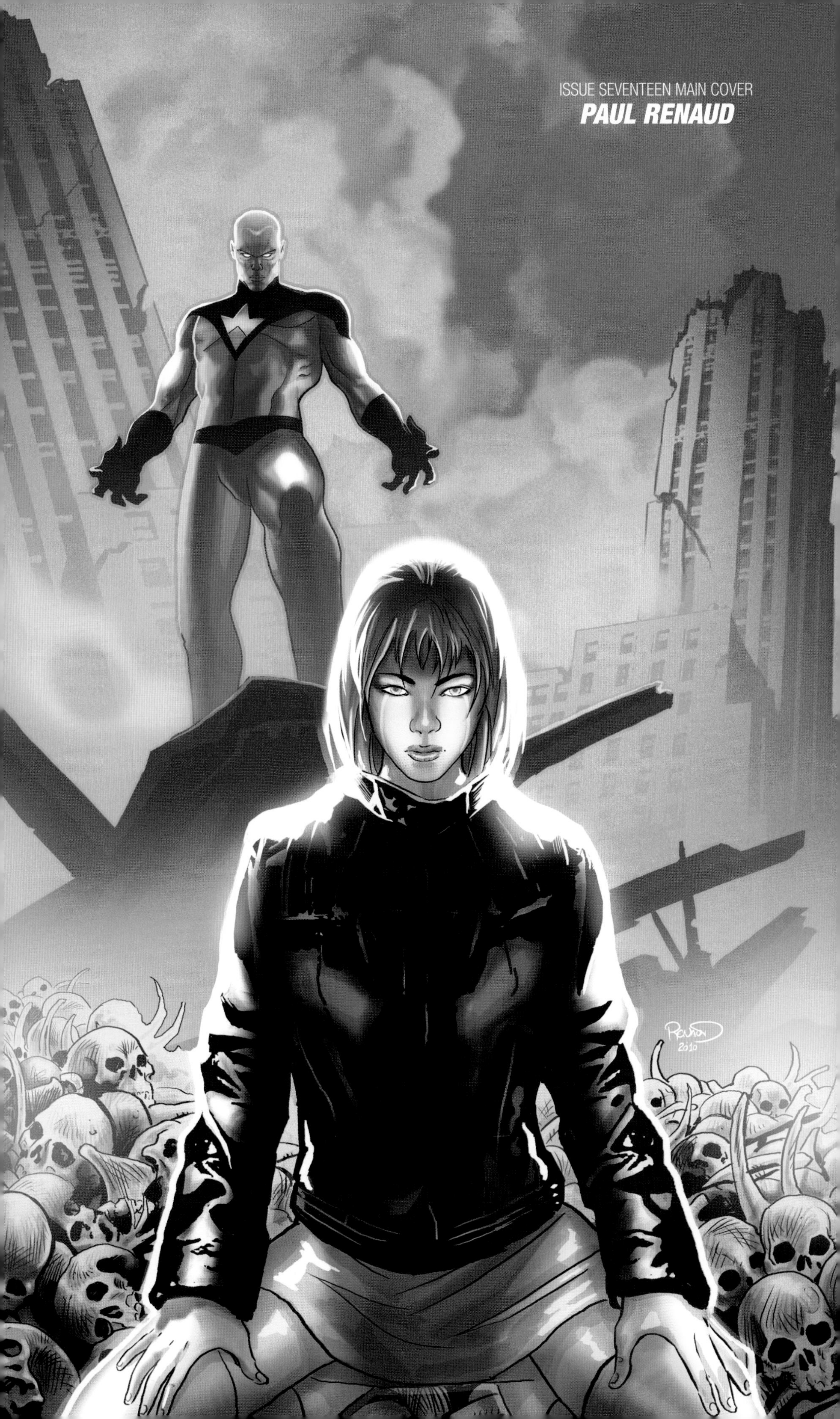

ISSUE SEVENTEEN MAIN COVER
PAUL RENAUD

ISSUE EIGHTEEN MAIN COVER
DAN PANOSIAN

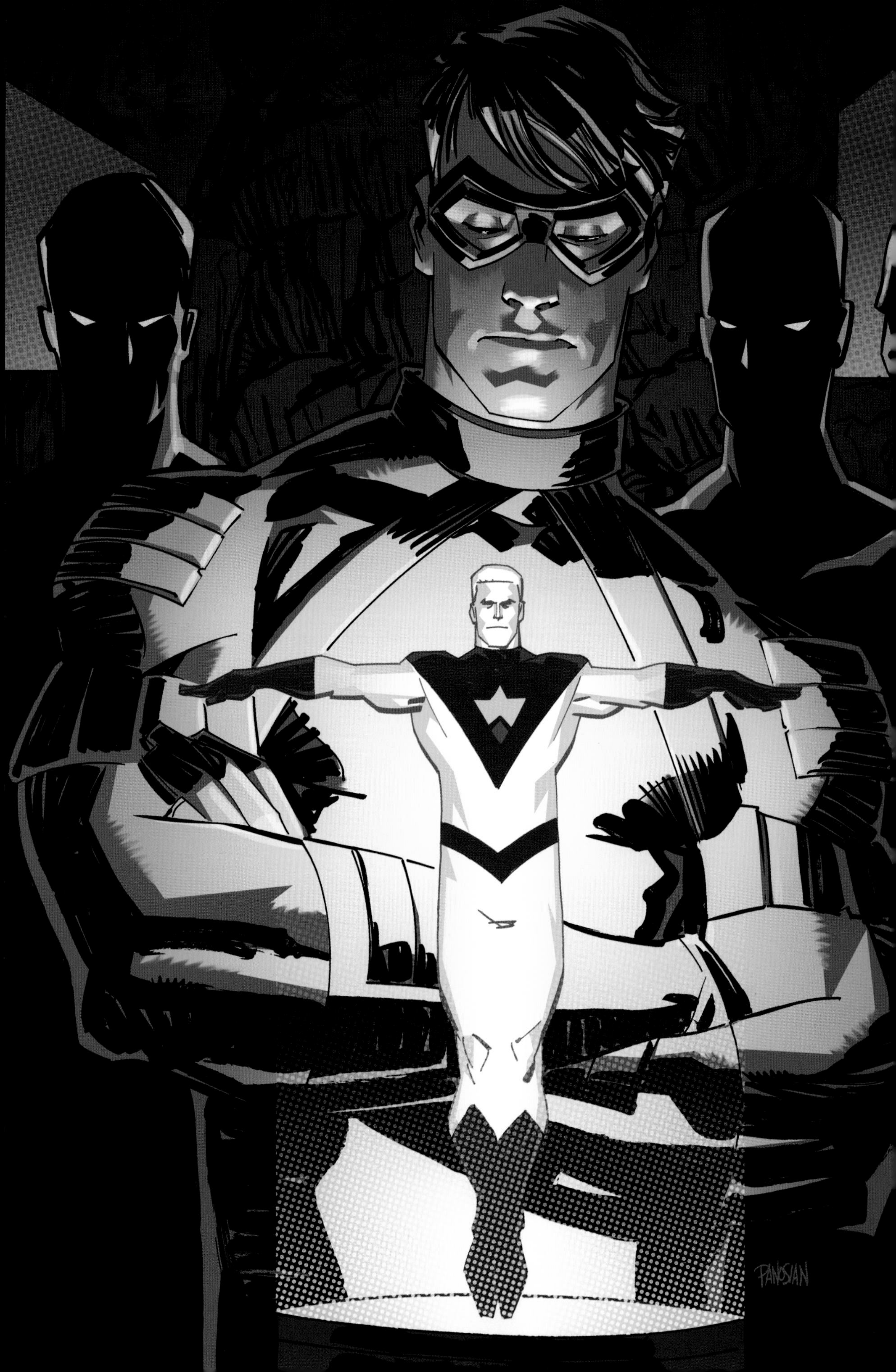
PANOSIAN

ISSUE NINETEEN MAIN COVER
DAN PANOSIAN

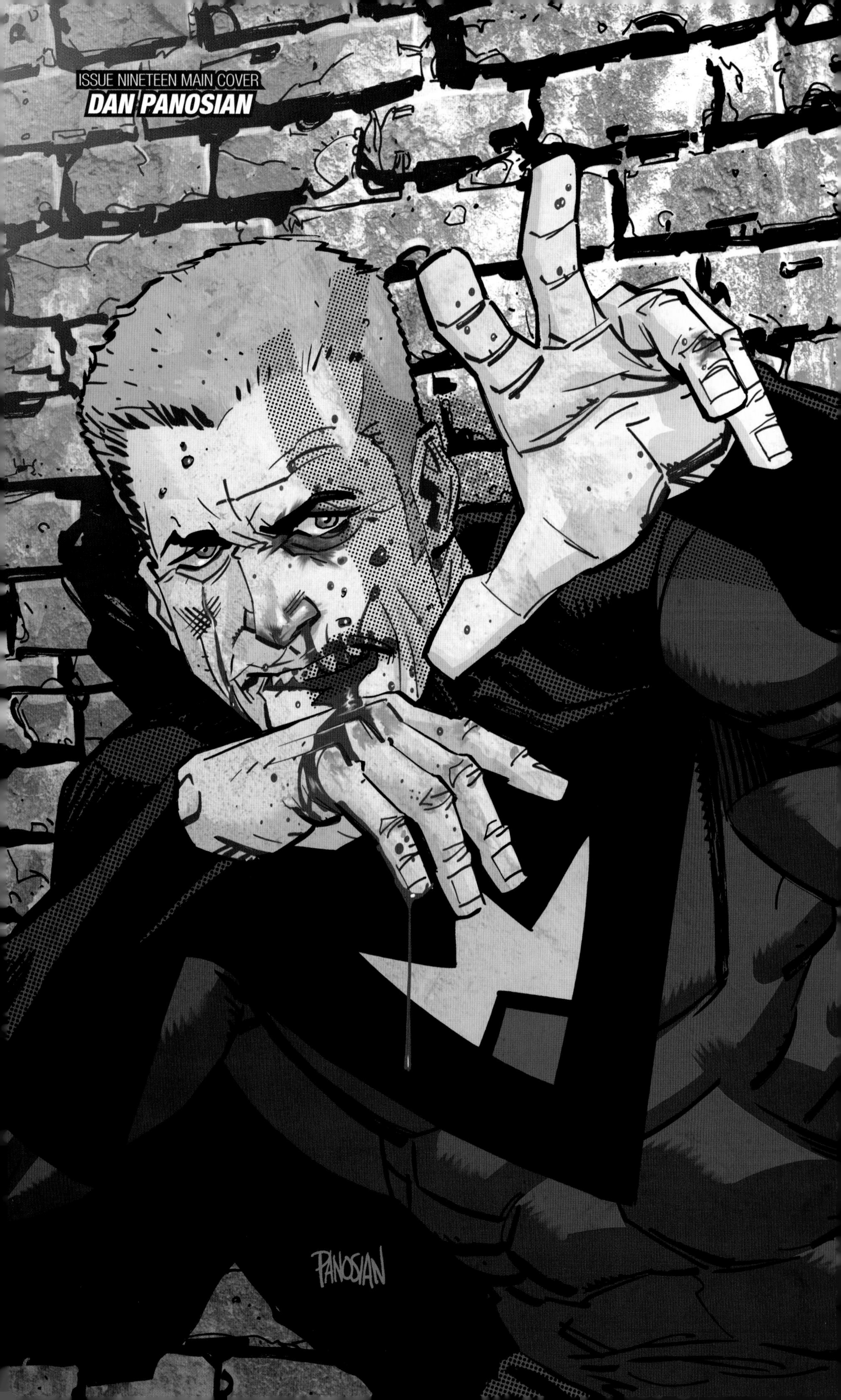
PANOSIAN

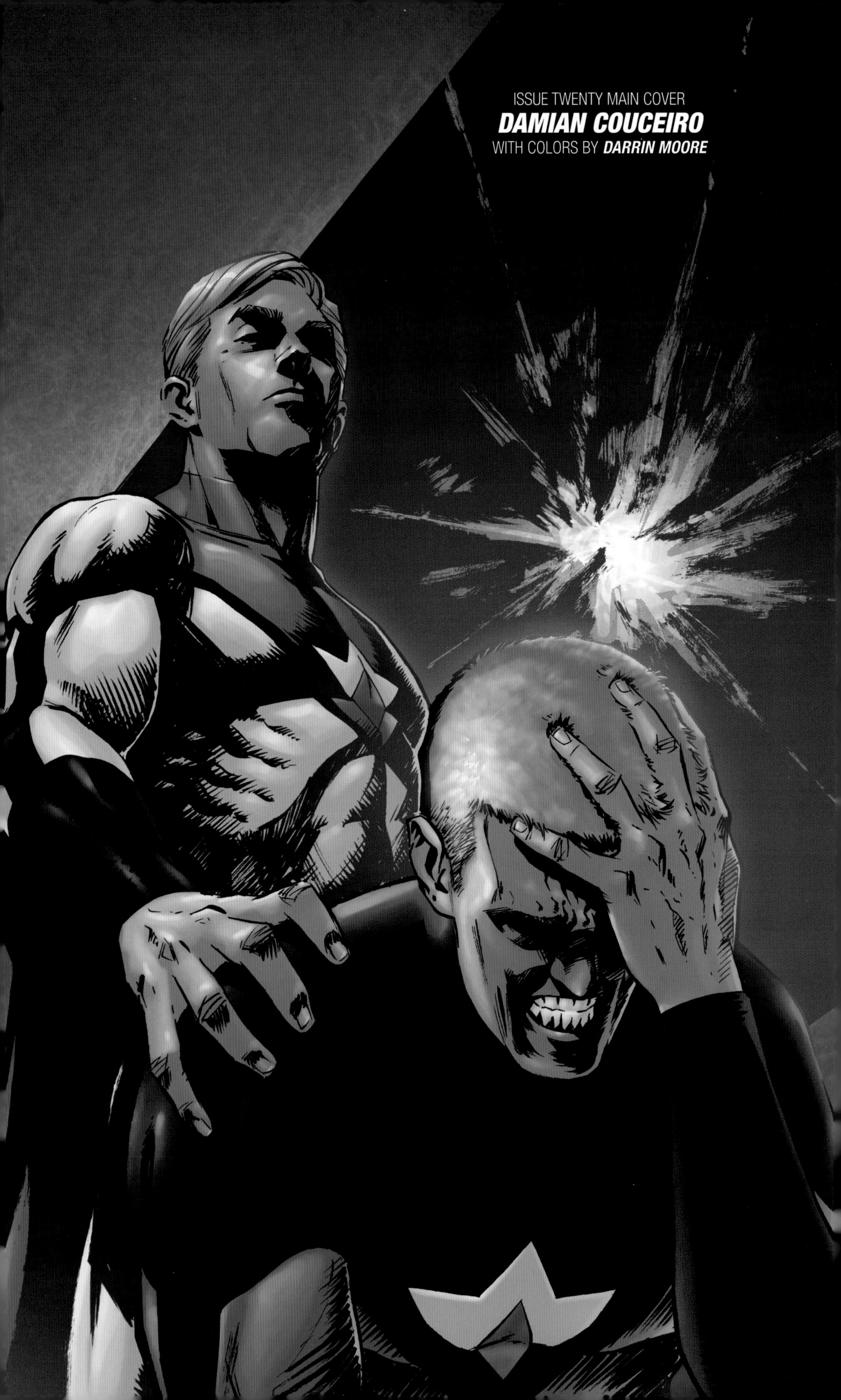

ISSUE TWENTY MAIN COVER
DAMIAN COUCEIRO
WITH COLORS BY ***DARRIN MOORE***

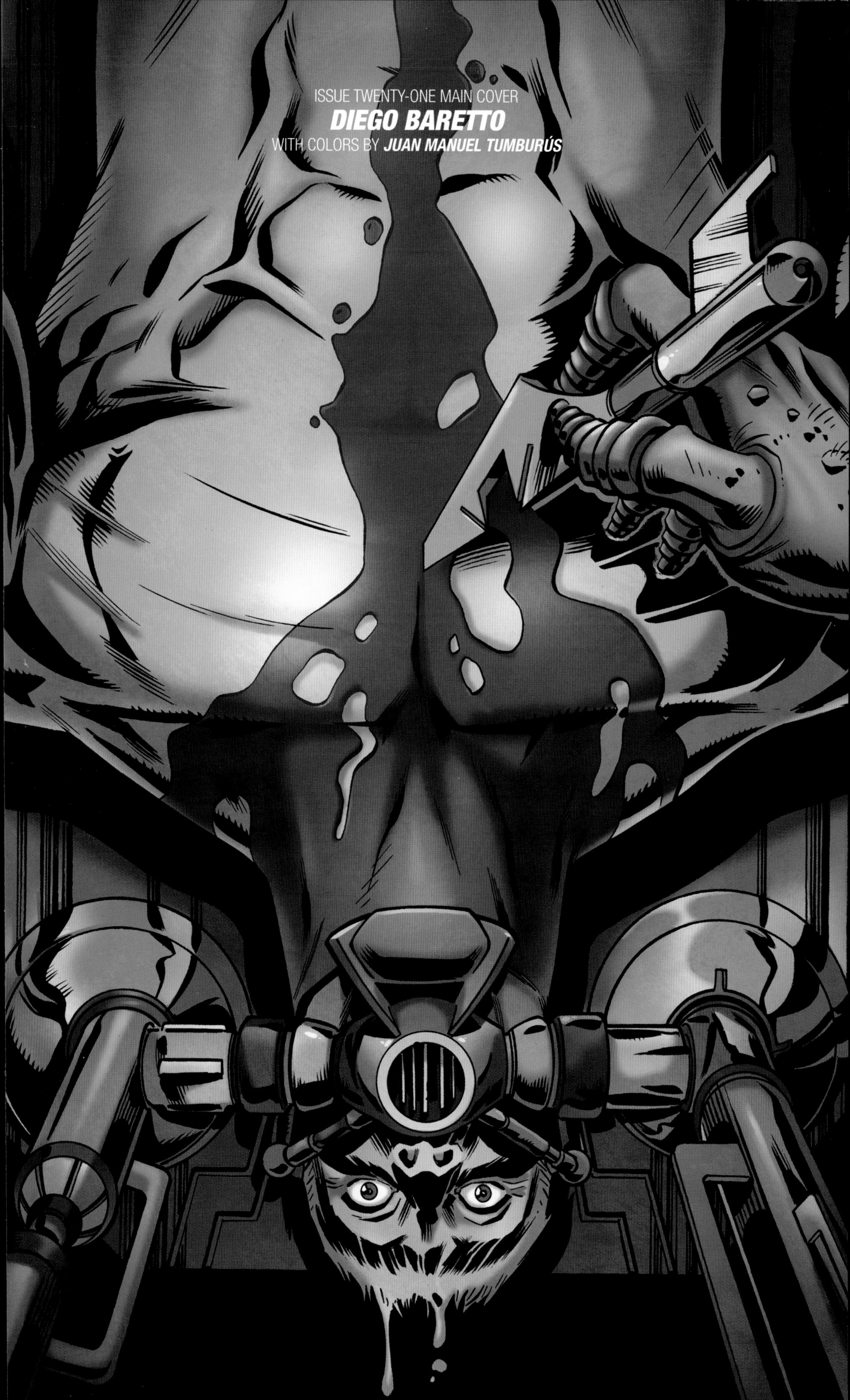

ISSUE TWENTY-ONE MAIN COVER
DIEGO BARETTO
WITH COLORS BY ***JUAN MANUEL TUMBURÚS***

ISSUE TWENTY-TWO MAIN COVER
SCOTT CLARK
WITH COLORS BY ***DAVE BEATY***

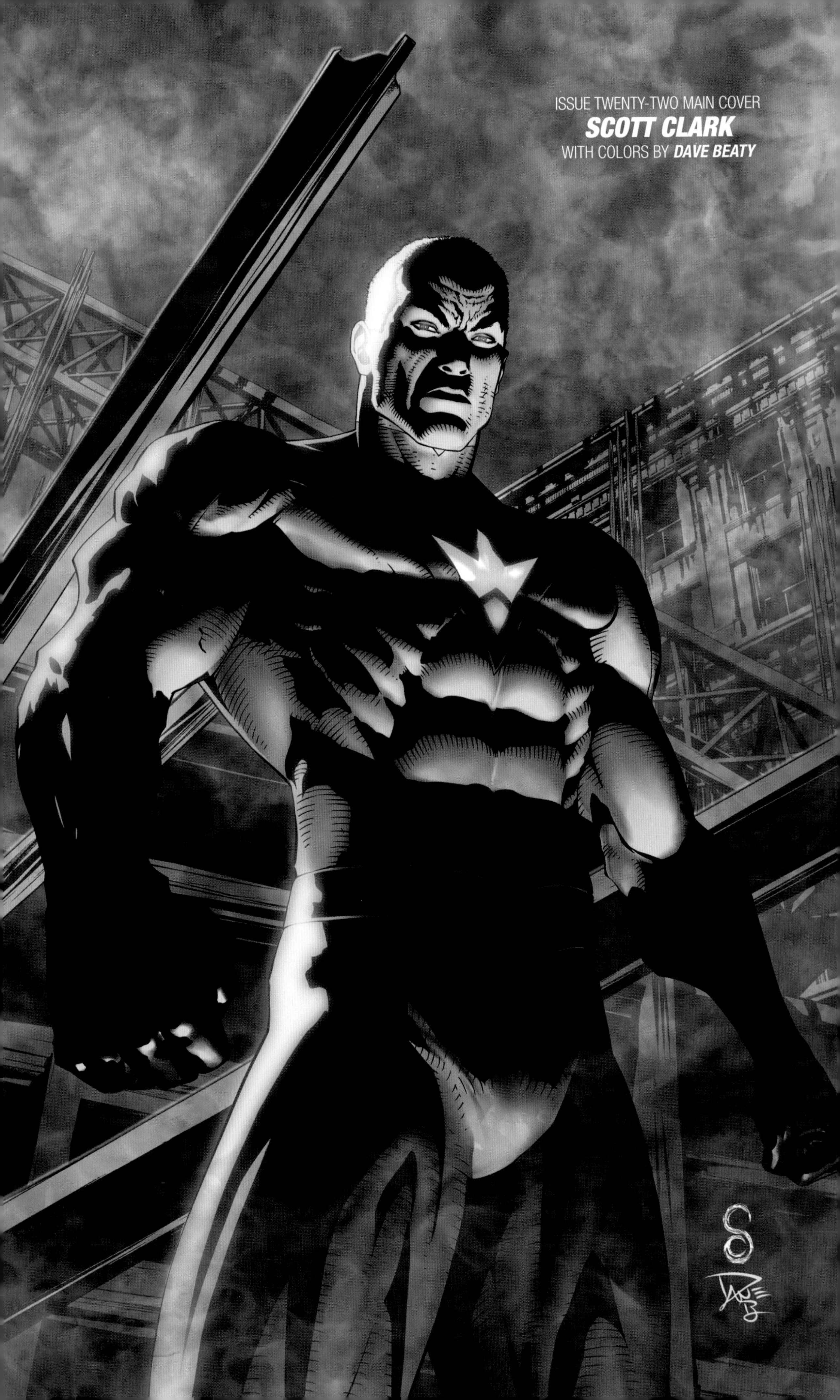

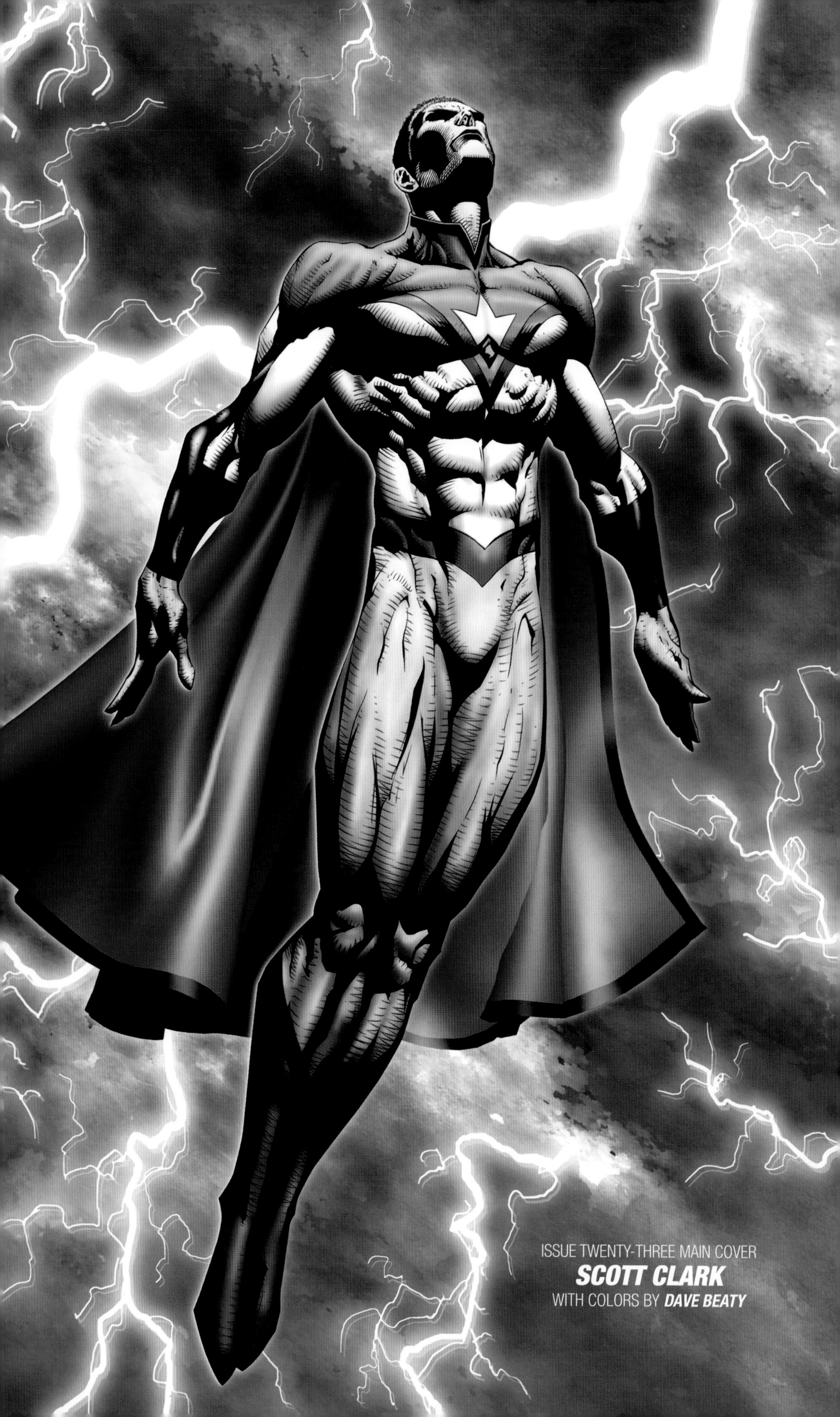

ISSUE TWENTY-THREE MAIN COVER
SCOTT CLARK
WITH COLORS BY ***DAVE BEATY***

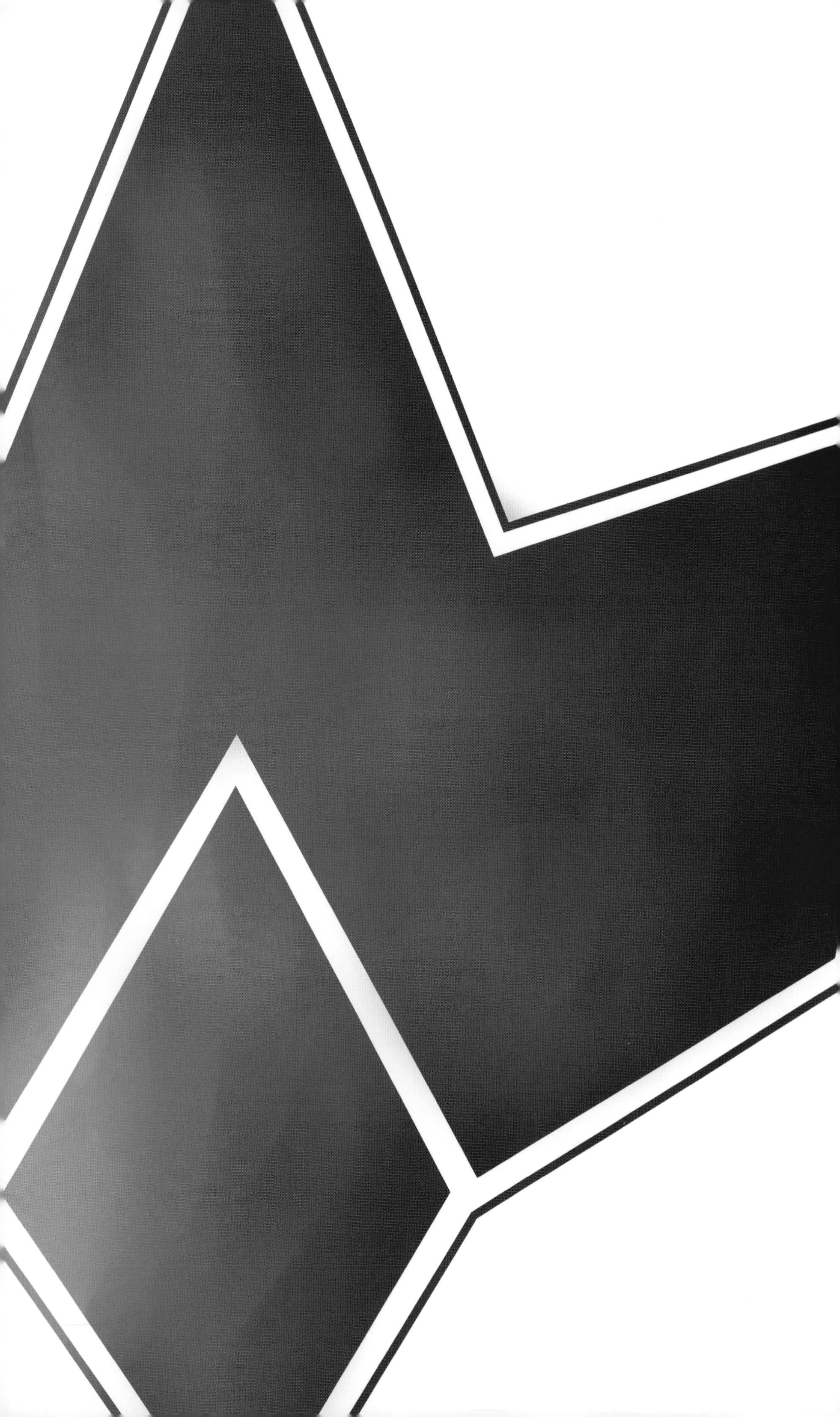